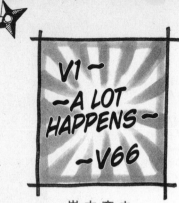

V1 ~
~A LOT
HAPPENS~
~V66

岸本斉史

Naruto is really starting to enter its climax. It's gone on longer than I expected, but it's definitely inching closer to the finale. This volume's cover is an updated version of the chapter 4 title page illustration from volume 1. The image I thought up back then is finally coming true in this volume...

—Masashi Kishimoto, 2013

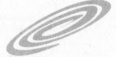

Author/artist Masashi Kishimoto was born in 1974 in rural Okayama Prefecture, Japan. After spending time in art college, he won the Hop Step Award for new manga artists with his manga **Karakuri** (Mechanism). Kishimoto decided to base his next story on traditional Japanese culture. His first version of **Naruto**, drawn in 1997, was a one-shot story about fox spirits; his final version, which debuted in **Weekly Shonen Jump** in 1999, quickly became the most popular ninja manga in Japan.

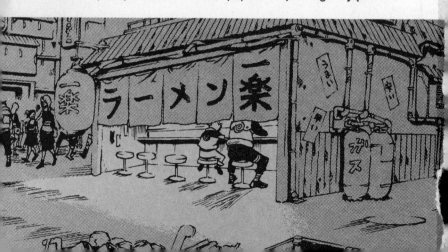

NARUTO VOL. 66
SHONEN JUMP Manga Edition

STORY AND ART BY MASASHI KISHIMOTO

Translation/Mari Morimoto
Touch-up Art & Lettering/John Hunt
Design/Sam Elzway
Editor/Alexis Kirsch

Printed in the U.S.A.

Published by VIZ Media, LLC
P.O. Box 77010
San Francisco, CA 94107

10 9 8 7 6 5 4 3 2 1
First printing, July 2014

SHONEN JUMP MANGA EDITION

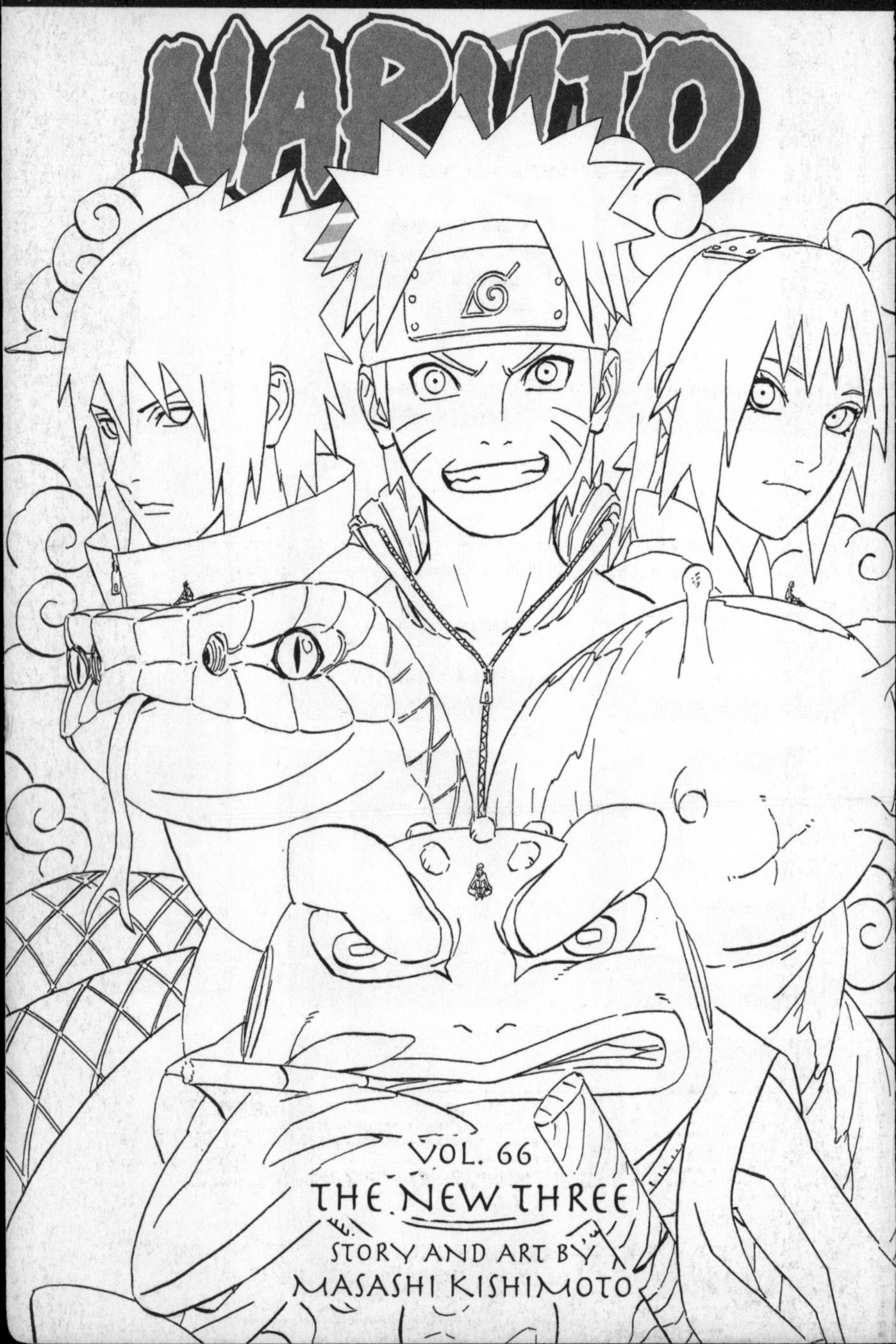
NARUTO
VOL. 66
THE NEW THREE
STORY AND ART BY
MASASHI KISHIMOTO

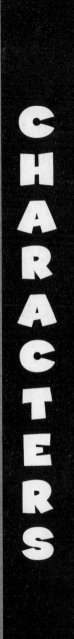

CHARACTERS

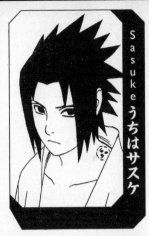

Naruto うずまきナルト

Sasuke うちはサスケ

Kakashi はたけカカシ

Sakura 春野サクラ

Sai サイ

Yamato ヤマト

Kurama 九喇嘛

Obito うちはオビト

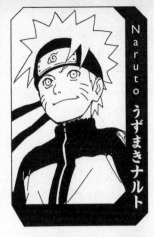

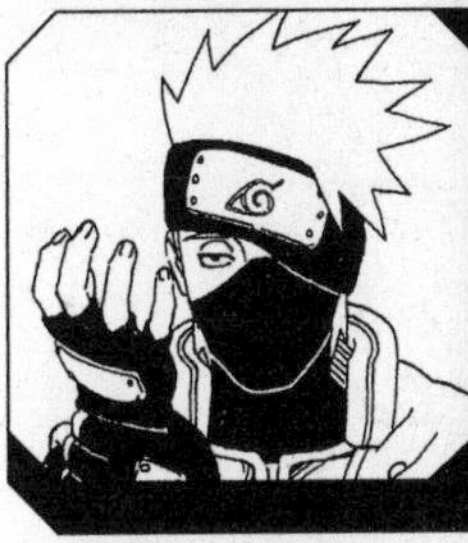

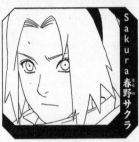

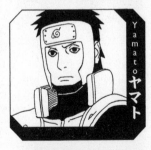

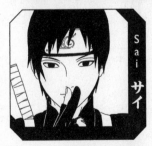

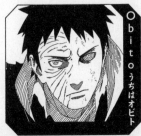

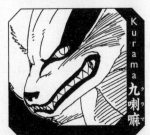

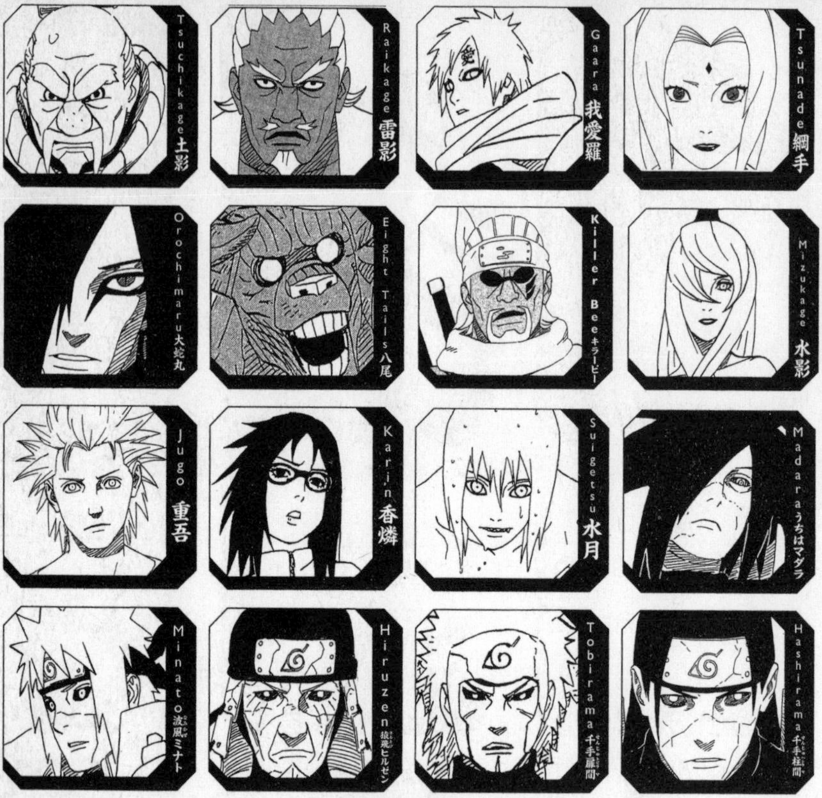
Tsunade 綱手
Gaara 我愛羅
Raikage 雷影
Tsuchikage 土影
Mizukage 水影
Killer Bee キラービー
Eight Tails 八尾
Orochimaru 大蛇丸
Madara うちはマダラ
Suigetsu 水月
Karin 香燐
Jugo 重吾
Hashirama 千手柱間
Tobirama 千手扉間
Hiruzen 猿飛ヒルゼン
Minato 波風ミナト

THE STORY SO FAR...

Naruto, the biggest troublemaker at the Ninja Academy in the Village of Konohagakure, finally becomes a ninja along with his classmates Sasuke and Sakura. They grow and mature through countless trials and battles. However, Sasuke, unable to give up his quest for vengeance, leaves Konohagakure to seek Orochimaru and his power…

Two years pass. Naruto grows up and engages in fierce battles against the Tailed Beast-targeting Akatsuki. And the Fourth Great Ninja War against the Akatsuki finally begins. Naruto and his companions face off against the reunited Obito and Madara in order to stop the resurrected Ten Tails! Meanwhile, Sasuke borrows the help of a revived Orochimaru to bring back the previous Hokage using Edotensei. After hearing the truth about the village and what shinobi are from Senju Hashirama, Sasuke adopts his brother's will and decides to head to the battlefield to protect his village!!

NARUTO

VOL. 66
THE NEW THREE

CONTENTS

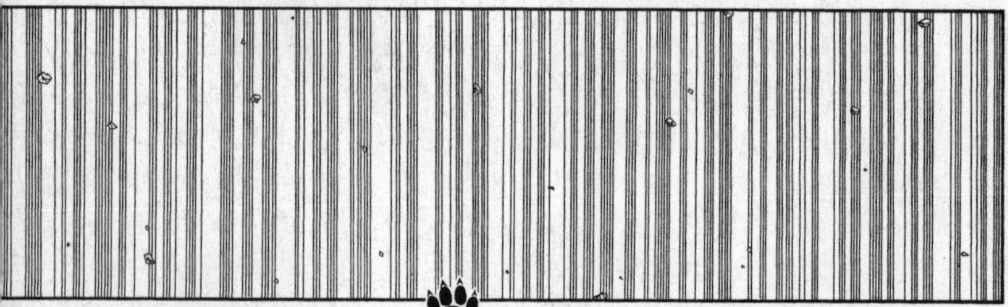

Number 628: Here and Now, and Hereafter

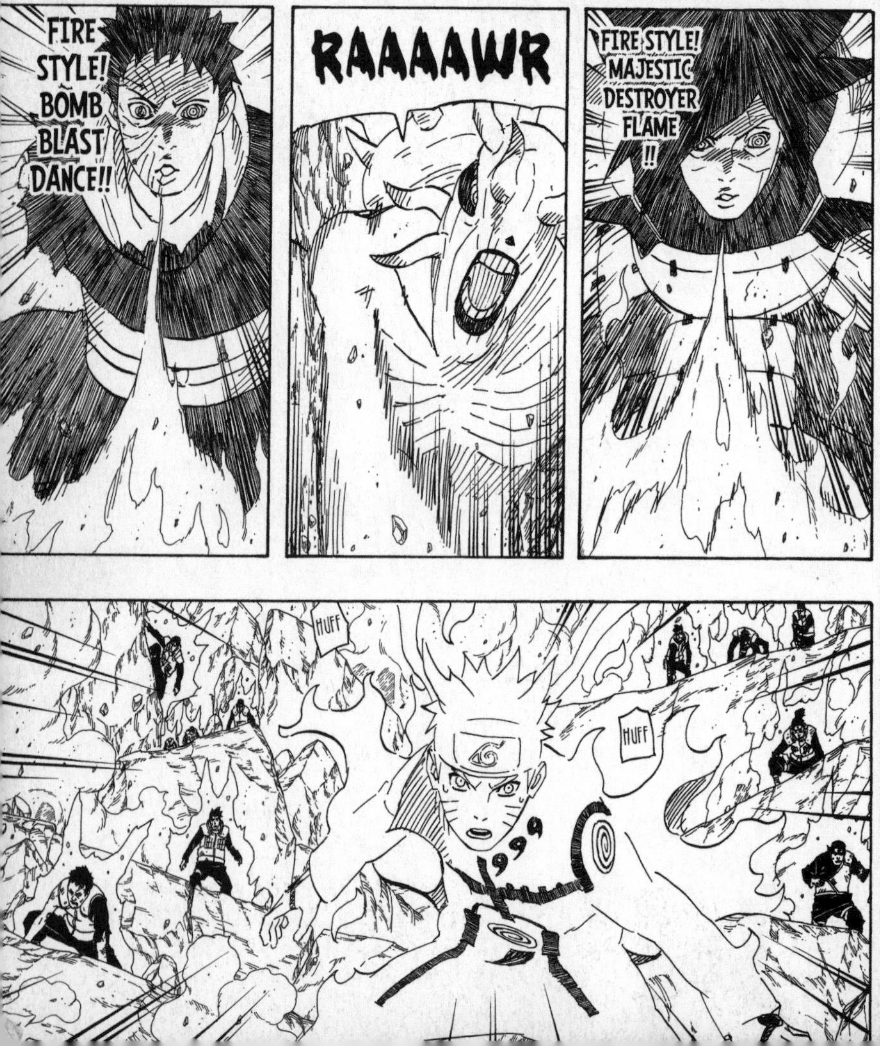
FIRE STYLE! MAJESTIC DESTROYER FLAME!!
RAAAAWR
FIRE STYLE! BOMB BLAST DANCE!!
HUFF
HUFF

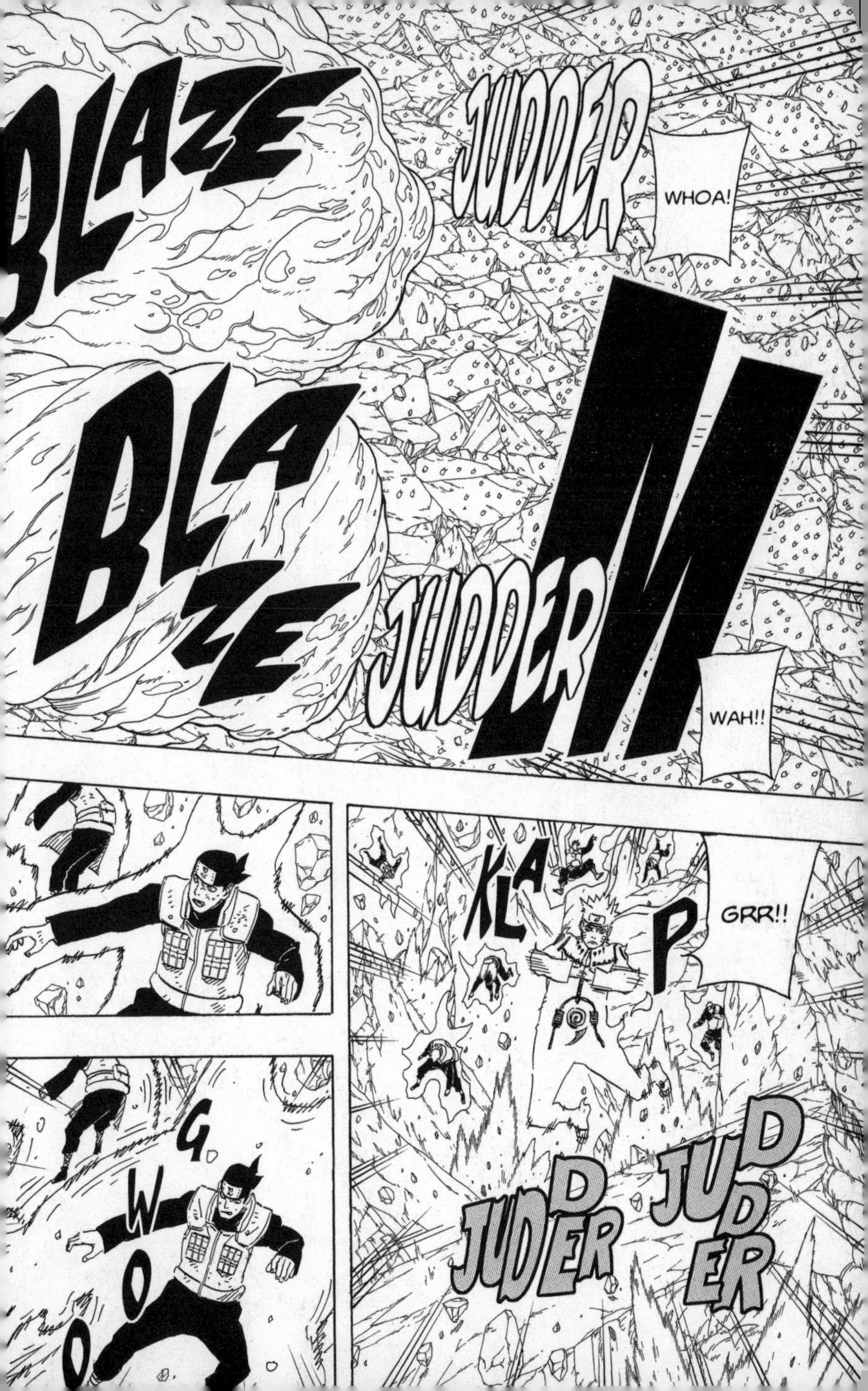
WHOA!
JUDDER
BLAZE
WAH!!
JUDDER
BLAZE
GRR!!
KLAP
JUDDER
JUDDER
GWOO

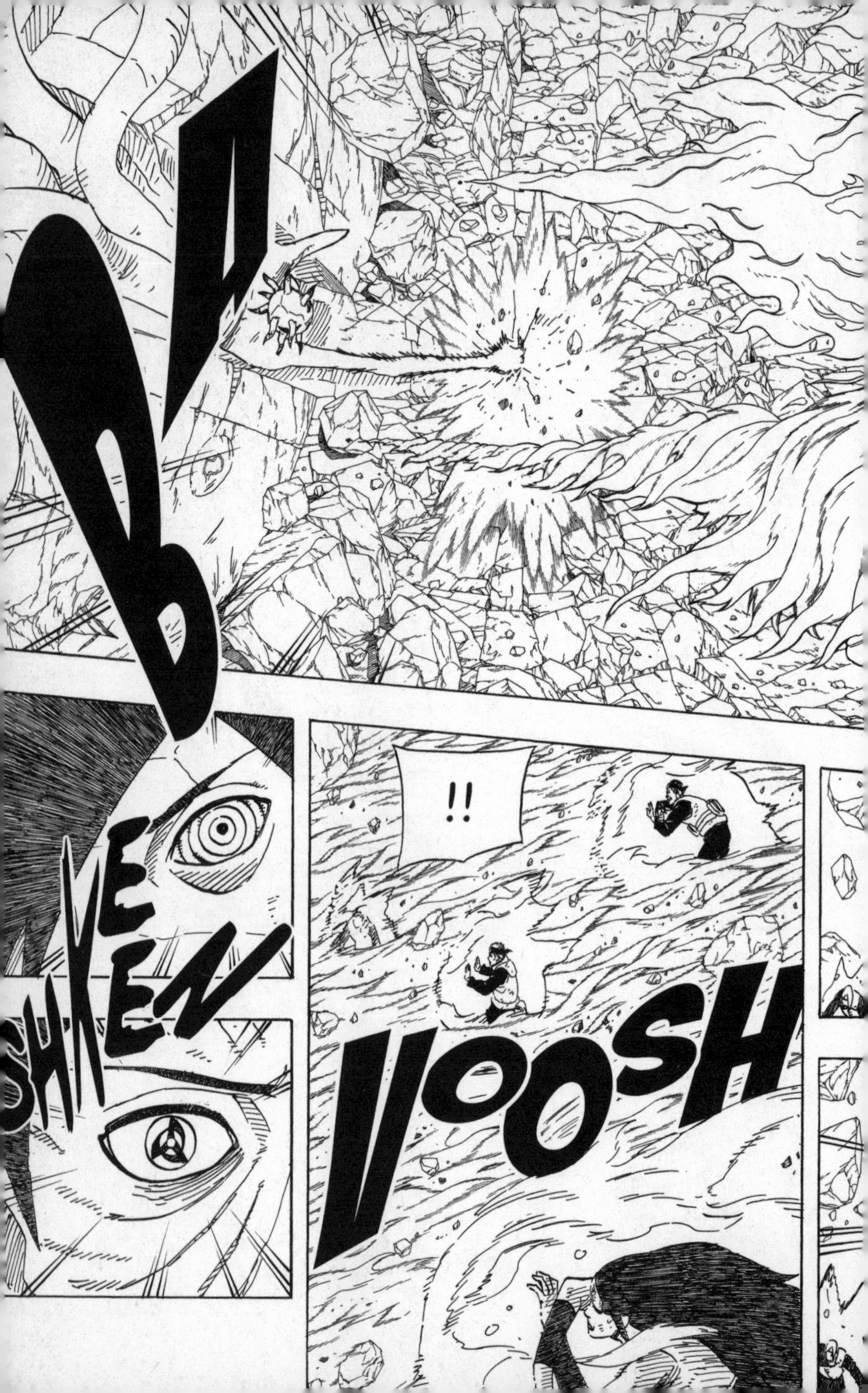
!!
VOOSH

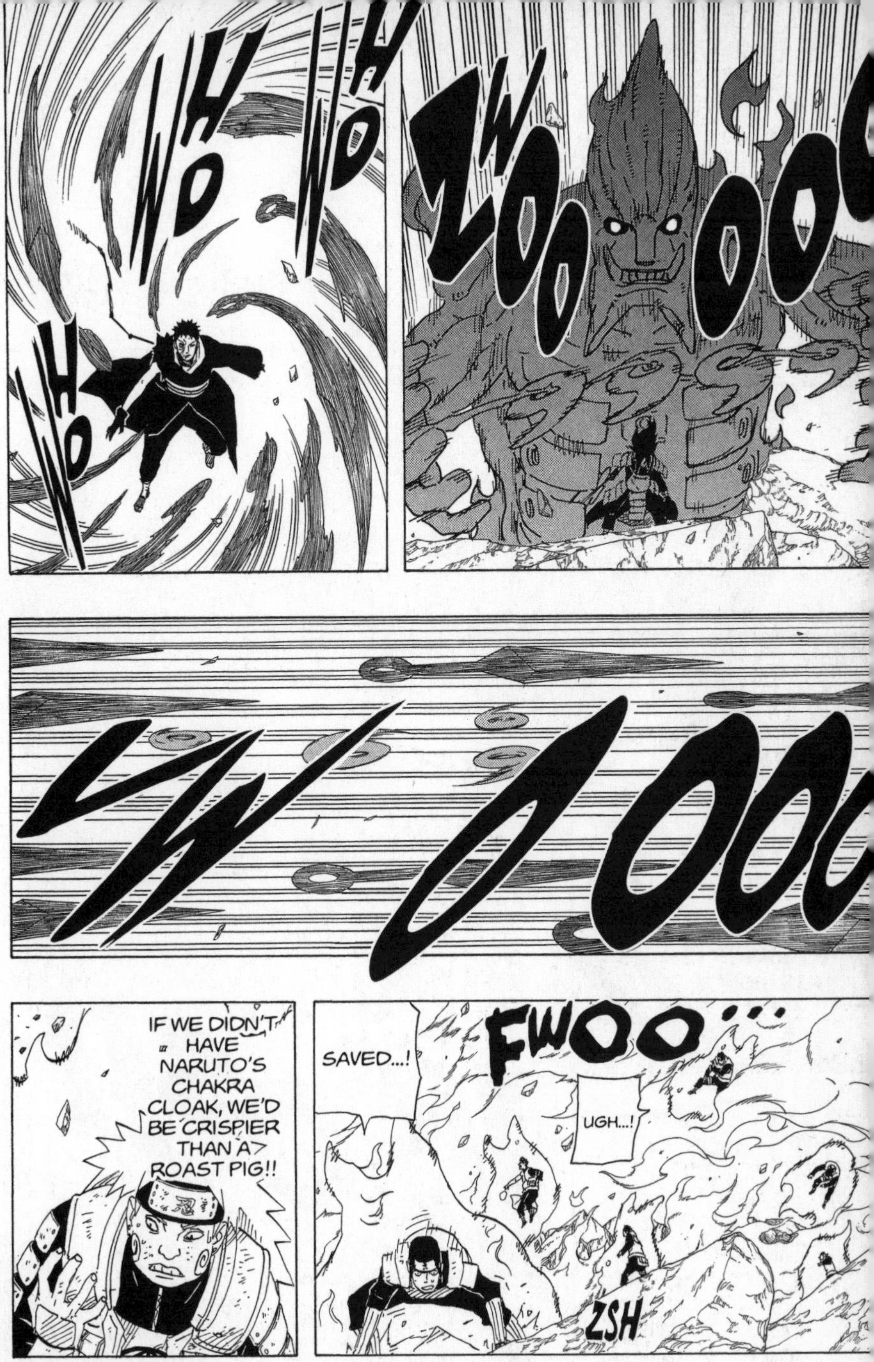

ZWOOOO
WHOO
WHOO
WHOO
SAVED...!
FWOO...
UGH...!
ZSH
IF WE DIDN'T HAVE NARUTO'S CHAKRA CLOAK, WE'D BE CRISPIER THAN A ROAST PIG!!

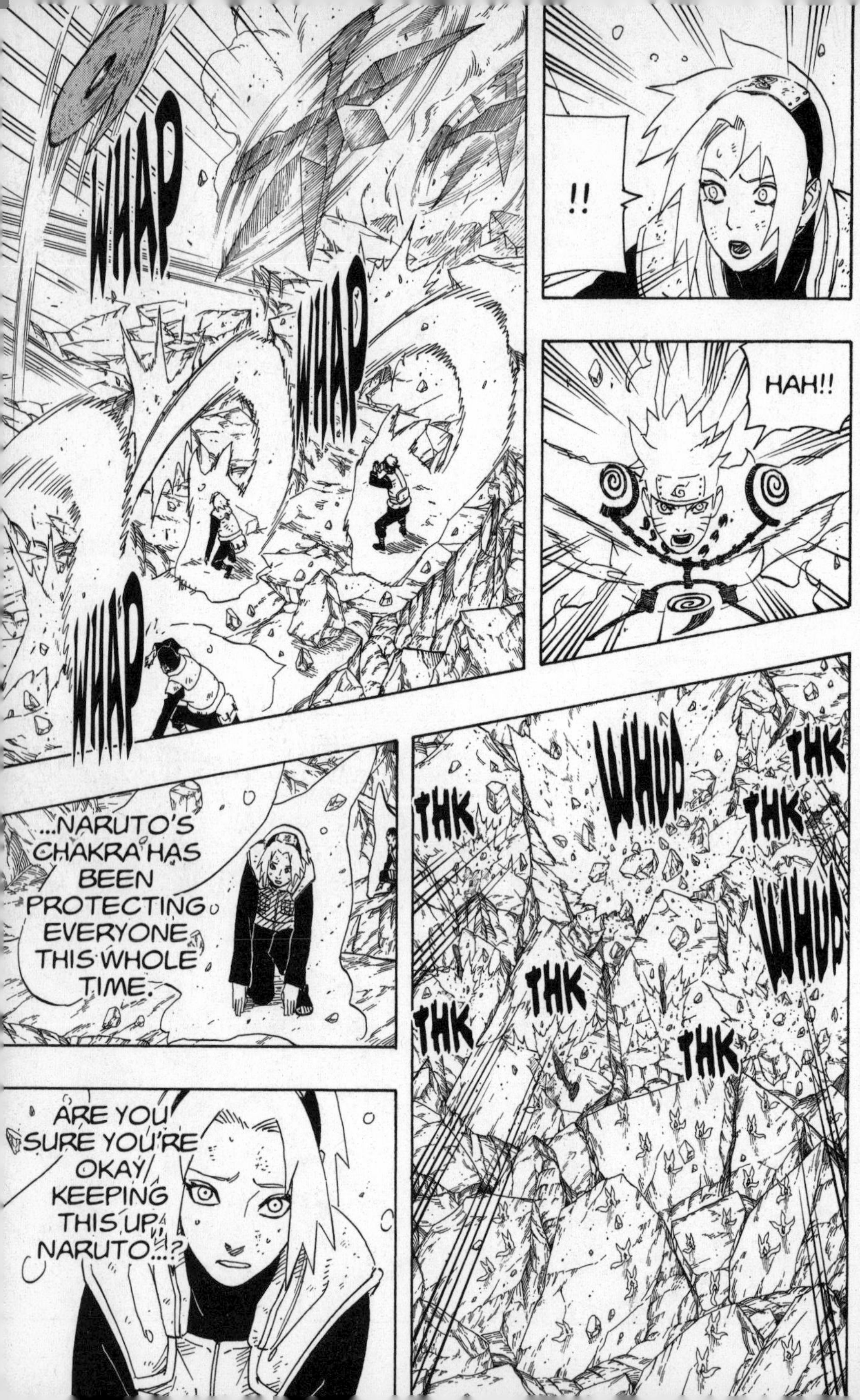
!!
HAH!!
WHAP
WHAP
WHAP
THK
THK
WHUD
THK
WHUD
THK
THK
THK
...NARUTO'S CHAKRA HAS BEEN PROTECTING EVERYONE THIS WHOLE TIME.
ARE YOU SURE YOU'RE OKAY KEEPING THIS UP, NARUTO...?

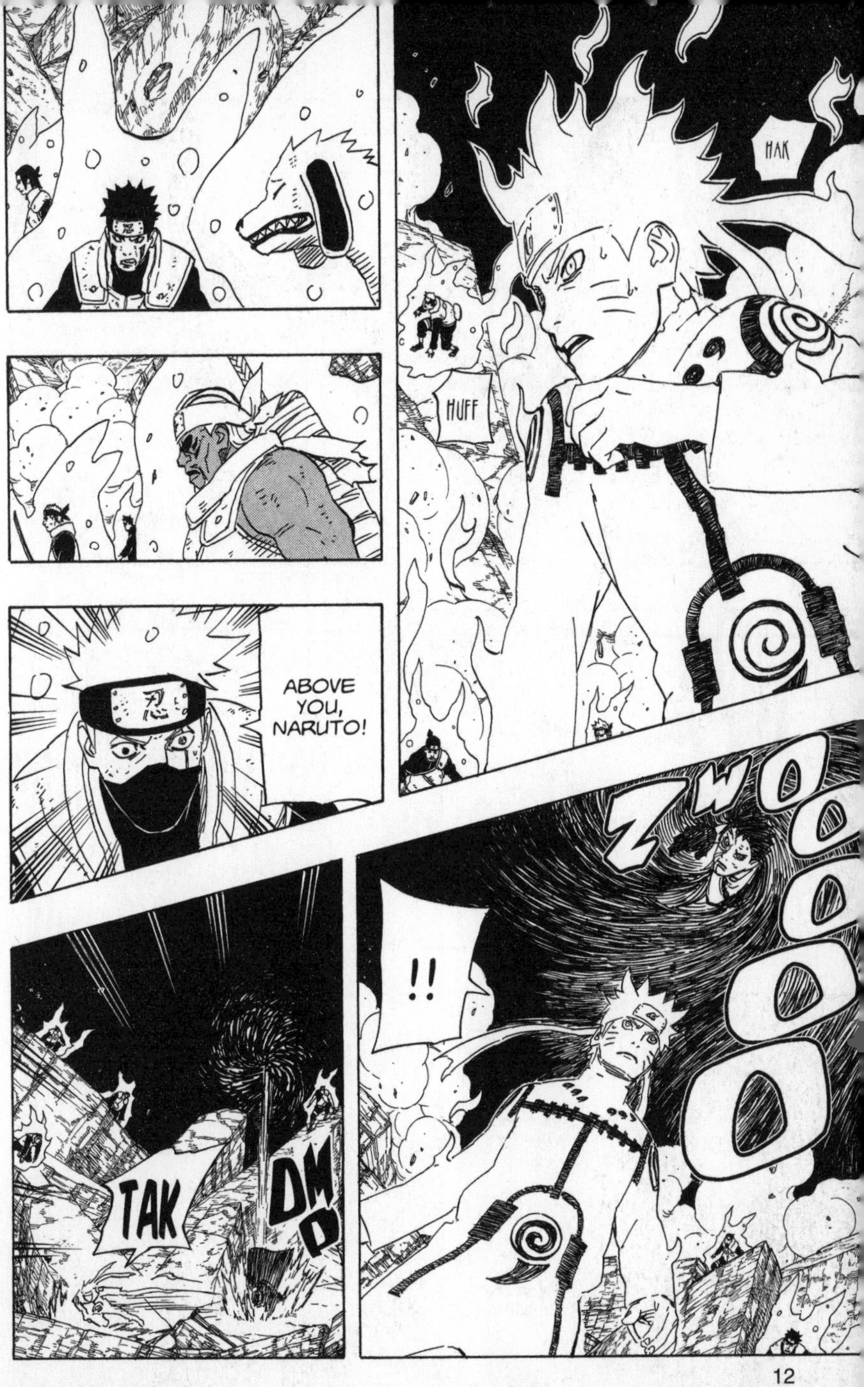

HAK
HUFF
ABOVE YOU, NARUTO!
ZWOOOOOOO
!!
DMP
TAK

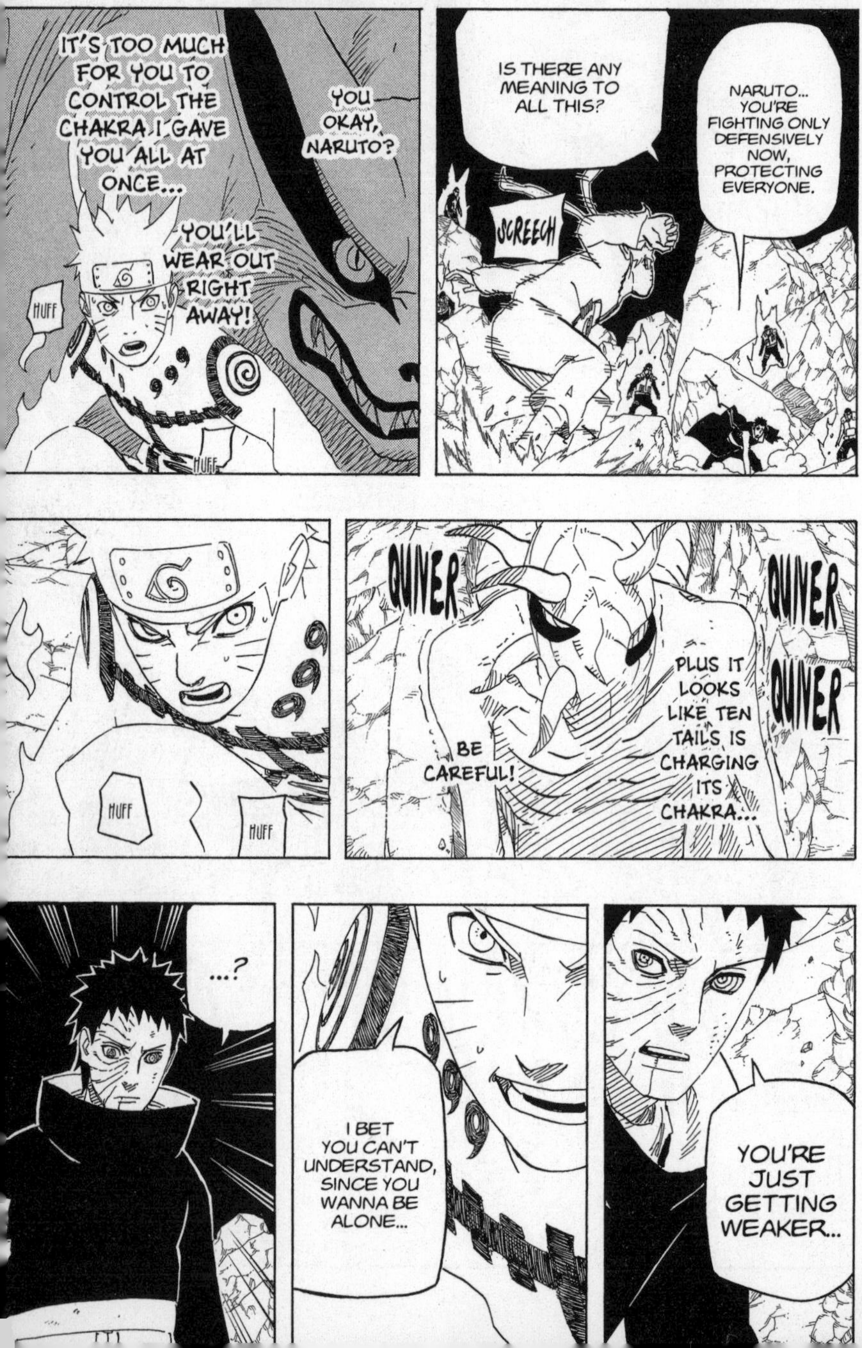
NARUTO... YOU'RE FIGHTING ONLY DEFENSIVELY NOW, PROTECTING EVERYONE.
IS THERE ANY MEANING TO ALL THIS?
SCREECH
YOU OKAY, NARUTO?
IT'S TOO MUCH FOR YOU TO CONTROL THE CHAKRA I GAVE YOU ALL AT ONCE...
YOU'LL WEAR OUT RIGHT AWAY!
HUFF
HUFF
QUIVER
QUIVER
PLUS IT LOOKS LIKE TEN TAILS IS CHARGING ITS CHAKRA...
BE CAREFUL!
QUIVER
HUFF
HUFF
YOU'RE JUST GETTING WEAKER...
I BET YOU CAN'T UNDERSTAND, SINCE YOU WANNA BE ALONE...
...?

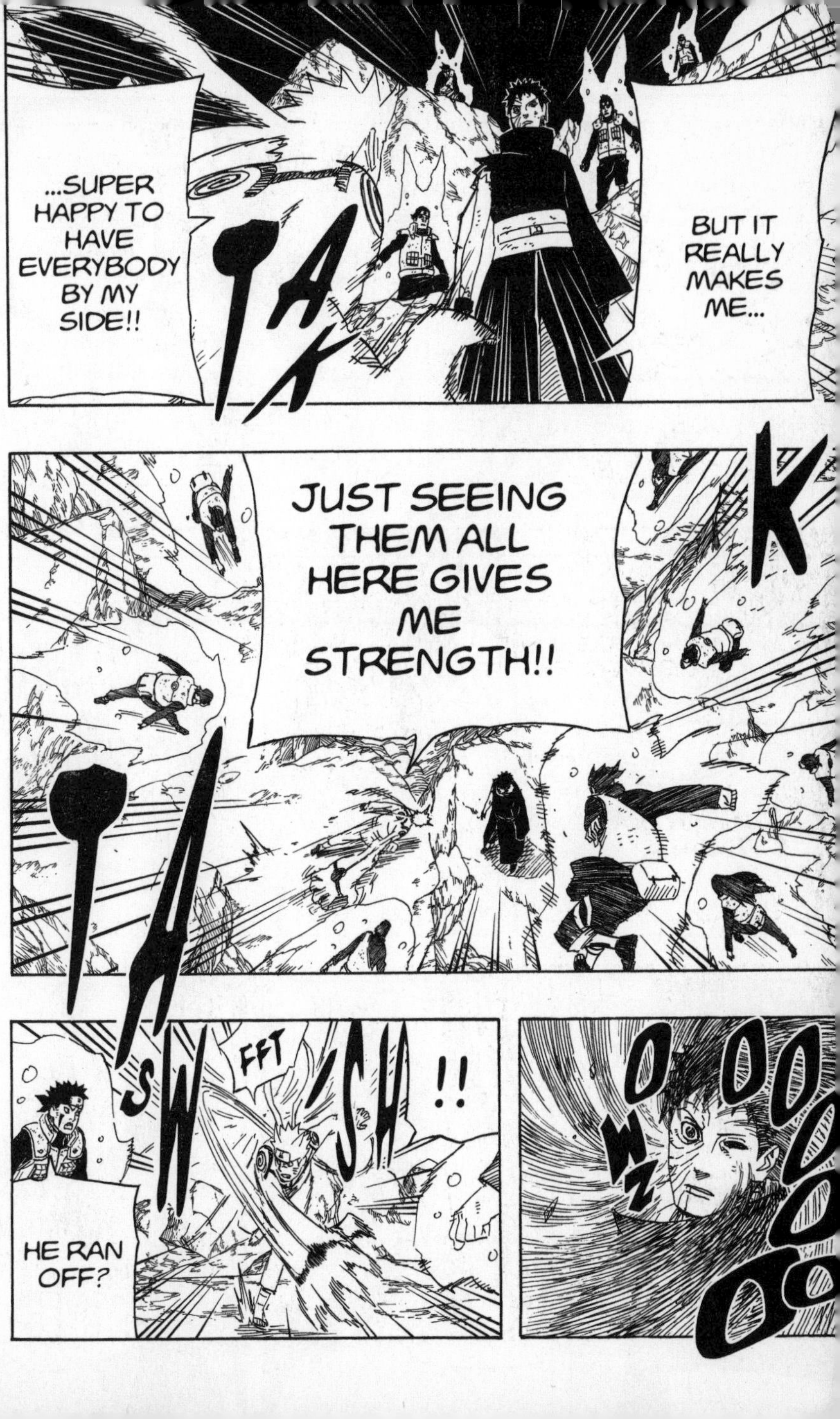
BUT IT REALLY MAKES ME...
...SUPER HAPPY TO HAVE EVERYBODY BY MY SIDE!!
TAK
JUST SEEING THEM ALL HERE GIVES ME STRENGTH!!
SWISH
FFT
!!
HE RAN OFF?

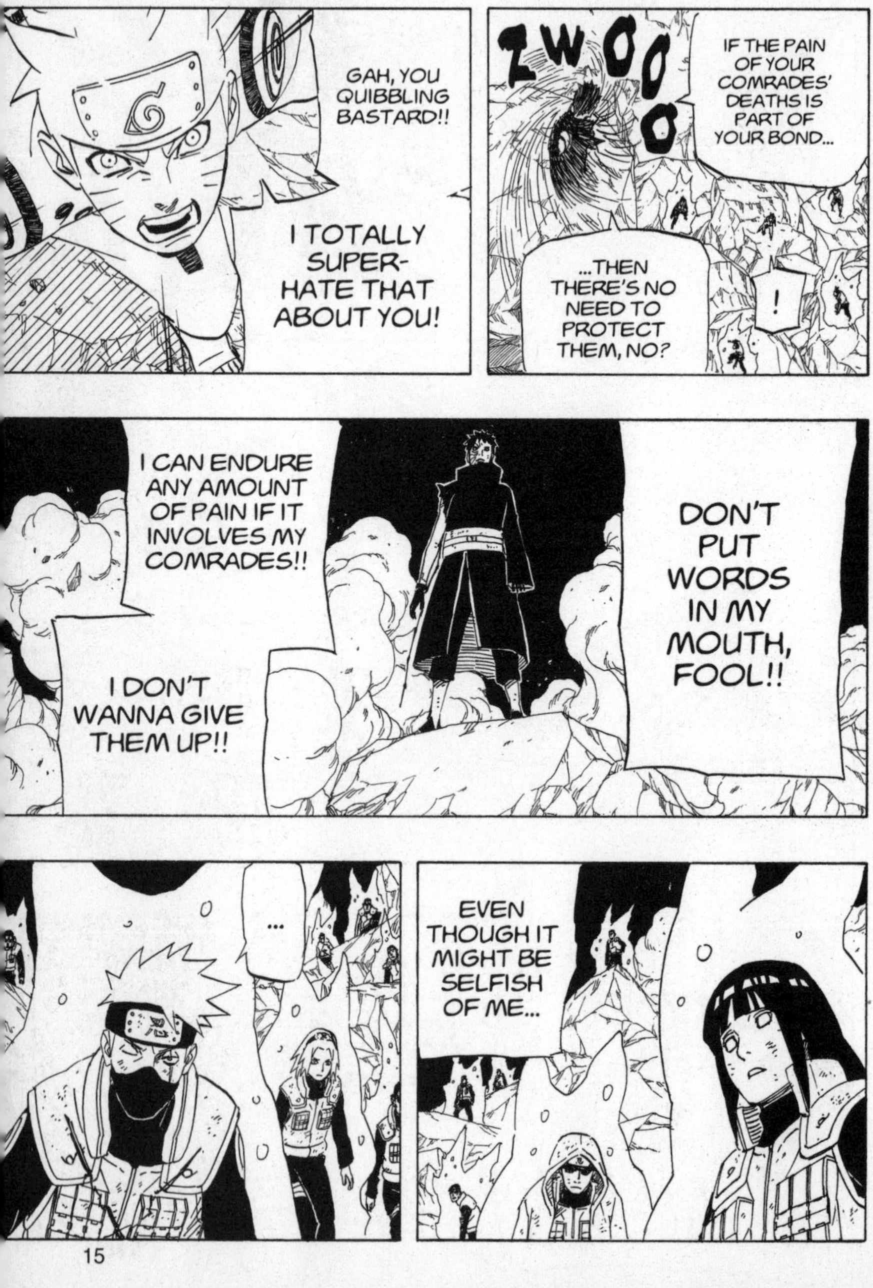
ZWOOO
IF THE PAIN OF YOUR COMRADES' DEATHS IS PART OF YOUR BOND...
...THEN THERE'S NO NEED TO PROTECT THEM, NO?
!
GAH, YOU QUIBBLING BASTARD!!
I TOTALLY SUPER-HATE THAT ABOUT YOU!
DON'T PUT WORDS IN MY MOUTH, FOOL!!
I CAN ENDURE ANY AMOUNT OF PAIN IF IT INVOLVES MY COMRADES!!
I DON'T WANNA GIVE THEM UP!!
EVEN THOUGH IT MIGHT BE SELFISH OF ME...
...

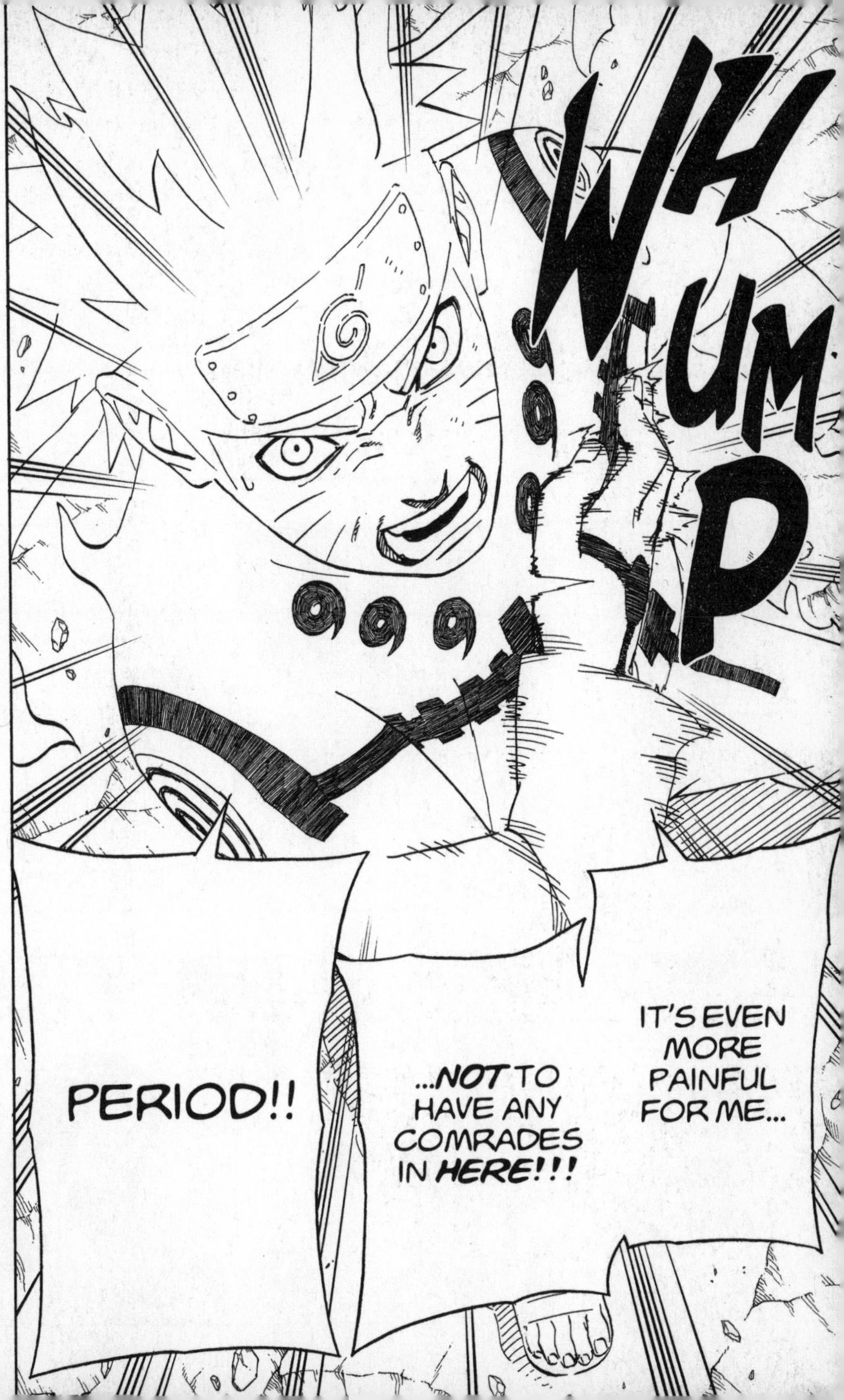
WHUMP
IT'S EVEN MORE PAINFUL FOR ME...
...NOT TO HAVE ANY COMRADES IN HERE!!!
PERIOD!!

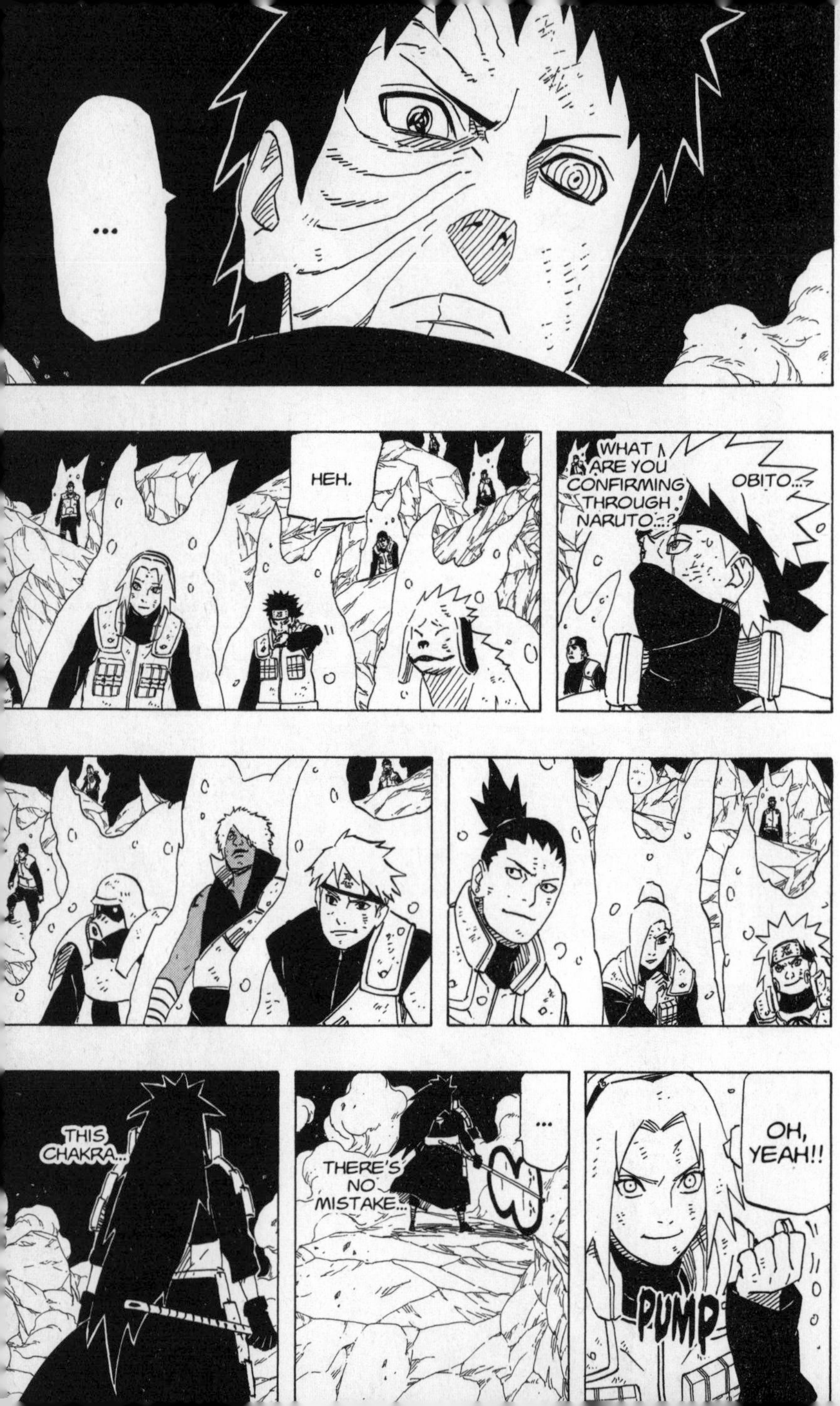
...
WHAT ARE YOU CONFIRMING THROUGH NARUTO...?
OBITO...?
HEH.
OH, YEAH!!
PUMP
...
THERE'S NO MISTAKE...
THIS CHAKRA...

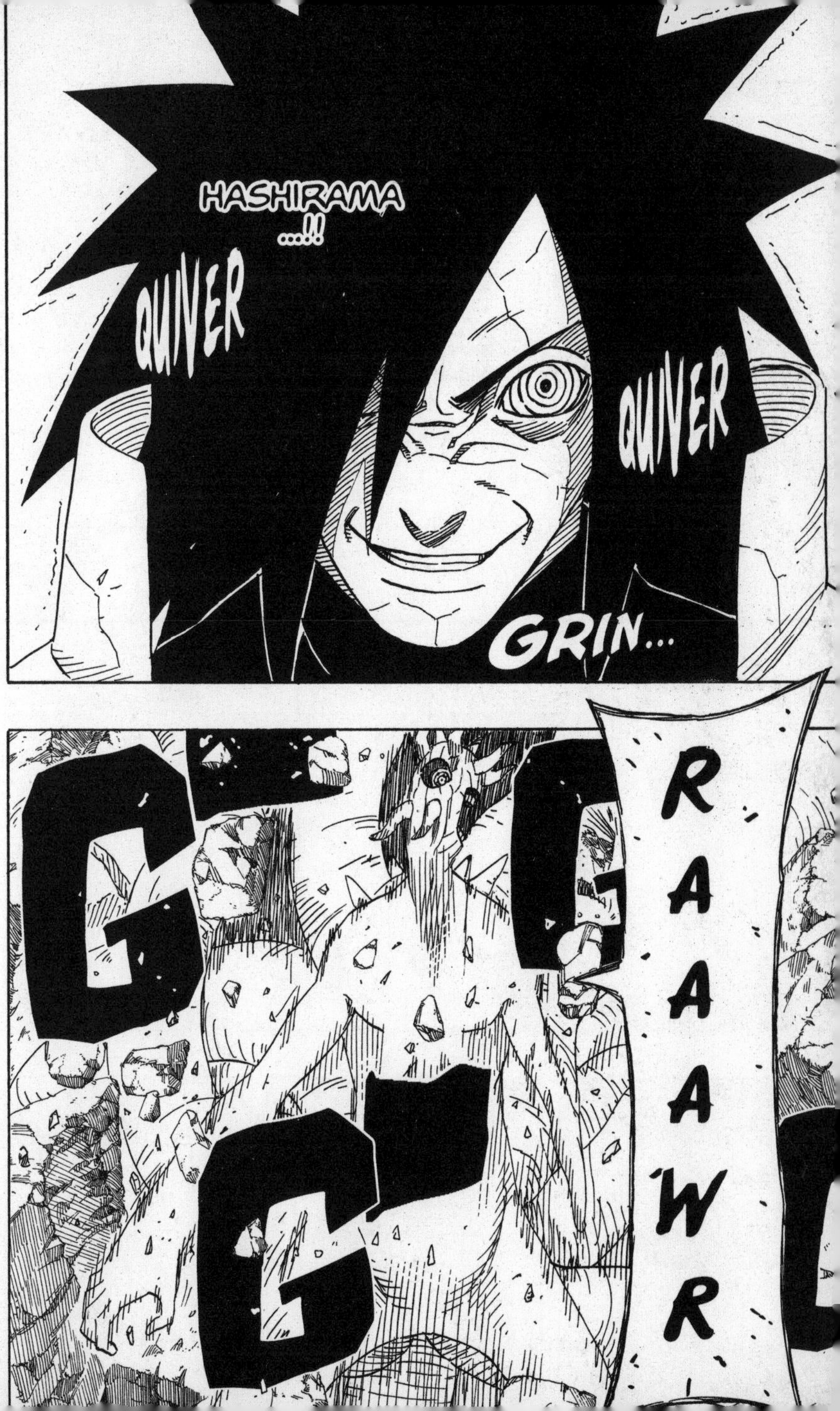
HASHIRAMA ...!!
QUIVER
QUIVER
GRIN...
RAAAWR
GGG

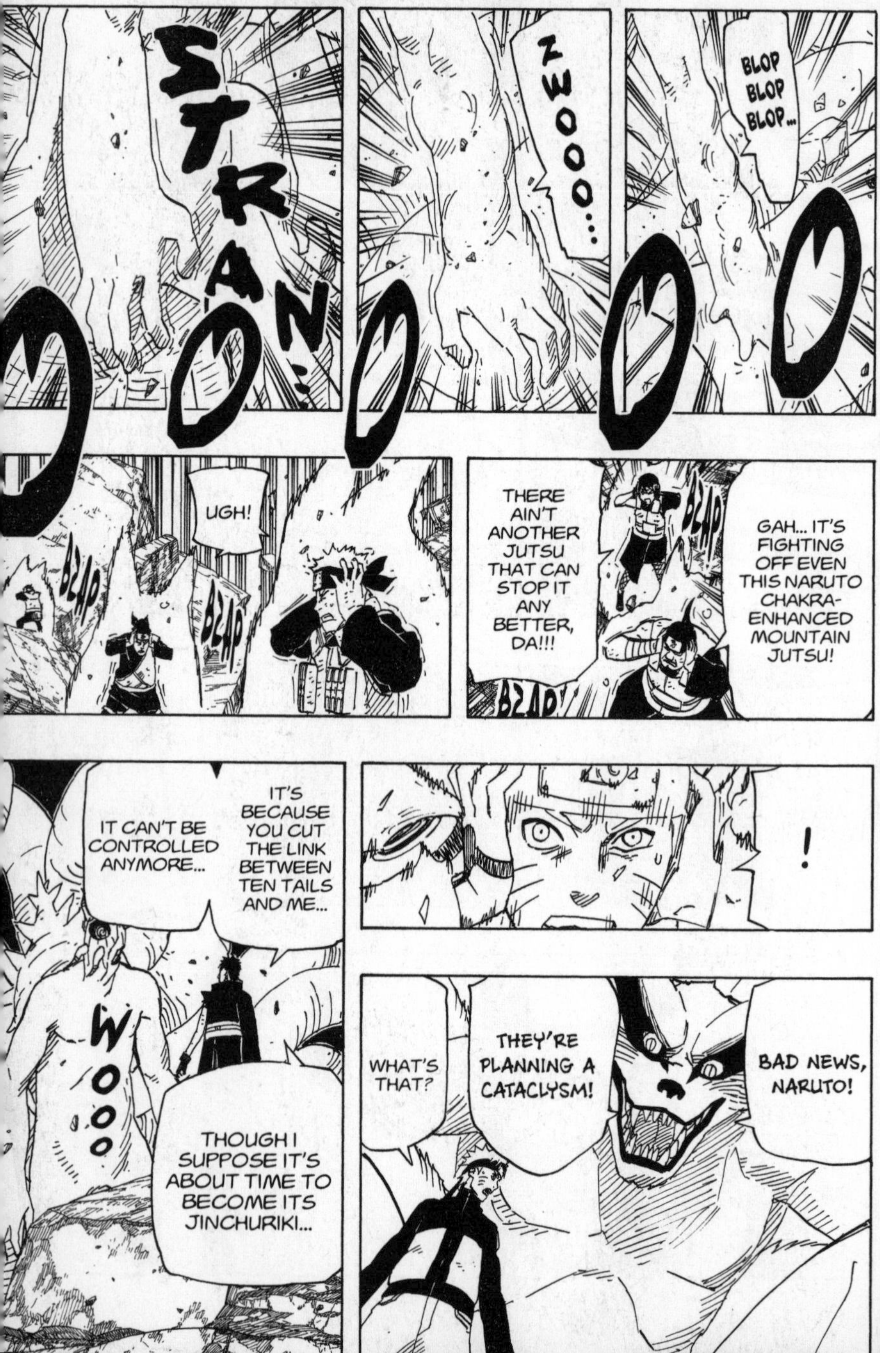

BLOP BLOP BLOP...
ZWOOO...
STRAN...
GAH... IT'S FIGHTING OFF EVEN THIS NARUTO CHAKRA-ENHANCED MOUNTAIN JUTSU!
THERE AIN'T ANOTHER JUTSU THAT CAN STOP IT ANY BETTER, DA!!!
BZAP
BZAP
UGH!
BZAP
BZAP
!
BAD NEWS, NARUTO!
THEY'RE PLANNING A CATACLYSM!
WHAT'S THAT?
IT'S BECAUSE YOU CUT THE LINK BETWEEN TEN TAILS AND ME...
IT CAN'T BE CONTROLLED ANYMORE...
THOUGH I SUPPOSE IT'S ABOUT TIME TO BECOME ITS JINCHURIKI...
WOOO

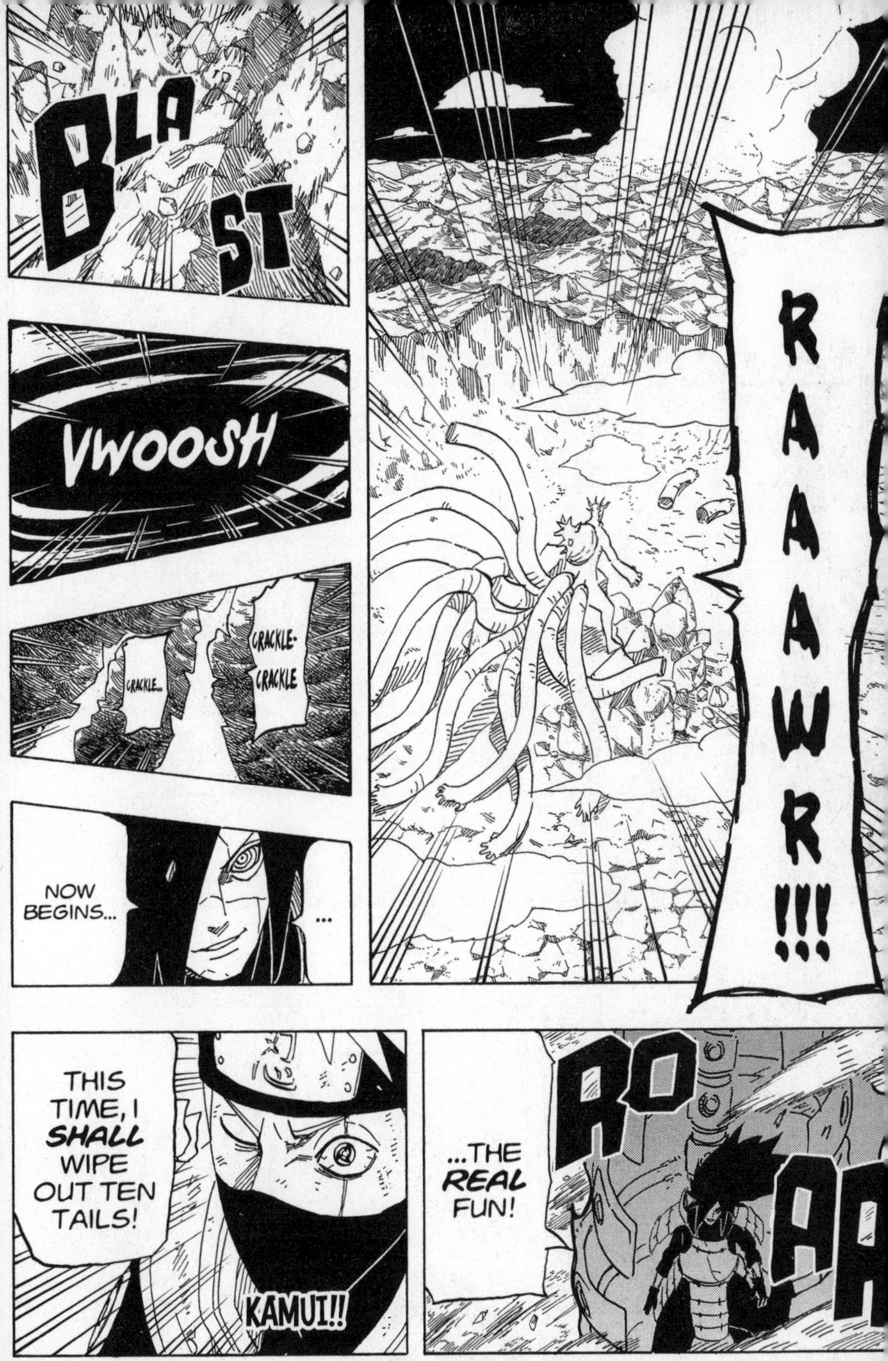
RAAAAWR!!!
BLAST
VWOOSH
CRACKLE-CRACKLE
CRACKLE...
NOW BEGINS...
...
...THE REAL FUN!
ROAR
THIS TIME, I SHALL WIPE OUT TEN TAILS!
KAMUI!!

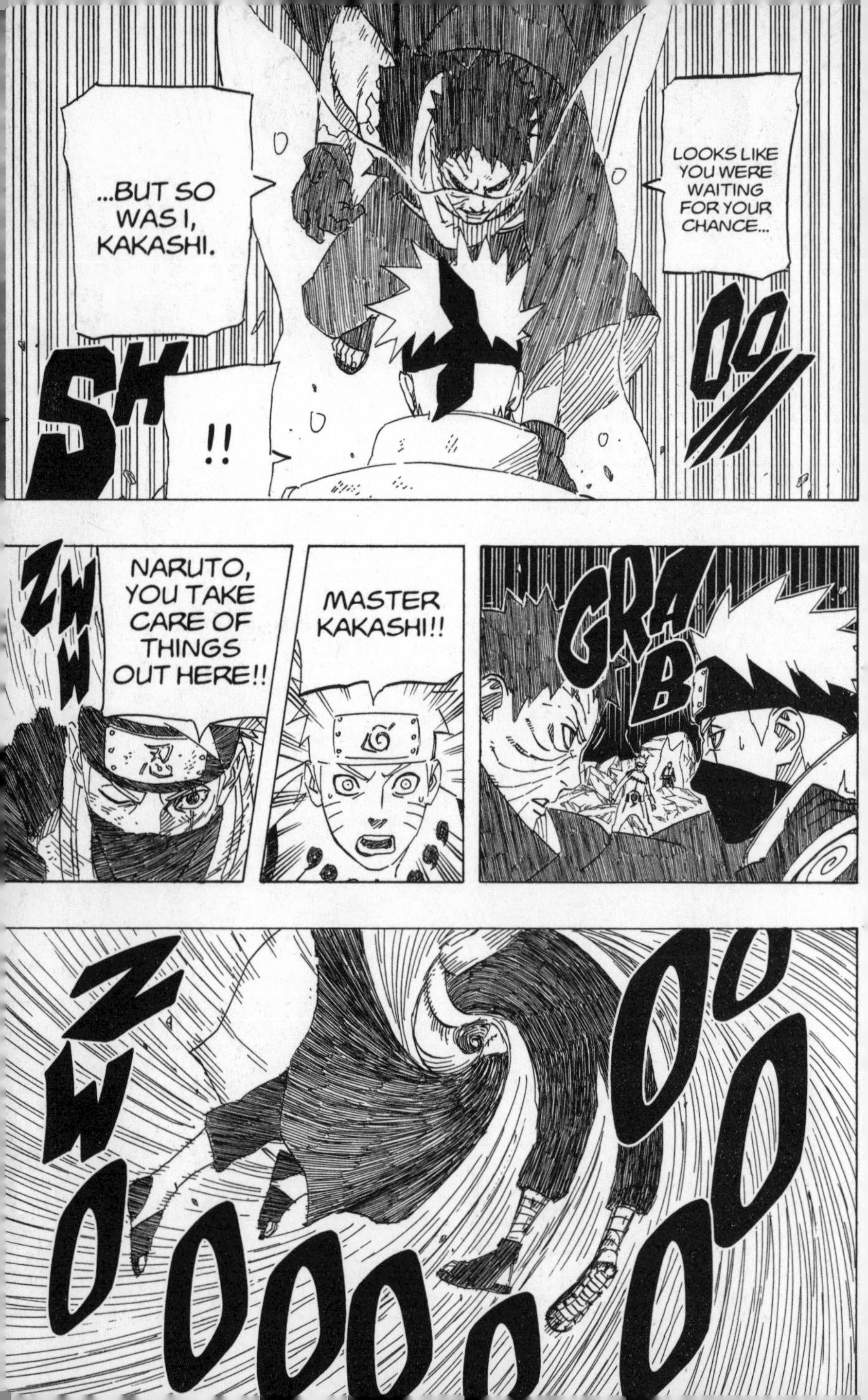
LOOKS LIKE YOU WERE WAITING FOR YOUR CHANCE...
...BUT SO WAS I, KAKASHI.
SH
!!
GRAB
MASTER KAKASHI!!
NARUTO, YOU TAKE CARE OF THINGS OUT HERE!!

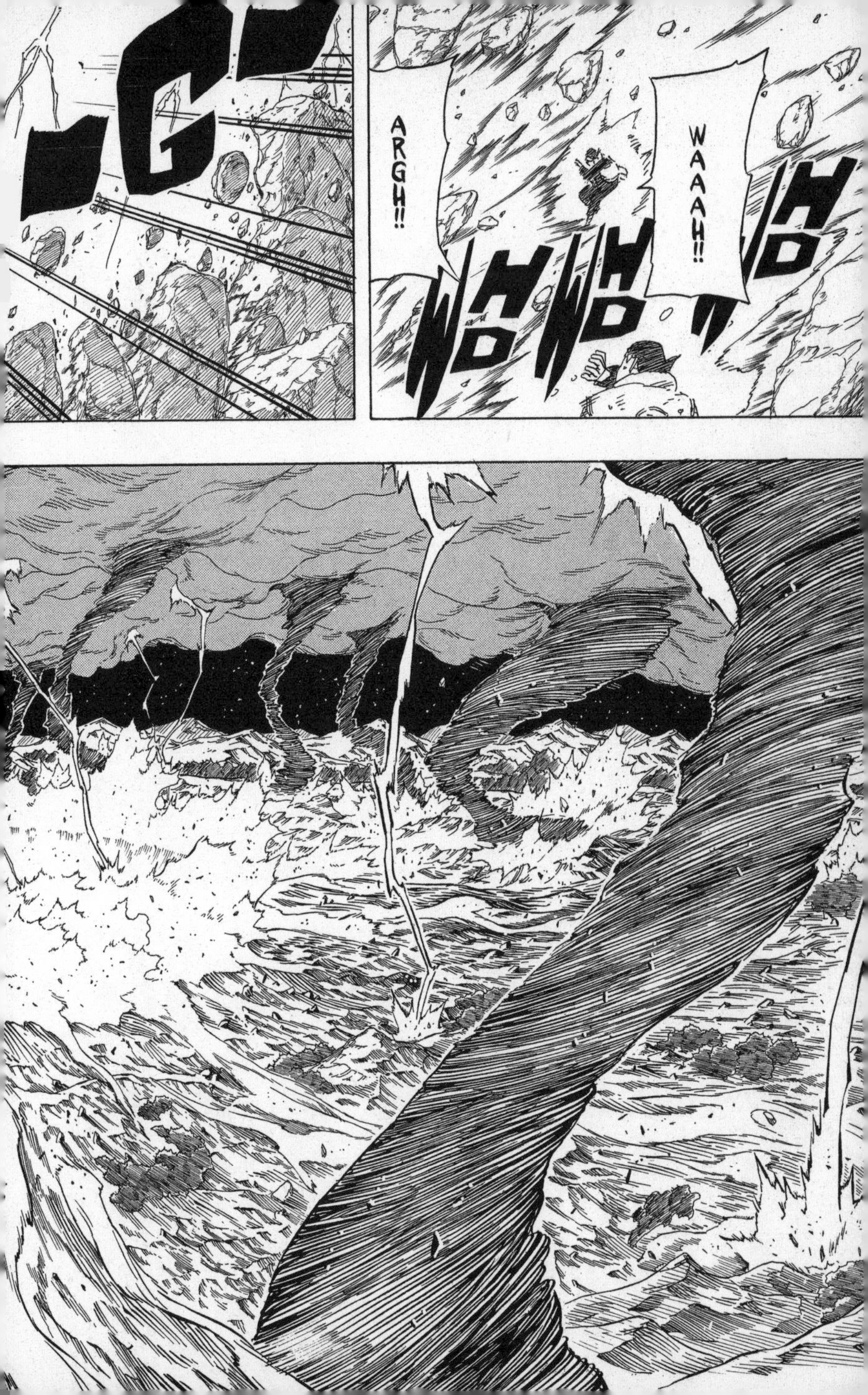
WAAAH!!
ARGH!!

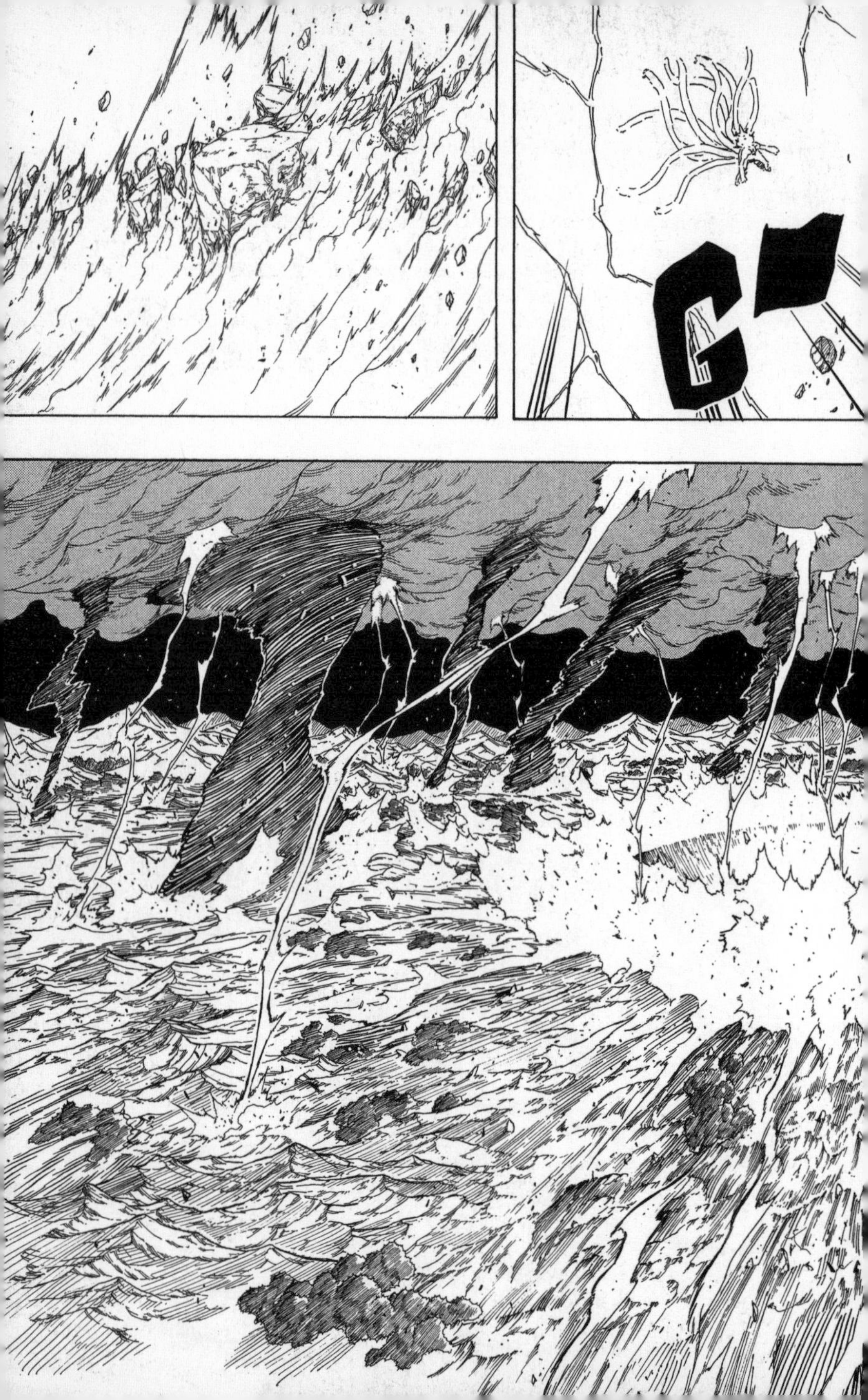
G

MEET MASASHI KISHIMOTO'S ASSISTANTS, PART 13
Assistant No. 13: Takahiro Hiraishi

PROFILE

- An indulgent parent who can't stop grinning when talking about his kids.
- More scheming and wicked than first thought.
- A basketball player who looks a lot like Japanese National Soccer Team goalkeeper Eiji Kawashima... So complicated.
- We're treating him like a newbie here, but it's actually been quite a while since he entered the workplace... He loves basketball but looks like the captain of Tomica Hero Rescue Force and was annoyed because I wasn't getting around to assistant introductions... So complicated.
- In short, this means GK Eiji Kawashima and the Rescue Force captain also look alike, but...he's right between the two of them.
- Always walks around on the tips of his toes.
- Fundamentally nice.

[Tasks] Coloring, screentone, backgrounds

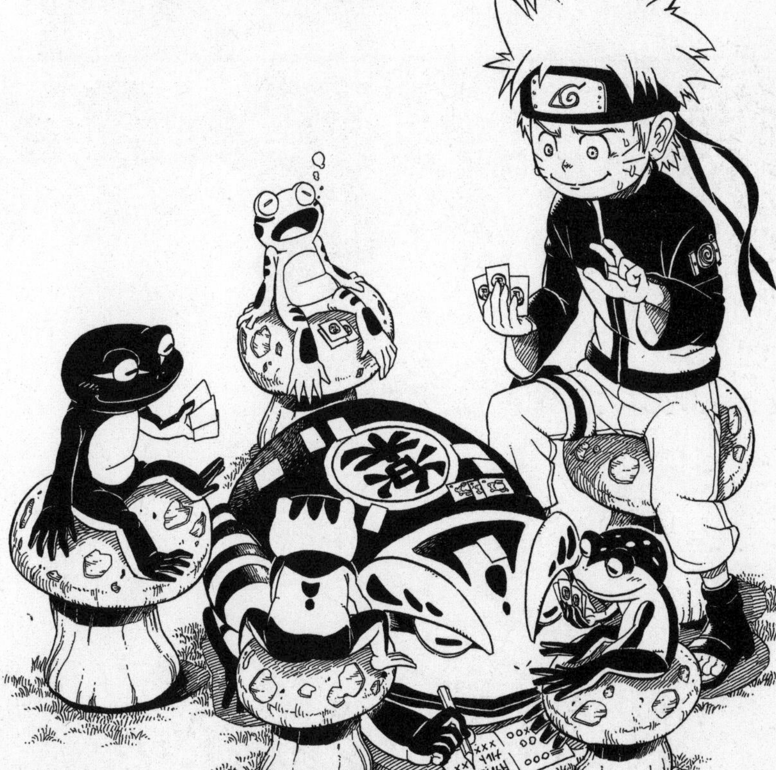

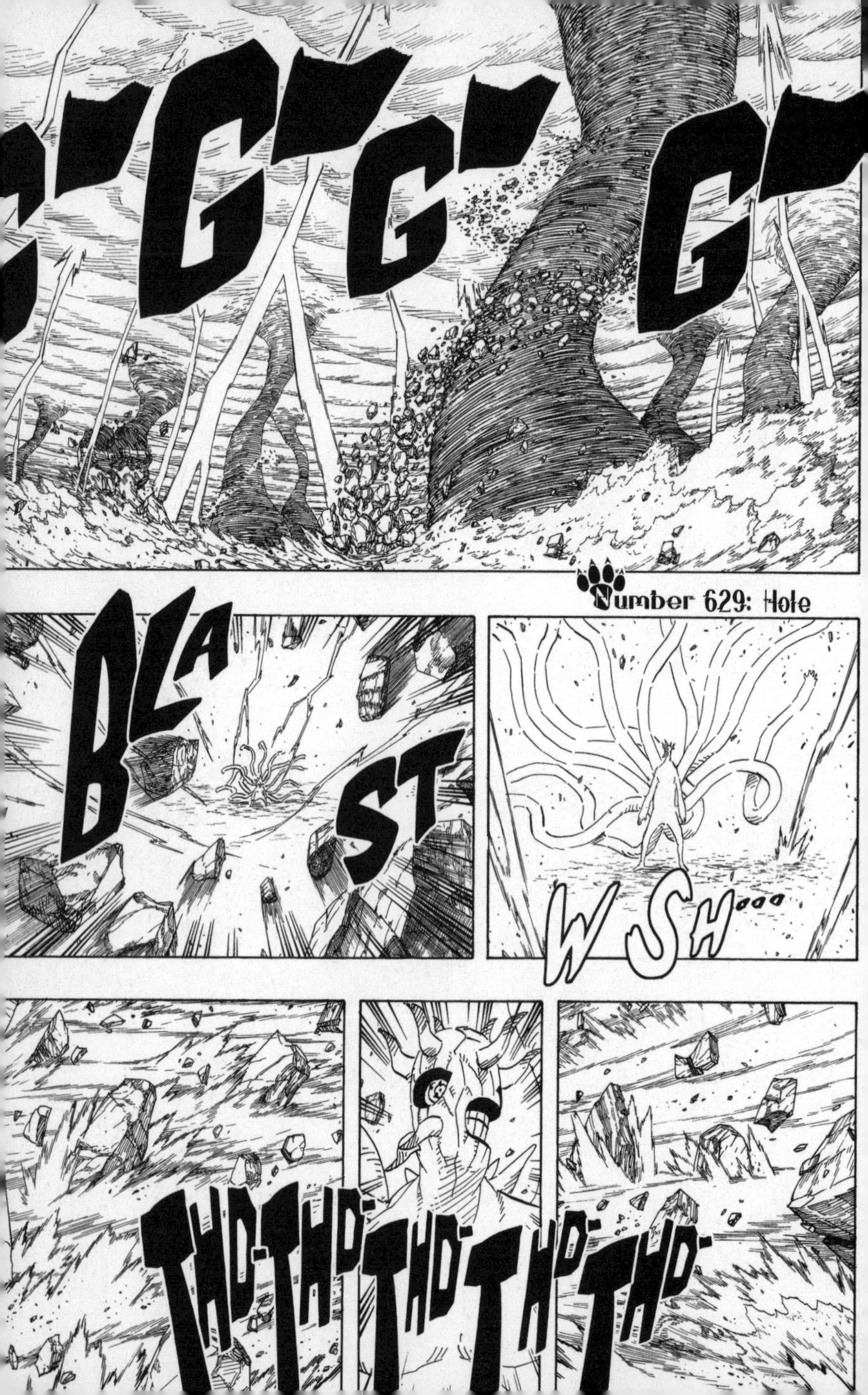
GGGG
Number 629: Hole
WSH...
BLAST
THD-THD-THD-THD-THD-THD-

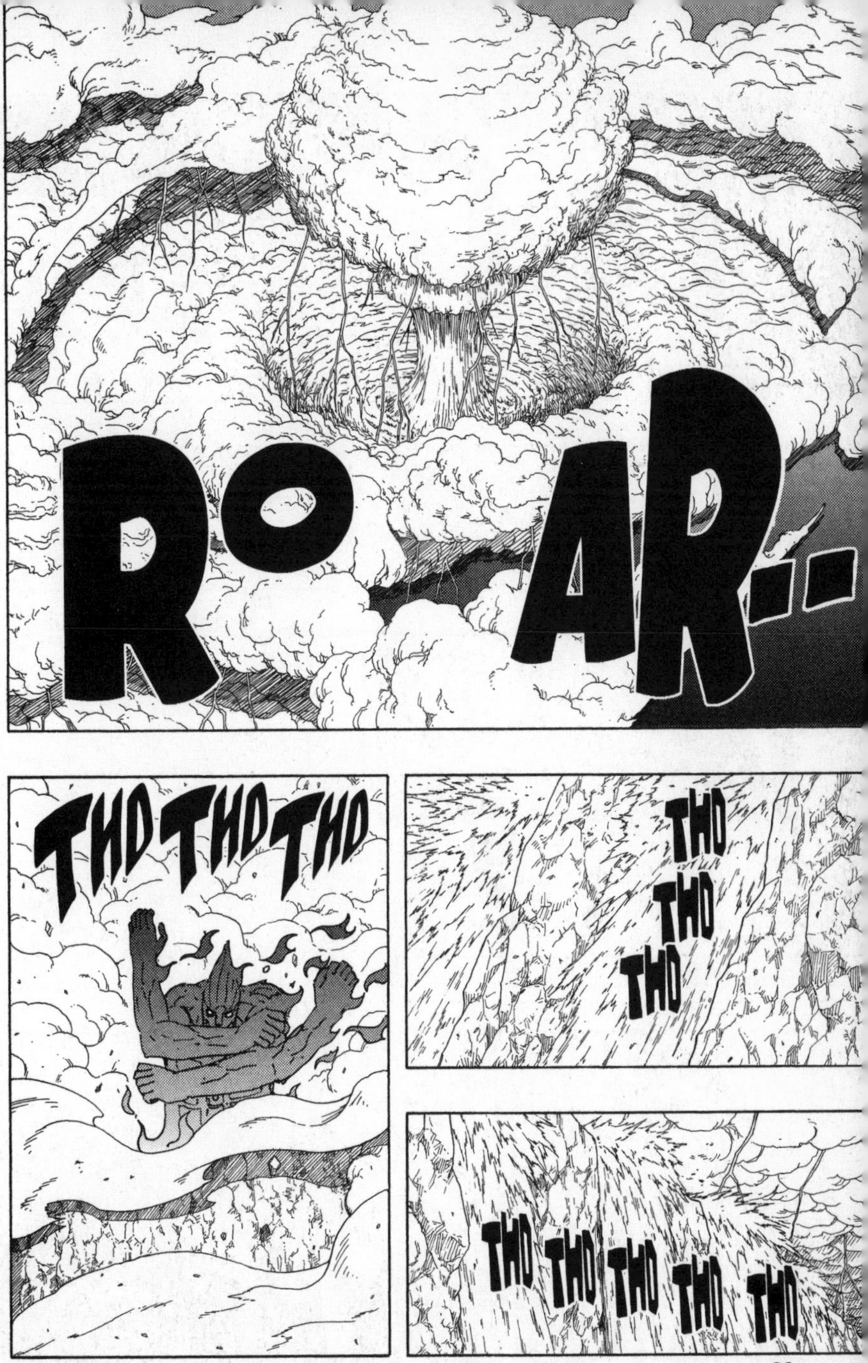
ROAR..
THD THD THD
THD THD THD THD THD
THD THD THD

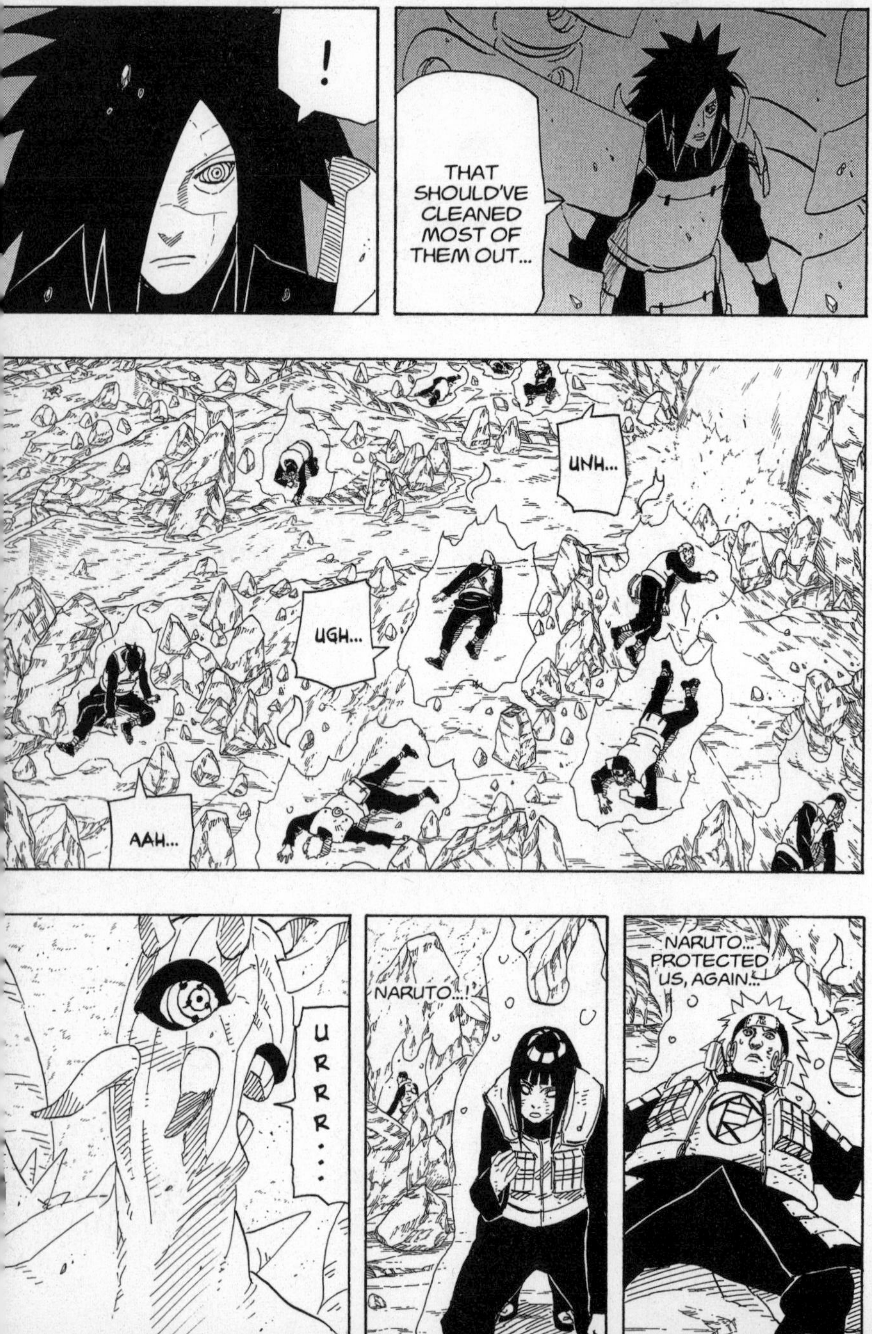
THAT SHOULD'VE CLEANED MOST OF THEM OUT...
!
UNH...
UGH...
AAH...
NARUTO... PROTECTED US, AGAIN...
NARUTO...!
URRR...

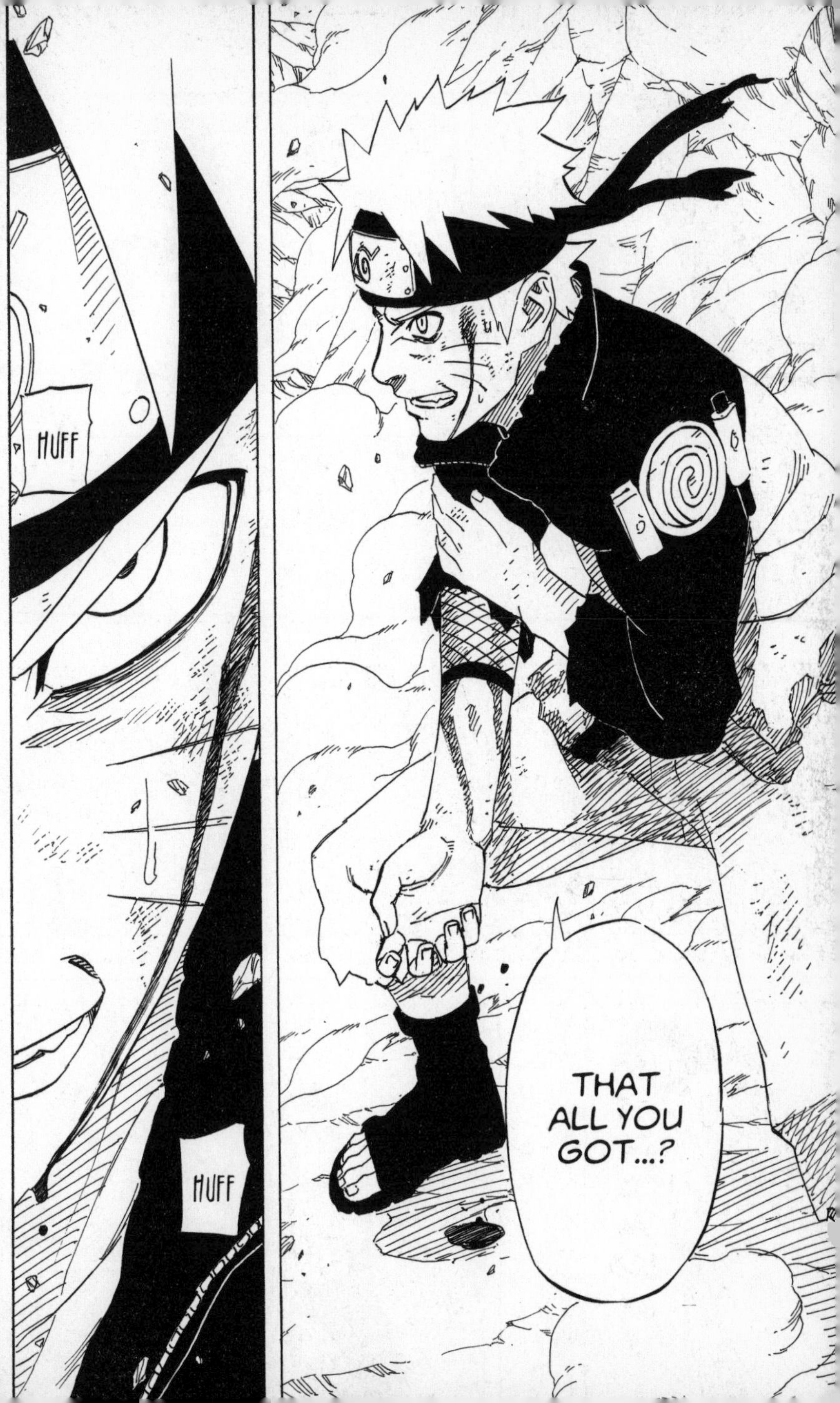
THAT ALL YOU GOT...?
HUFF
HUFF

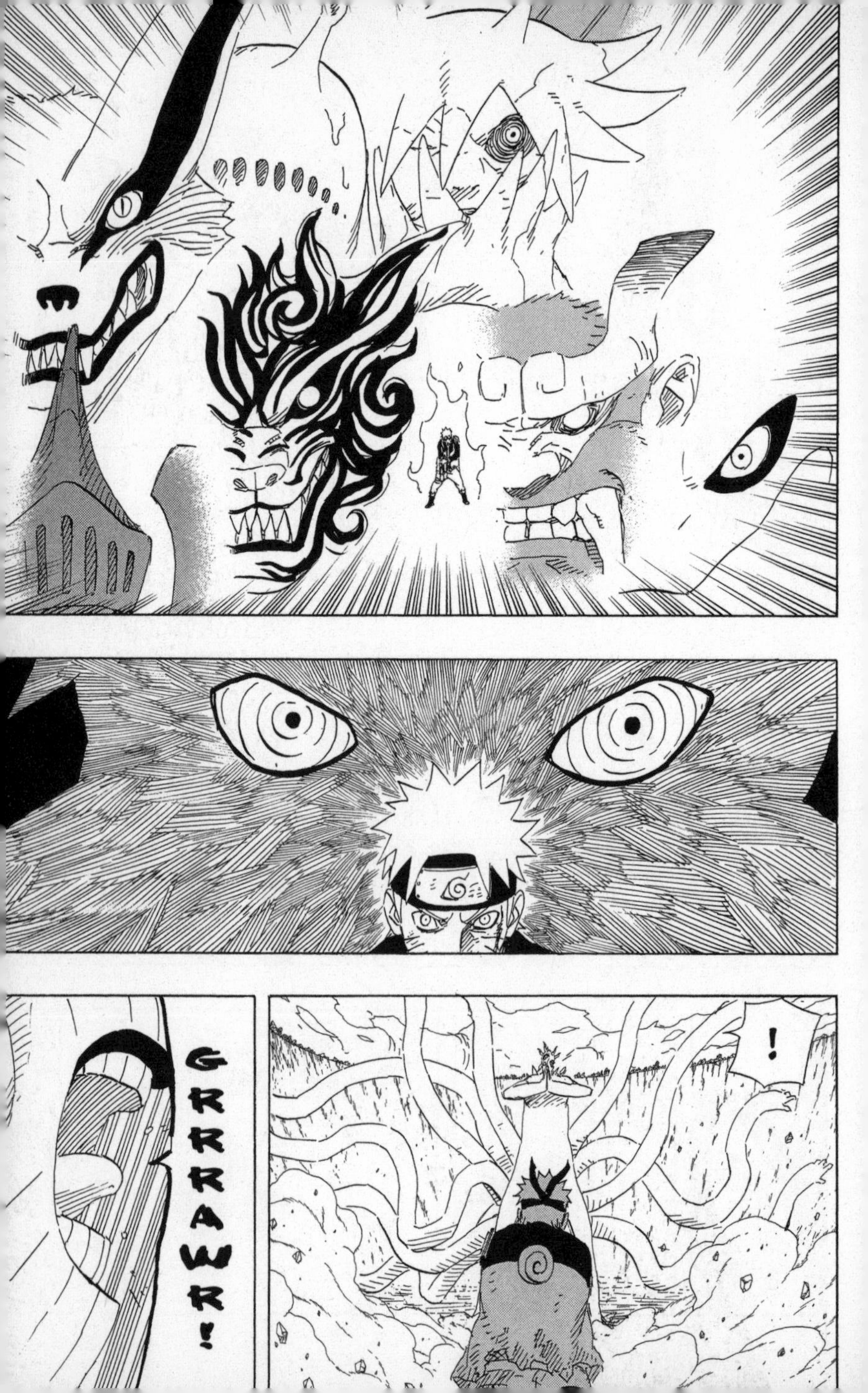
....
!
GRRRAWR!

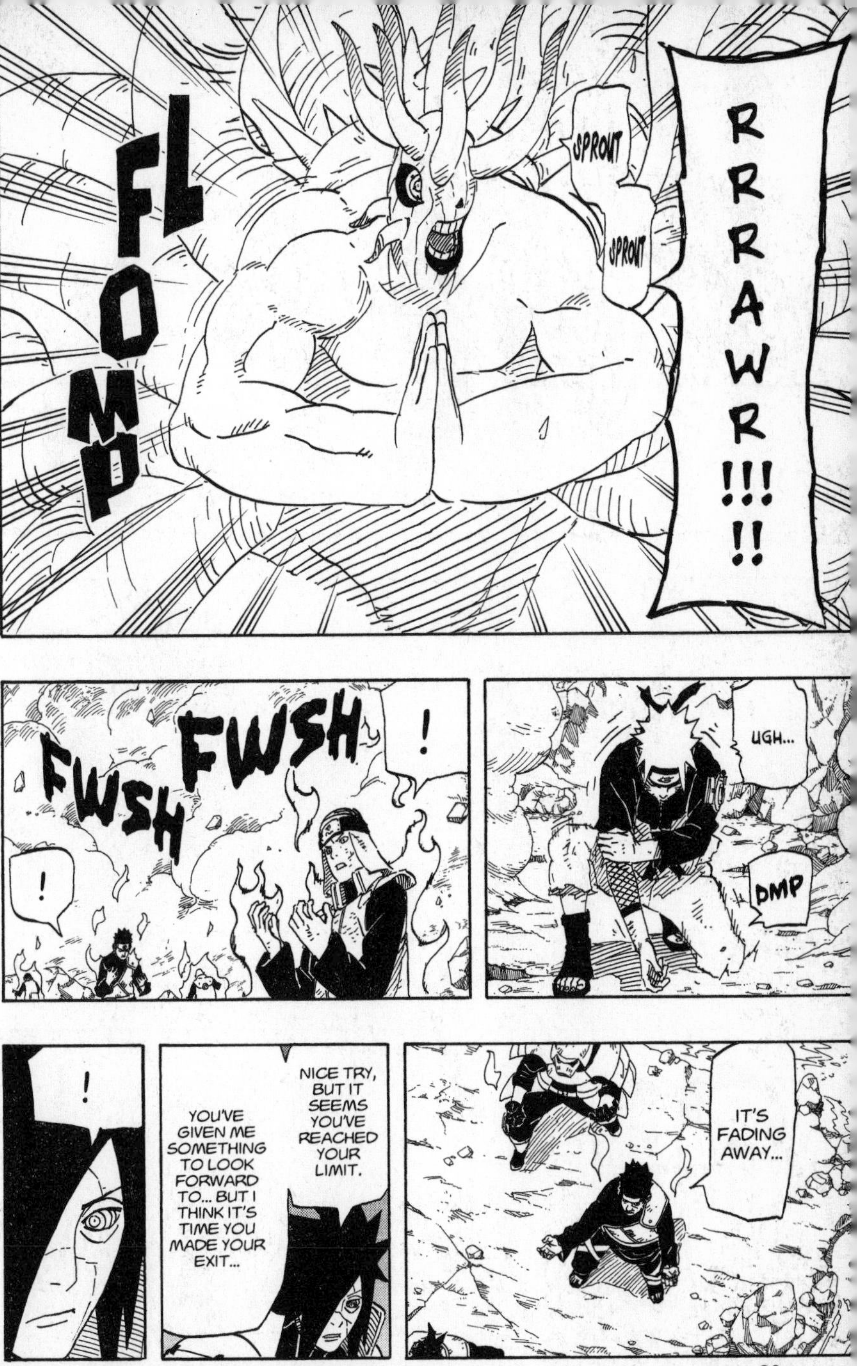
RRRAWR!!!!!
SPROUT
SPROUT
FLOMP
UGH...
DMP
!
FWSH
FWSH
!
IT'S FADING AWAY...
NICE TRY, BUT IT SEEMS YOU'VE REACHED YOUR LIMIT.
YOU'VE GIVEN ME SOMETHING TO LOOK FORWARD TO... BUT I THINK IT'S TIME YOU MADE YOUR EXIT...
!

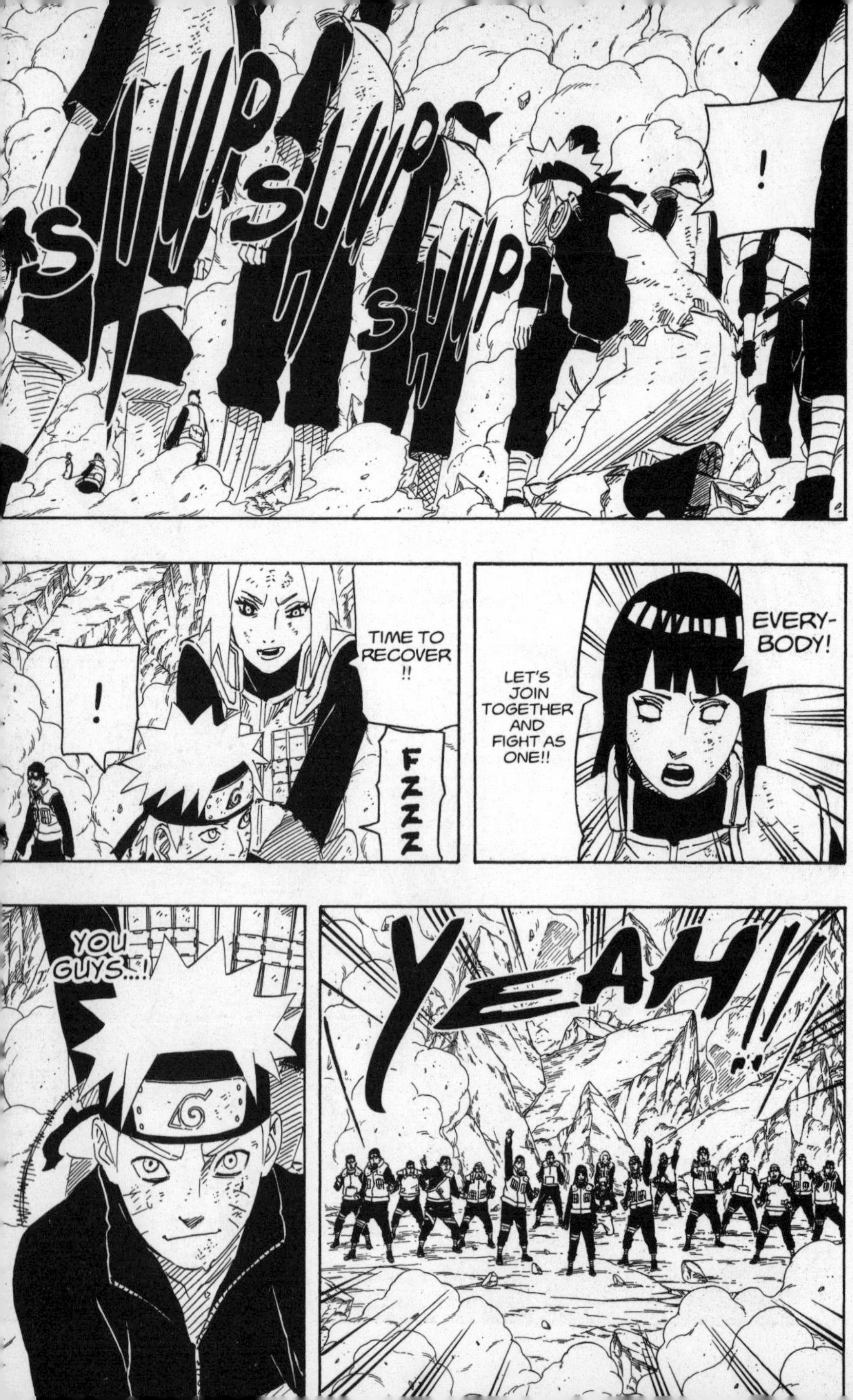
!
SHUP
SHUP
SHUP
SHUP
EVERY-BODY!
LET'S JOIN TOGETHER AND FIGHT AS ONE!!
TIME TO RECOVER!!
FZZZ
!
YEAH!!
YOU GUYS...!

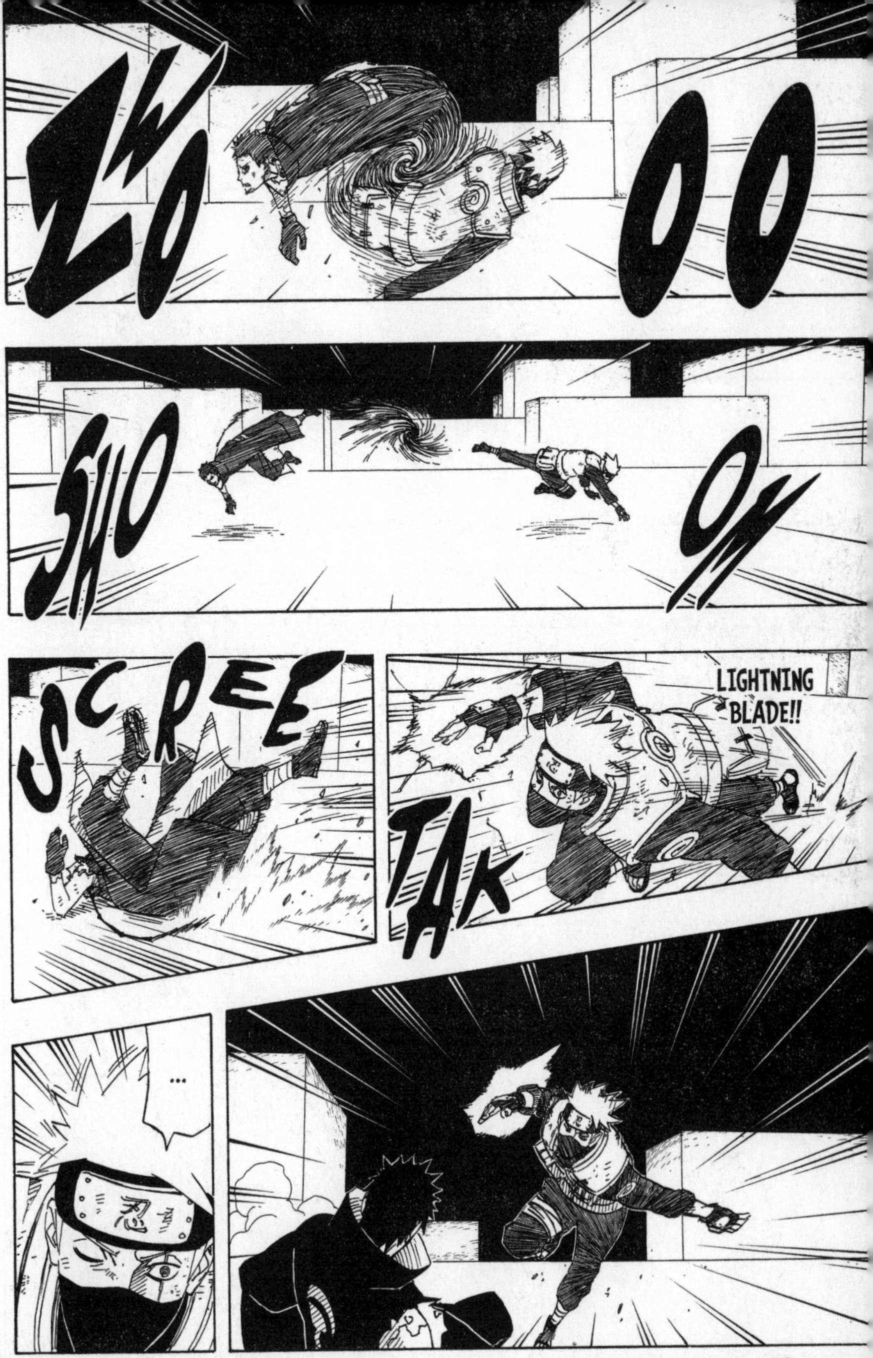
ZWO
OO
SHO
OM
LIGHTNING BLADE!!
TAK
SCREE
...

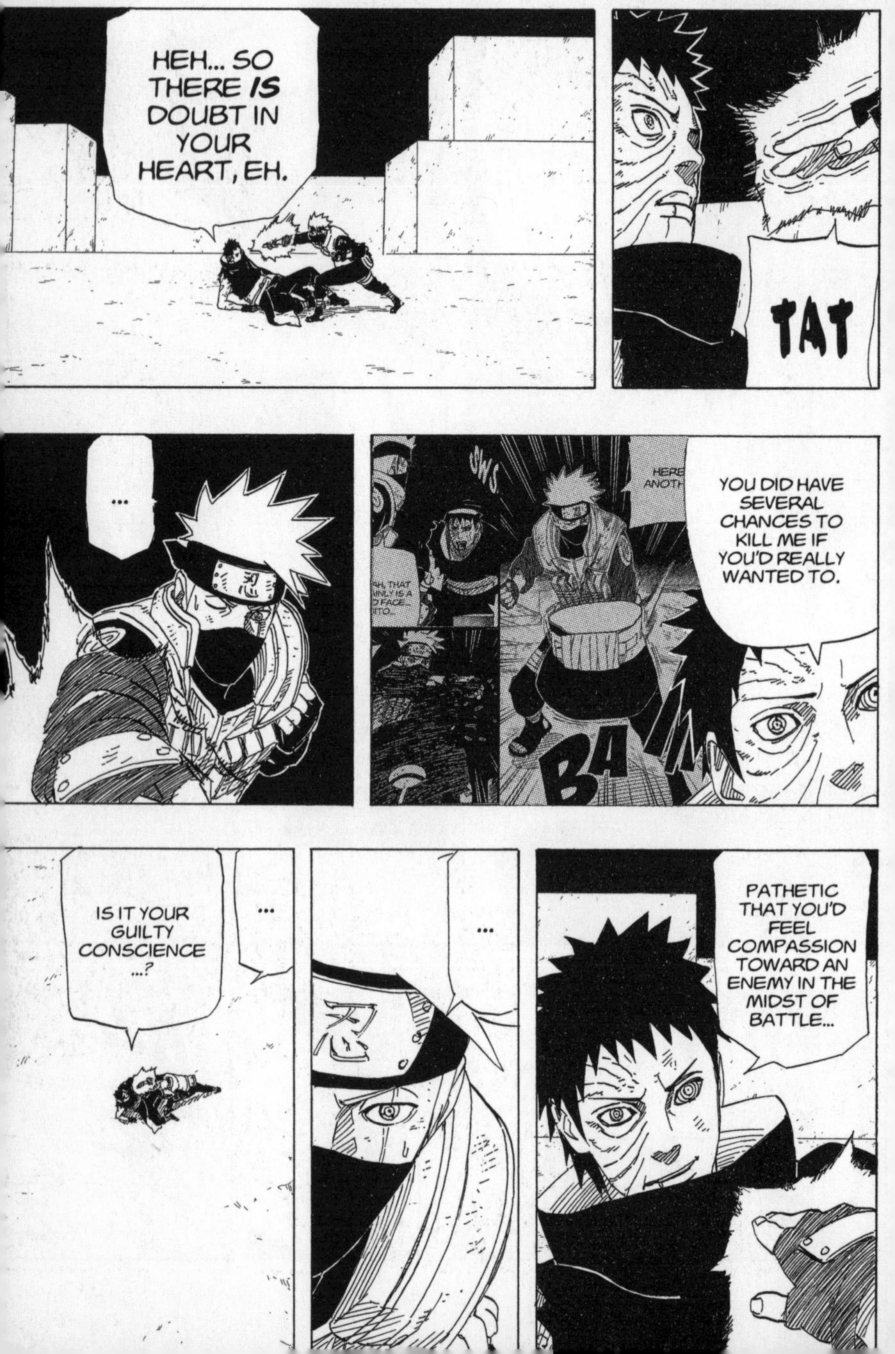
TAT
HEH... SO THERE *IS* DOUBT IN YOUR HEART, EH.
YOU DID HAVE SEVERAL CHANCES TO KILL ME IF YOU'D REALLY WANTED TO.
SWS
BA
...
PATHETIC THAT YOU'D FEEL COMPASSION TOWARD AN ENEMY IN THE MIDST OF BATTLE...
...
...
IS IT YOUR GUILTY CONSCIENCE ...?

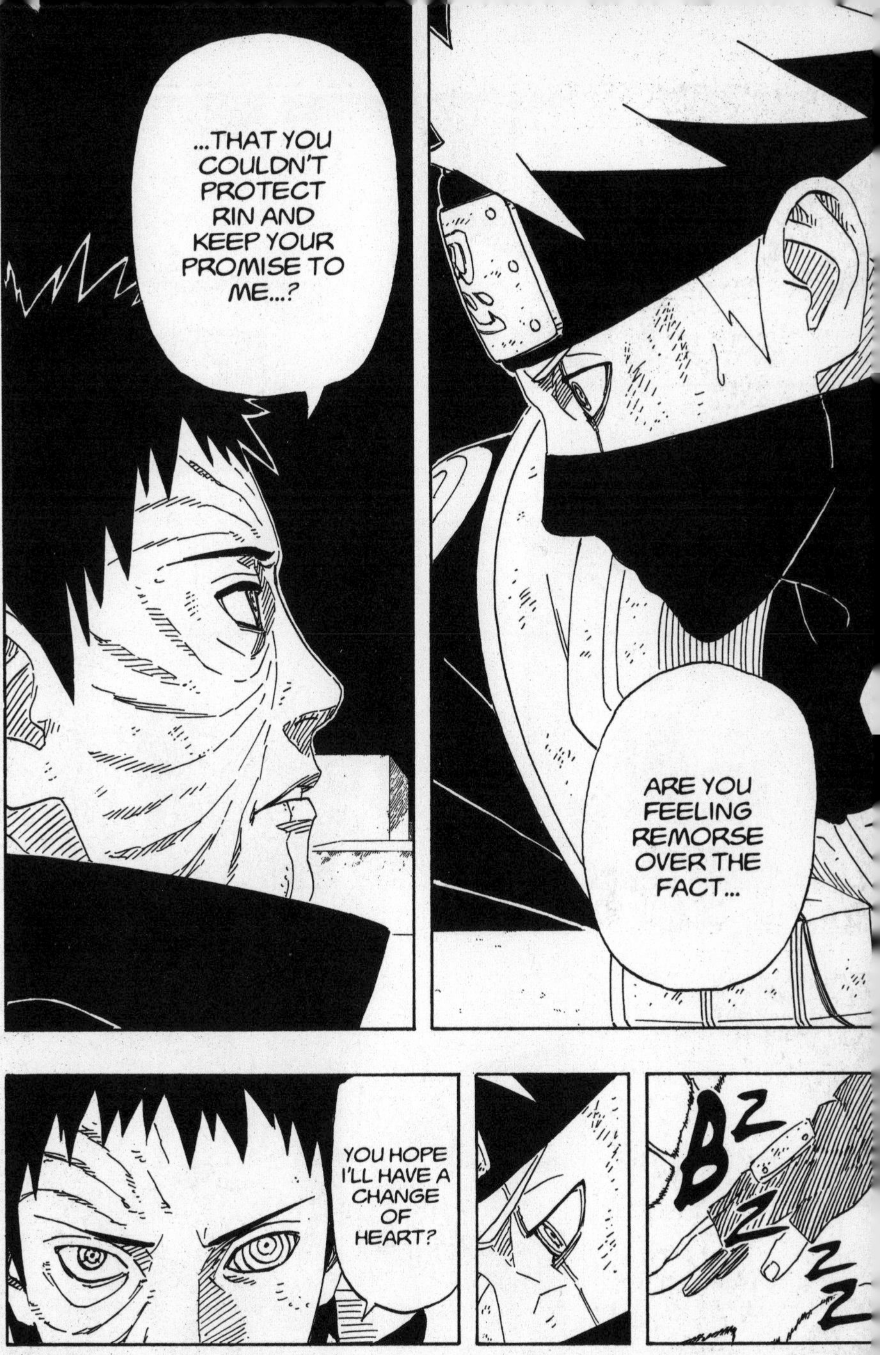
ARE YOU FEELING REMORSE OVER THE FACT...
...THAT YOU COULDN'T PROTECT RIN AND KEEP YOUR PROMISE TO ME...?
BZZZZ
YOU HOPE I'LL HAVE A CHANGE OF HEART?

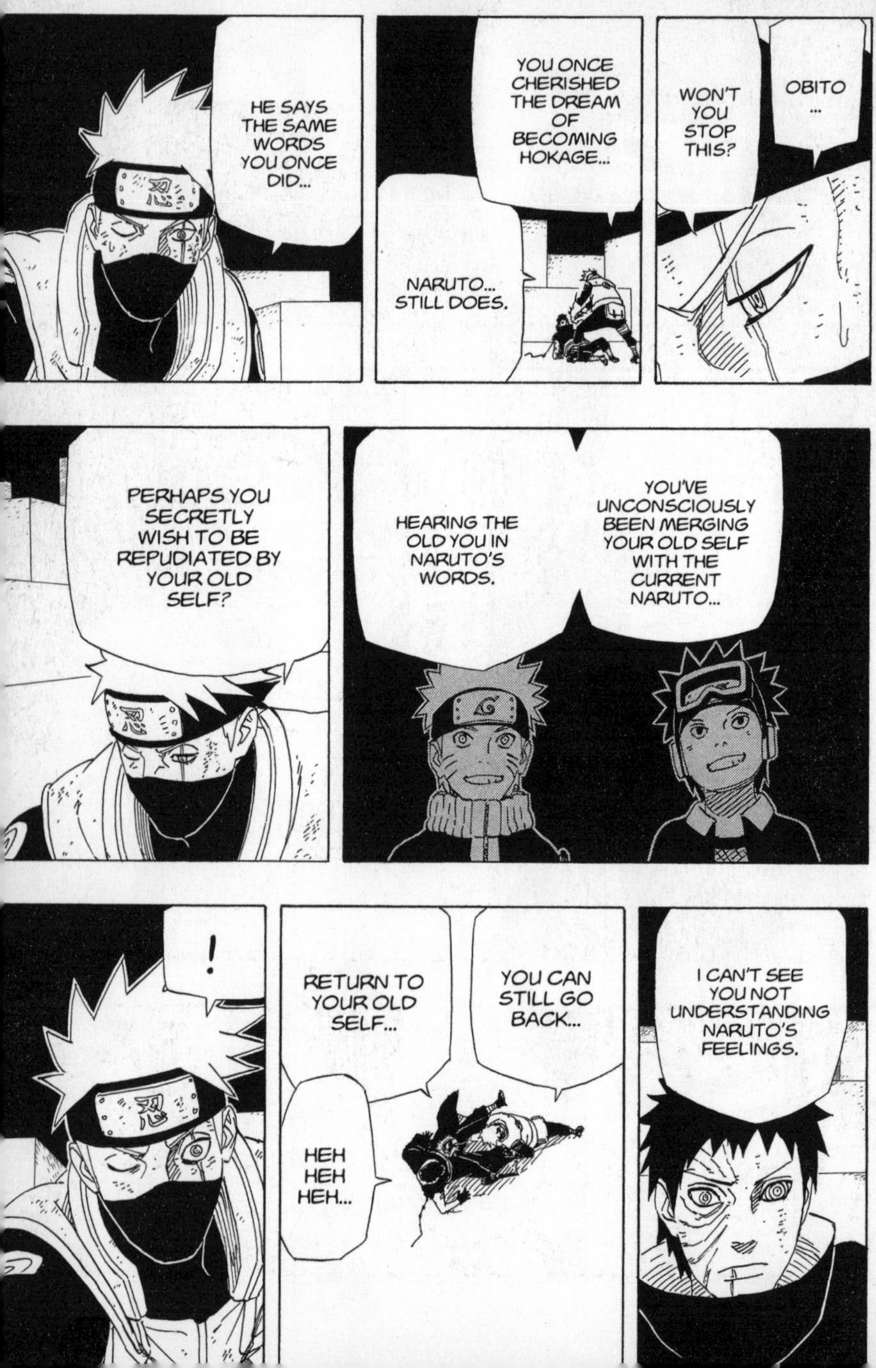
OBITO ...
WON'T YOU STOP THIS?
YOU ONCE CHERISHED THE DREAM OF BECOMING HOKAGE...
NARUTO... STILL DOES.
HE SAYS THE SAME WORDS YOU ONCE DID...
YOU'VE UNCONSCIOUSLY BEEN MERGING YOUR OLD SELF WITH THE CURRENT NARUTO...
HEARING THE OLD YOU IN NARUTO'S WORDS.
PERHAPS YOU SECRETLY WISH TO BE REPUDIATED BY YOUR OLD SELF?
I CAN'T SEE YOU NOT UNDERSTANDING NARUTO'S FEELINGS.
YOU CAN STILL GO BACK...
RETURN TO YOUR OLD SELF...
HEH HEH HEH...
!

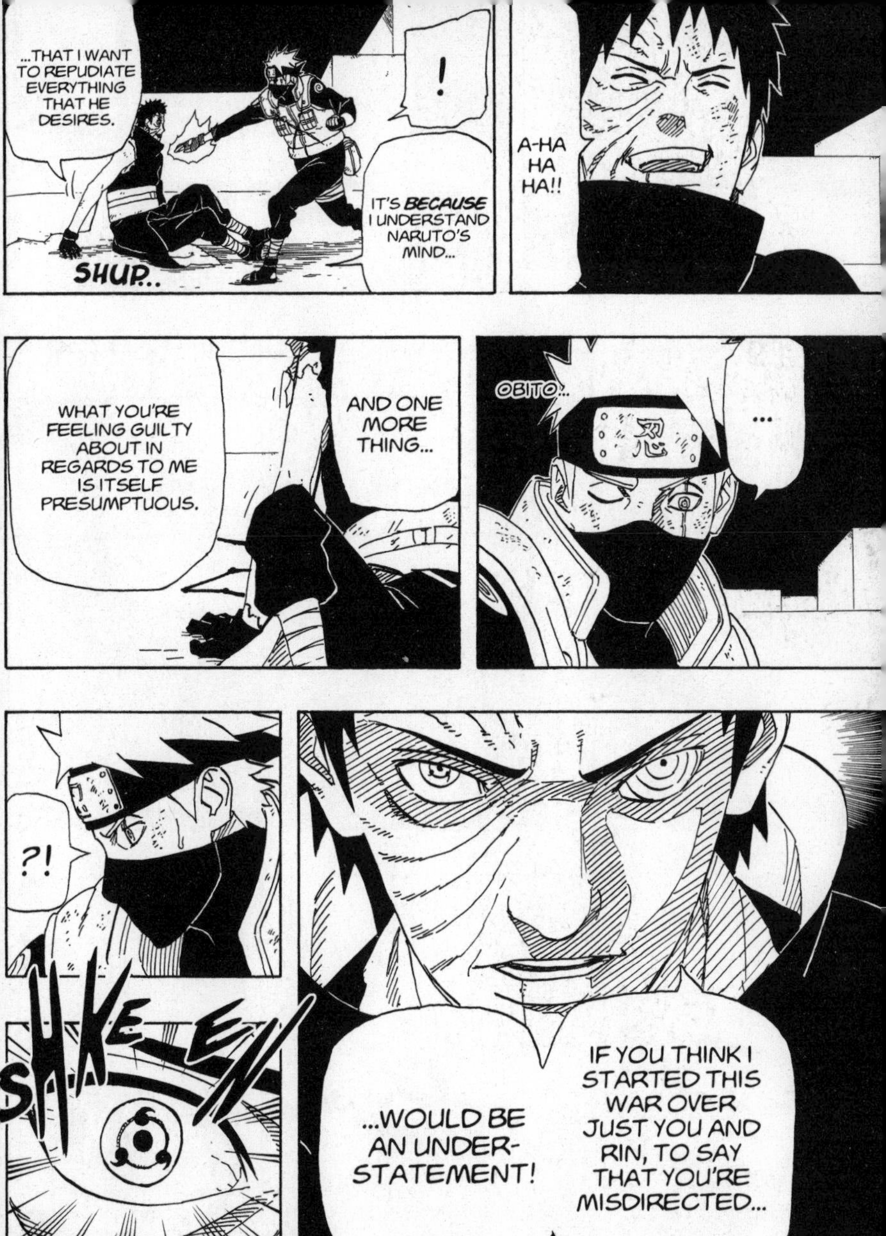

A-HA HA HA!!
!
IT'S BECAUSE I UNDERSTAND NARUTO'S MIND...
...THAT I WANT TO REPUDIATE EVERYTHING THAT HE DESIRES.
SHUP...
...
OBITO...
AND ONE MORE THING...
WHAT YOU'RE FEELING GUILTY ABOUT IN REGARDS TO ME IS ITSELF PRESUMPTUOUS.
IF YOU THINK I STARTED THIS WAR OVER JUST YOU AND RIN, TO SAY THAT YOU'RE MISDIRECTED...
...WOULD BE AN UNDER-STATEMENT!
?!
SHKE-EN

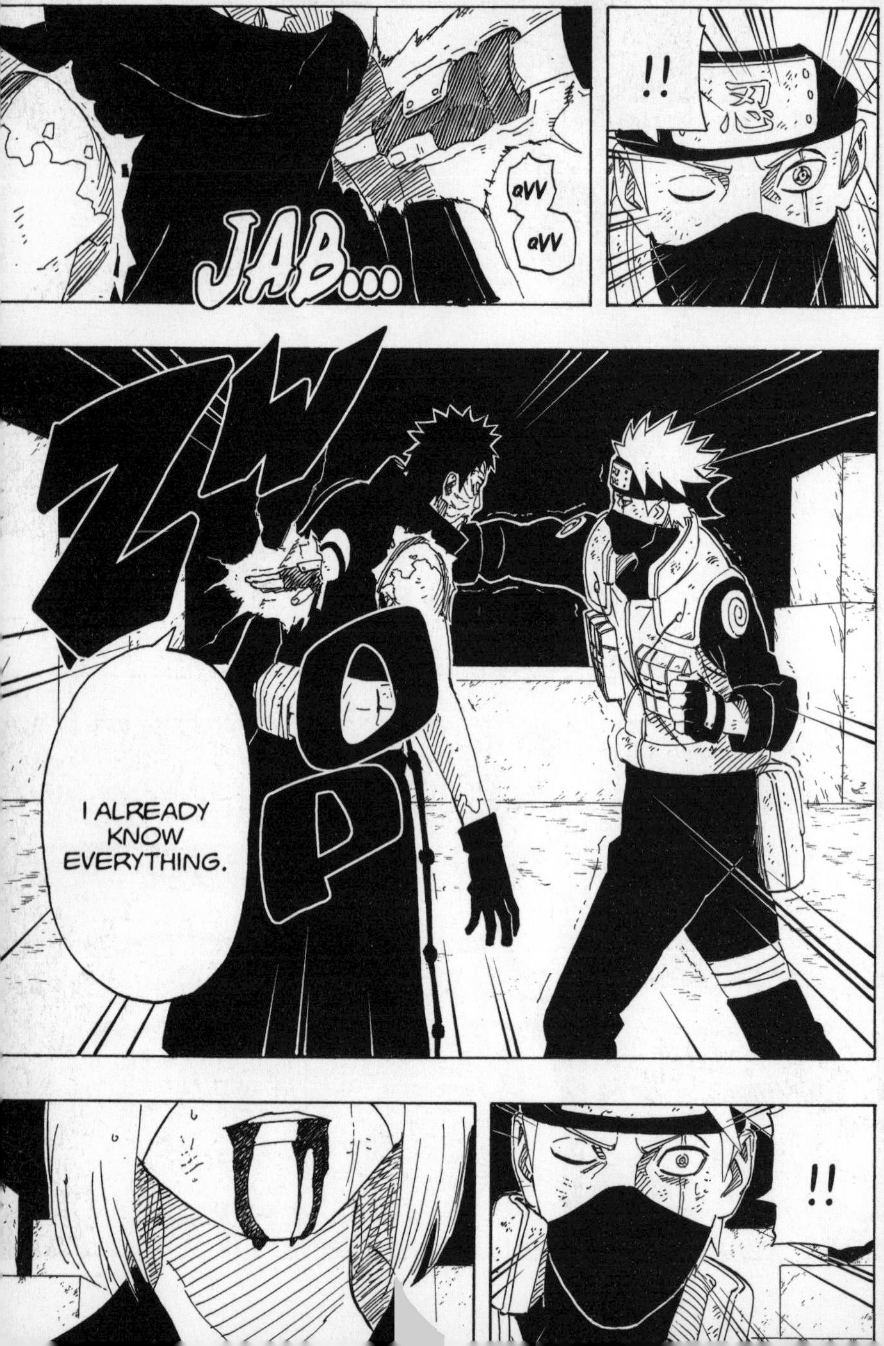
!!
QVV
QVV
JAB...
ZWOP
I ALREADY KNOW EVERYTHING.
!!

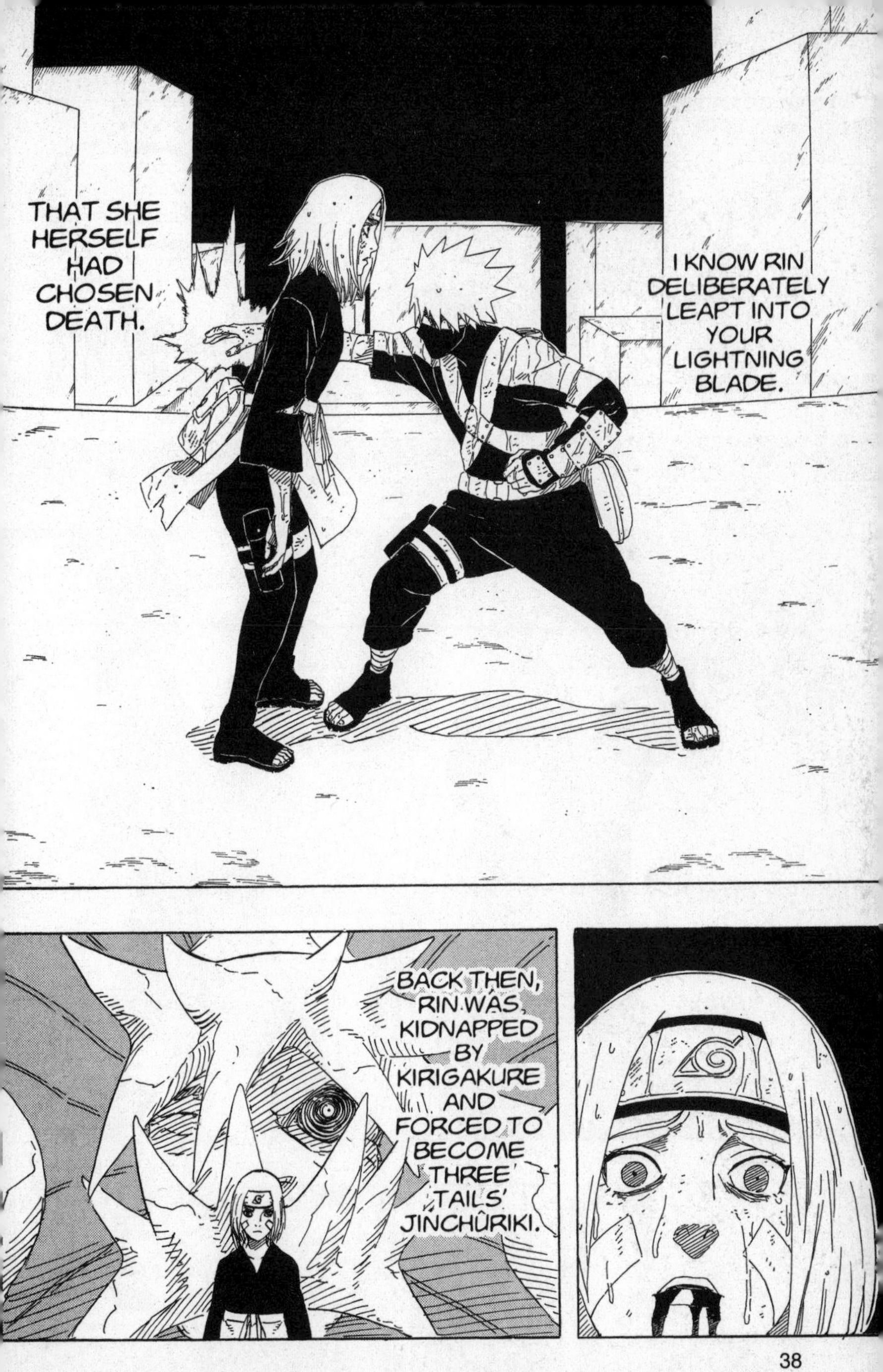
I KNOW RIN DELIBERATELY LEAPT INTO YOUR LIGHTNING BLADE.
THAT SHE HERSELF HAD CHOSEN DEATH.
BACK THEN, RIN WAS KIDNAPPED BY KIRIGAKURE AND FORCED TO BECOME THREE TAILS' JINCHÛRIKI.

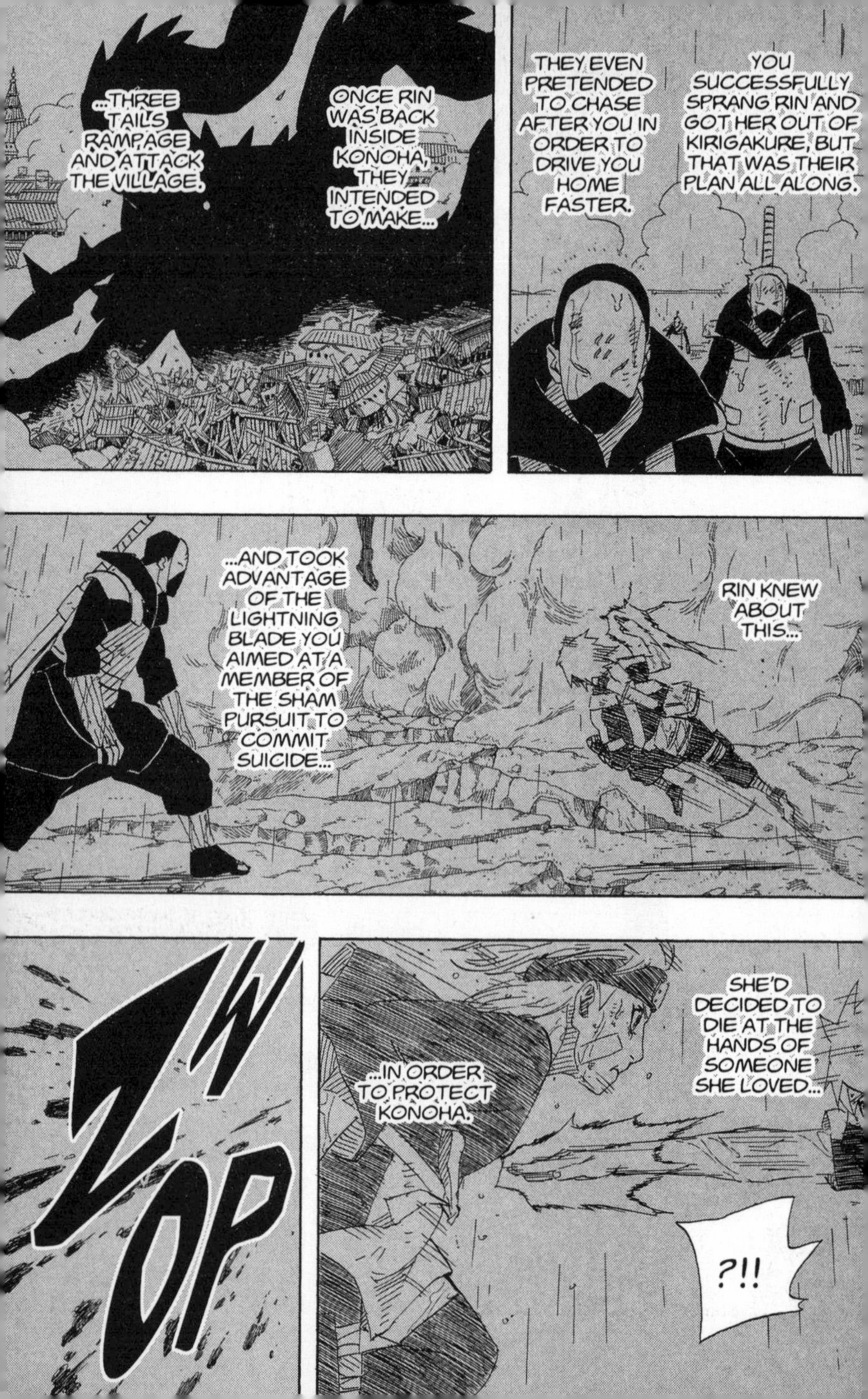
YOU SUCCESSFULLY SPRANG RIN AND GOT HER OUT OF KIRIGAKURE, BUT THAT WAS THEIR PLAN ALL ALONG.
THEY EVEN PRETENDED TO CHASE AFTER YOU IN ORDER TO DRIVE YOU HOME FASTER.
ONCE RIN WAS BACK INSIDE KONOHA, THEY INTENDED TO MAKE...
...THREE TAILS RAMPAGE AND ATTACK THE VILLAGE.
RIN KNEW ABOUT THIS...
...AND TOOK ADVANTAGE OF THE LIGHTNING BLADE YOU AIMED AT A MEMBER OF THE SHAM PURSUIT TO COMMIT SUICIDE...
SHE'D DECIDED TO DIE AT THE HANDS OF SOMEONE SHE LOVED...
...IN ORDER TO PROTECT KONOHA.
?!!
ZWOP

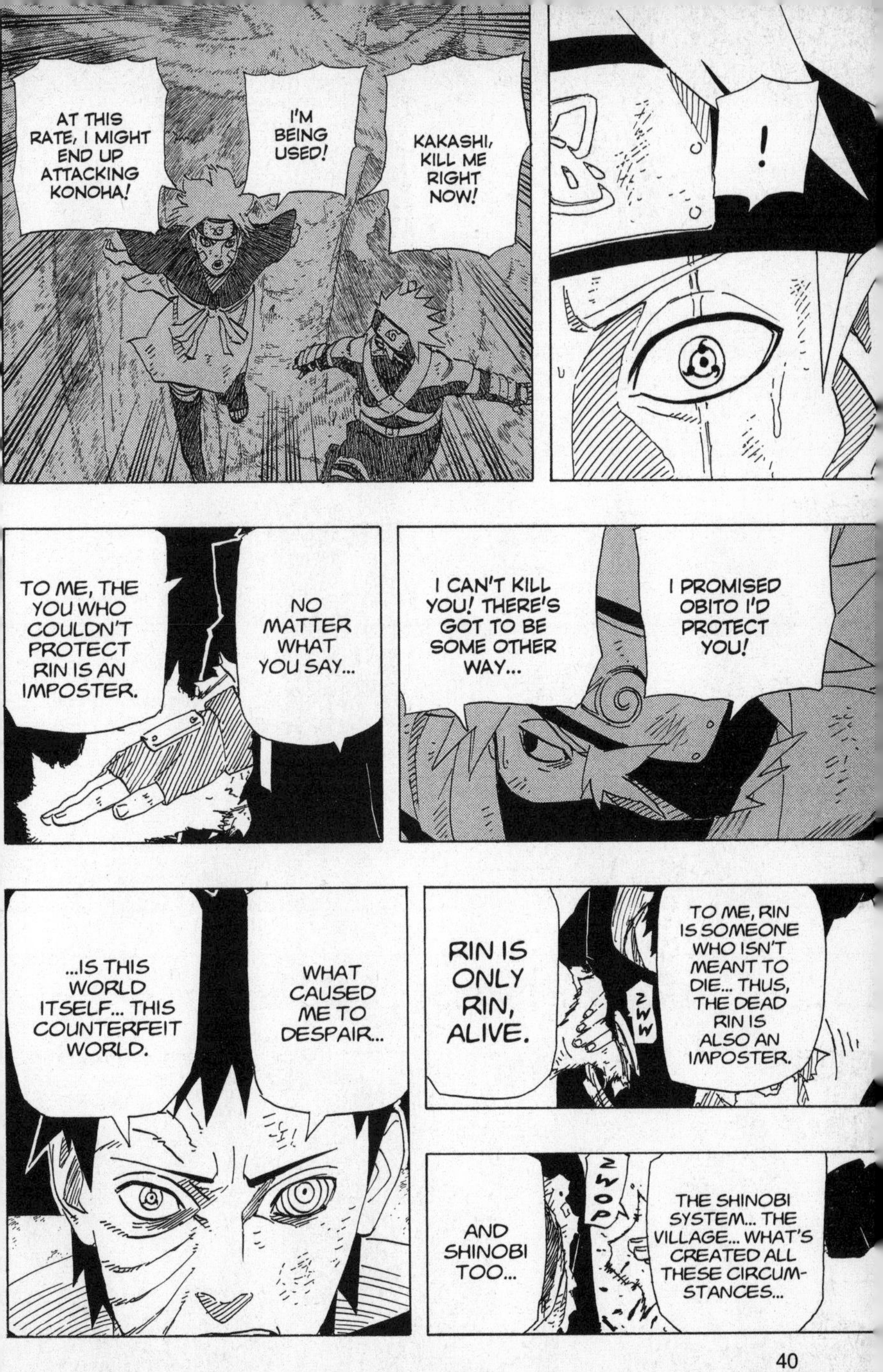
!
KAKASHI, KILL ME RIGHT NOW!
I'M BEING USED!
AT THIS RATE, I MIGHT END UP ATTACKING KONOHA!
I PROMISED OBITO I'D PROTECT YOU!
I CAN'T KILL YOU! THERE'S GOT TO BE SOME OTHER WAY...
NO MATTER WHAT YOU SAY...
TO ME, THE YOU WHO COULDN'T PROTECT RIN IS AN IMPOSTER.
TO ME, RIN IS SOMEONE WHO ISN'T MEANT TO DIE... THUS, THE DEAD RIN IS ALSO AN IMPOSTER.
ZWW
RIN IS ONLY RIN, ALIVE.
THE SHINOBI SYSTEM... THE VILLAGE... WHAT'S CREATED ALL THESE CIRCUM-STANCES...
ZWOP
AND SHINOBI TOO...
WHAT CAUSED ME TO DESPAIR...
...IS THIS WORLD ITSELF... THIS COUNTERFEIT WORLD.

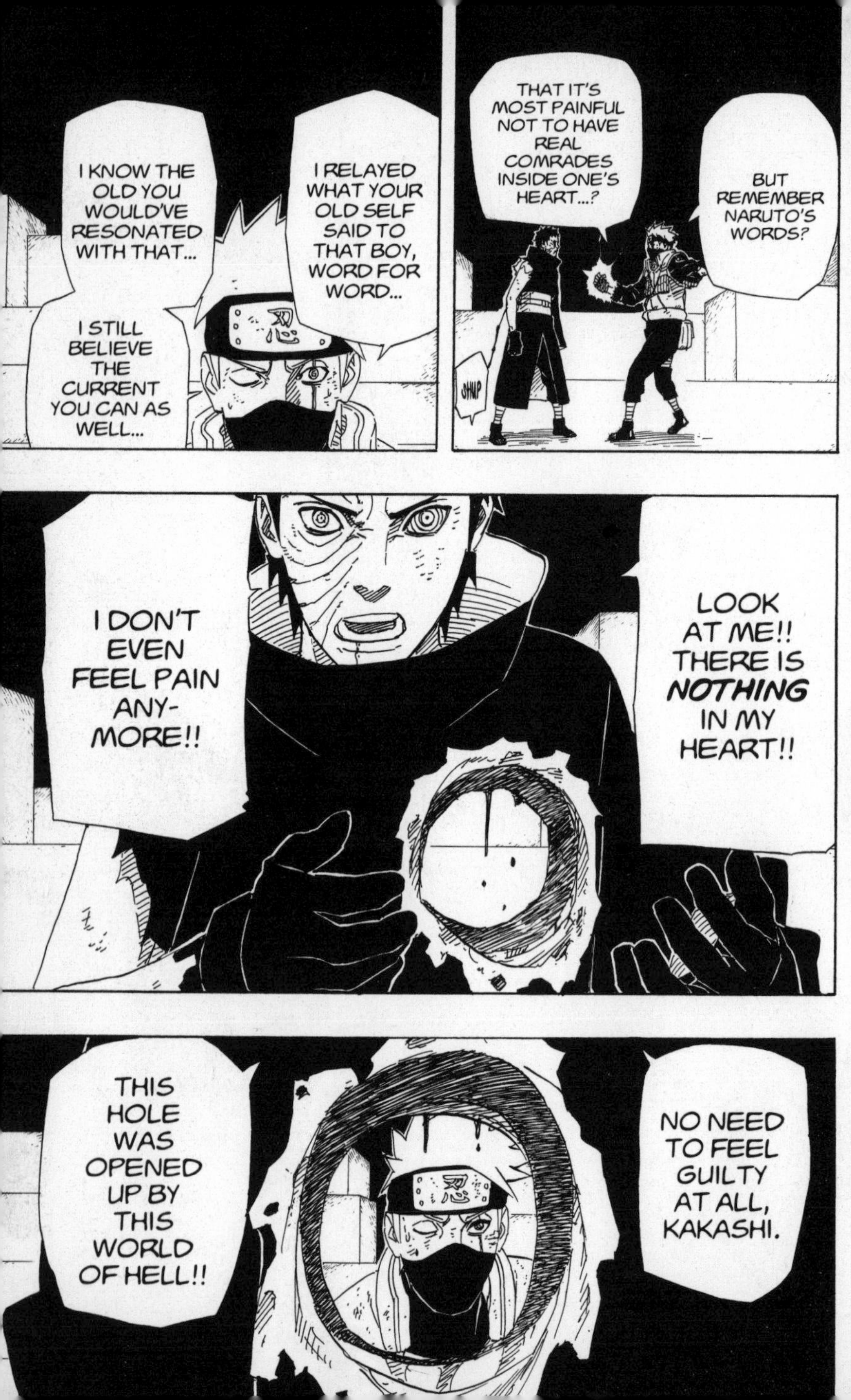
BUT REMEMBER NARUTO'S WORDS?
THAT IT'S MOST PAINFUL NOT TO HAVE REAL COMRADES INSIDE ONE'S HEART...?
I RELAYED WHAT YOUR OLD SELF SAID TO THAT BOY, WORD FOR WORD...
I KNOW THE OLD YOU WOULD'VE RESONATED WITH THAT...
I STILL BELIEVE THE CURRENT YOU CAN AS WELL...
LOOK AT ME!! THERE IS ***NOTHING*** IN MY HEART!!
I DON'T EVEN FEEL PAIN ANY-MORE!!
NO NEED TO FEEL GUILTY AT ALL, KAKASHI.
THIS HOLE WAS OPENED UP BY THIS WORLD OF HELL!!

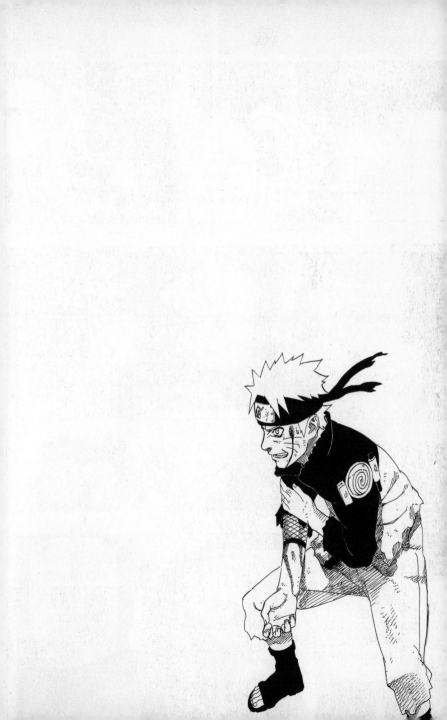

Number 630: Something to Fill the Hole

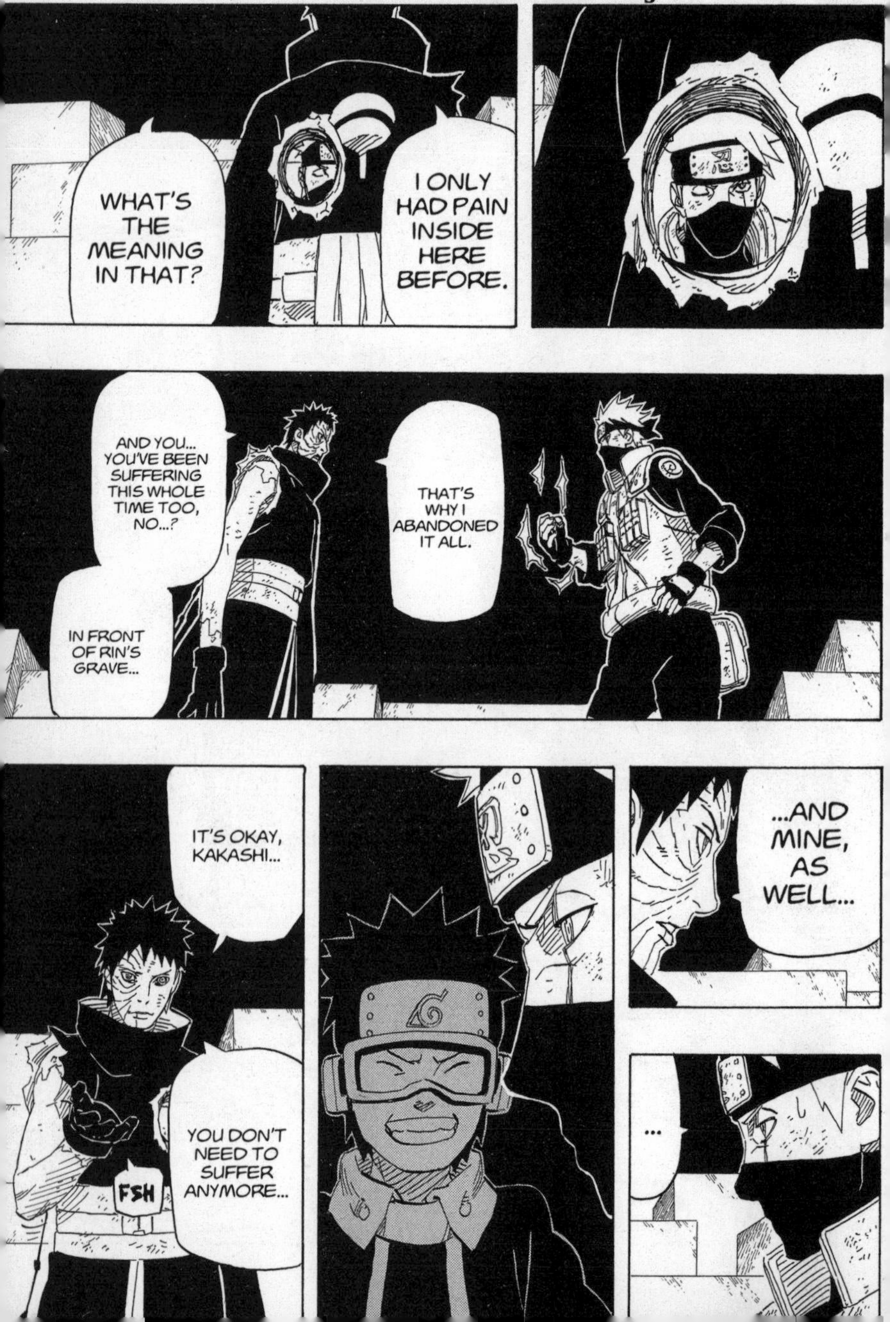
I ONLY HAD PAIN INSIDE HERE BEFORE.
WHAT'S THE MEANING IN THAT?
THAT'S WHY I ABANDONED IT ALL.
AND YOU... YOU'VE BEEN SUFFERING THIS WHOLE TIME TOO, NO...?
IN FRONT OF RIN'S GRAVE...
...AND MINE, AS WELL...
...
IT'S OKAY, KAKASHI...
FSH
YOU DON'T NEED TO SUFFER ANYMORE...

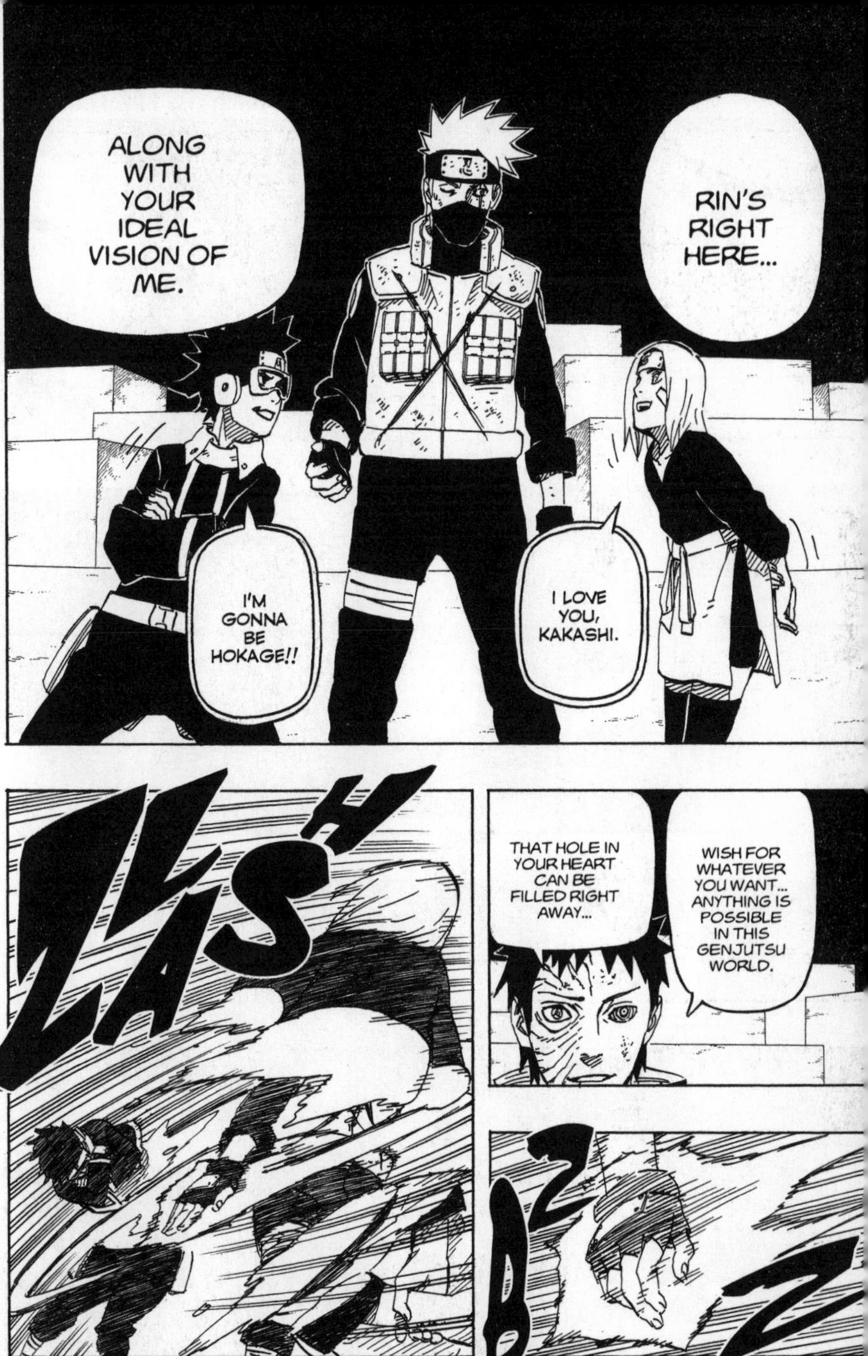
RIN'S RIGHT HERE...
ALONG WITH YOUR IDEAL VISION OF ME.
I LOVE YOU, KAKASHI.
I'M GONNA BE HOKAGE!!
WISH FOR WHATEVER YOU WANT... ANYTHING IS POSSIBLE IN THIS GENJUTSU WORLD.
THAT HOLE IN YOUR HEART CAN BE FILLED RIGHT AWAY...
ZASH
BZZ

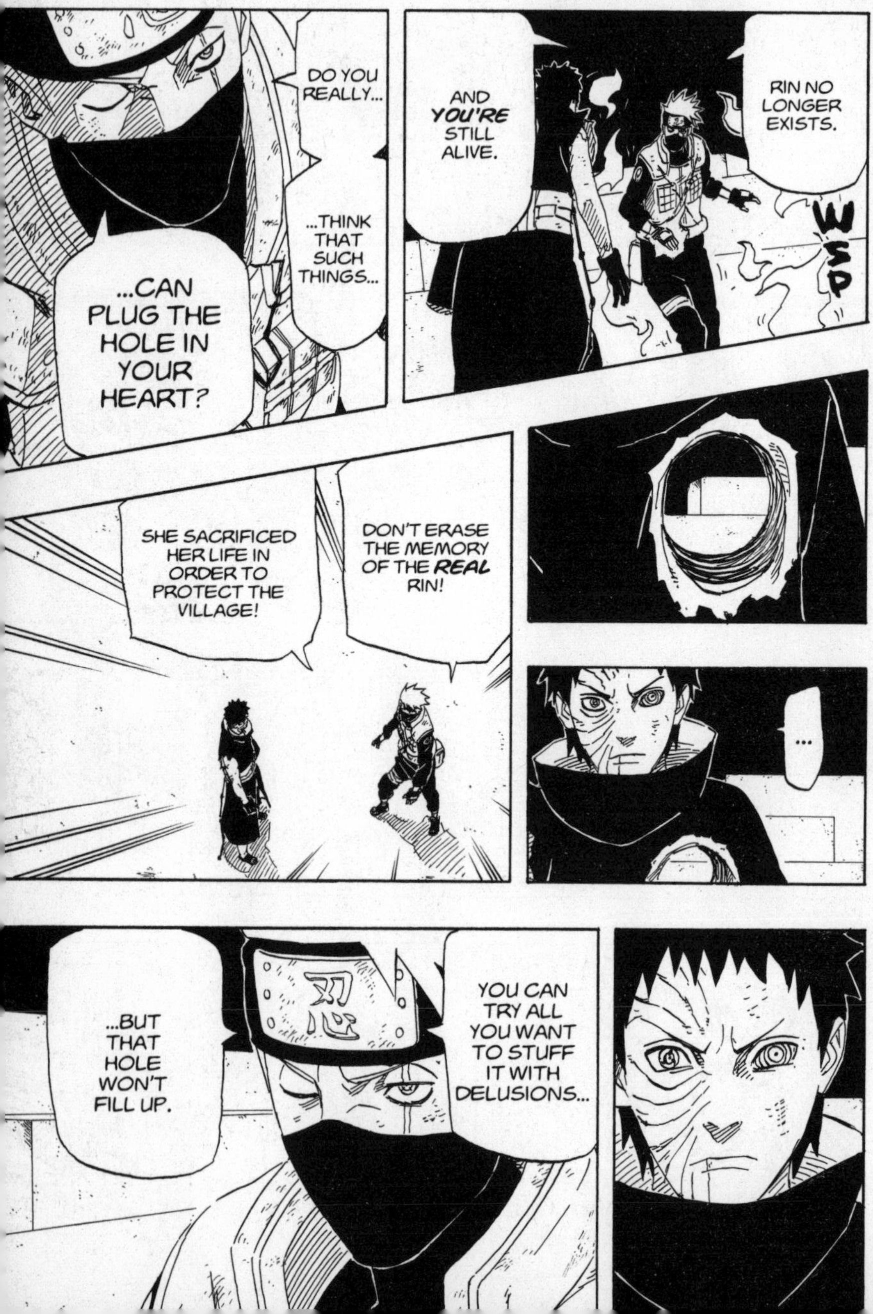
RIN NO LONGER EXISTS.
WSP
AND YOU'RE STILL ALIVE.
DO YOU REALLY...
...THINK THAT SUCH THINGS...
...CAN PLUG THE HOLE IN YOUR HEART?
...
DON'T ERASE THE MEMORY OF THE REAL RIN!
SHE SACRIFICED HER LIFE IN ORDER TO PROTECT THE VILLAGE!
YOU CAN TRY ALL YOU WANT TO STUFF IT WITH DELUSIONS...
...BUT THAT HOLE WON'T FILL UP.

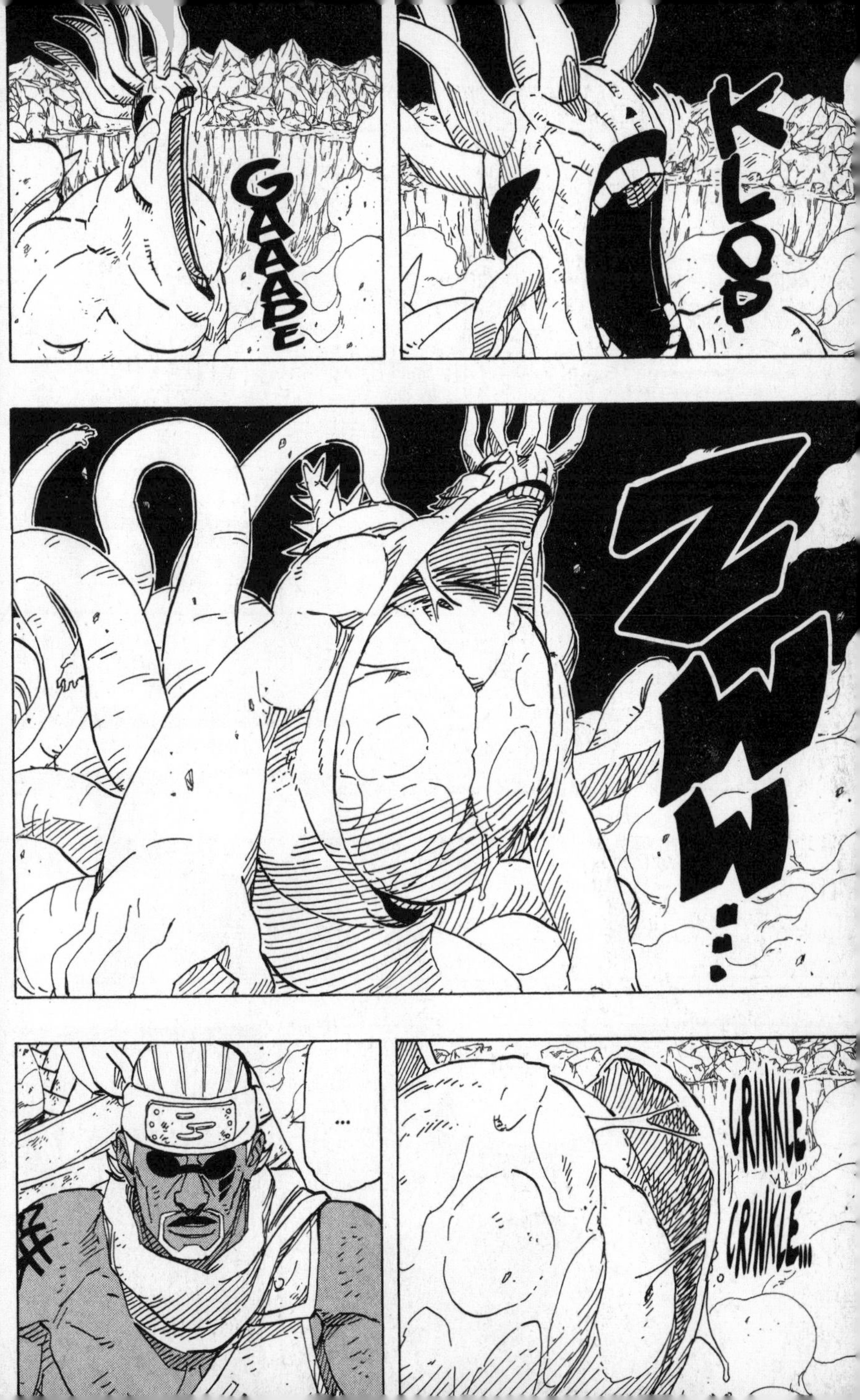
KLOP
GAAADE
ZWWW...
CRINKLE CRINKLE...
...

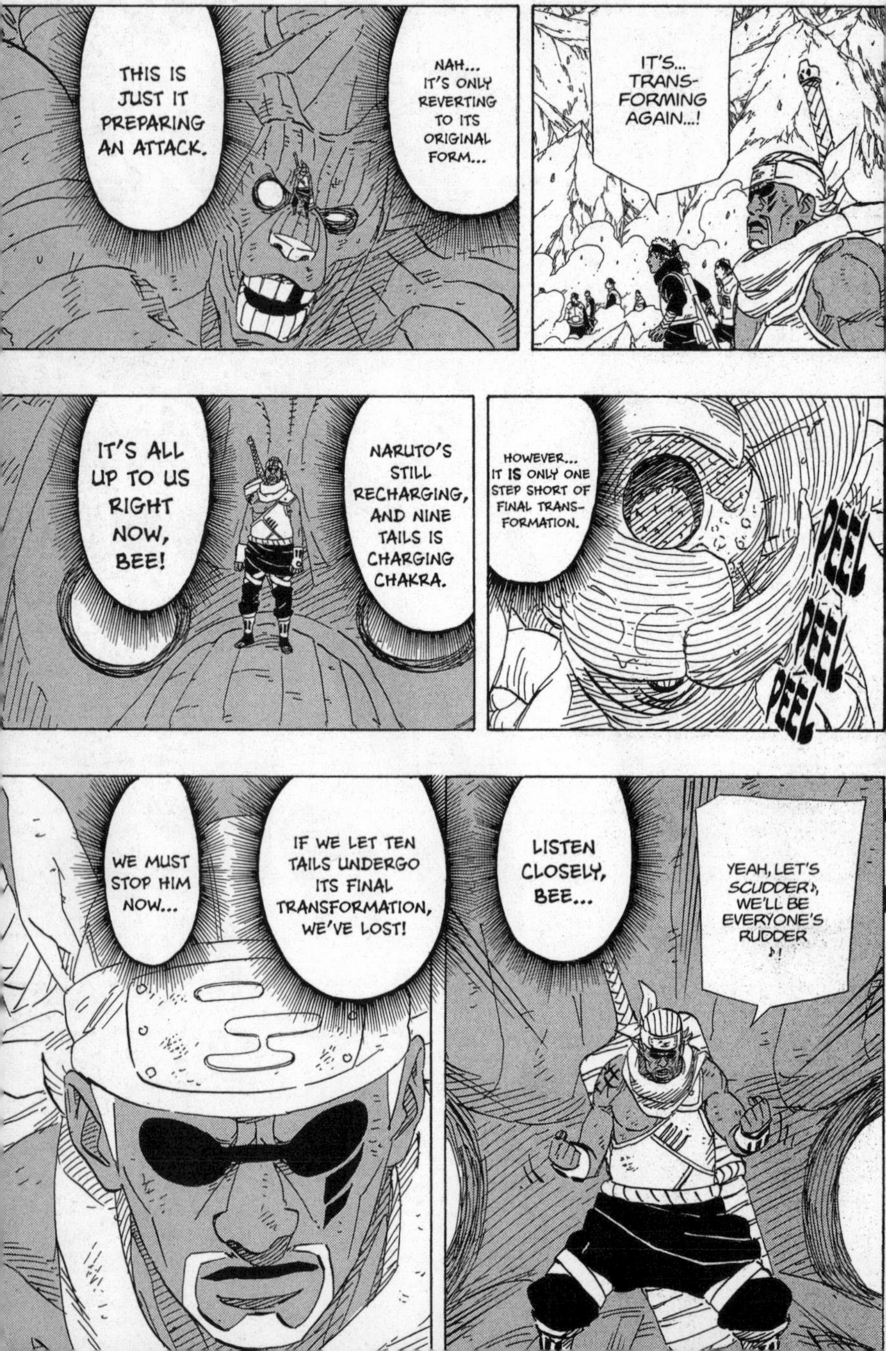
IT'S... TRANS-FORMING AGAIN...!
NAH... IT'S ONLY REVERTING TO ITS ORIGINAL FORM...
THIS IS JUST IT PREPARING AN ATTACK.
HOWEVER... IT IS ONLY ONE STEP SHORT OF FINAL TRANS-FORMATION.
PEEL PEEL PEEL
NARUTO'S STILL RECHARGING, AND NINE TAILS IS CHARGING CHAKRA.
IT'S ALL UP TO US RIGHT NOW, BEE!
YEAH, LET'S SCUDDER♪, WE'LL BE EVERYONE'S RUDDER ♪!
LISTEN CLOSELY, BEE...
IF WE LET TEN TAILS UNDERGO ITS FINAL TRANSFORMATION, WE'VE LOST!
WE MUST STOP HIM NOW...

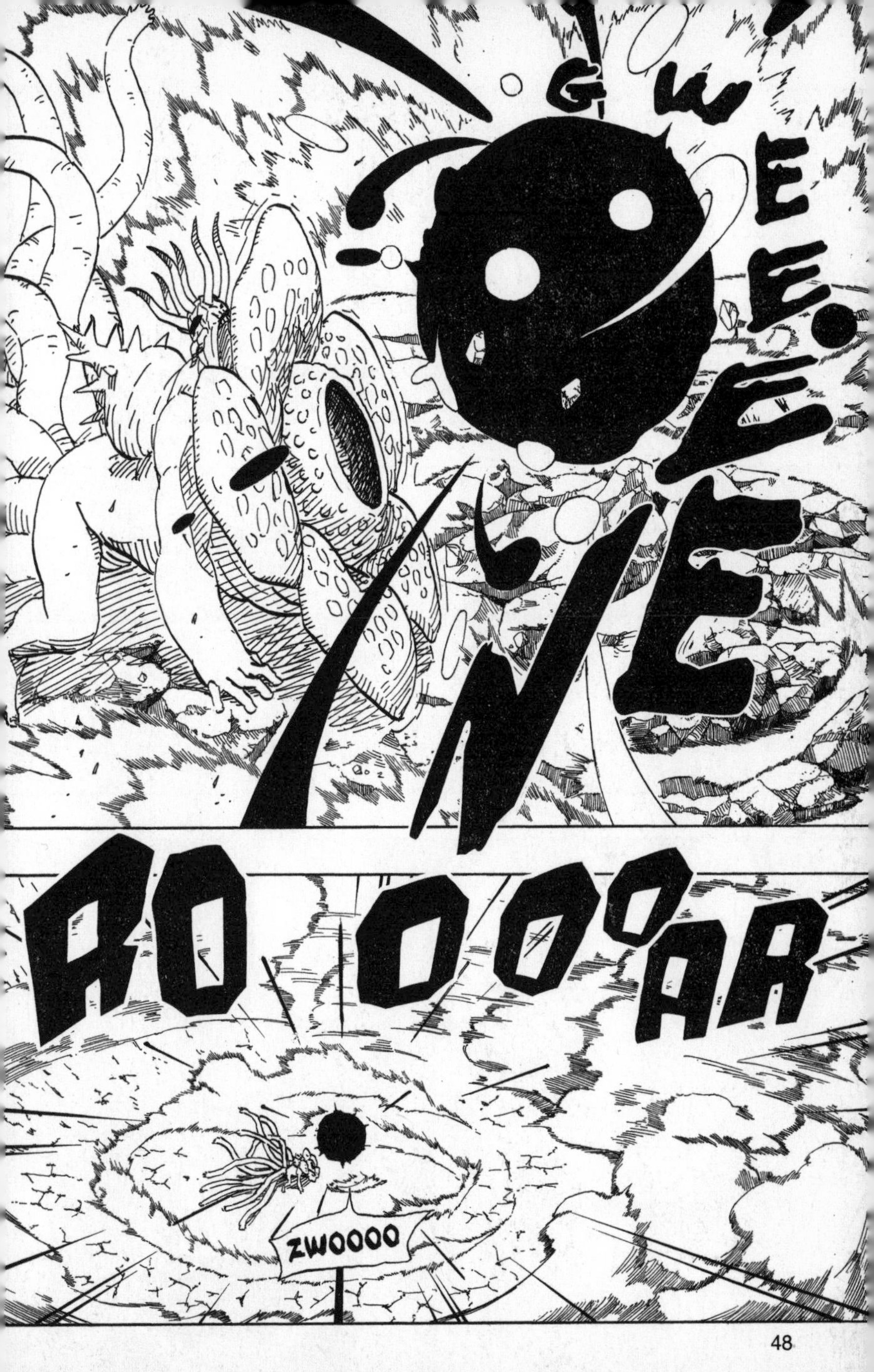
ROOOOAR
ZWOOOO

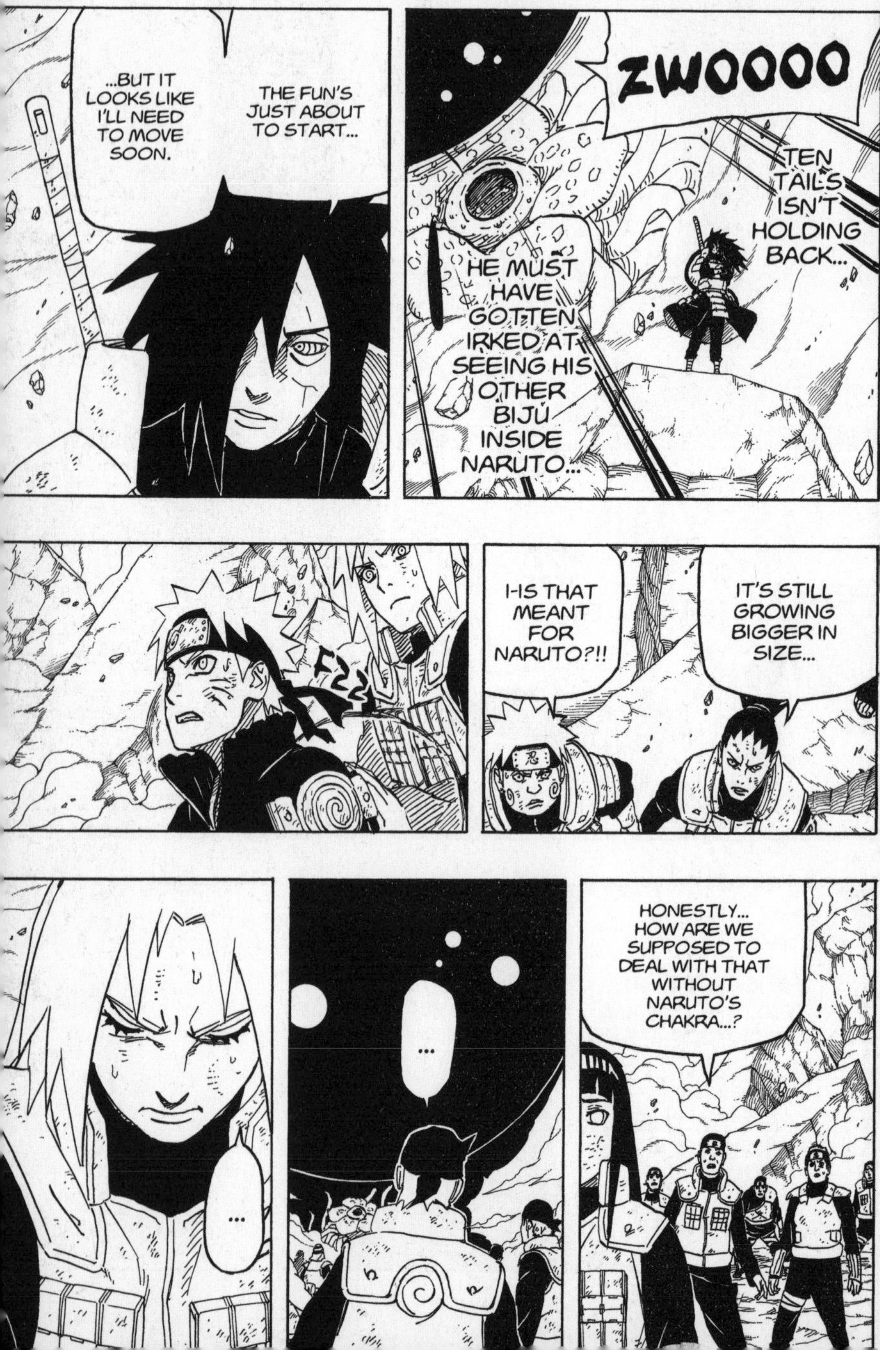
ZWOOOO
TEN TAILS ISN'T HOLDING BACK...
HE MUST HAVE GOTTEN IRKED AT SEEING HIS OTHER BIJŪ INSIDE NARUTO...
THE FUN'S JUST ABOUT TO START...
...BUT IT LOOKS LIKE I'LL NEED TO MOVE SOON.
IT'S STILL GROWING BIGGER IN SIZE...
I-IS THAT MEANT FOR NARUTO?!!
FZZ
HONESTLY... HOW ARE WE SUPPOSED TO DEAL WITH THAT WITHOUT NARUTO'S CHAKRA...?
...
...

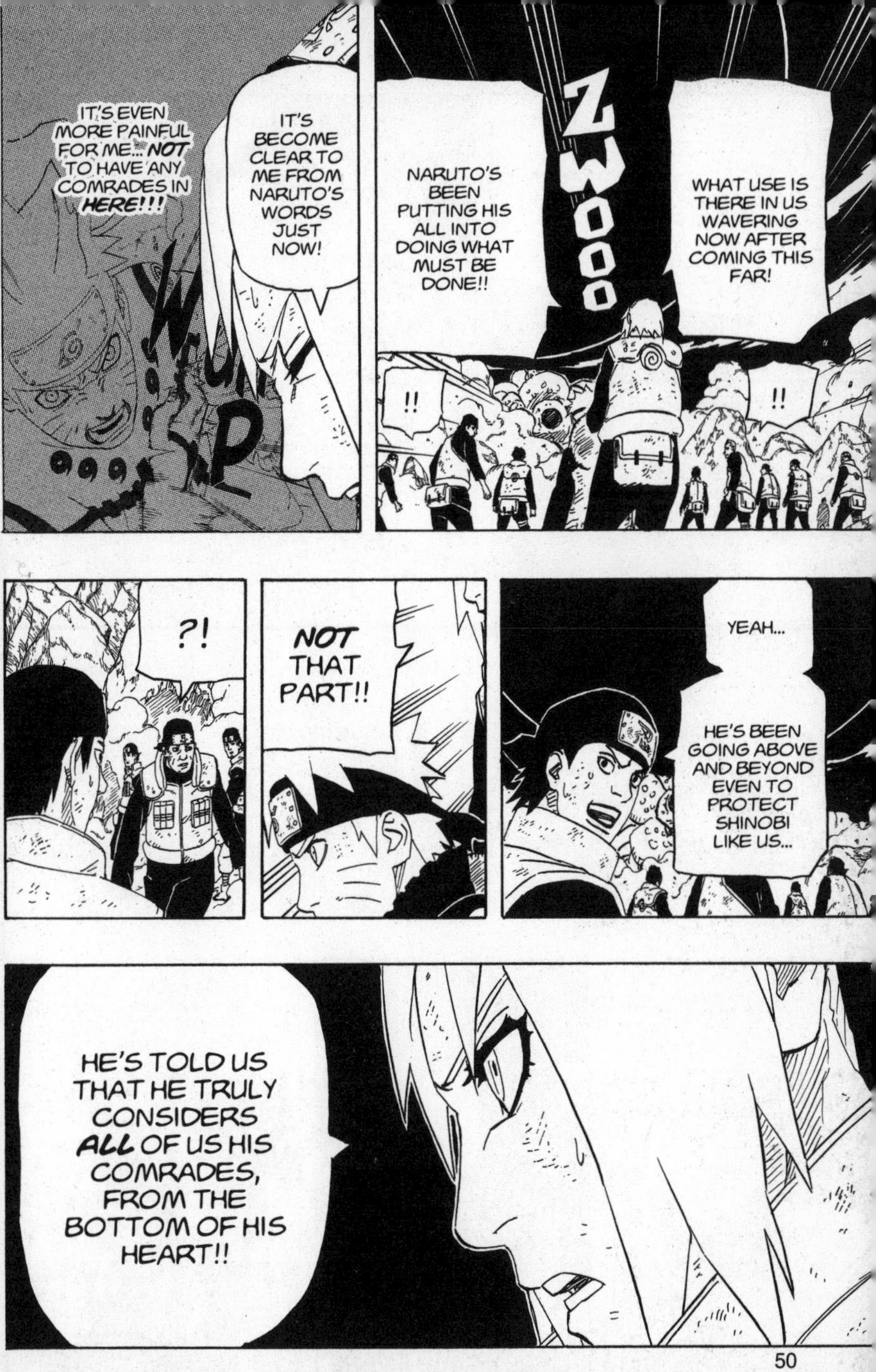
WHAT USE IS THERE IN US WAVERING NOW AFTER COMING THIS FAR!
NARUTO'S BEEN PUTTING HIS ALL INTO DOING WHAT MUST BE DONE!!
ZWOOO
!!
!!
IT'S BECOME CLEAR TO ME FROM NARUTO'S WORDS JUST NOW!
IT'S EVEN MORE PAINFUL FOR ME... NOT TO HAVE ANY COMRADES IN HERE!!!
WHUMP
YEAH...
HE'S BEEN GOING ABOVE AND BEYOND EVEN TO PROTECT SHINOBI LIKE US...
NOT THAT PART!!
?!
HE'S TOLD US THAT HE TRULY CONSIDERS ALL OF US HIS COMRADES, FROM THE BOTTOM OF HIS HEART!!

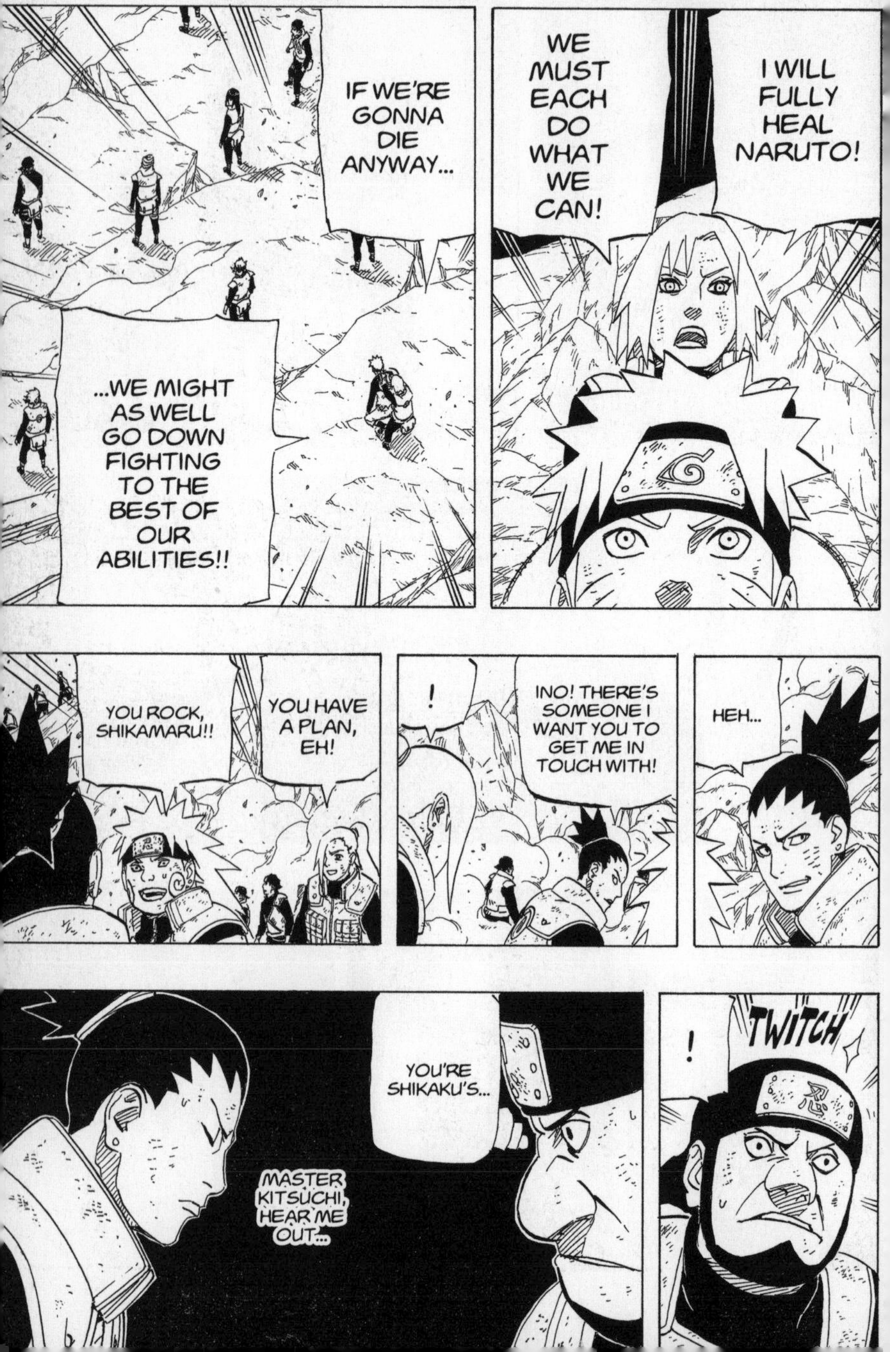
I WILL FULLY HEAL NARUTO!
WE MUST EACH DO WHAT WE CAN!
IF WE'RE GONNA DIE ANYWAY...
...WE MIGHT AS WELL GO DOWN FIGHTING TO THE BEST OF OUR ABILITIES!!
HEH...
INO! THERE'S SOMEONE I WANT YOU TO GET ME IN TOUCH WITH!
!
YOU HAVE A PLAN, EH!
YOU ROCK, SHIKAMARU!!
TWITCH
!
YOU'RE SHIKAKU'S...
MASTER KITSUCHI, HEAR ME OUT...

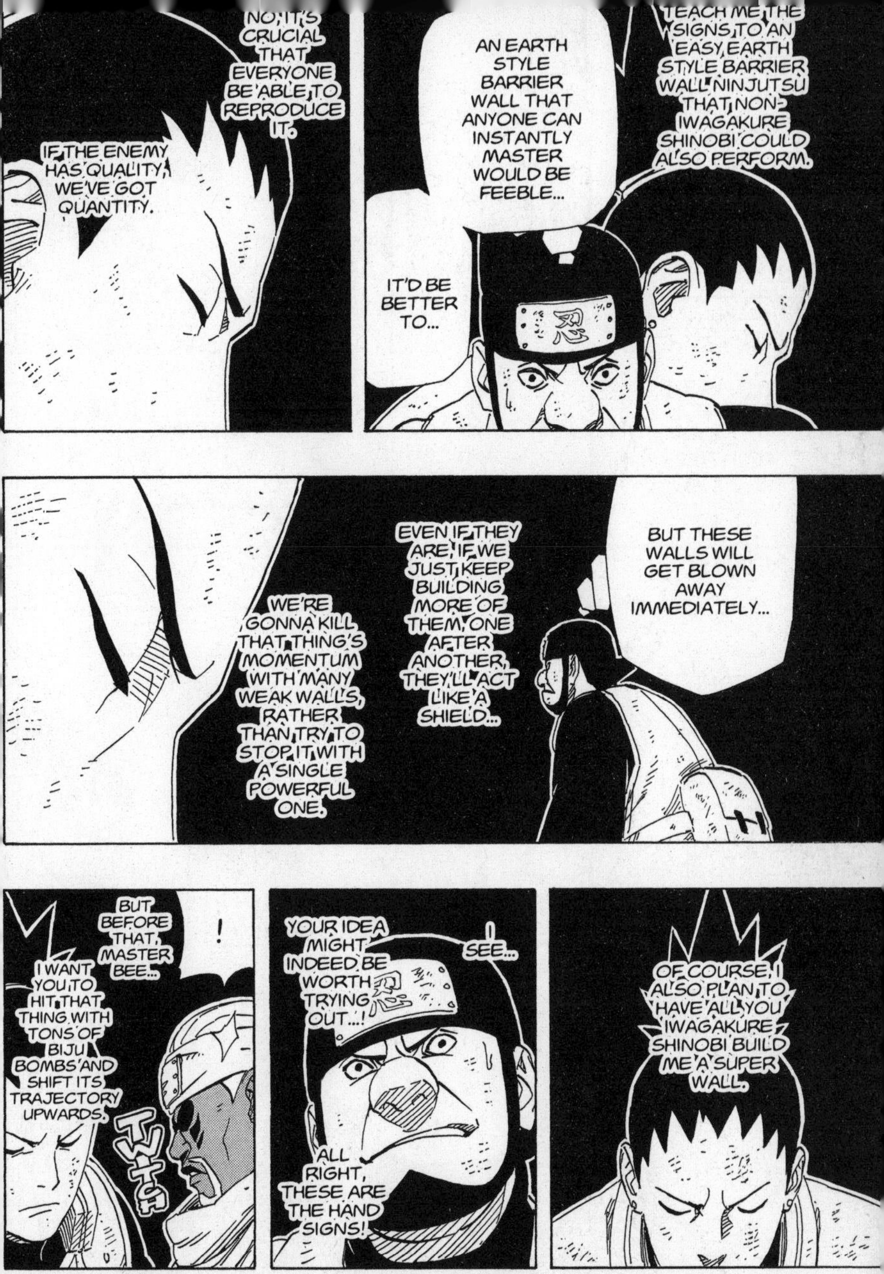
TEACH ME THE SIGNS TO AN EASY EARTH STYLE BARRIER WALL NINJUTSU THAT NON-IWAGAKURE SHINOBI COULD ALSO PERFORM.
AN EARTH STYLE BARRIER WALL THAT ANYONE CAN INSTANTLY MASTER WOULD BE FEEBLE...
IT'D BE BETTER TO...
NO, IT'S CRUCIAL THAT EVERYONE BE ABLE TO REPRODUCE IT.
IF THE ENEMY HAS QUALITY, WE'VE GOT QUANTITY.
BUT THESE WALLS WILL GET BLOWN AWAY IMMEDIATELY...
EVEN IF THEY ARE, IF WE JUST KEEP BUILDING MORE OF THEM, ONE AFTER ANOTHER, THEY'LL ACT LIKE A SHIELD...
WE'RE GONNA KILL THAT THING'S MOMENTUM WITH MANY WEAK WALLS, RATHER THAN TRY TO STOP IT WITH A SINGLE POWERFUL ONE.
OF COURSE, I ALSO PLAN TO HAVE ALL YOU IWAGAKURE SHINOBI BUILD ME A SUPER WALL.
I SEE...
YOUR IDEA MIGHT INDEED BE WORTH TRYING OUT...!
ALL RIGHT, THESE ARE THE HAND SIGNS!
!
BUT BEFORE THAT, MASTER BEE...
I WANT YOU TO HIT THAT THING WITH TONS OF BIJU BOMBS AND SHIFT ITS TRAJECTORY UPWARDS.
TWITCH

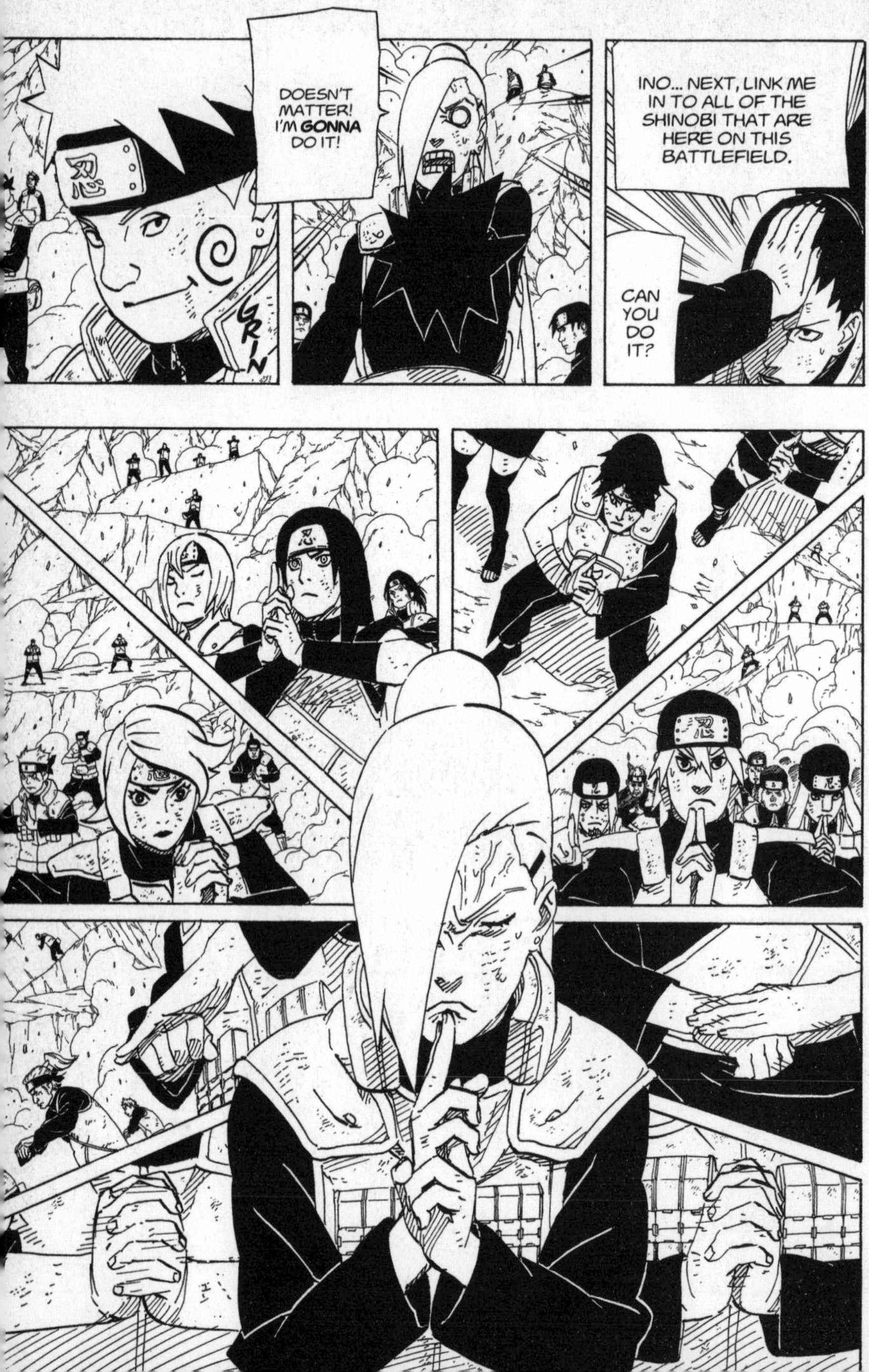
INO... NEXT, LINK ME IN TO ALL OF THE SHINOBI THAT ARE HERE ON THIS BATTLEFIELD.
CAN YOU DO IT?
DOESN'T MATTER! I'M **GONNA** DO IT!
GRIN

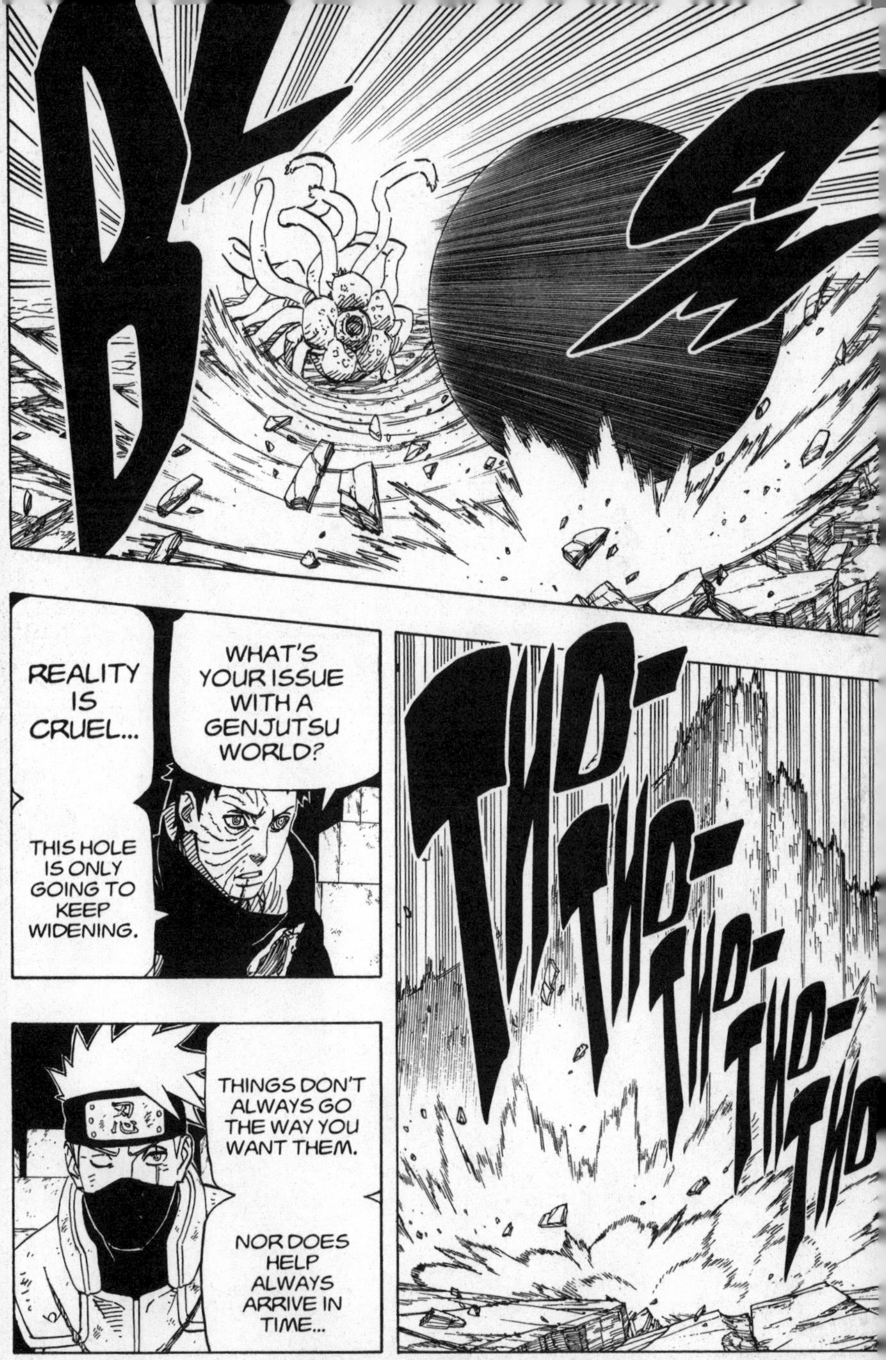
BLAM
THO-THO-THO-THO-THO
WHAT'S YOUR ISSUE WITH A GENJUTSU WORLD?
REALITY IS CRUEL...
THIS HOLE IS ONLY GOING TO KEEP WIDENING.
THINGS DON'T ALWAYS GO THE WAY YOU WANT THEM.
NOR DOES HELP ALWAYS ARRIVE IN TIME...

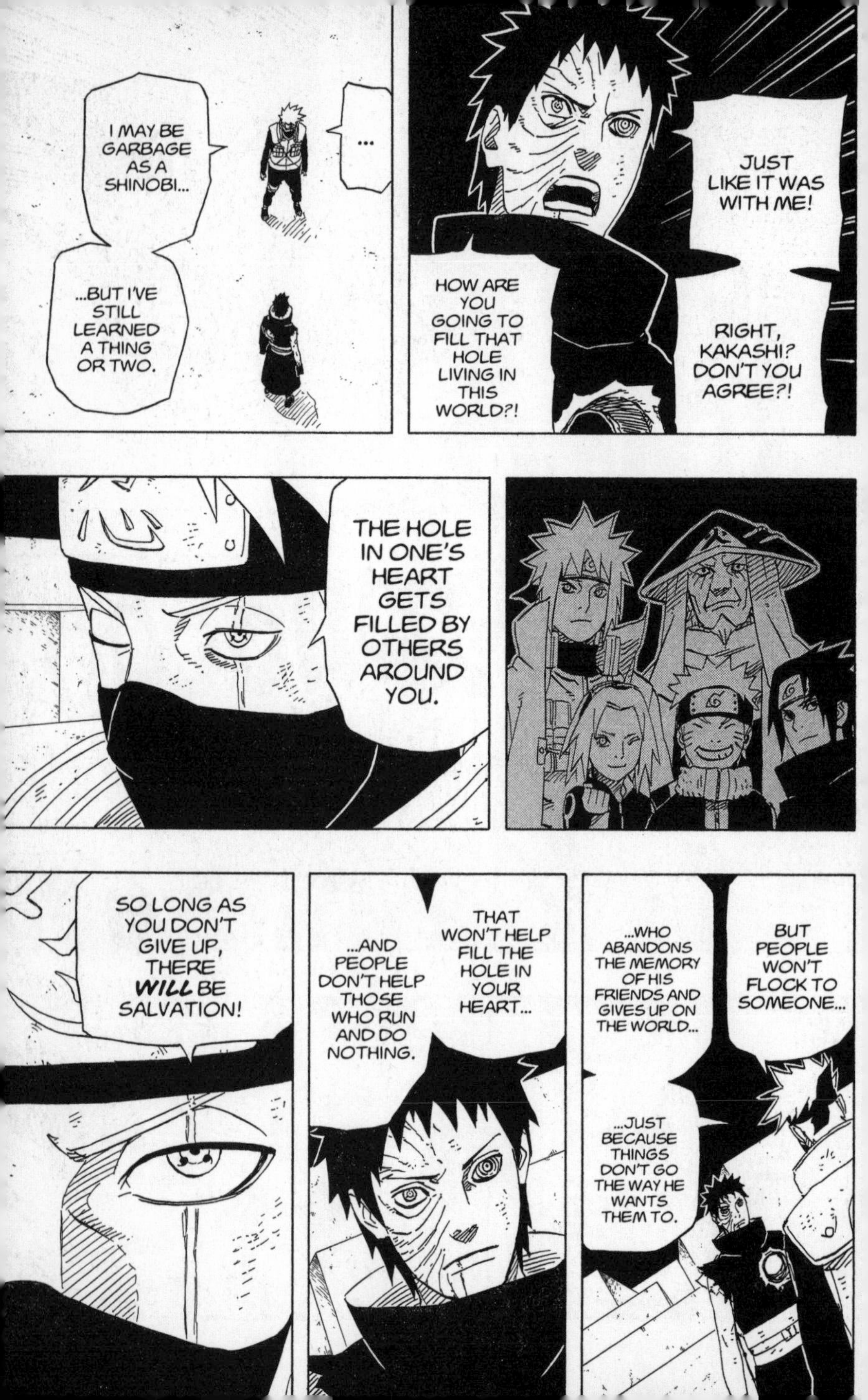
JUST LIKE IT WAS WITH ME!
HOW ARE YOU GOING TO FILL THAT HOLE LIVING IN THIS WORLD?!
RIGHT, KAKASHI? DON'T YOU AGREE?!
...
I MAY BE GARBAGE AS A SHINOBI...
...BUT I'VE STILL LEARNED A THING OR TWO.
THE HOLE IN ONE'S HEART GETS FILLED BY OTHERS AROUND YOU.
BUT PEOPLE WON'T FLOCK TO SOMEONE...
...WHO ABANDONS THE MEMORY OF HIS FRIENDS AND GIVES UP ON THE WORLD...
...JUST BECAUSE THINGS DON'T GO THE WAY HE WANTS THEM TO.
THAT WON'T HELP FILL THE HOLE IN YOUR HEART...
...AND PEOPLE DON'T HELP THOSE WHO RUN AND DO NOTHING.
SO LONG AS YOU DON'T GIVE UP, THERE **WILL** BE SALVATION!

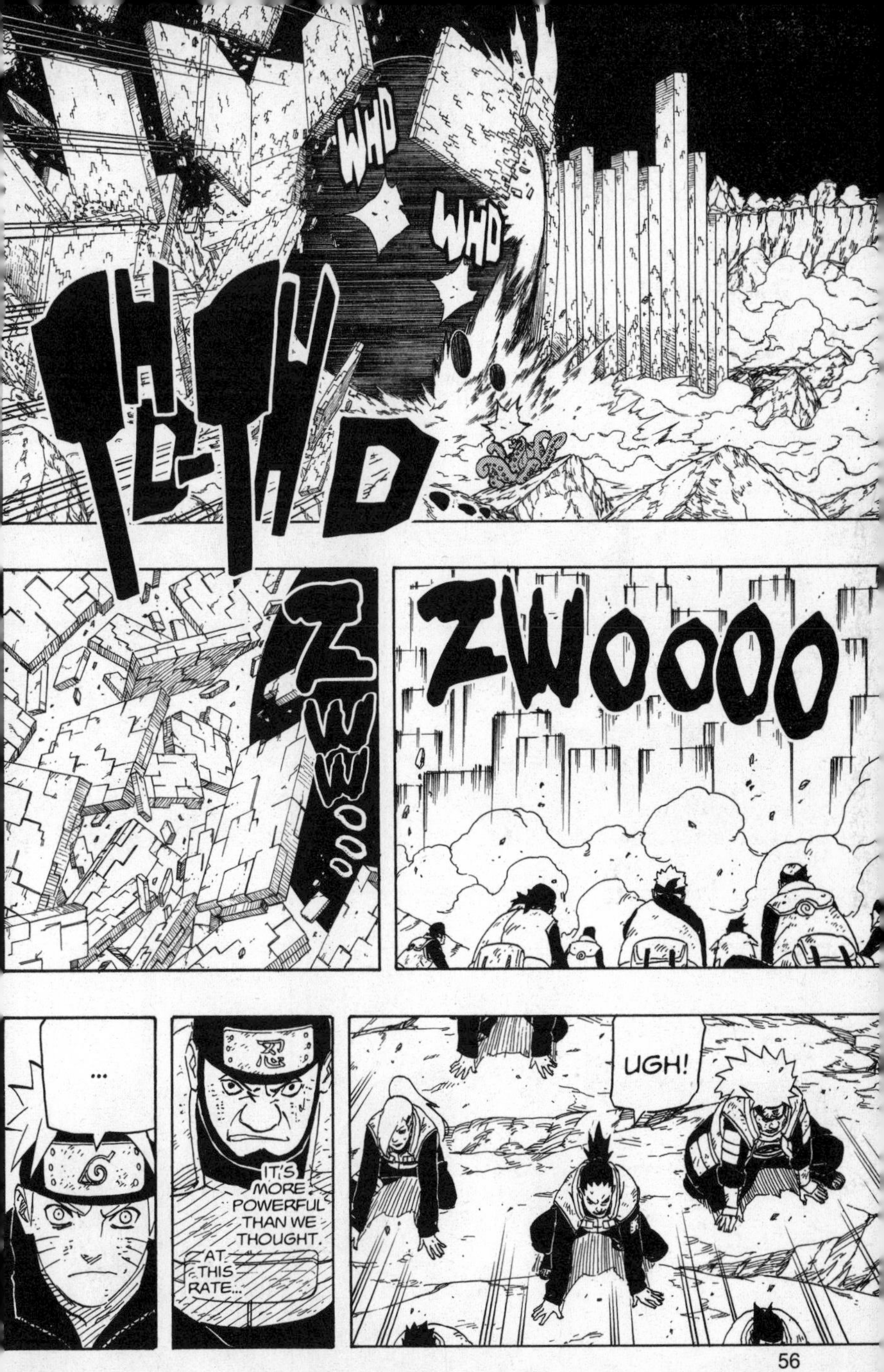
WHD
WHD
ZWOOOO
ZWWWOOOO...
UGH!
IT'S MORE POWERFUL THAN WE THOUGHT.
AT THIS RATE...
...

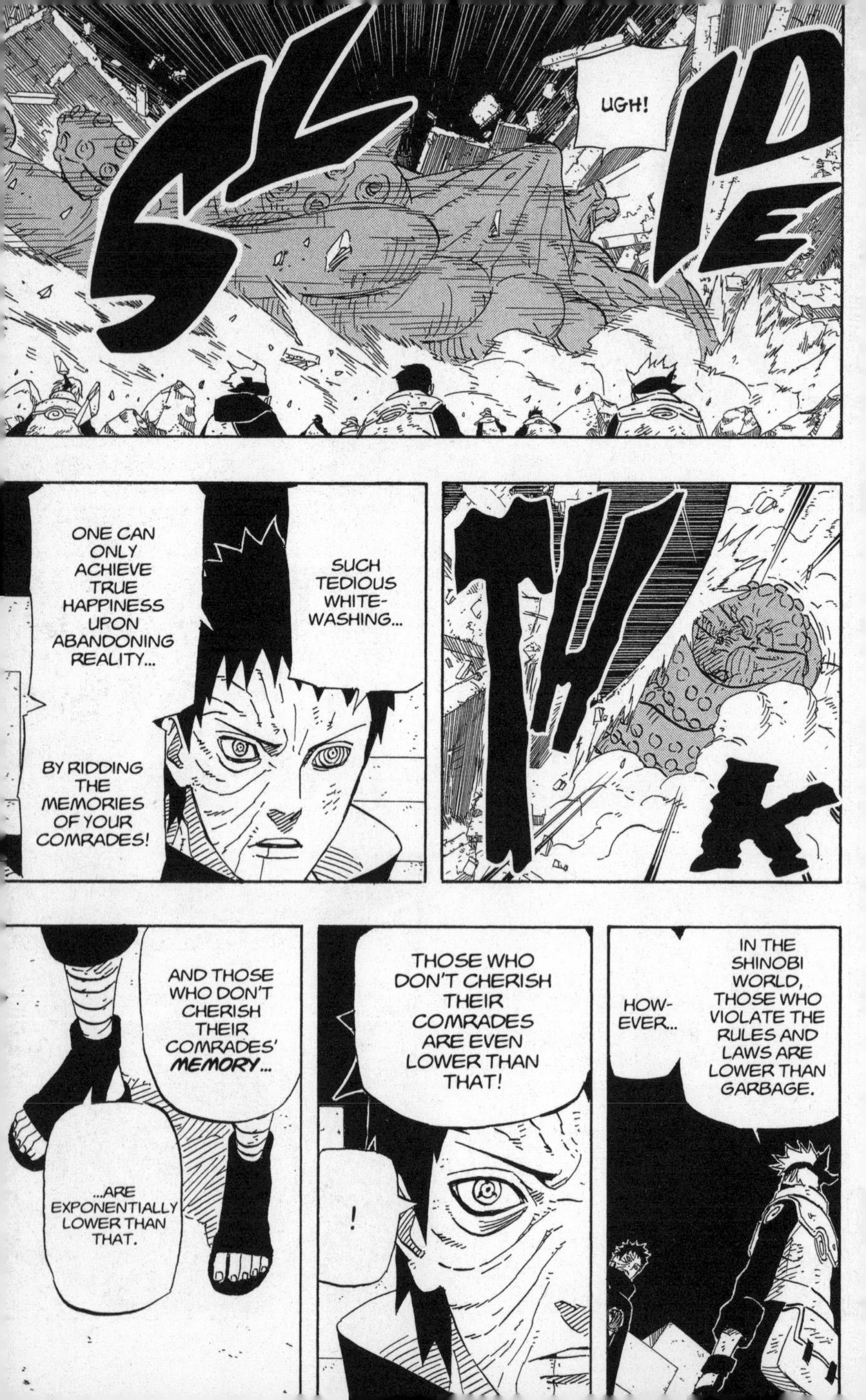
SLIDE
UGH!
SUCH TEDIOUS WHITE-WASHING...
ONE CAN ONLY ACHIEVE TRUE HAPPINESS UPON ABANDONING REALITY...
BY RIDDING THE MEMORIES OF YOUR COMRADES!
IN THE SHINOBI WORLD, THOSE WHO VIOLATE THE RULES AND LAWS ARE LOWER THAN GARBAGE.
HOW-EVER...
THOSE WHO DON'T CHERISH THEIR COMRADES ARE EVEN LOWER THAN THAT!
!
AND THOSE WHO DON'T CHERISH THEIR COMRADES' *MEMORY*...
...ARE EXPONENTIALLY LOWER THAN THAT.

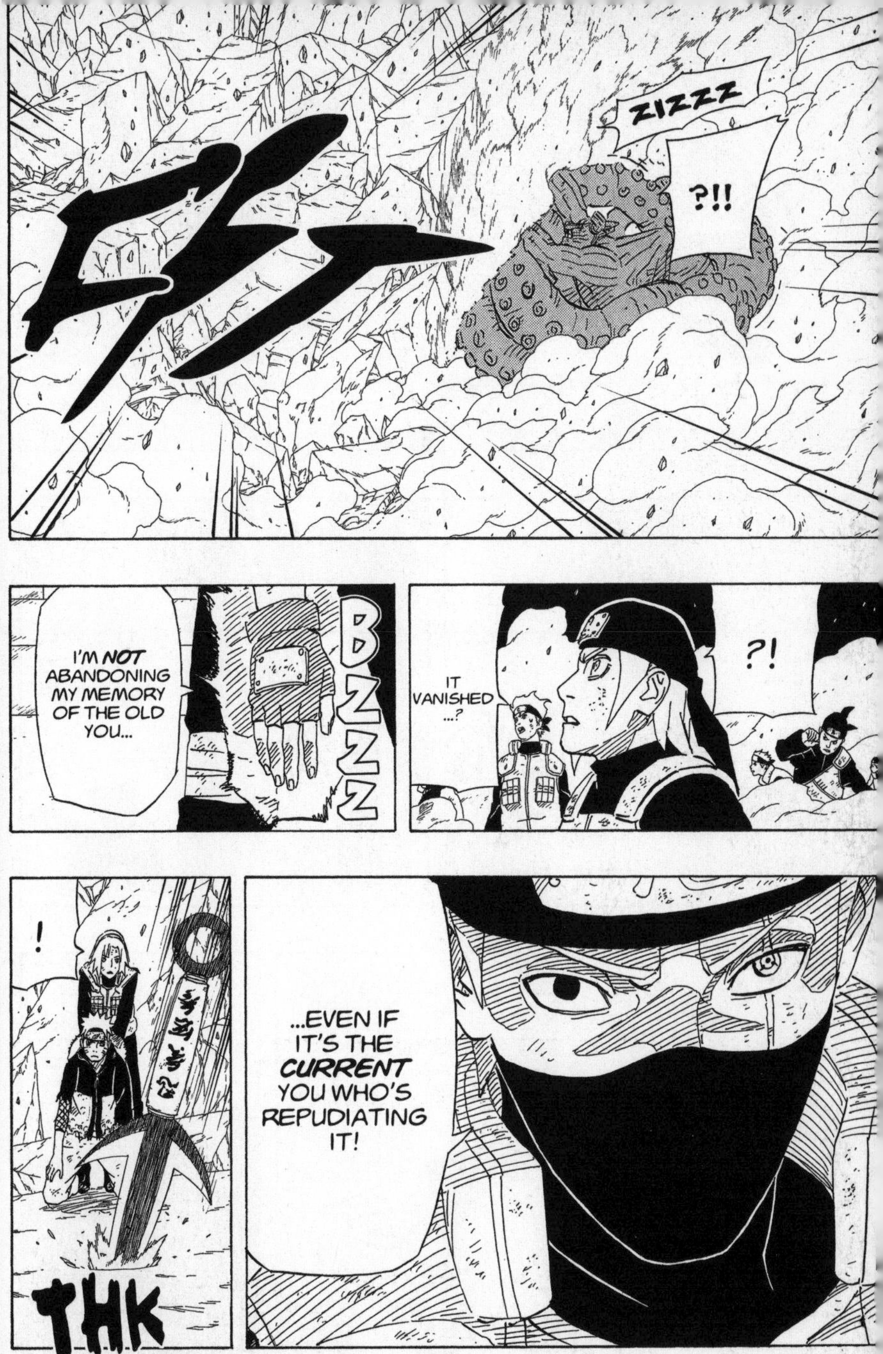
ZIZZZ
?!!
?!
IT VANISHED ...?
BZZZ
I'M NOT ABANDONING MY MEMORY OF THE OLD YOU...
...EVEN IF IT'S THE CURRENT YOU WHO'S REPUDIATING IT!
!
THK

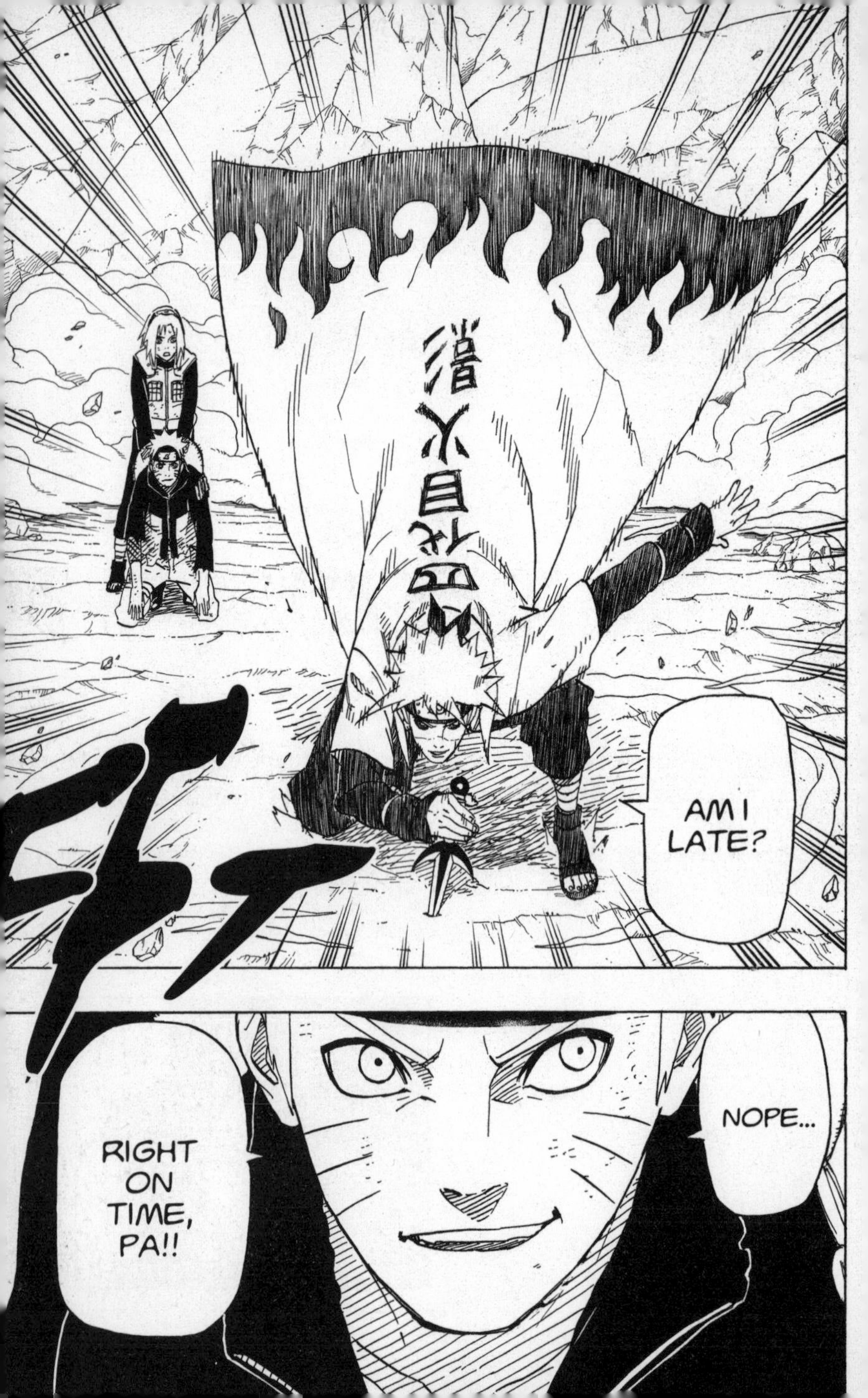
AM I LATE?
NOPE...
RIGHT ON TIME, PA!!

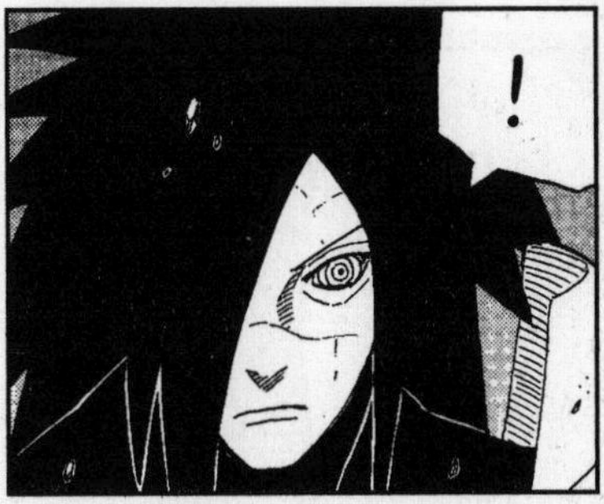

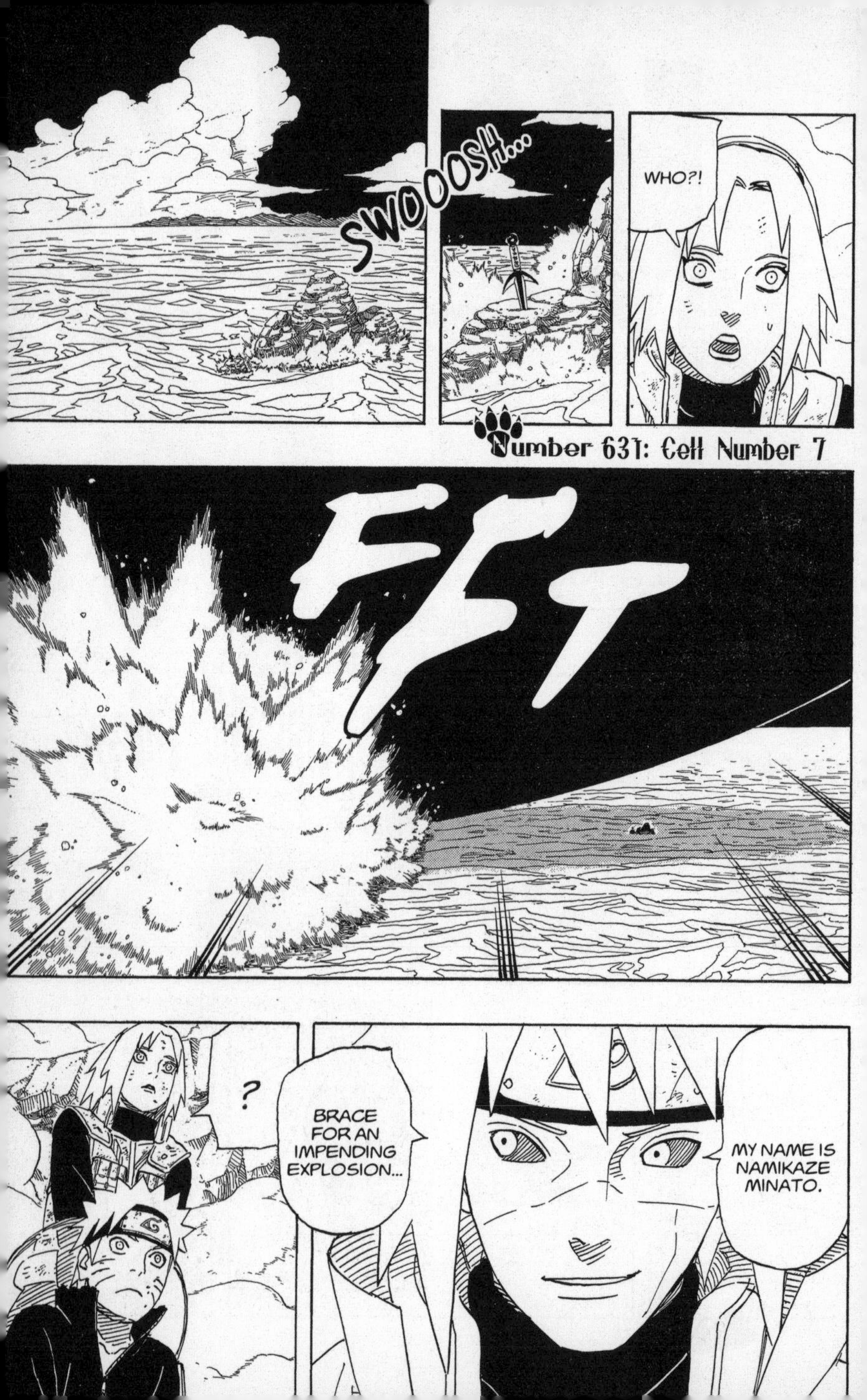
WHO?!
SWOOOSH...
Number 631: Cell Number 7
FFT
MY NAME IS NAMIKAZE MINATO.
BRACE FOR AN IMPENDING EXPLOSION...
?

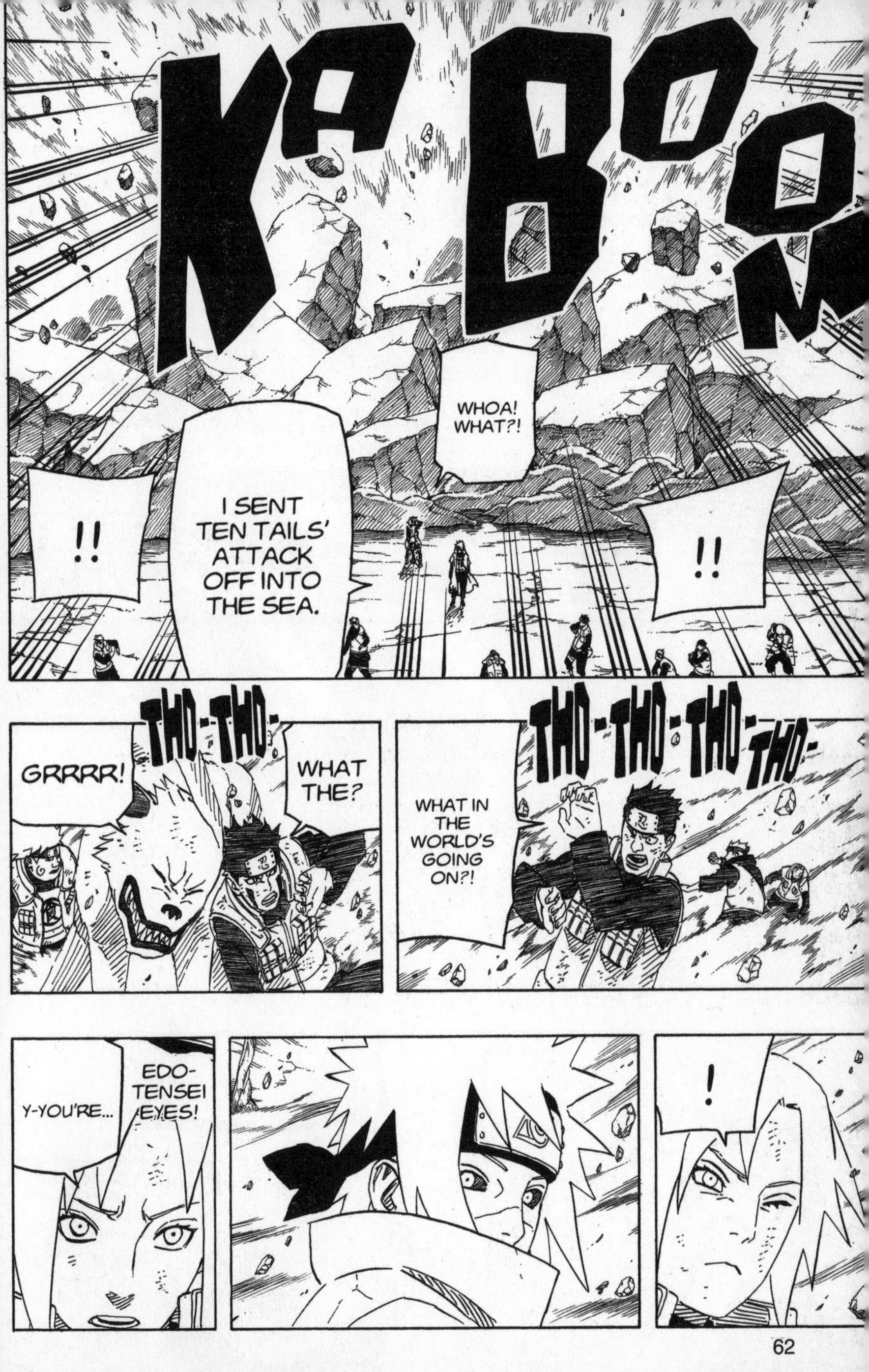

KA BOOM
!!
WHOA! WHAT?!
I SENT TEN TAILS' ATTACK OFF INTO THE SEA.
!!
THO-THO-THO-THO-
WHAT IN THE WORLD'S GOING ON?!
THO-THO-
WHAT THE?
GRRRR!
!
EDO-TENSEI EYES!
Y-YOU'RE...

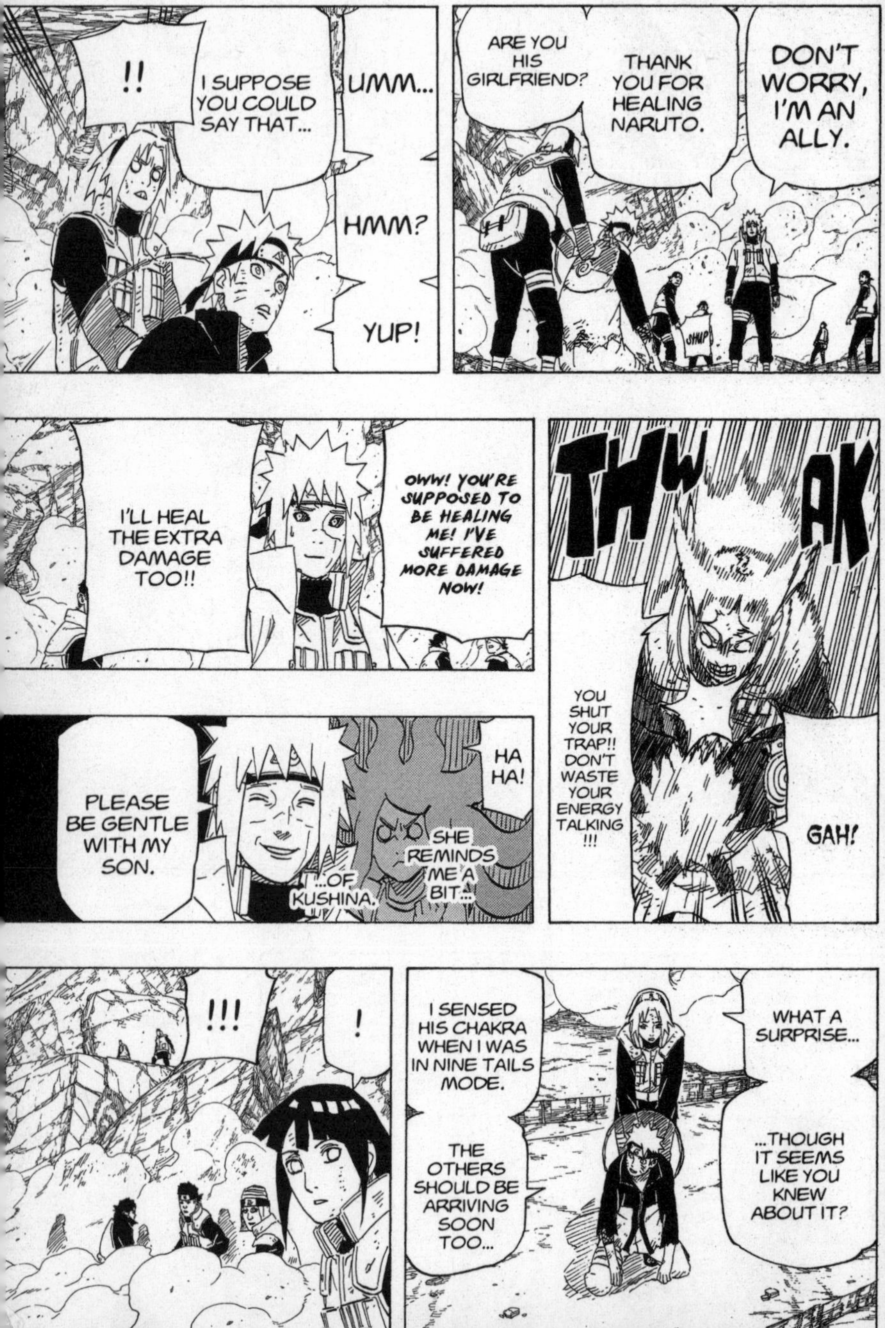
DON'T WORRY, I'M AN ALLY.
THANK YOU FOR HEALING NARUTO.
ARE YOU HIS GIRLFRIEND?
SHUP
UMM...
I SUPPOSE YOU COULD SAY THAT...
HMM?
!!
YUP!
THWAK
GAH!
YOU SHUT YOUR TRAP!! DON'T WASTE YOUR ENERGY TALKING!!!
OWW! YOU'RE SUPPOSED TO BE HEALING ME! I'VE SUFFERED MORE DAMAGE NOW!
I'LL HEAL THE EXTRA DAMAGE TOO!!
HA HA!
SHE REMINDS ME A BIT...
...OF KUSHINA.
PLEASE BE GENTLE WITH MY SON.
WHAT A SURPRISE...
...THOUGH IT SEEMS LIKE YOU KNEW ABOUT IT?
I SENSED HIS CHAKRA WHEN I WAS IN NINE TAILS MODE.
THE OTHERS SHOULD BE ARRIVING SOON TOO...
!
!!!

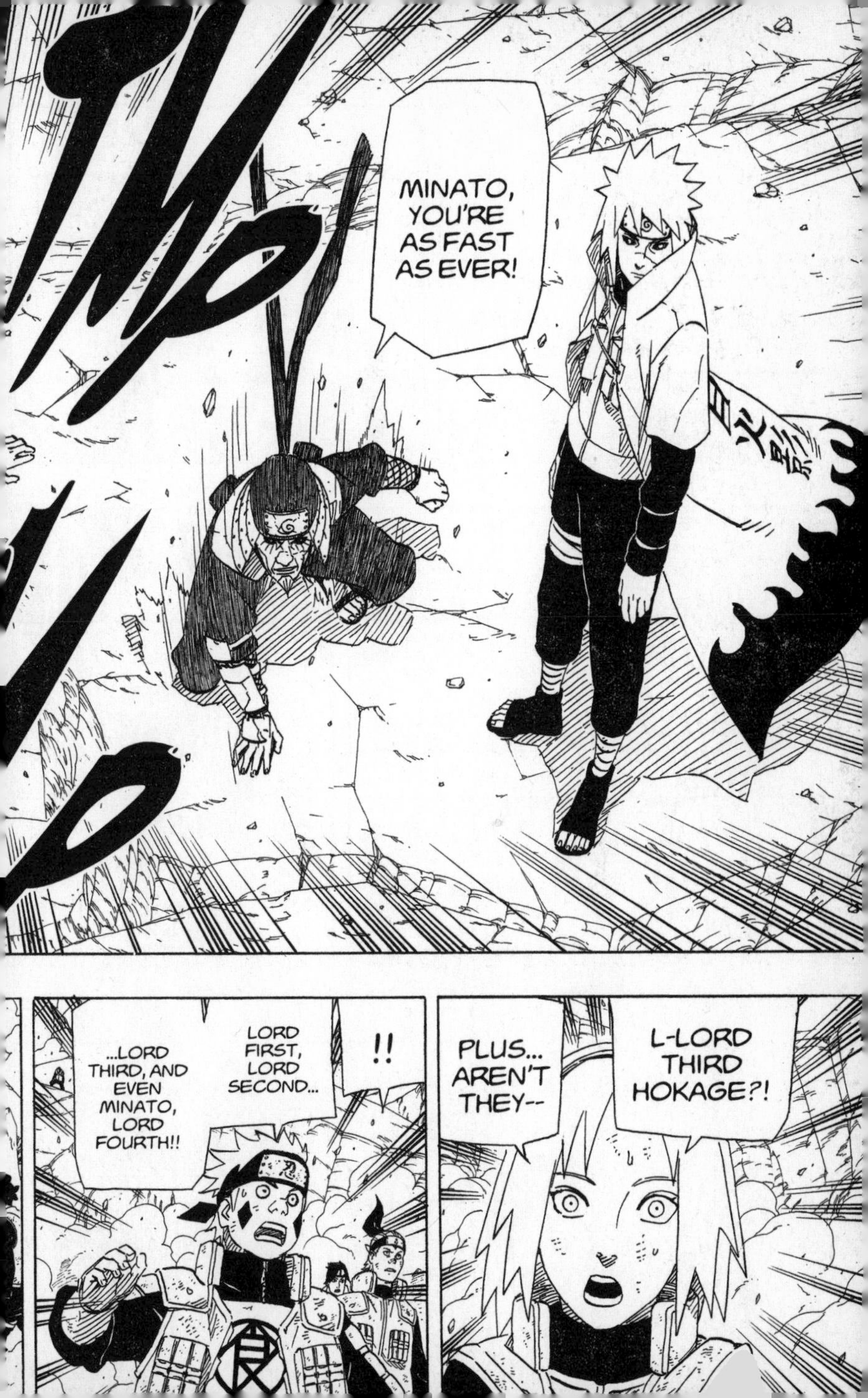
MINATO, YOU'RE AS FAST AS EVER!
L-LORD THIRD HOKAGE?!
PLUS... AREN'T THEY--
!!
LORD FIRST, LORD SECOND...
...LORD THIRD, AND EVEN MINATO, LORD FOURTH!!

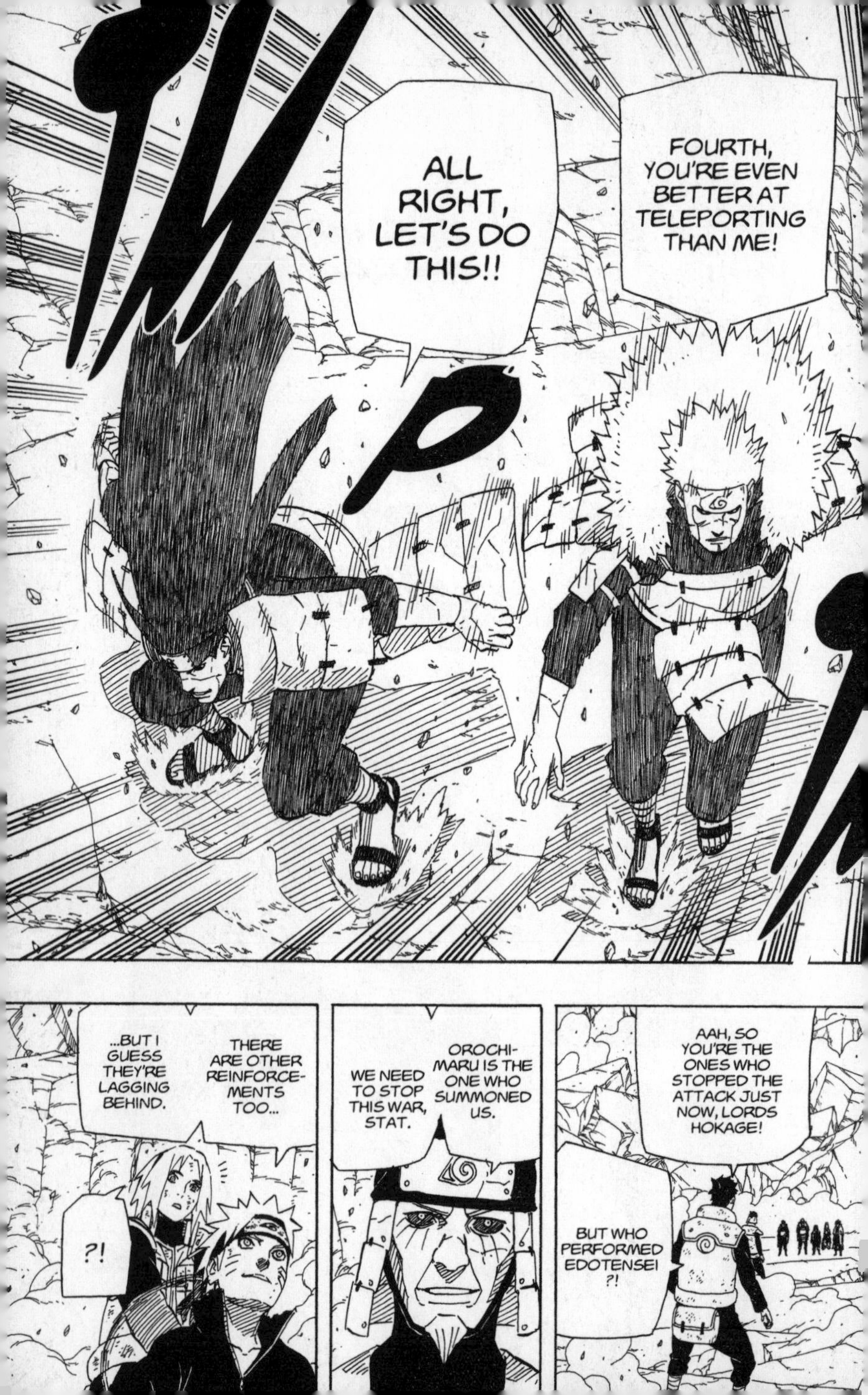
FOURTH, YOU'RE EVEN BETTER AT TELEPORTING THAN ME!
ALL RIGHT, LET'S DO THIS!!
AAH, SO YOU'RE THE ONES WHO STOPPED THE ATTACK JUST NOW, LORDS HOKAGE!
BUT WHO PERFORMED EDOTENSEI ?!
OROCHI-MARU IS THE ONE WHO SUMMONED US.
WE NEED TO STOP THIS WAR, STAT.
THERE ARE OTHER REINFORCE-MENTS TOO...
...BUT I GUESS THEY'RE LAGGING BEHIND.
?!

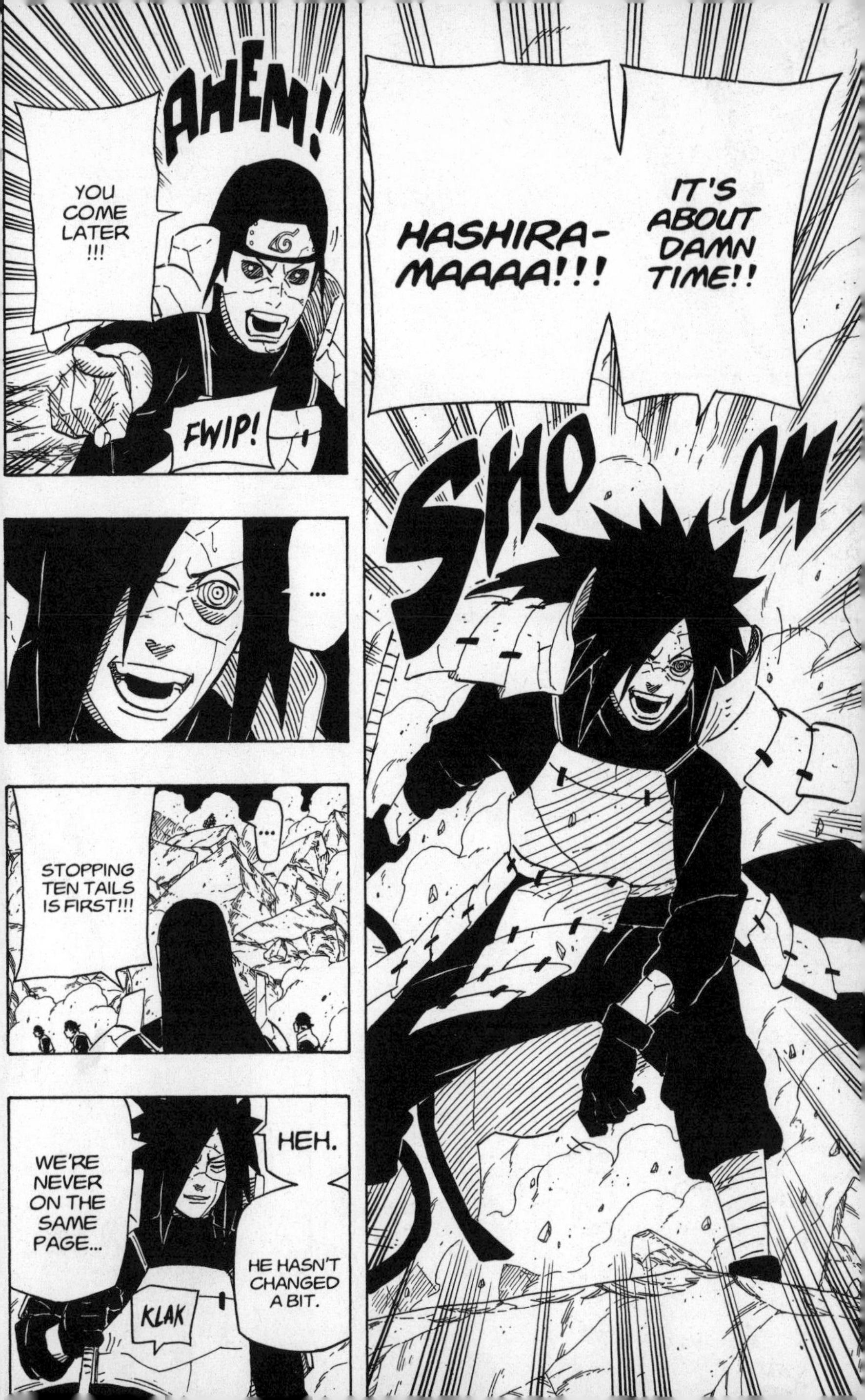
IT'S ABOUT DAMN TIME!!
HASHIRA-MAAAAA!!!
SHO OM
AHEM!
YOU COME LATER !!!
FWIP!
...
...
STOPPING TEN TAILS IS FIRST!!!
HEH.
WE'RE NEVER ON THE SAME PAGE...
HE HASN'T CHANGED A BIT.
KLAK

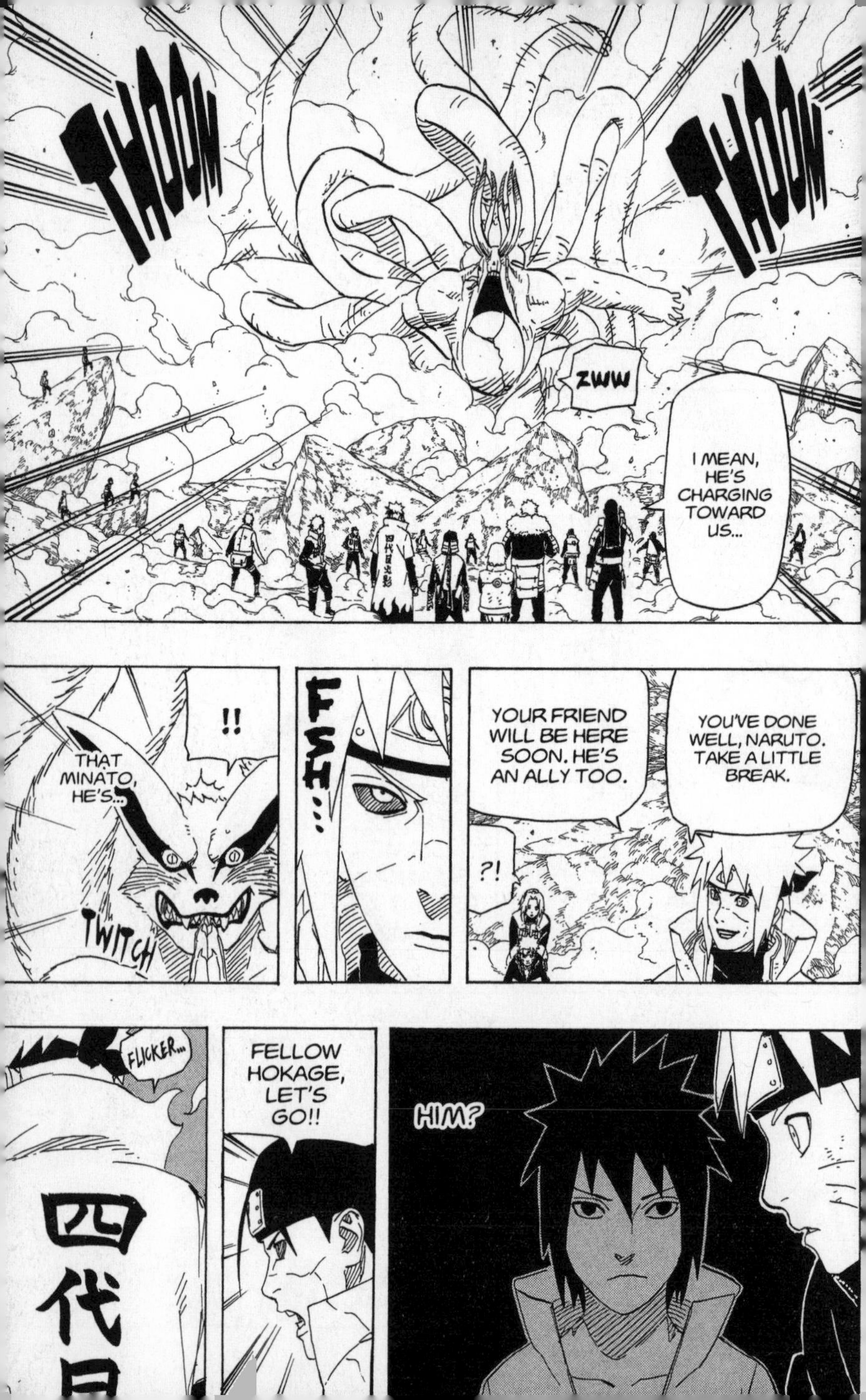
THOOM
THOOM
ZWW
I MEAN, HE'S CHARGING TOWARD US...
YOU'VE DONE WELL, NARUTO. TAKE A LITTLE BREAK.
YOUR FRIEND WILL BE HERE SOON. HE'S AN ALLY TOO.
?!
FSH...
!!
THAT MINATO, HE'S...
TWITCH
HIM?
FELLOW HOKAGE, LET'S GO!!
FLICKER...
四代

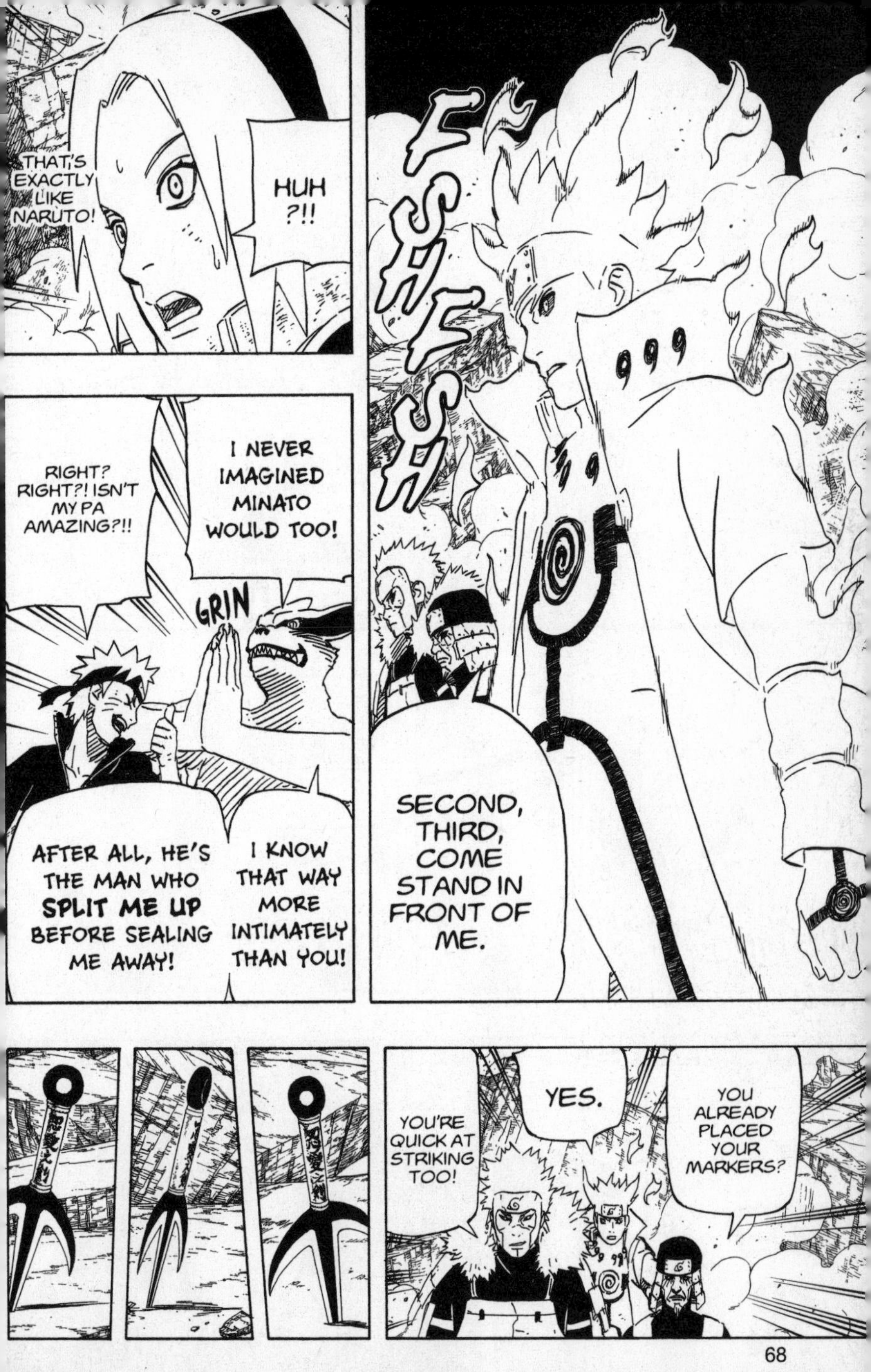
FSHFSH
SECOND, THIRD, COME STAND IN FRONT OF ME.
HUH ?!!
THAT'S EXACTLY LIKE NARUTO!
I NEVER IMAGINED MINATO WOULD TOO!
RIGHT? RIGHT?! ISN'T MY PA AMAZING?!!
GRIN
I KNOW THAT WAY MORE INTIMATELY THAN YOU!
AFTER ALL, HE'S THE MAN WHO **SPLIT ME UP** BEFORE SEALING ME AWAY!
YOU ALREADY PLACED YOUR MARKERS?
YES.
YOU'RE QUICK AT STRIKING TOO!

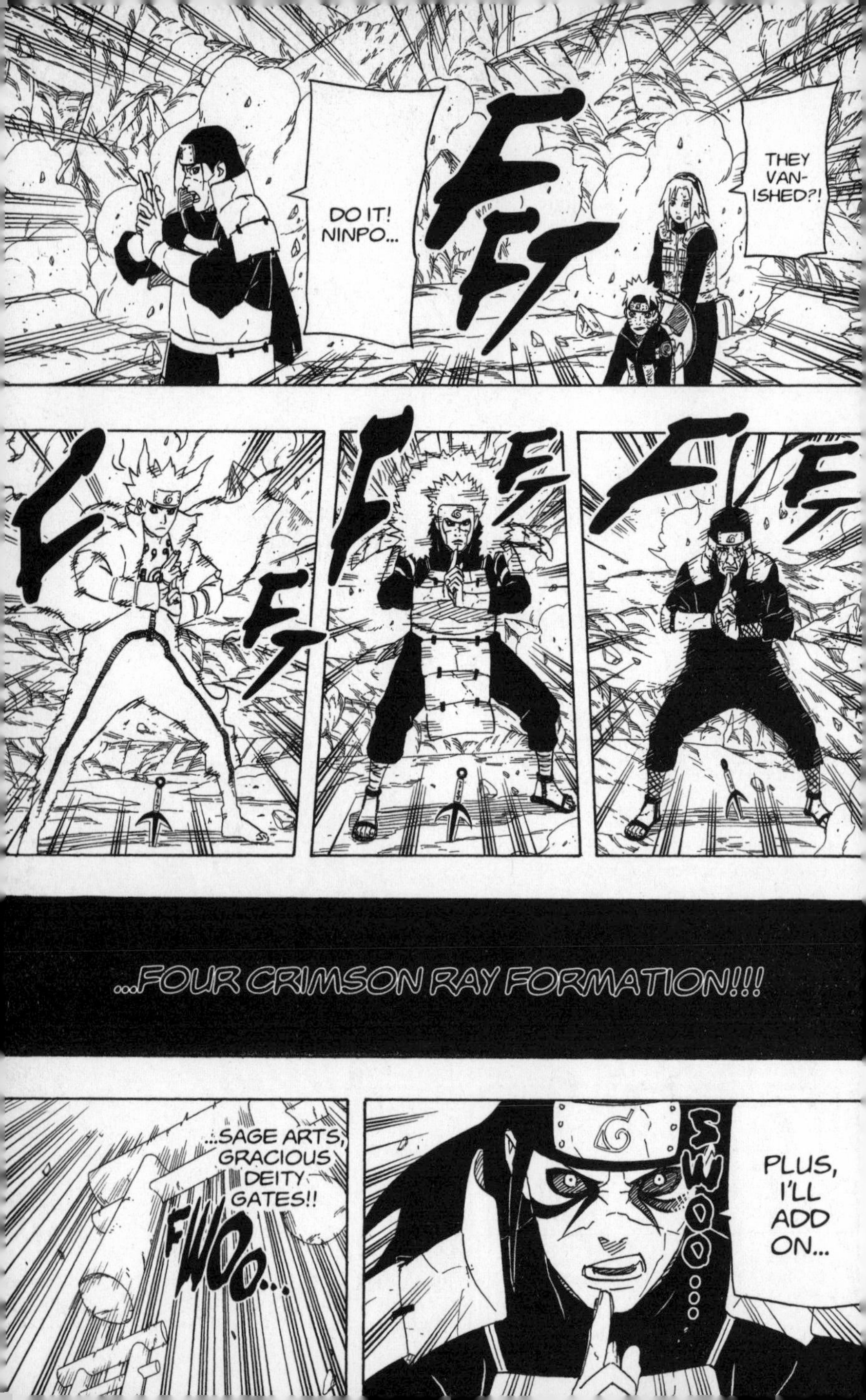
THEY VANISHED?!
DO IT! NINPO...
...FOUR CRIMSON RAY FORMATION!!!
SWOO...
PLUS, I'LL ADD ON...
...SAGE ARTS, GRACIOUS DEITY GATES!!
FWOO...

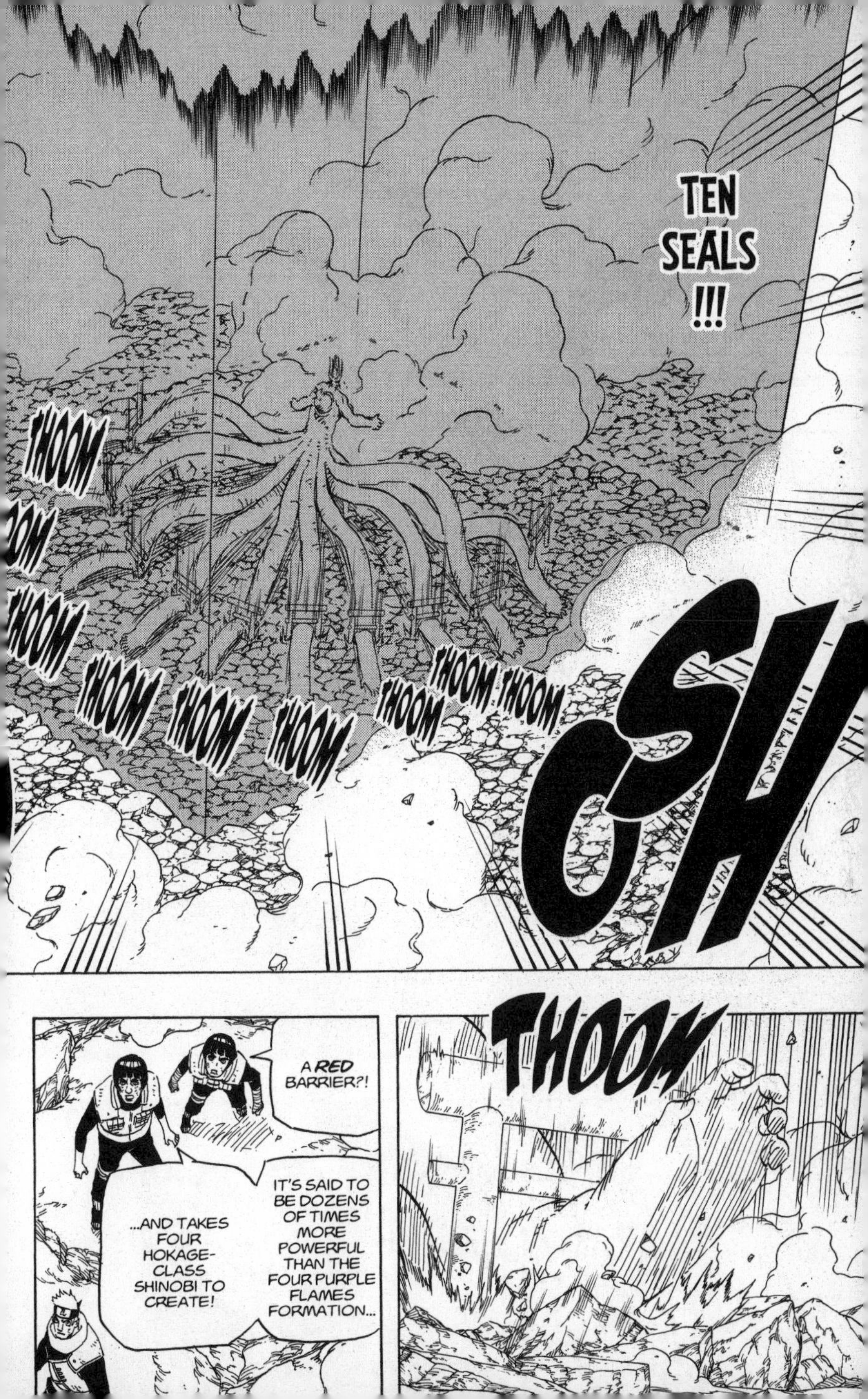
TEN SEALS!!!
CSH
THOOM THOOM
THOOM
THOOM
THOOM
THOOM
THOOM
OOM
THOOM
THOOM
A RED BARRIER?!
IT'S SAID TO BE DOZENS OF TIMES MORE POWERFUL THAN THE FOUR PURPLE FLAMES FORMATION...
...AND TAKES FOUR HOKAGE-CLASS SHINOBI TO CREATE!

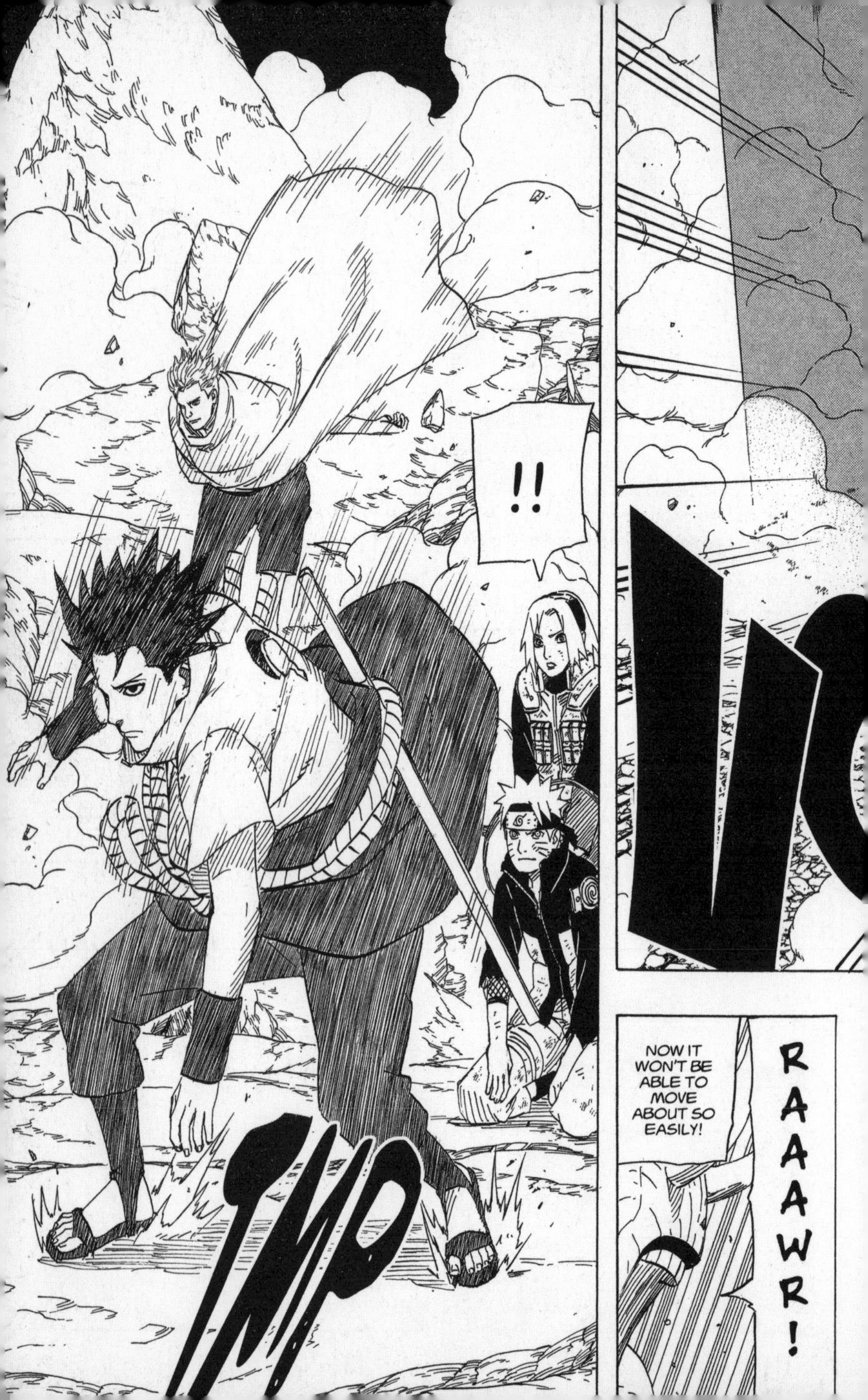
RAAAWR!
NOW IT WON'T BE ABLE TO MOVE ABOUT SO EASILY!
!!

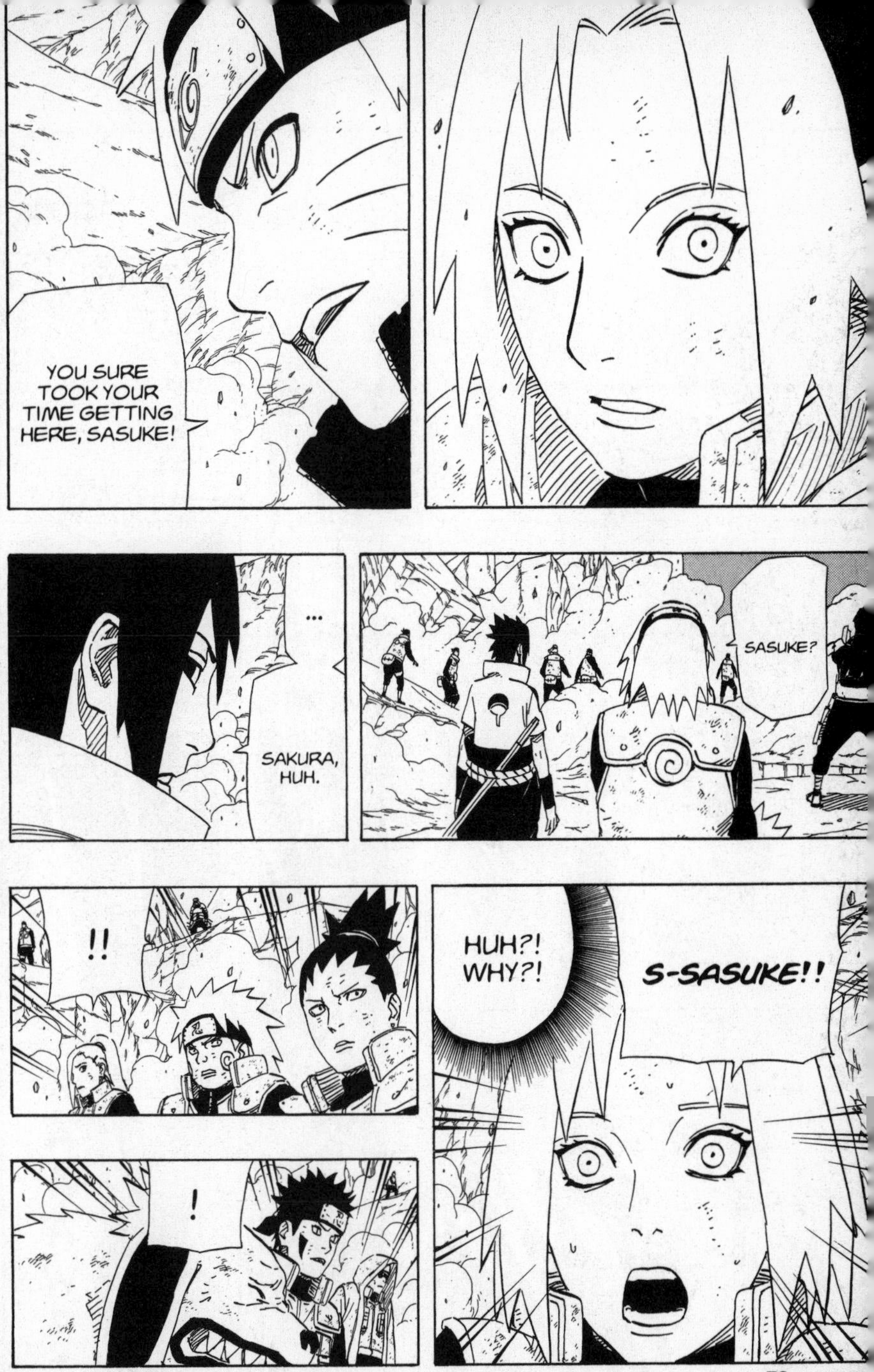
YOU SURE TOOK YOUR TIME GETTING HERE, SASUKE!
SASUKE?
...
SAKURA, HUH.
S-SASUKE!!
HUH?! WHY?!
!!
!

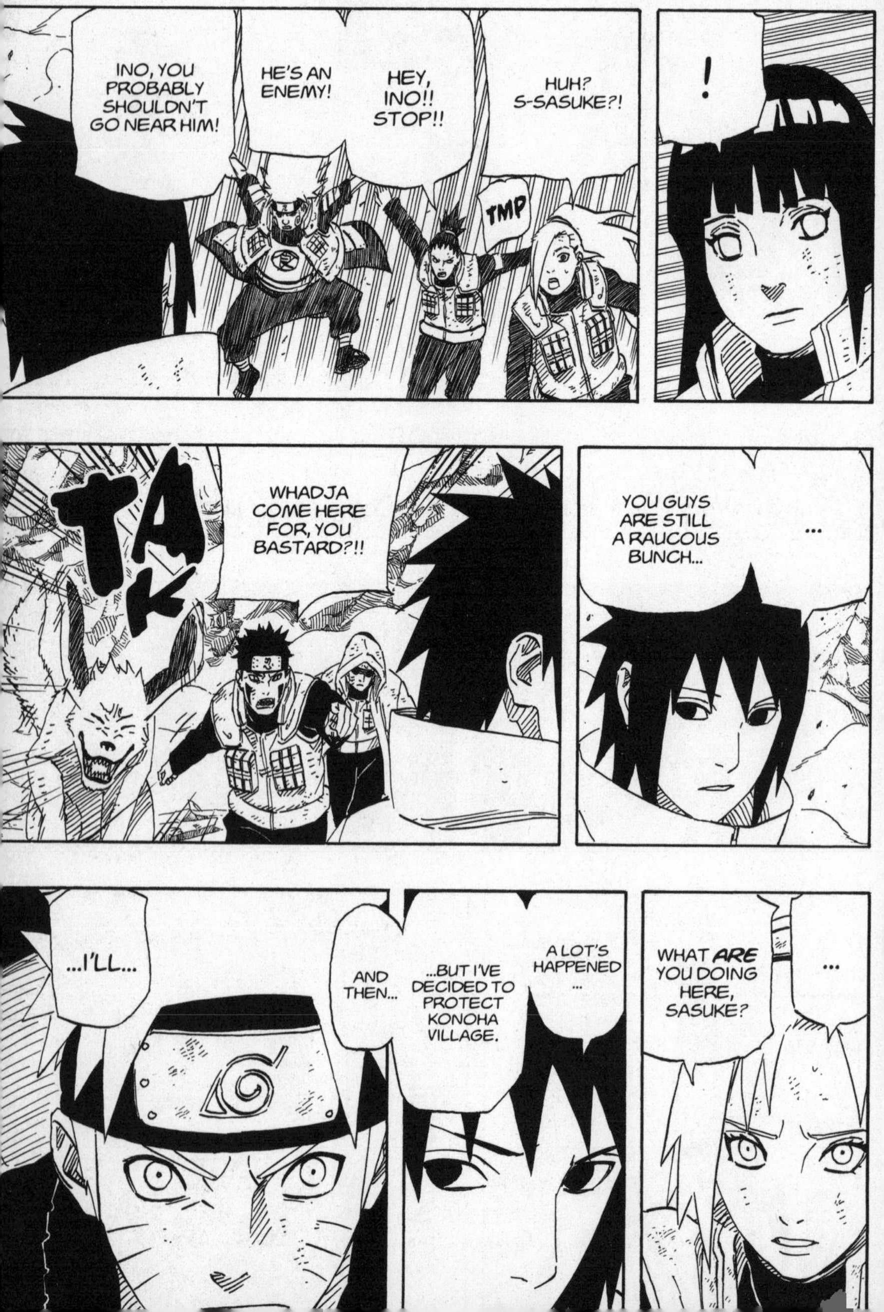
!
HUH? S-SASUKE?!
TMP
HEY, INO!! STOP!!
HE'S AN ENEMY!
INO, YOU PROBABLY SHOULDN'T GO NEAR HIM!
...
YOU GUYS ARE STILL A RAUCOUS BUNCH...
WHADJA COME HERE FOR, YOU BASTARD?!!
TAK
...
WHAT **ARE** YOU DOING HERE, SASUKE?
A LOT'S HAPPENED ...
...BUT I'VE DECIDED TO PROTECT KONOHA VILLAGE.
AND THEN...
...I'LL...

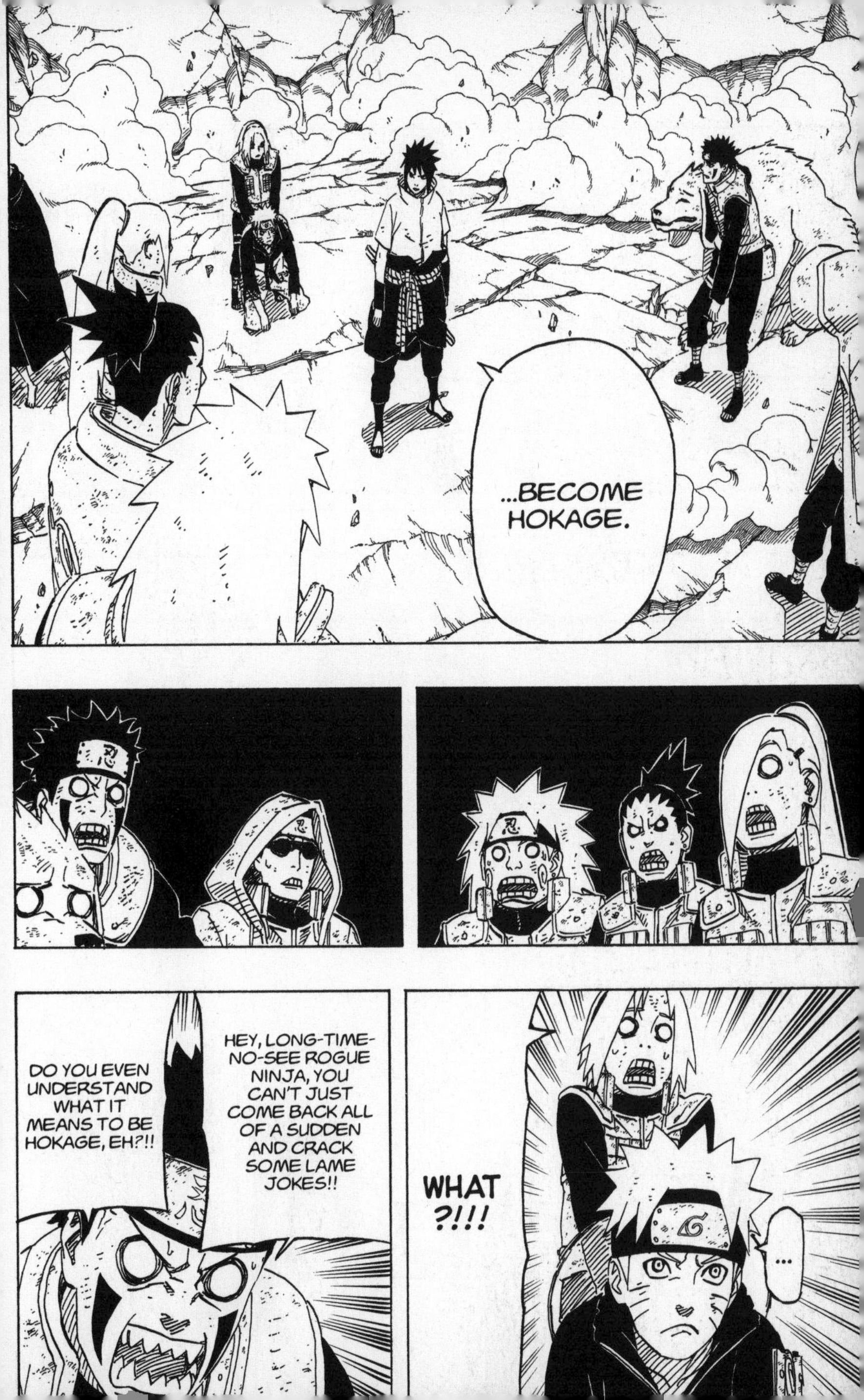
...BECOME HOKAGE.
...
WHAT ?!!!
HEY, LONG-TIME-NO-SEE ROGUE NINJA, YOU CAN'T JUST COME BACK ALL OF A SUDDEN AND CRACK SOME LAME JOKES!!
DO YOU EVEN UNDERSTAND WHAT IT MEANS TO BE HOKAGE, EH?!!

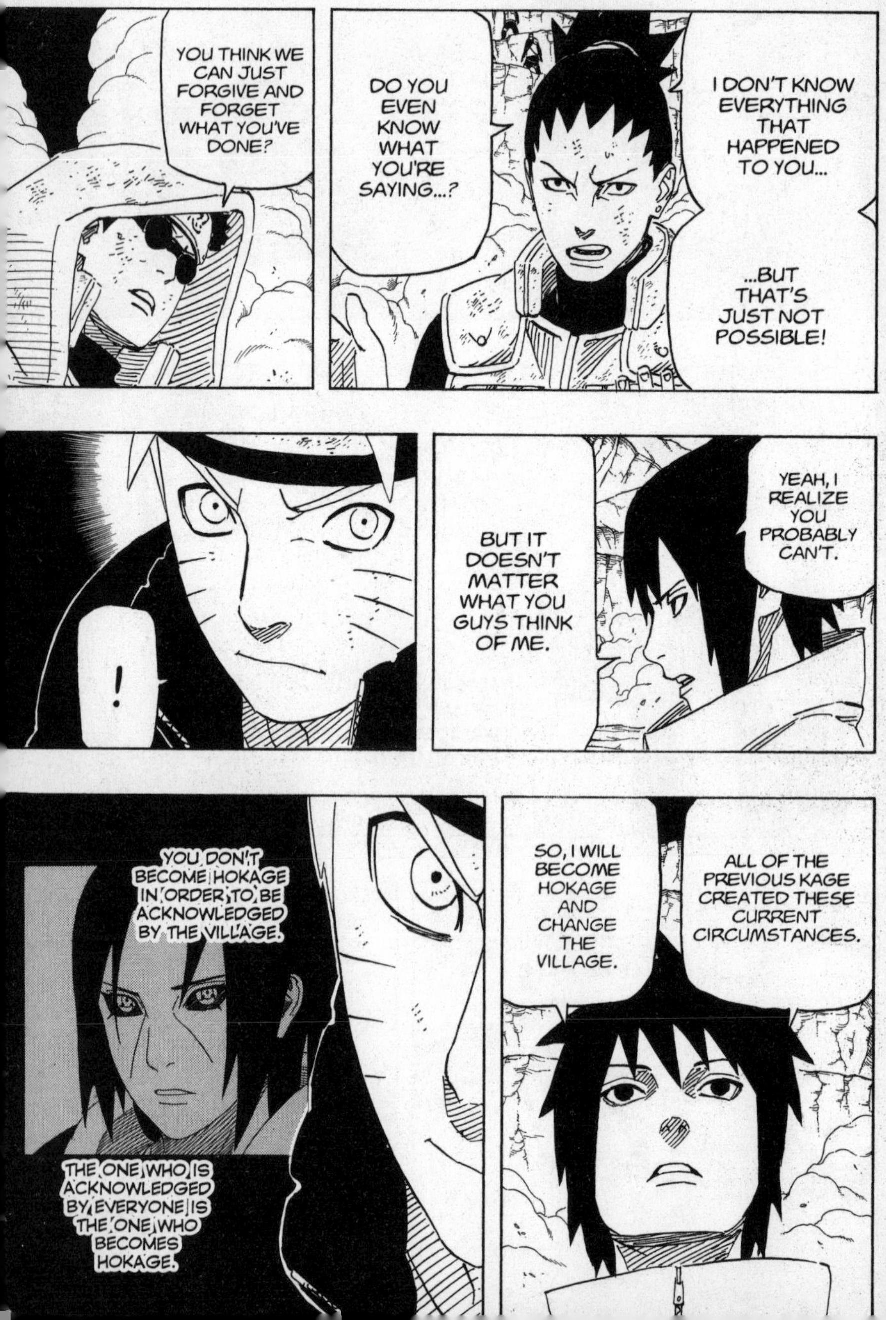
I DON'T KNOW EVERYTHING THAT HAPPENED TO YOU...
DO YOU EVEN KNOW WHAT YOU'RE SAYING...?
...BUT THAT'S JUST NOT POSSIBLE!
YOU THINK WE CAN JUST FORGIVE AND FORGET WHAT YOU'VE DONE?
YEAH, I REALIZE YOU PROBABLY CAN'T.
BUT IT DOESN'T MATTER WHAT YOU GUYS THINK OF ME.
!
ALL OF THE PREVIOUS KAGE CREATED THESE CURRENT CIRCUMSTANCES.
SO, I WILL BECOME HOKAGE AND CHANGE THE VILLAGE.
YOU DON'T BECOME HOKAGE IN ORDER TO BE ACKNOWLEDGED BY THE VILLAGE.
THE ONE WHO IS ACKNOWLEDGED BY EVERYONE IS THE ONE WHO BECOMES HOKAGE.

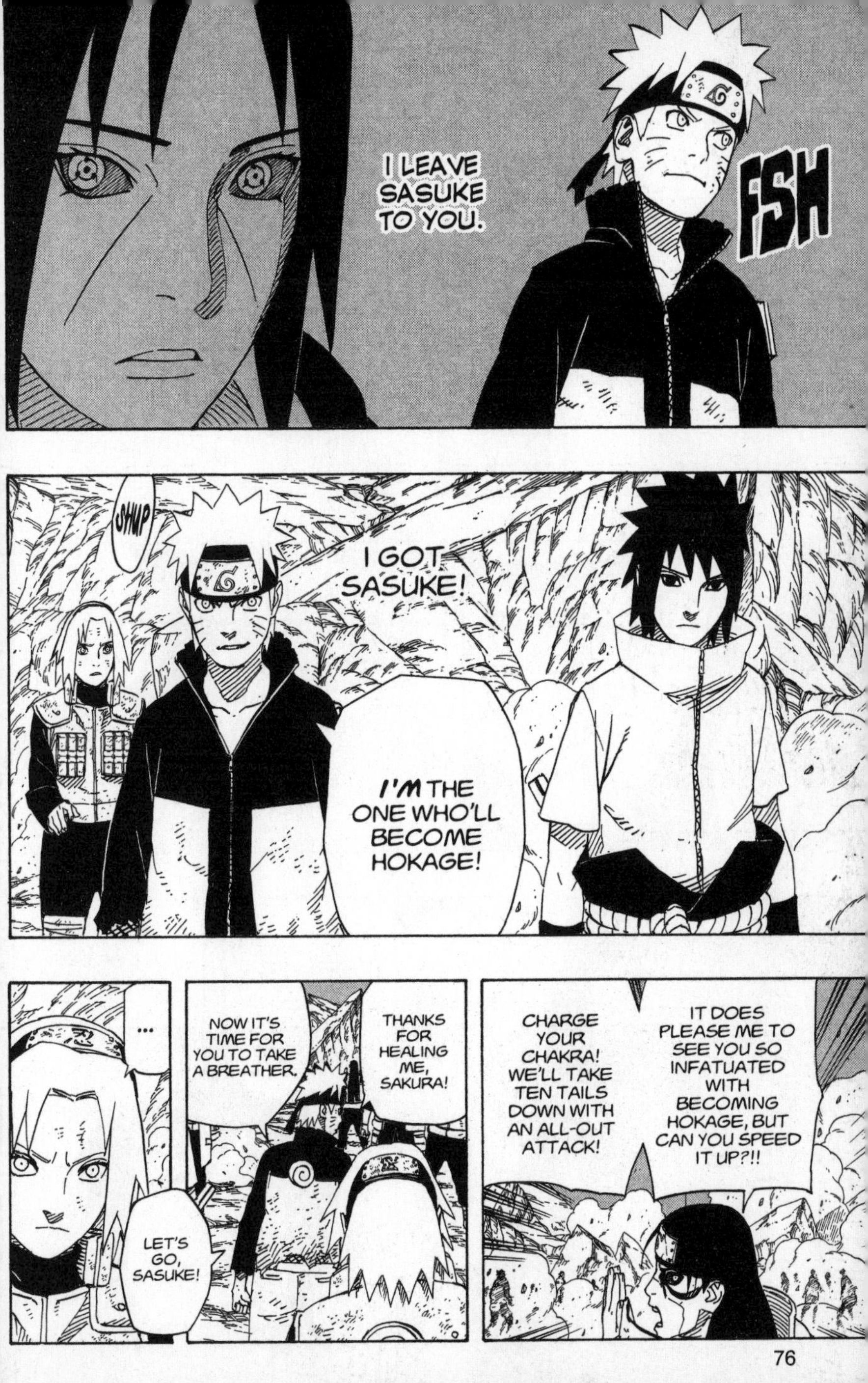
FSH
I LEAVE SASUKE TO YOU.
I GOT SASUKE!
I'M THE ONE WHO'LL BECOME HOKAGE!
SHUP
IT DOES PLEASE ME TO SEE YOU SO INFATUATED WITH BECOMING HOKAGE, BUT CAN YOU SPEED IT UP?!!
CHARGE YOUR CHAKRA! WE'LL TAKE TEN TAILS DOWN WITH AN ALL-OUT ATTACK!
THANKS FOR HEALING ME, SAKURA!
NOW IT'S TIME FOR YOU TO TAKE A BREATHER.
LET'S GO, SASUKE!
...

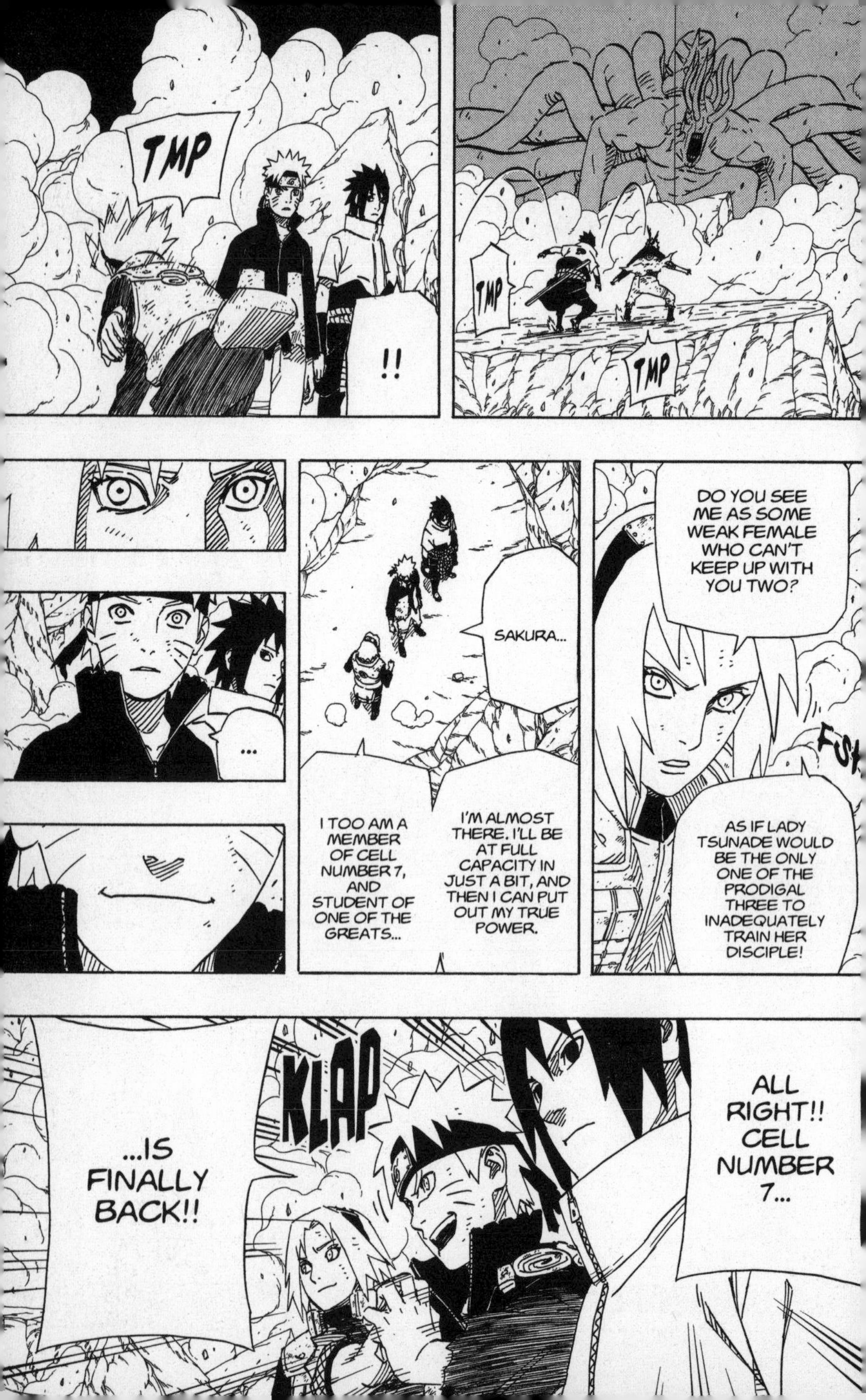
TMP
TMP
TMP
!!
DO YOU SEE ME AS SOME WEAK FEMALE WHO CAN'T KEEP UP WITH YOU TWO?
AS IF LADY TSUNADE WOULD BE THE ONLY ONE OF THE PRODIGAL THREE TO INADEQUATELY TRAIN HER DISCIPLE!
SAKURA...
I'M ALMOST THERE. I'LL BE AT FULL CAPACITY IN JUST A BIT, AND THEN I CAN PUT OUT MY TRUE POWER.
I TOO AM A MEMBER OF CELL NUMBER 7, AND STUDENT OF ONE OF THE GREATS...
...
ALL RIGHT!! CELL NUMBER 7...
KLAP
...IS FINALLY BACK!!

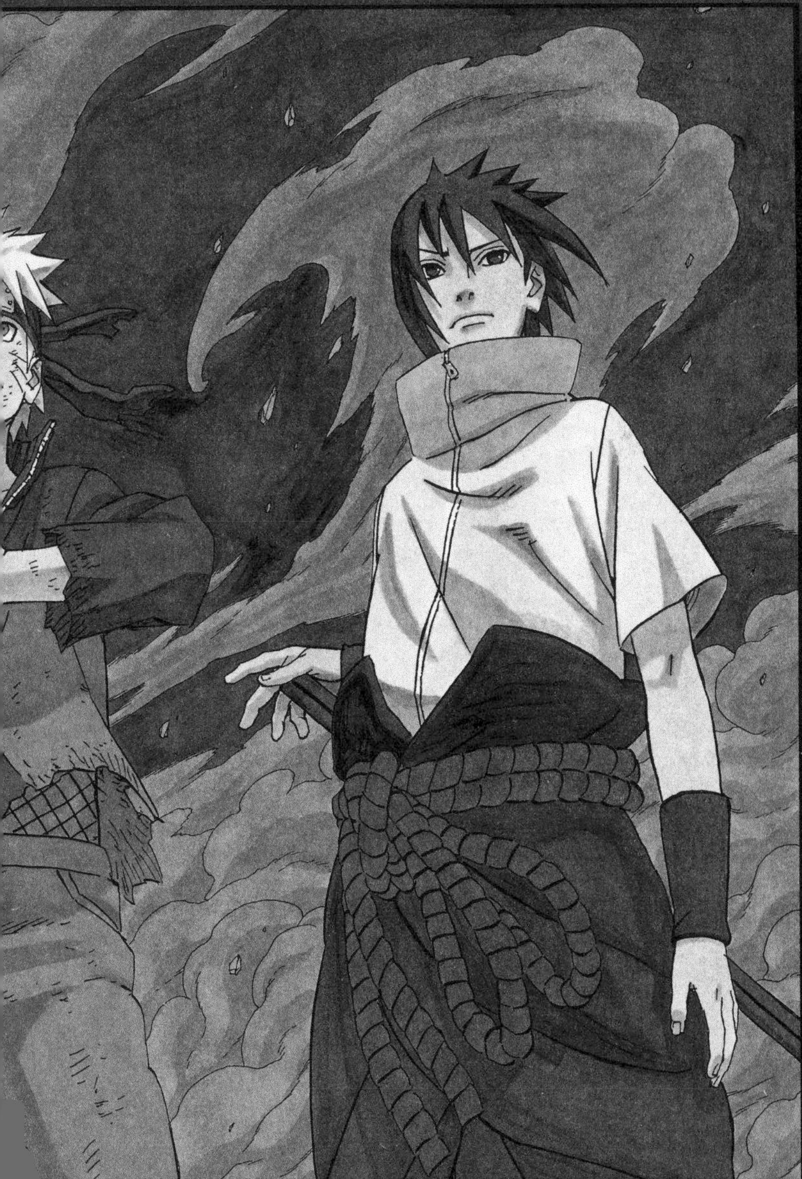

Number 632: A United Front

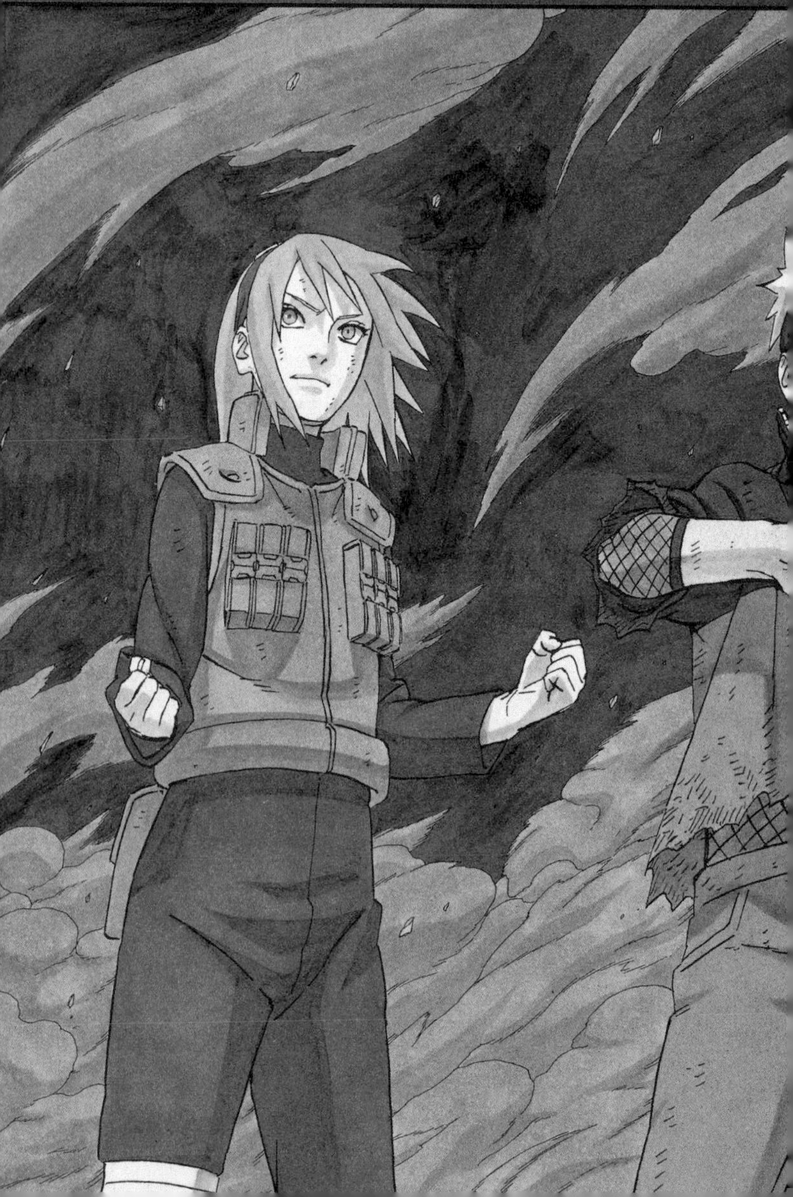

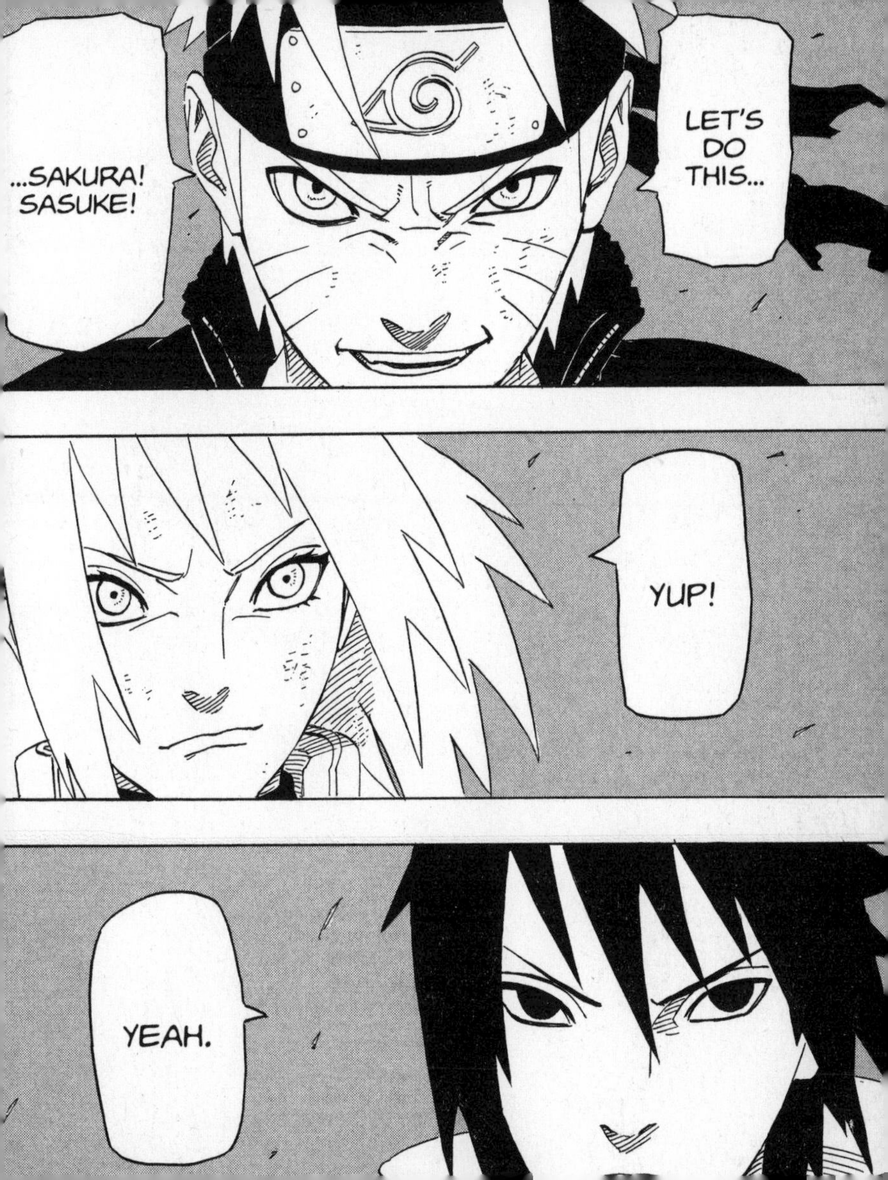
LET'S DO THIS...
...SAKURA! SASUKE!
YUP!
YEAH.

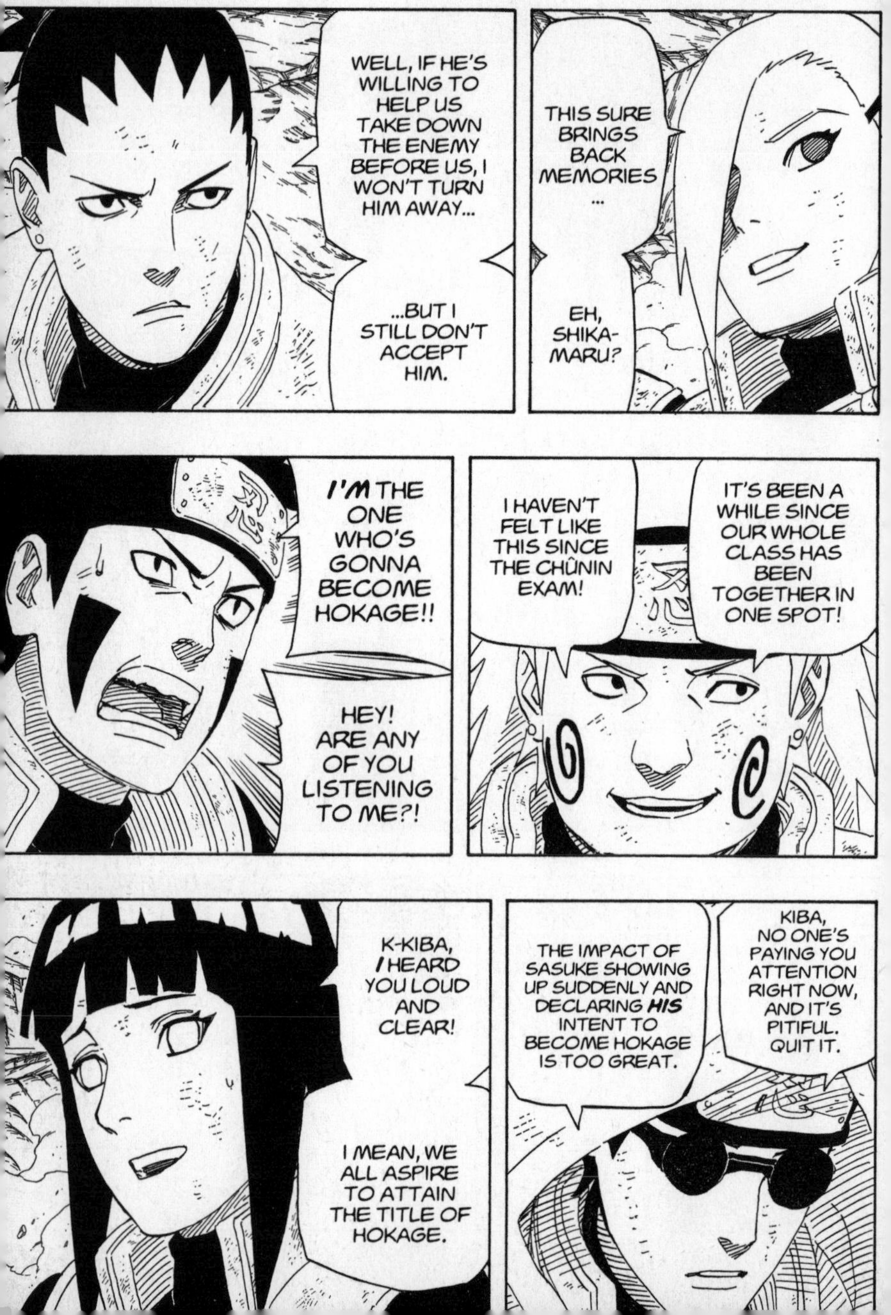
THIS SURE BRINGS BACK MEMORIES ...
EH, SHIKA-MARU?
WELL, IF HE'S WILLING TO HELP US TAKE DOWN THE ENEMY BEFORE US, I WON'T TURN HIM AWAY...
...BUT I STILL DON'T ACCEPT HIM.
IT'S BEEN A WHILE SINCE OUR WHOLE CLASS HAS BEEN TOGETHER IN ONE SPOT!
I HAVEN'T FELT LIKE THIS SINCE THE CHŪNIN EXAM!
I'M THE ONE WHO'S GONNA BECOME HOKAGE!!
HEY! ARE ANY OF YOU LISTENING TO ME?!
KIBA, NO ONE'S PAYING YOU ATTENTION RIGHT NOW, AND IT'S PITIFUL. QUIT IT.
THE IMPACT OF SASUKE SHOWING UP SUDDENLY AND DECLARING *HIS* INTENT TO BECOME HOKAGE IS TOO GREAT.
K-KIBA, *I* HEARD YOU LOUD AND CLEAR!
I MEAN, WE ALL ASPIRE TO ATTAIN THE TITLE OF HOKAGE.

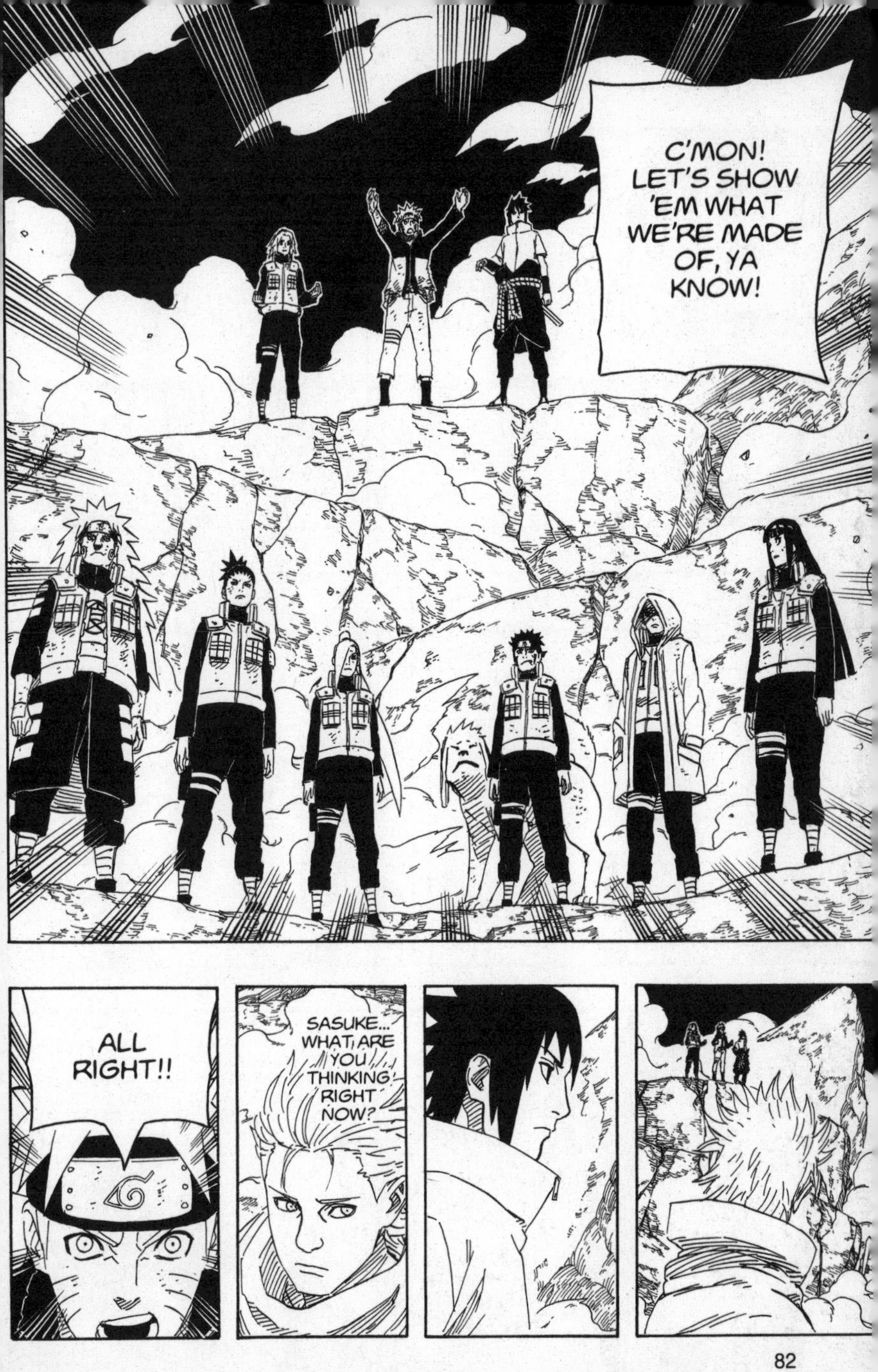
C'MON! LET'S SHOW 'EM WHAT WE'RE MADE OF, YA KNOW!
SASUKE... WHAT ARE YOU THINKING RIGHT NOW?
ALL RIGHT!!

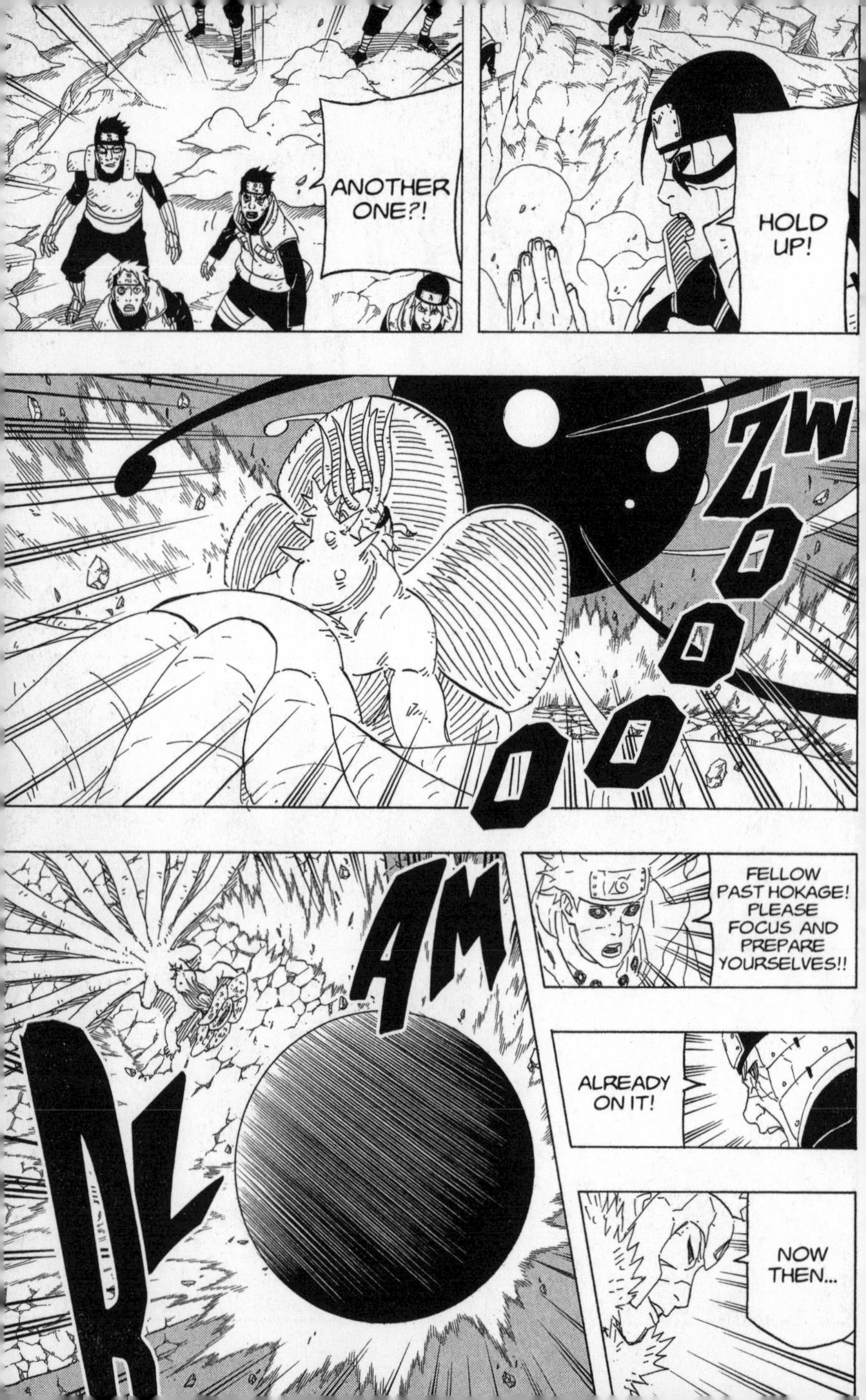
HOLD UP!
ANOTHER ONE?!
ZWOOOO
FELLOW PAST HOKAGE! PLEASE FOCUS AND PREPARE YOURSELVES!!
ALREADY ON IT!
NOW THEN...

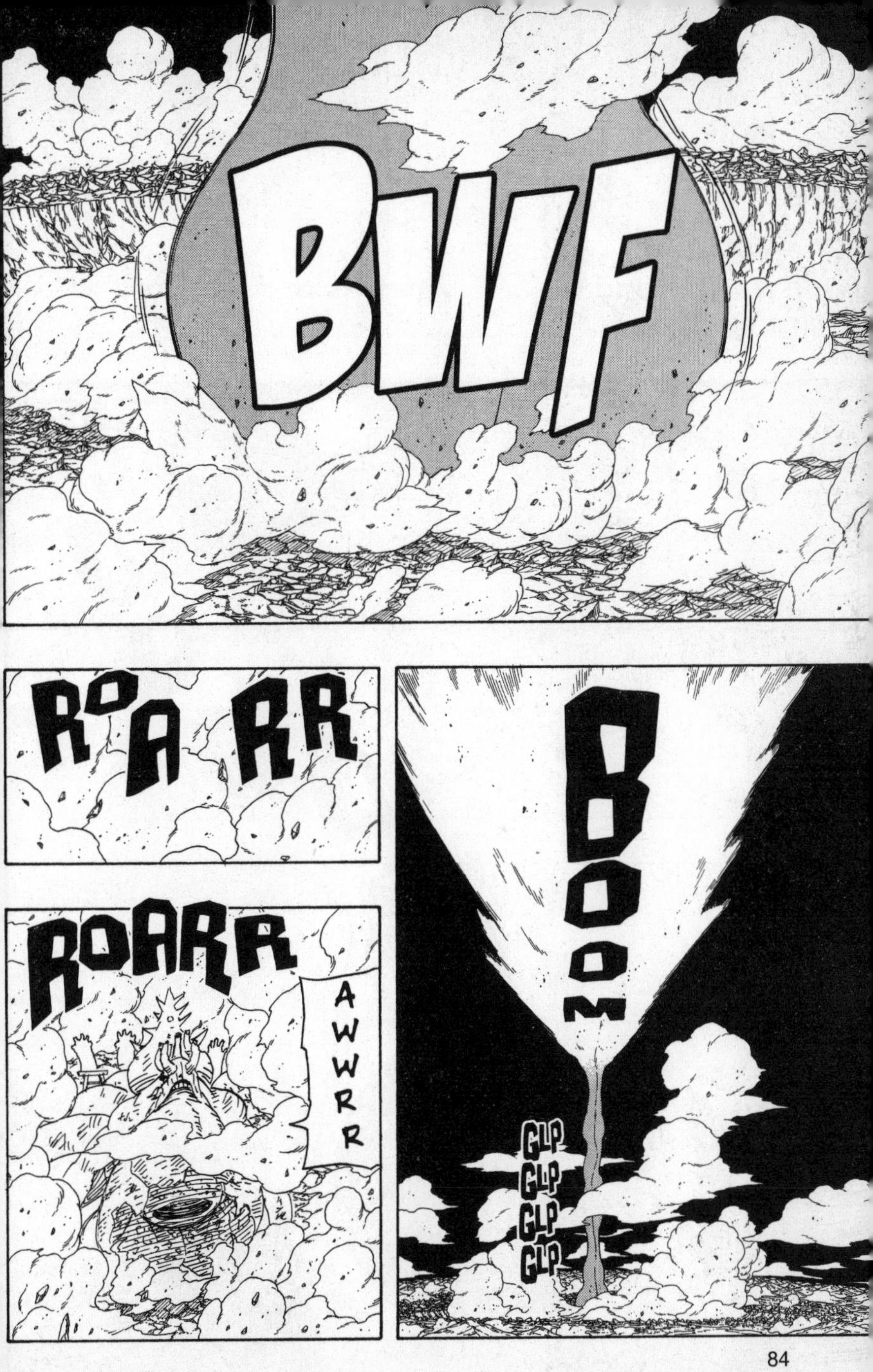
BWF
BOOM
GLP
GLP
GLP
GLP
ROARR
ROARR
AWWRR

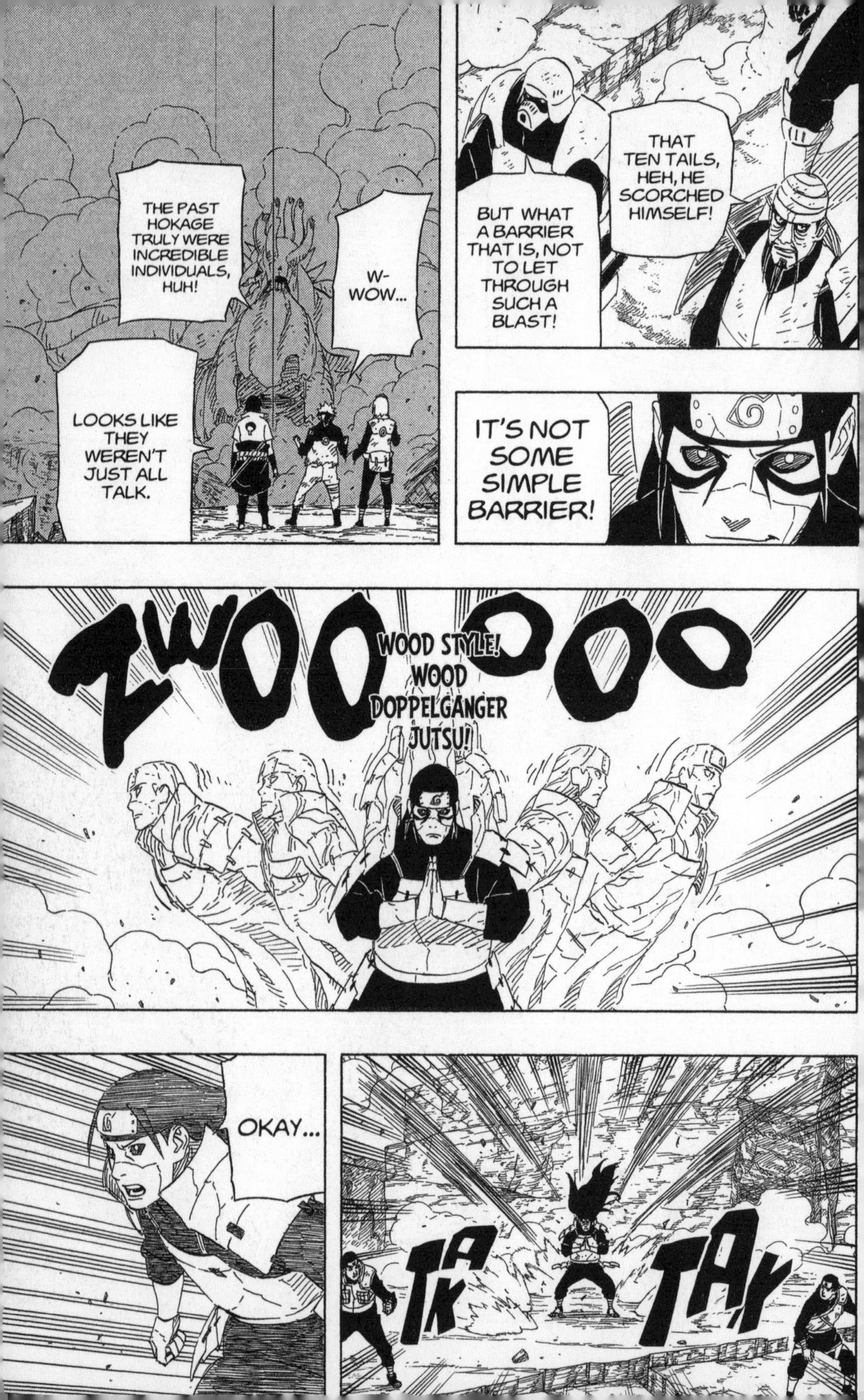
THAT TEN TAILS, HEH, HE SCORCHED HIMSELF!
BUT WHAT A BARRIER THAT IS, NOT TO LET THROUGH SUCH A BLAST!
IT'S NOT SOME SIMPLE BARRIER!
W-WOW...
THE PAST HOKAGE TRULY WERE INCREDIBLE INDIVIDUALS, HUH!
LOOKS LIKE THEY WEREN'T JUST ALL TALK.
ZWOOOOOO
WOOD STYLE! WOOD DOPPELGANGER JUTSU!
TA
TAK
OKAY...

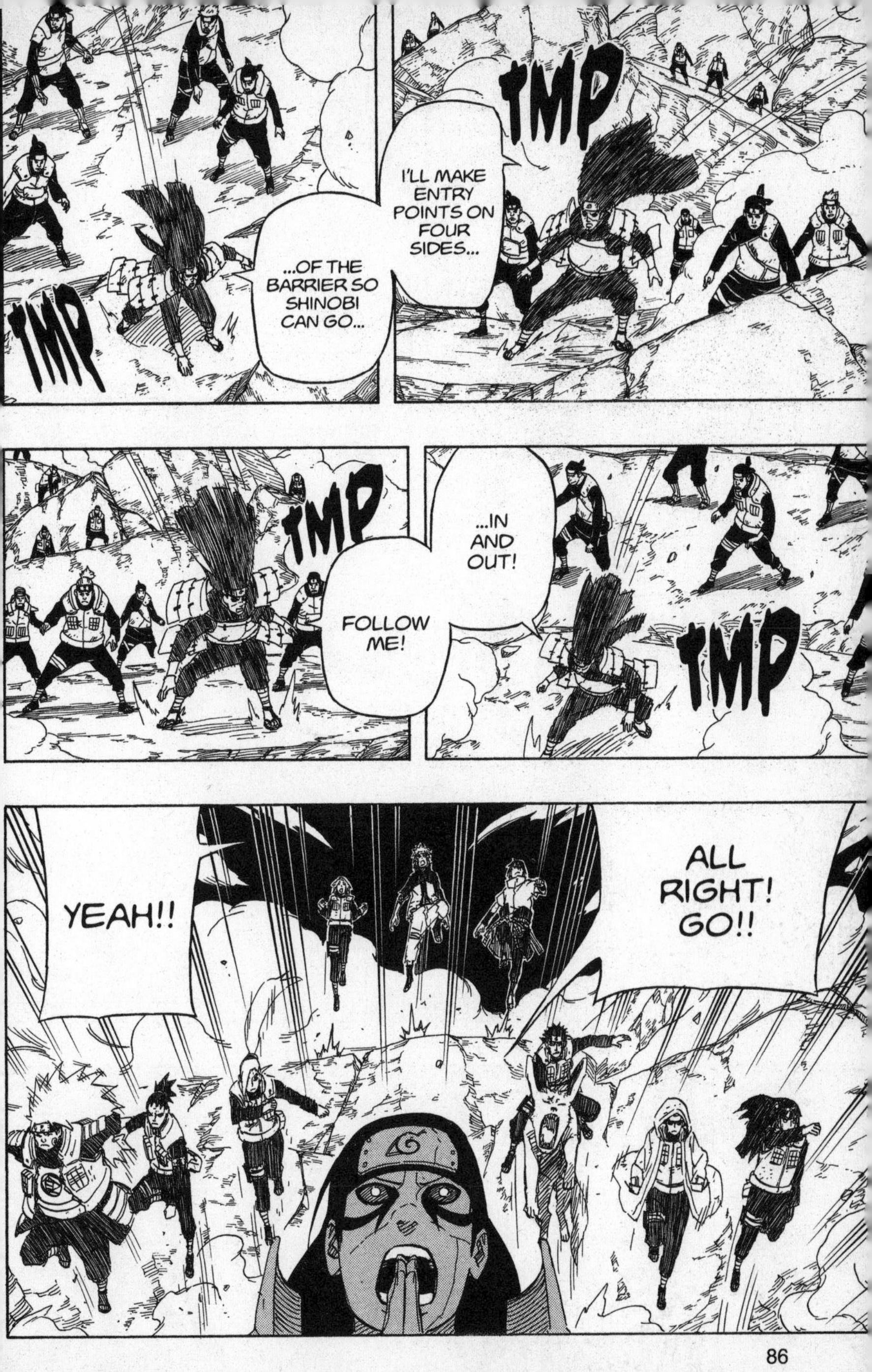
TMP
I'LL MAKE ENTRY POINTS ON FOUR SIDES...
...OF THE BARRIER SO SHINOBI CAN GO...
TMP
...IN AND OUT!
TMP
FOLLOW ME!
TMP
ALL RIGHT! GO!!
YEAH!!

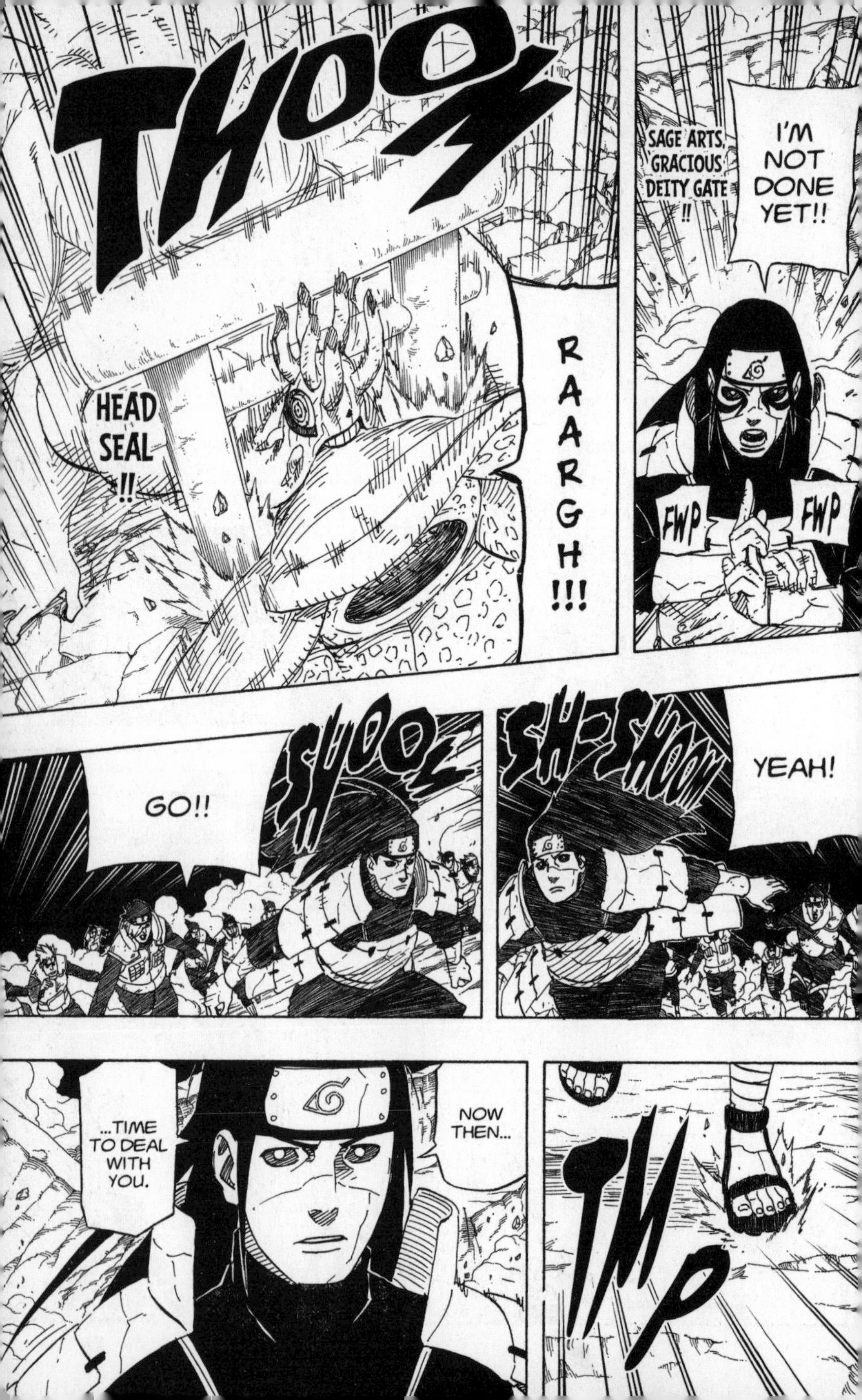
I'M NOT DONE YET!!
SAGE ARTS, GRACIOUS DEITY GATE!!
FWP
FWP
THOOM
RAAARGH!!!
HEAD SEAL!!
YEAH!
SH-SHOOM
SHOOM
GO!!
THMP
NOW THEN...
...TIME TO DEAL WITH YOU.

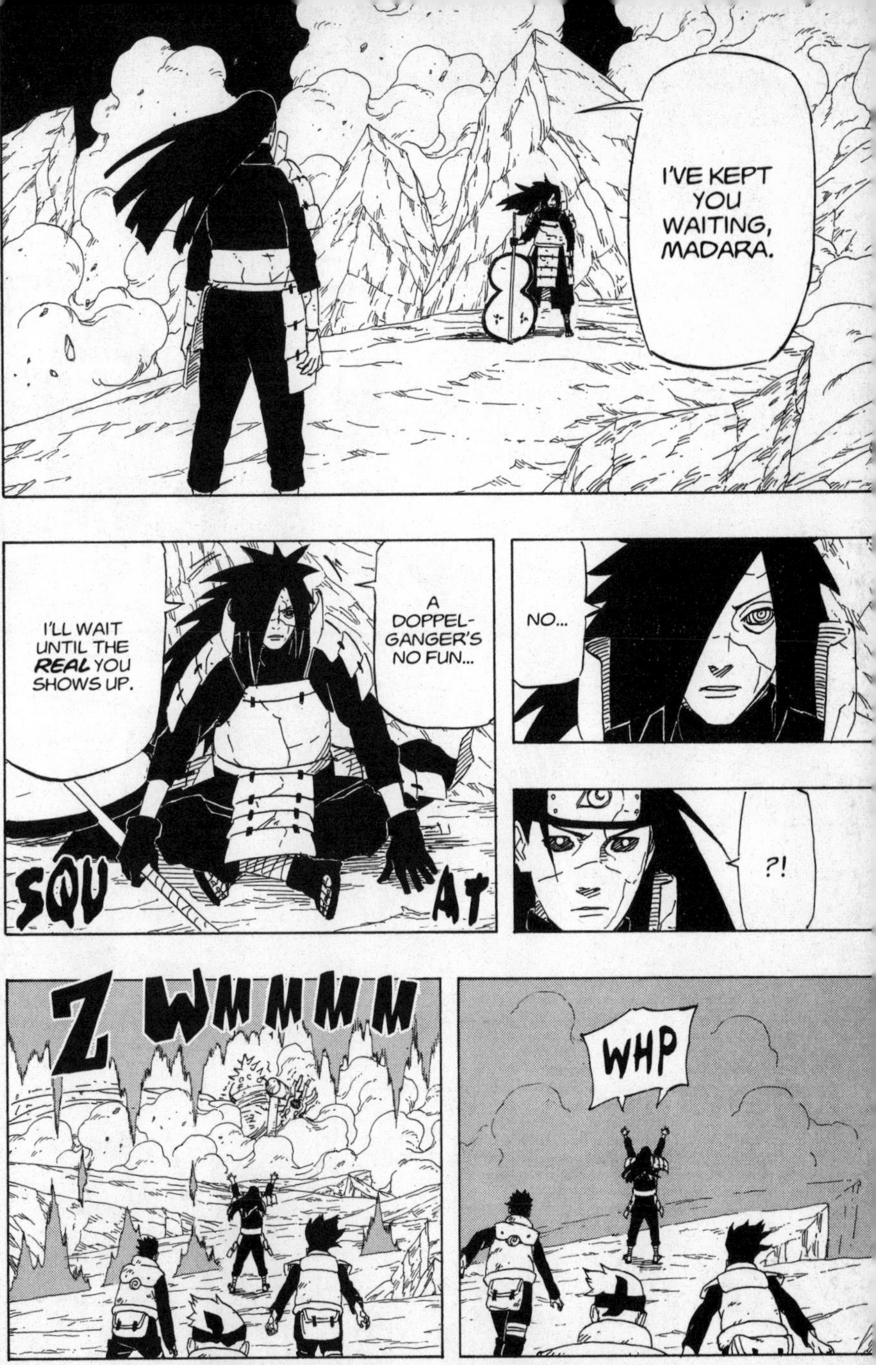
I'VE KEPT YOU WAITING, MADARA.
NO...
?!
A DOPPEL-GANGER'S NO FUN...
I'LL WAIT UNTIL THE REAL YOU SHOWS UP.
SQUAT
WHP
ZWMMMM

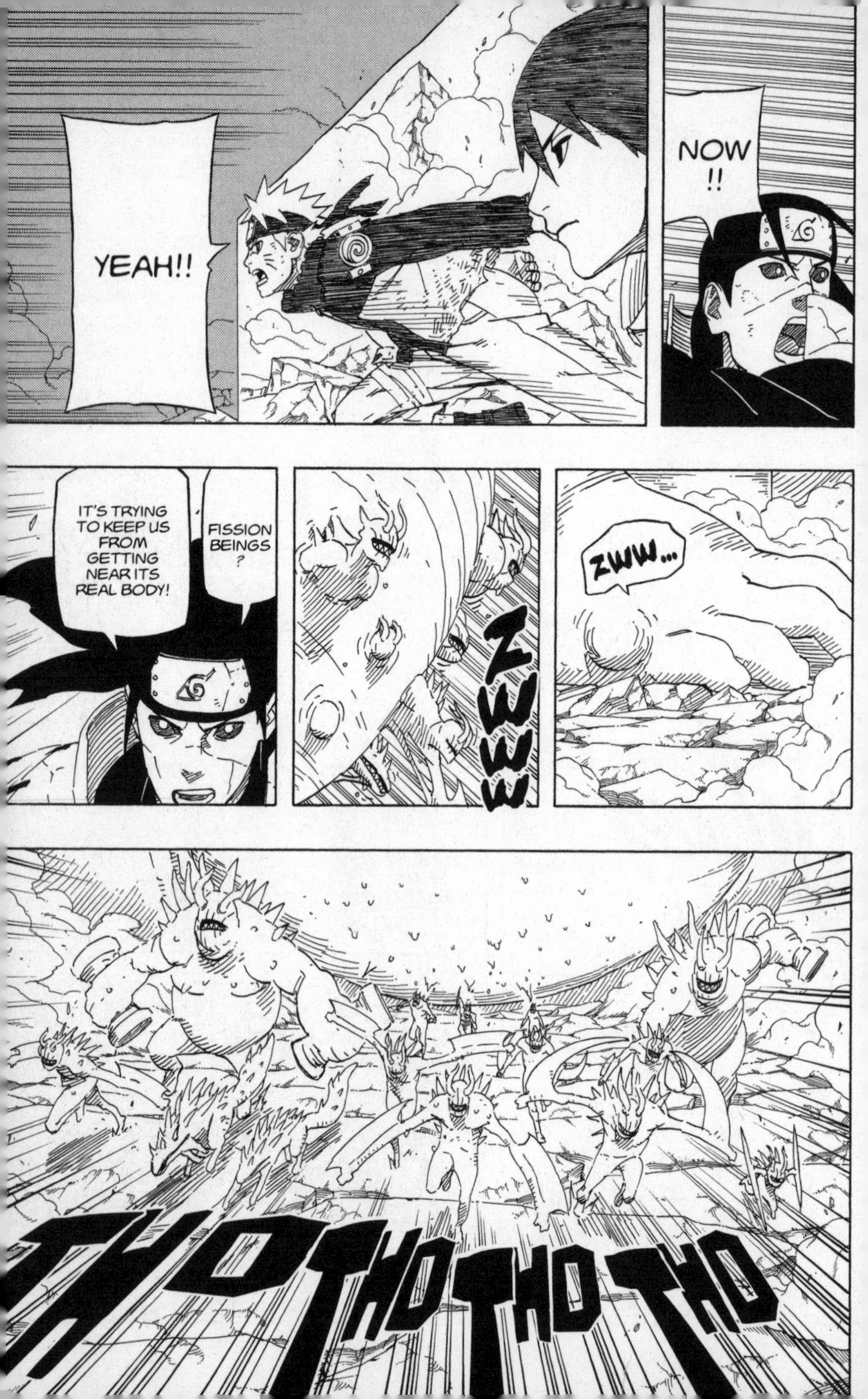
NOW !!
YEAH!!
ZWW...
ZWWW
FISSION BEINGS ?
IT'S TRYING TO KEEP US FROM GETTING NEAR ITS REAL BODY!
THO THO THO THO THO

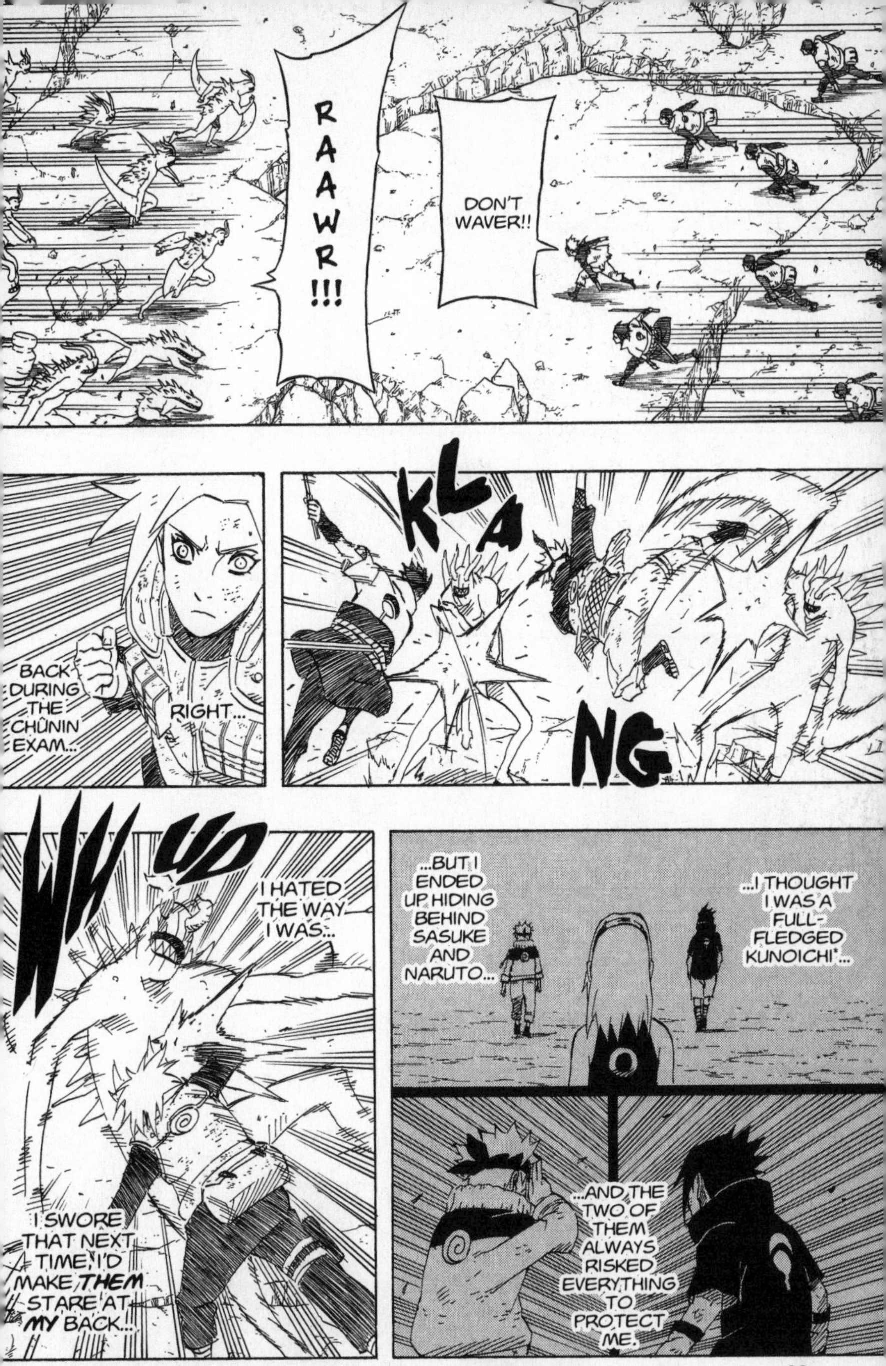
DON'T WAVER!!
RAAAWR!!!
KLANG
RIGHT...
BACK DURING THE CHŪNIN EXAM...
...I THOUGHT I WAS A FULL-FLEDGED KUNOICHI*...
...BUT I ENDED UP HIDING BEHIND SASUKE AND NARUTO...
...AND THE TWO OF THEM ALWAYS RISKED EVERYTHING TO PROTECT ME.
WHUD
I HATED THE WAY I WAS...
I SWORE THAT NEXT TIME, I'D MAKE ***THEM*** STARE AT ***MY*** BACK...!

*KUNOICHI = FEMALE NINJA

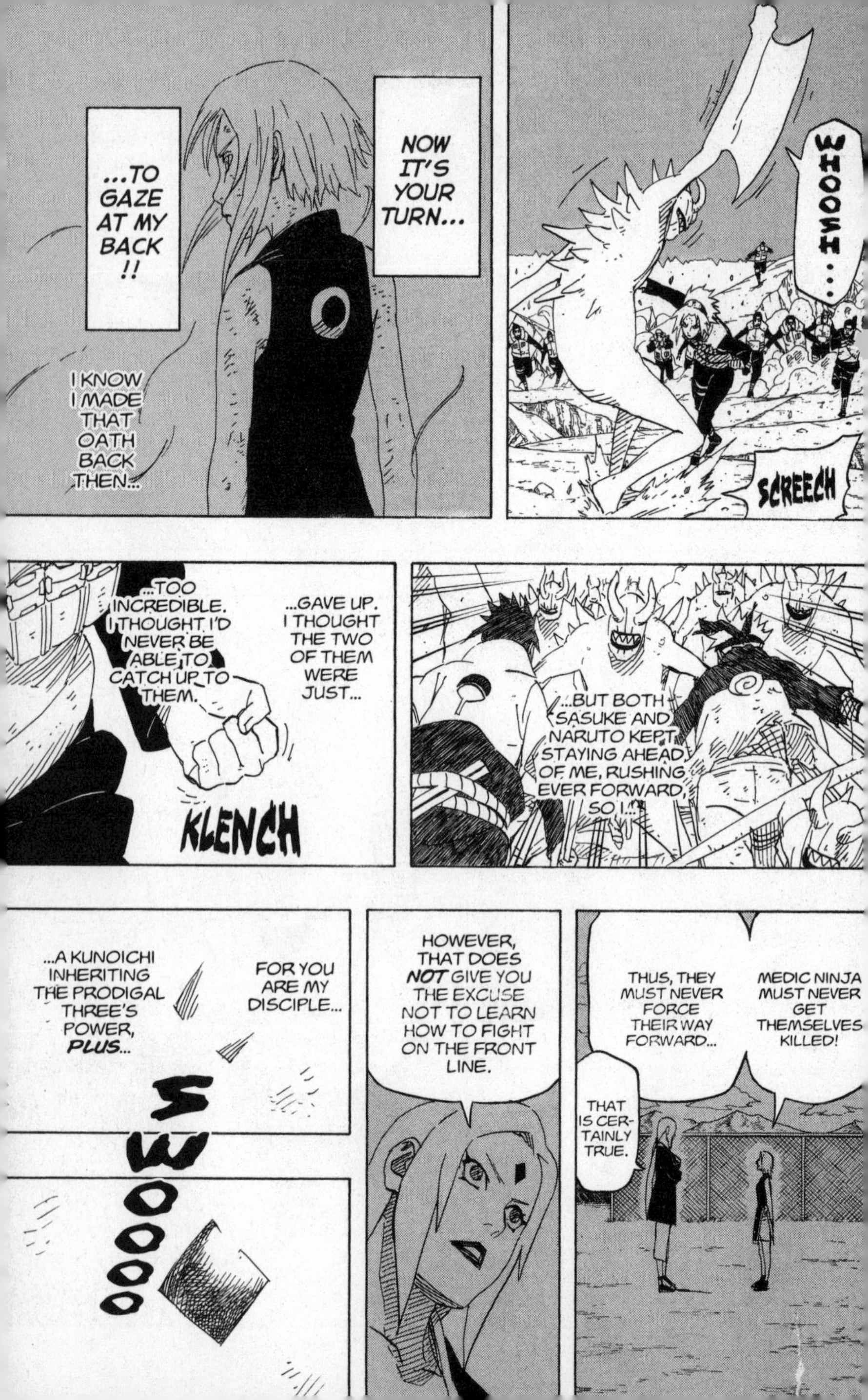
WHOOSH...
SCREECH
NOW IT'S YOUR TURN...
...TO GAZE AT MY BACK!!
I KNOW I MADE THAT OATH BACK THEN...
...BUT BOTH SASUKE AND NARUTO KEPT STAYING AHEAD OF ME, RUSHING EVER FORWARD, SO I...
...GAVE UP. I THOUGHT THE TWO OF THEM WERE JUST...
...TOO INCREDIBLE. I THOUGHT I'D NEVER BE ABLE TO CATCH UP TO THEM.
KLENCH
MEDIC NINJA MUST NEVER GET THEMSELVES KILLED!
THUS, THEY MUST NEVER FORCE THEIR WAY FORWARD...
THAT IS CERTAINLY TRUE.
HOWEVER, THAT DOES NOT GIVE YOU THE EXCUSE NOT TO LEARN HOW TO FIGHT ON THE FRONT LINE.
FOR YOU ARE MY DISCIPLE...
...A KUNOICHI INHERITING THE PRODIGAL THREE'S POWER, PLUS...
SWOOOOO

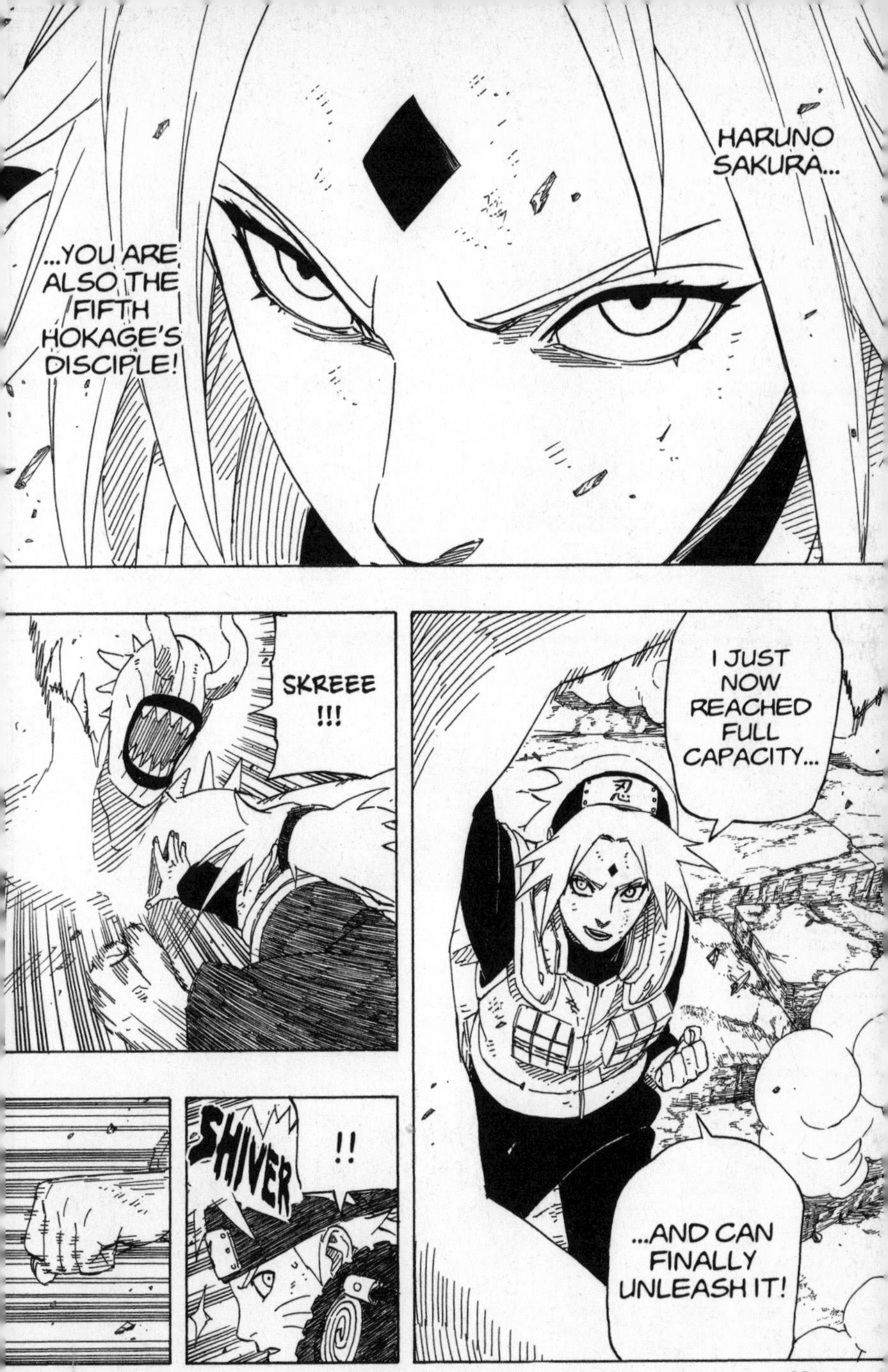
HARUNO SAKURA...
...YOU ARE ALSO THE FIFTH HOKAGE'S DISCIPLE!
I JUST NOW REACHED FULL CAPACITY...
...AND CAN FINALLY UNLEASH IT!
SKREEE !!!
SHIVER
!!

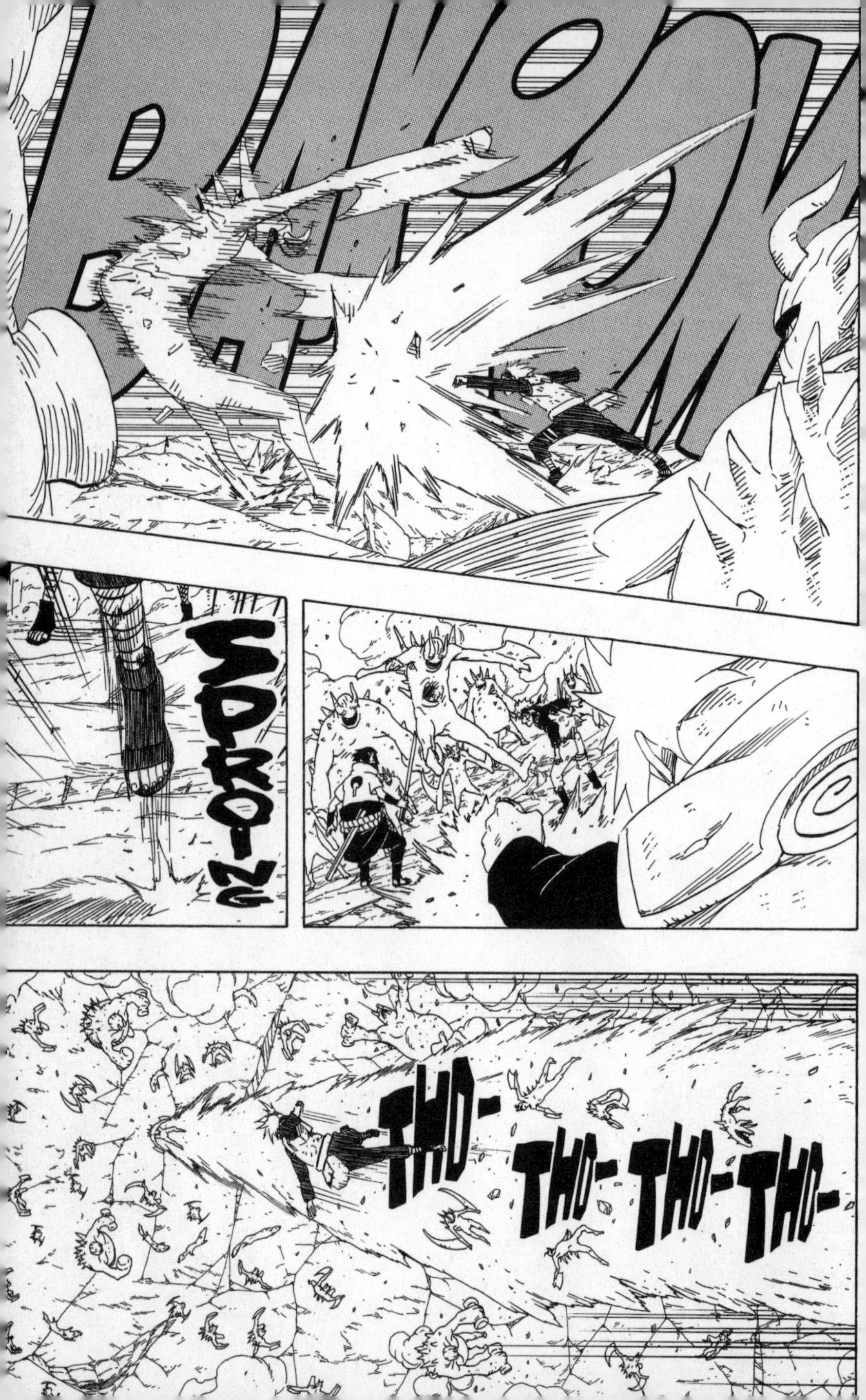
SPROING
THO- THO- THO- THO-

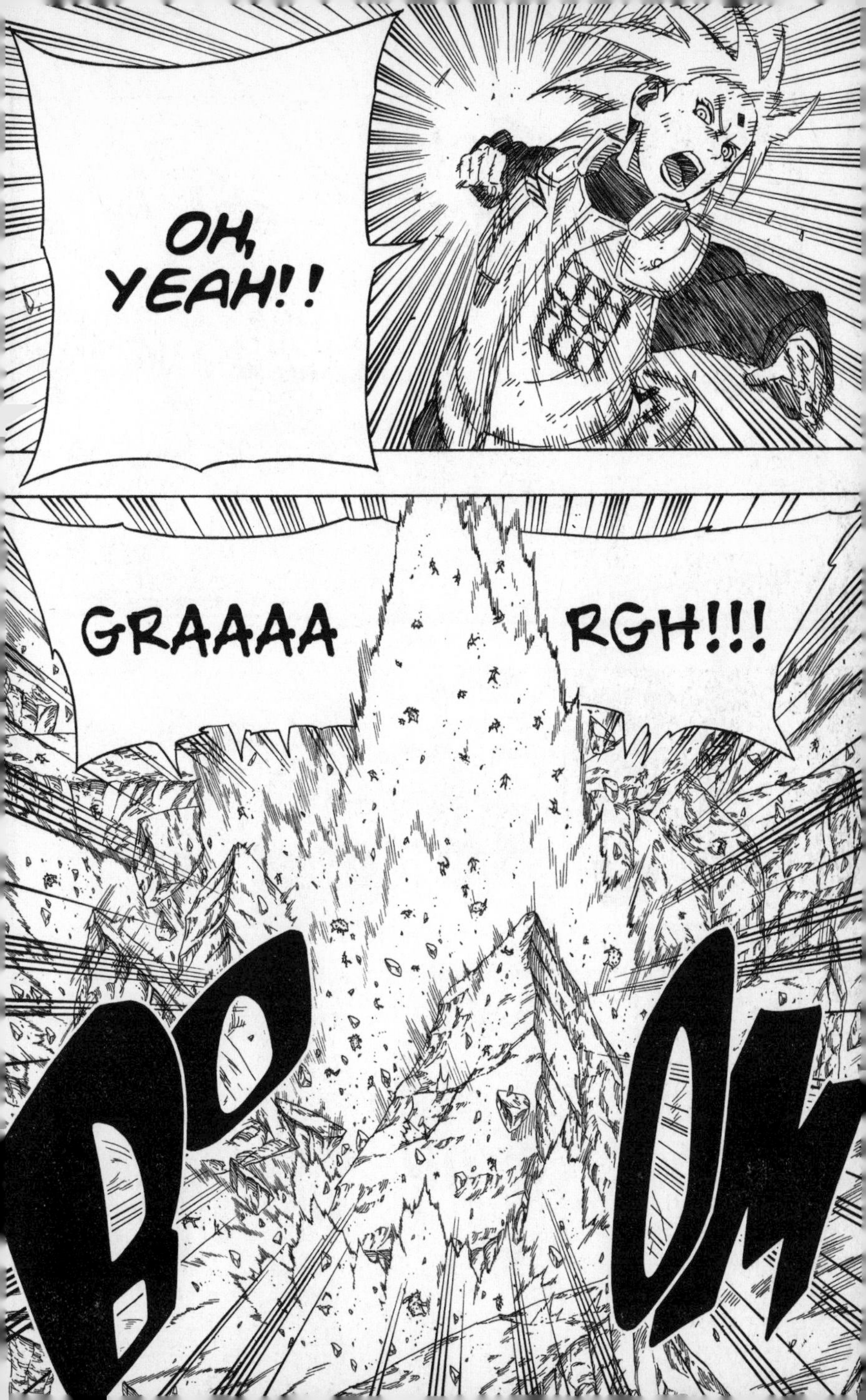
OH, YEAH!!
GRAAAA RGH!!!
BOOM

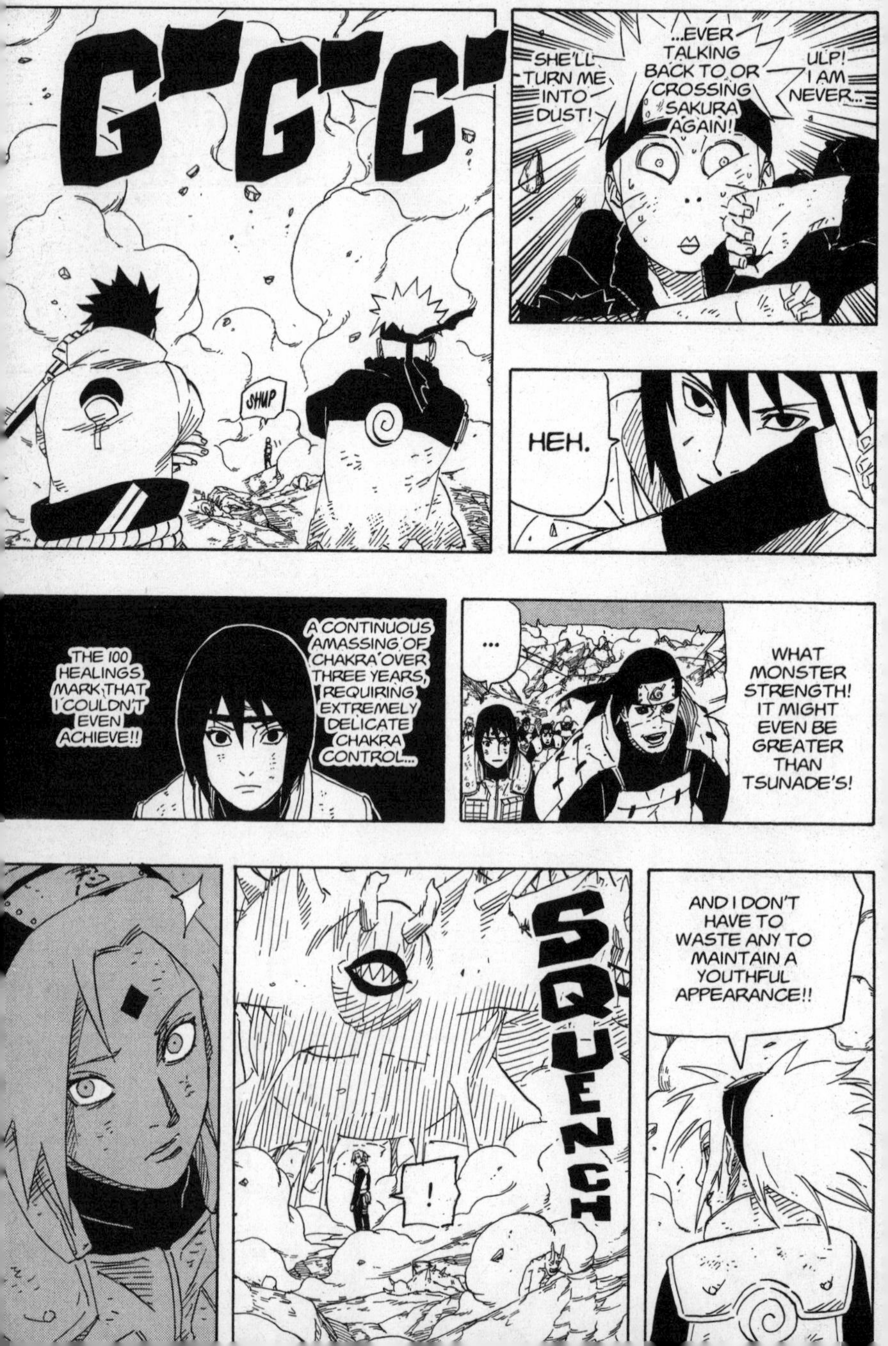
ULP! I AM NEVER...
...EVER TALKING BACK TO OR CROSSING SAKURA AGAIN!
SHE'LL TURN ME INTO DUST!
HEH.
G'G'G'
SHUP
WHAT MONSTER STRENGTH! IT MIGHT EVEN BE GREATER THAN TSUNADE'S!
...
A CONTINUOUS AMASSING OF CHAKRA OVER THREE YEARS, REQUIRING EXTREMELY DELICATE CHAKRA CONTROL...
THE 100 HEALINGS MARK THAT I COULDN'T EVEN ACHIEVE!!
AND I DON'T HAVE TO WASTE ANY TO MAINTAIN A YOUTHFUL APPEARANCE!!
SQUENCH
!

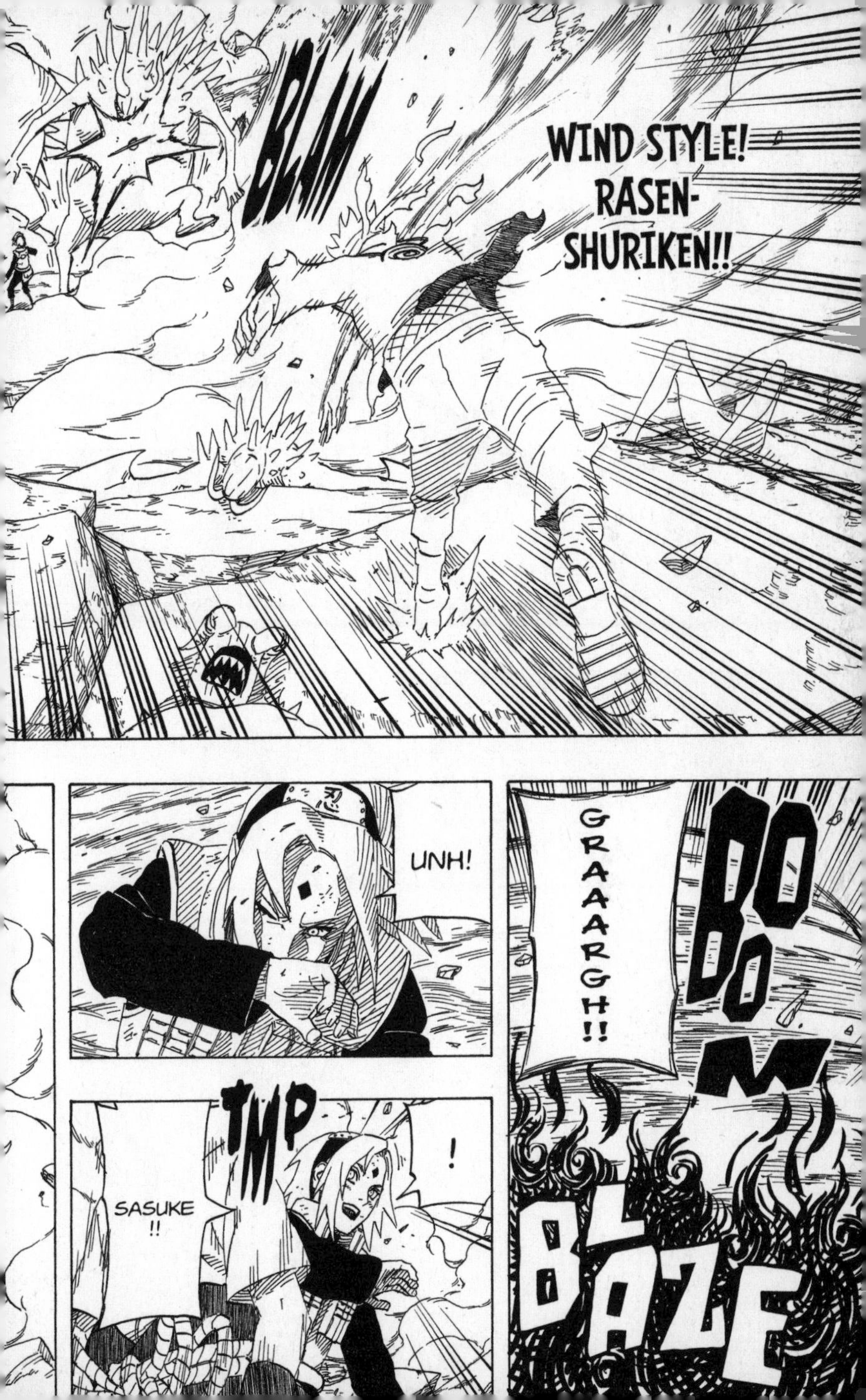
WIND STYLE! RASEN-SHURIKEN!!
BLAM
GRAAAARGH!!
BOOM
BLAZE
UNH!
TMP
!
SASUKE!!

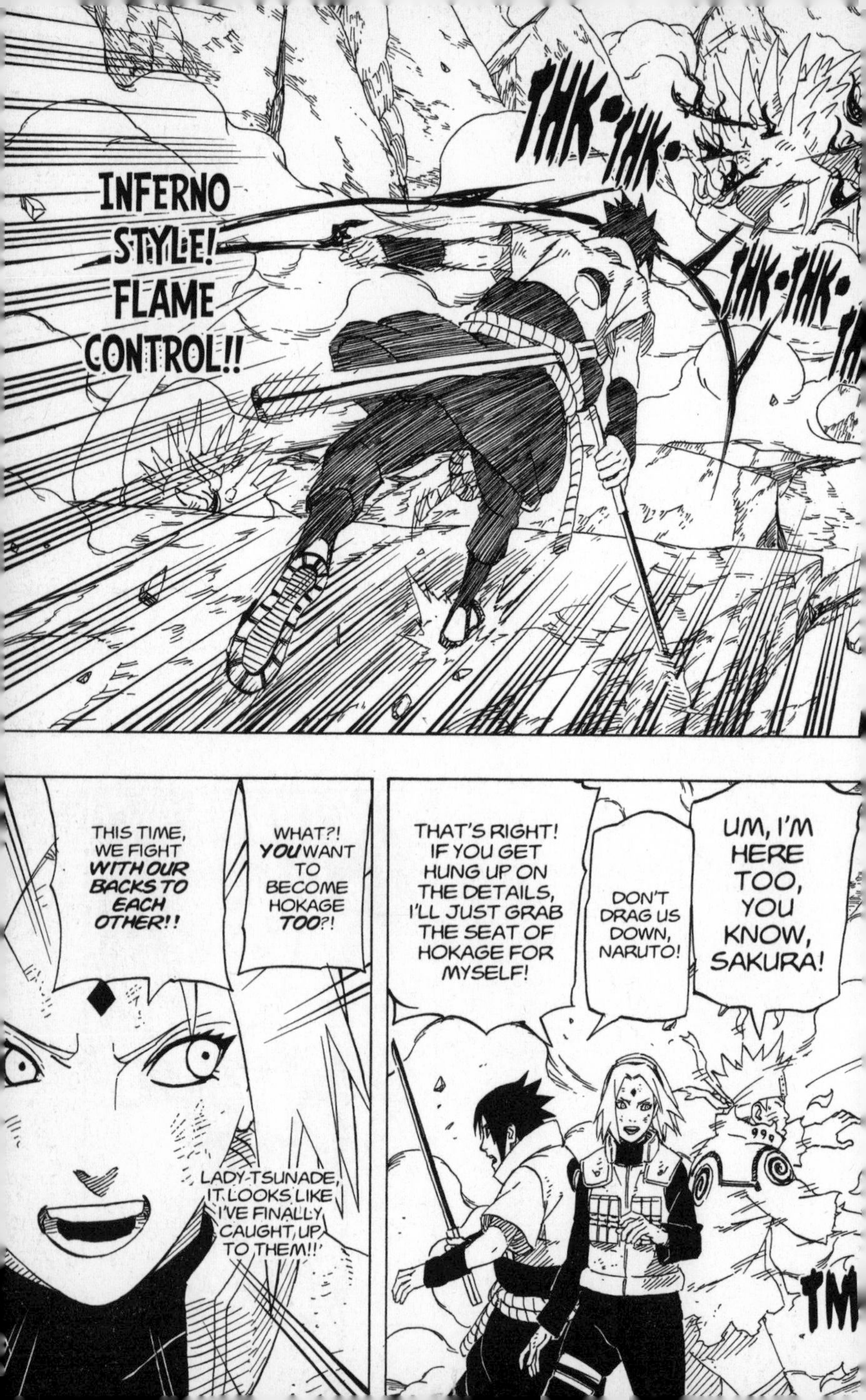
THK-THK-
THK-THK-TH
INFERNO STYLE! FLAME CONTROL!!
UM, I'M HERE TOO, YOU KNOW, SAKURA!
DON'T DRAG US DOWN, NARUTO!
THAT'S RIGHT! IF YOU GET HUNG UP ON THE DETAILS, I'LL JUST GRAB THE SEAT OF HOKAGE FOR MYSELF!
TM
WHAT?! YOU WANT TO BECOME HOKAGE TOO?!
THIS TIME, WE FIGHT WITH OUR BACKS TO EACH OTHER!!
LADY TSUNADE, IT LOOKS LIKE I'VE FINALLY CAUGHT UP TO THEM!!

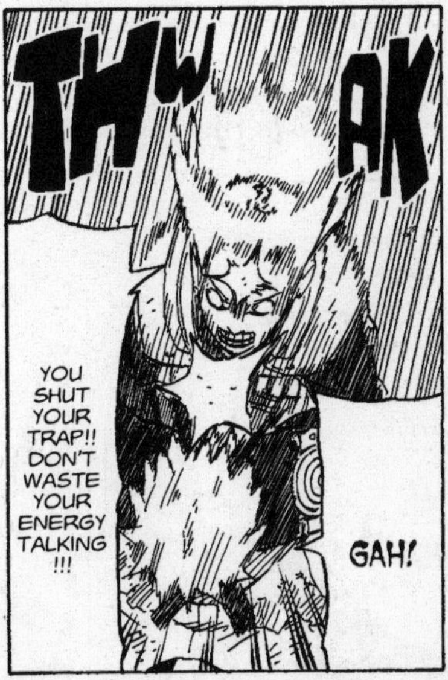
THWAK
YOU SHUT YOUR TRAP!! DON'T WASTE YOUR ENERGY TALKING !!!
GAH!

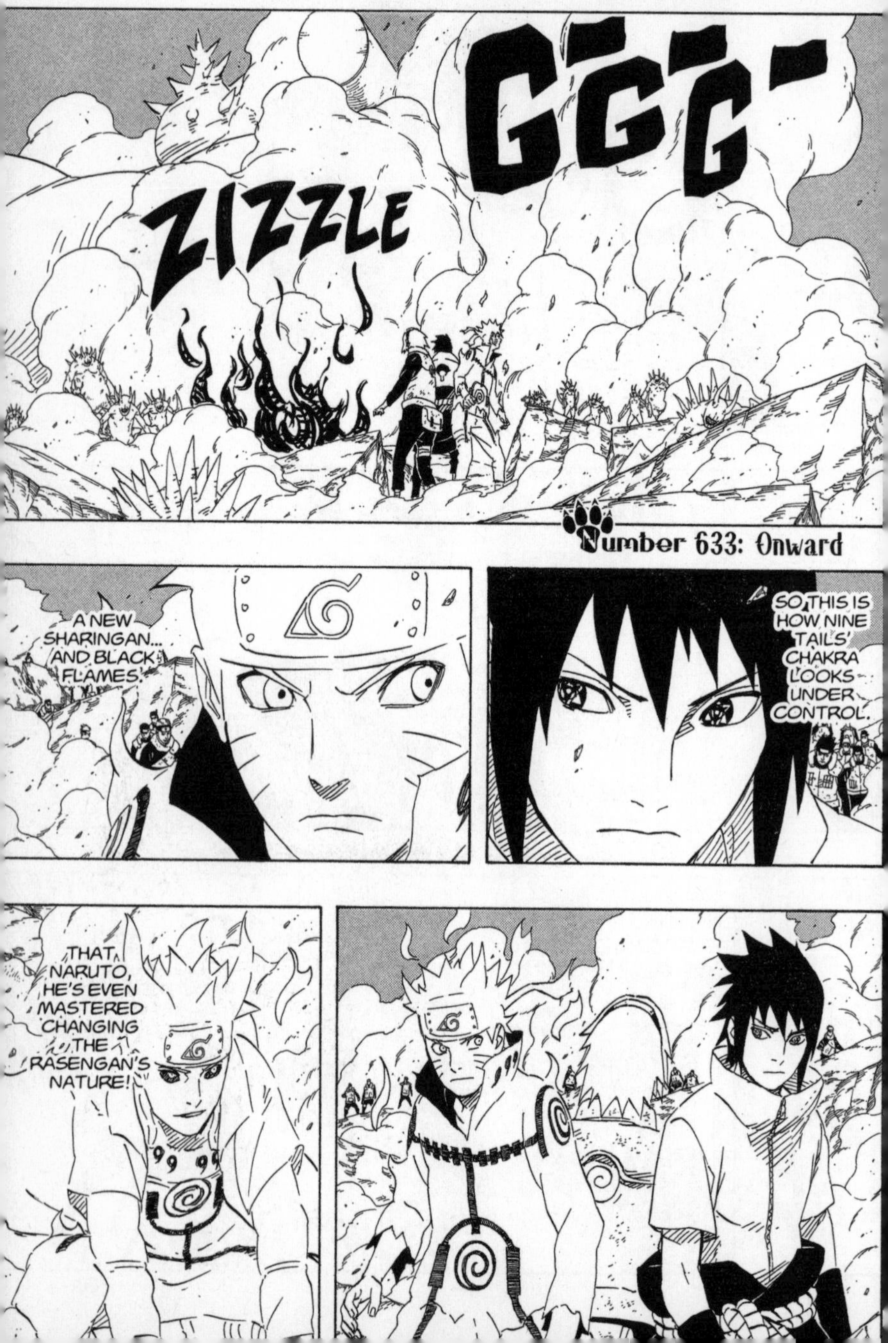
GGG
ZIZZLE
Number 633: Onward
SO THIS IS HOW NINE TAILS' CHAKRA LOOKS UNDER CONTROL.
A NEW SHARINGAN... AND BLACK FLAMES!
THAT NARUTO, HE'S EVEN MASTERED CHANGING THE RASENGAN'S NATURE!

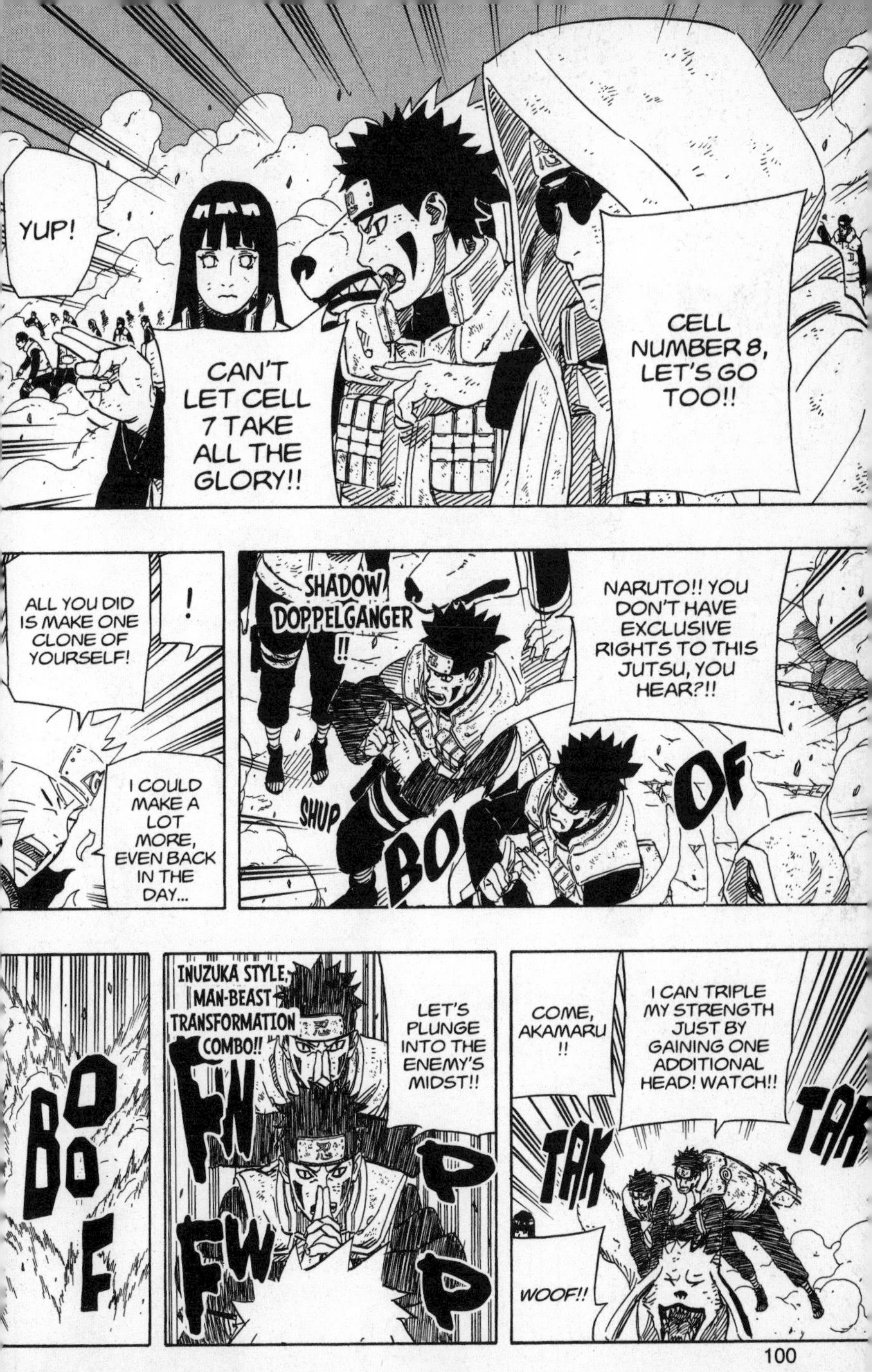
CELL NUMBER 8, LET'S GO TOO!!
CAN'T LET CELL 7 TAKE ALL THE GLORY!!
YUP!
NARUTO!! YOU DON'T HAVE EXCLUSIVE RIGHTS TO THIS JUTSU, YOU HEAR?!!
SHADOW DOPPELGANGER!!
SHUP
BOOF
!
ALL YOU DID IS MAKE ONE CLONE OF YOURSELF!
I COULD MAKE A LOT MORE, EVEN BACK IN THE DAY...
I CAN TRIPLE MY STRENGTH JUST BY GAINING ONE ADDITIONAL HEAD! WATCH!!
TAK
COME, AKAMARU!!
TAK
WOOF!!
LET'S PLUNGE INTO THE ENEMY'S MIDST!!
INUZUKA STYLE, MAN-BEAST TRANSFORMATION COMBO!!
FWP
FWP
BOOF

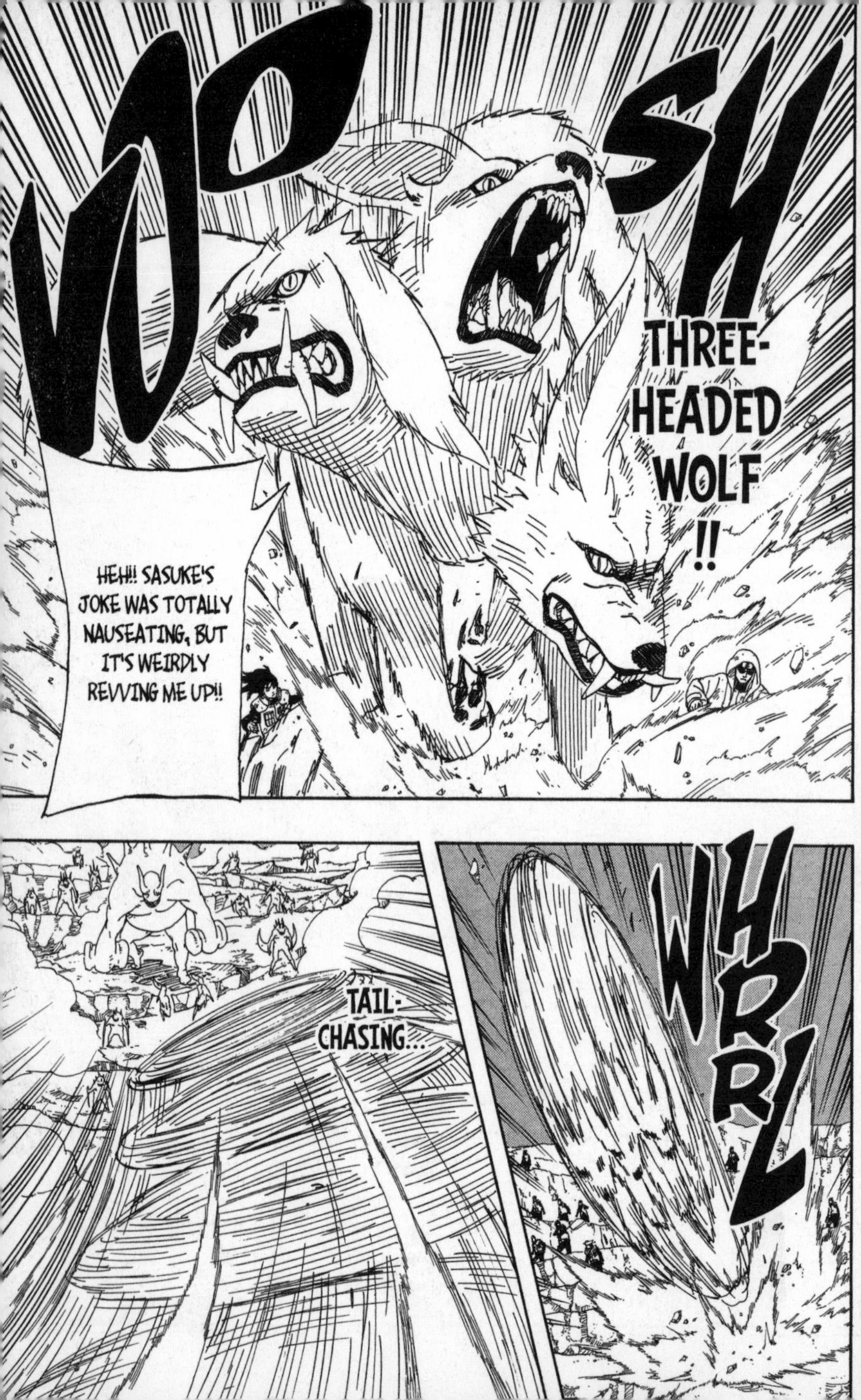
VOOSH
THREE-HEADED WOLF!!
HEH!! SASUKE'S JOKE WAS TOTALLY NAUSEATING, BUT IT'S WEIRDLY REVVING ME UP!!
WHRRL
TAIL-CHASING...

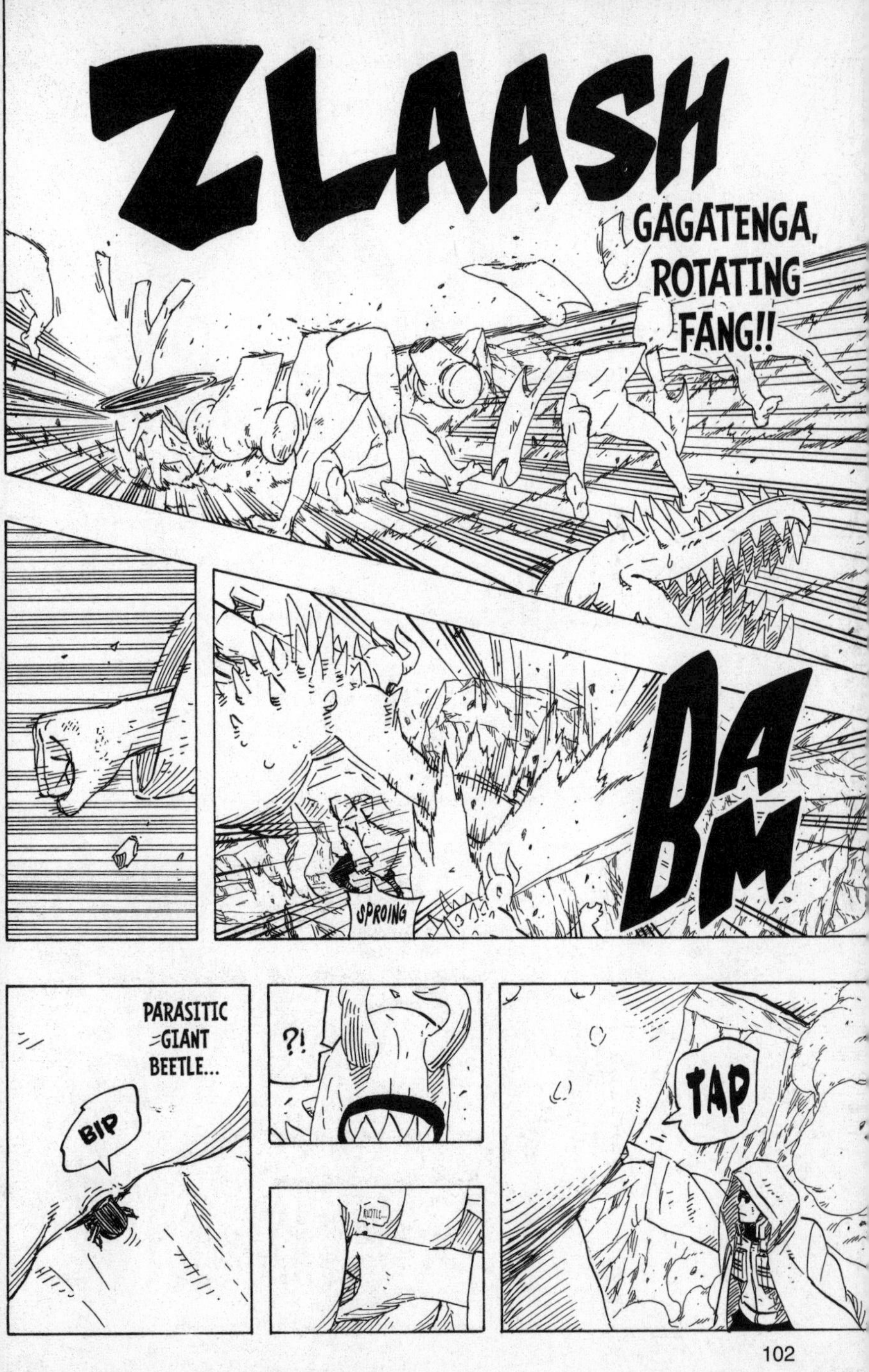
ZLAASH
GAGATENGA, ROTATING FANG!!
DABM
SPROING
TAP
?!
RUSTLE...
PARASITIC GIANT BEETLE...
BIP

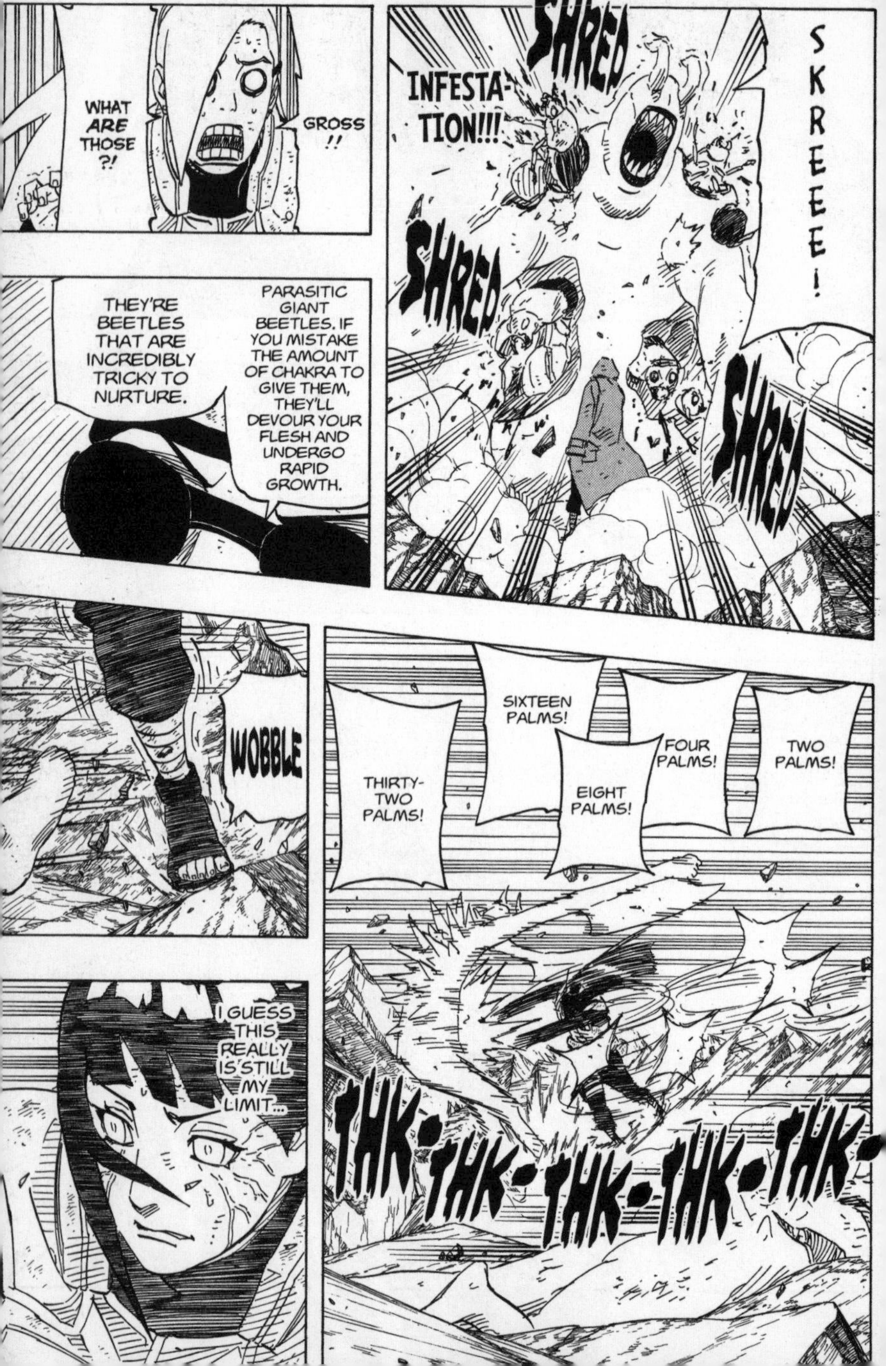
SHRED
SKREEE!
INFESTATION!!!
SHRED
SHRED
GROSS!!
WHAT ARE THOSE?!
PARASITIC GIANT BEETLES. IF YOU MISTAKE THE AMOUNT OF CHAKRA TO GIVE THEM, THEY'LL DEVOUR YOUR FLESH AND UNDERGO RAPID GROWTH.
THEY'RE BEETLES THAT ARE INCREDIBLY TRICKY TO NURTURE.
TWO PALMS!
FOUR PALMS!
EIGHT PALMS!
SIXTEEN PALMS!
THIRTY-TWO PALMS!
THK-THK-THK-THK-THK-
WOBBLE
I GUESS THIS REALLY IS STILL MY LIMIT...

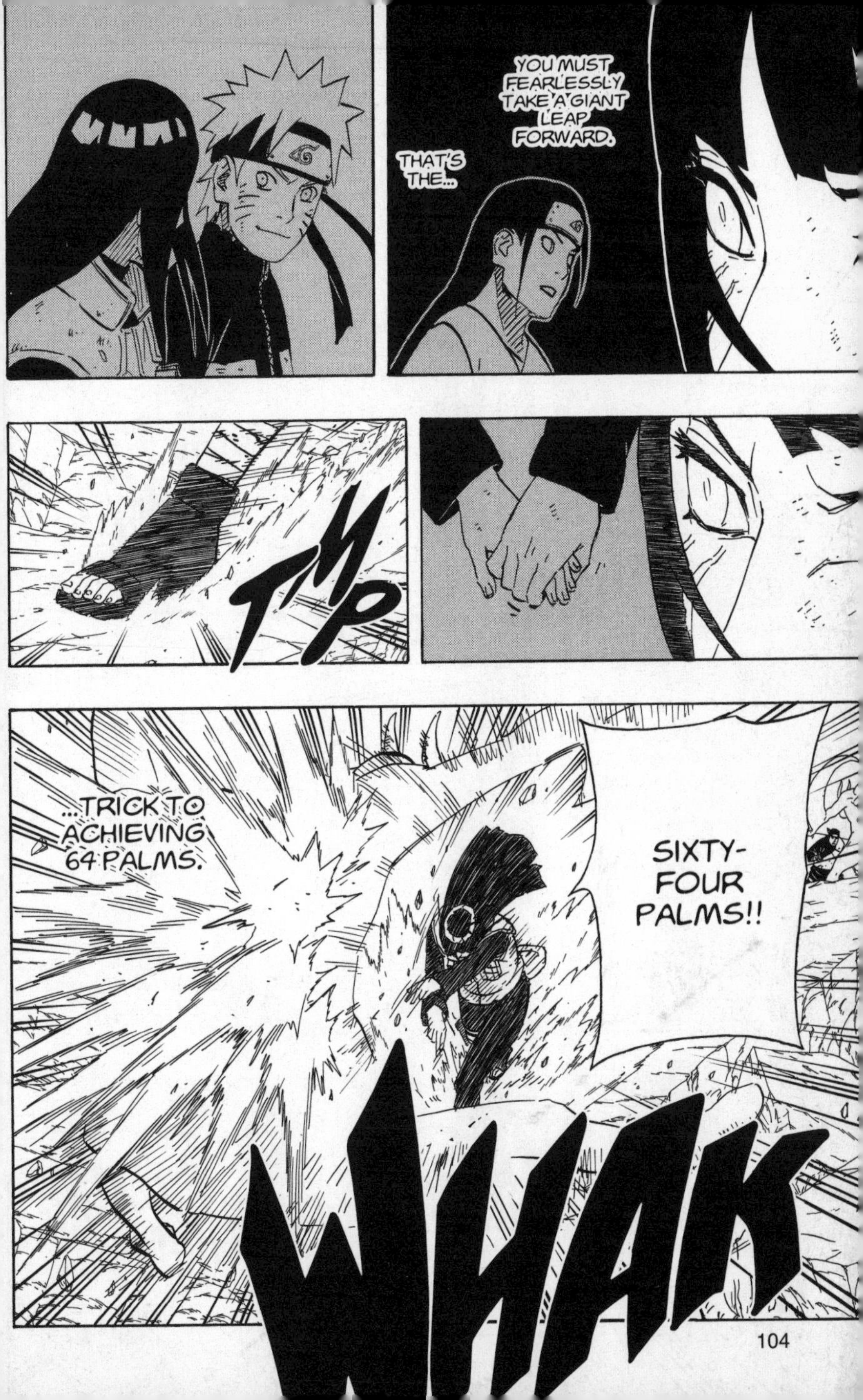
YOU MUST FEARLESSLY TAKE A GIANT LEAP FORWARD.
THAT'S THE...
TMP
SIXTY-FOUR PALMS!!
...TRICK TO ACHIEVING 64 PALMS.
WHAK

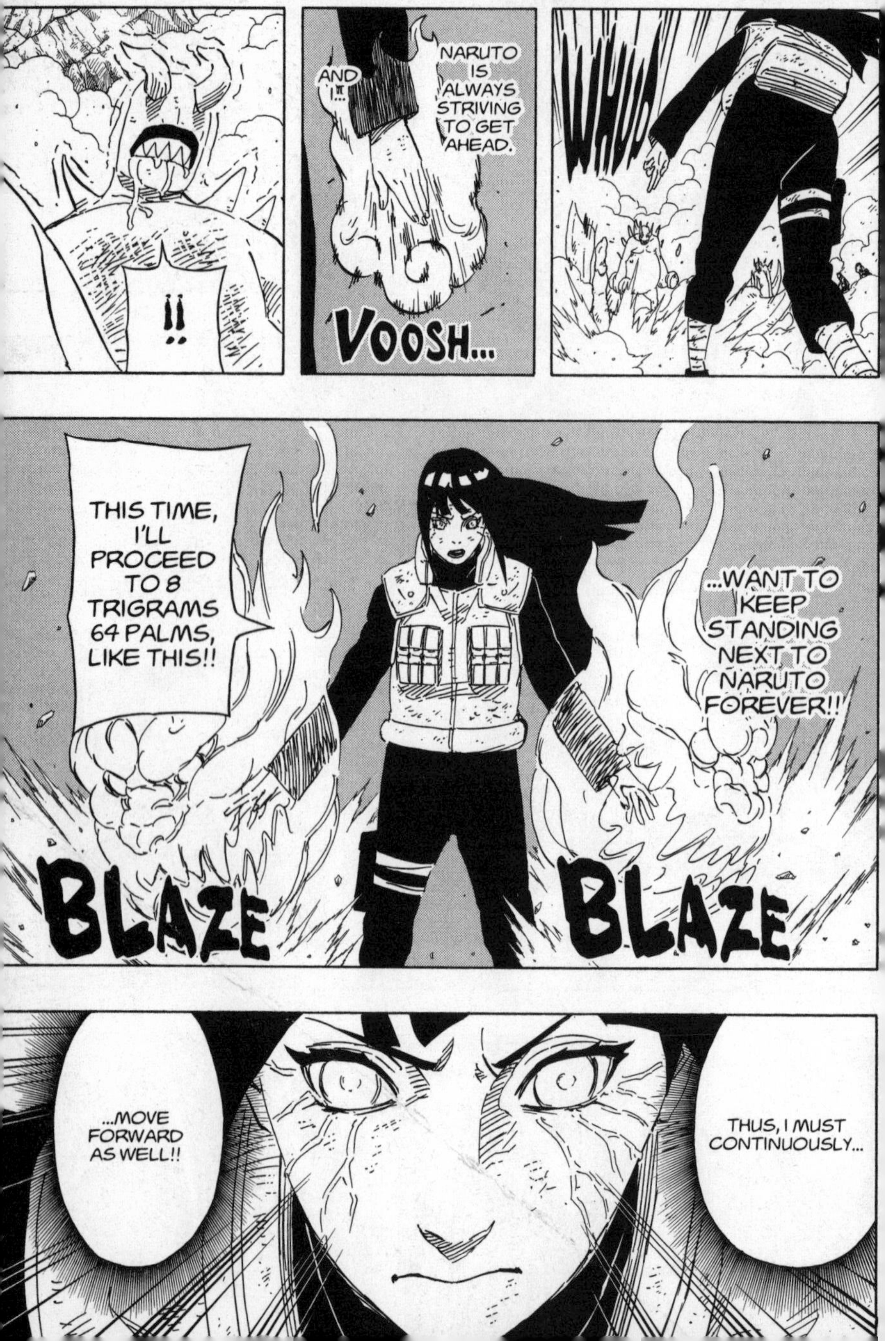
NARUTO IS ALWAYS STRIVING TO GET AHEAD.
AND I...
VOOSH...
!!
...WANT TO KEEP STANDING NEXT TO NARUTO FOREVER!!
THIS TIME, I'LL PROCEED TO 8 TRIGRAMS 64 PALMS, LIKE THIS!!
BLAZE
BLAZE
THUS, I MUST CONTINUOUSLY...
...MOVE FORWARD AS WELL!!

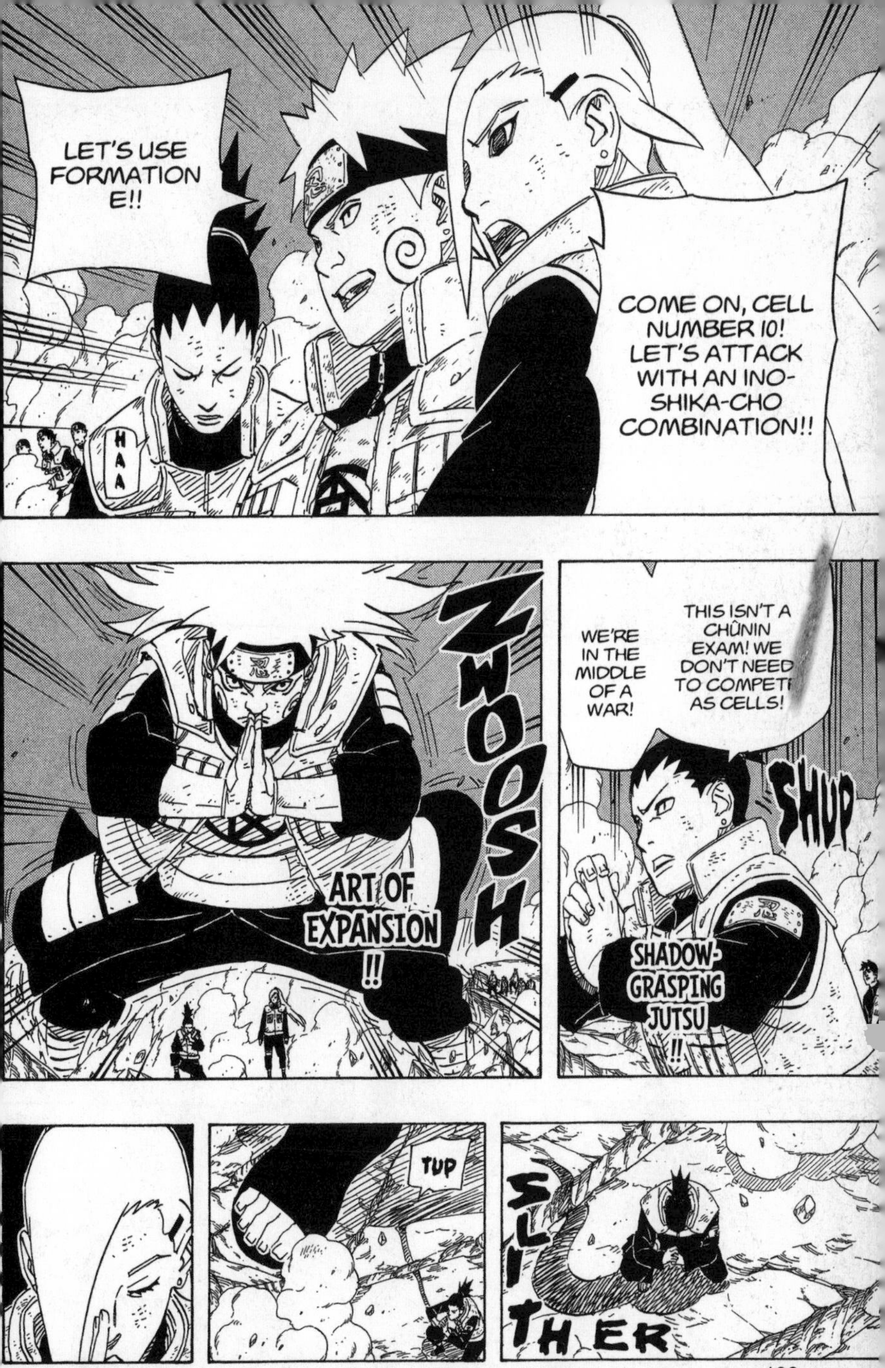
COME ON, CELL NUMBER 10! LET'S ATTACK WITH AN INO-SHIKA-CHO COMBINATION!!
LET'S USE FORMATION E!!
HAA
THIS ISN'T A CHÛNIN EXAM! WE DON'T NEED TO COMPET AS CELLS!
WE'RE IN THE MIDDLE OF A WAR!
SHUP
SHADOW-GRASPING JUTSU!!
WHOOSH
ART OF EXPANSION!!
SLITHER
TUP

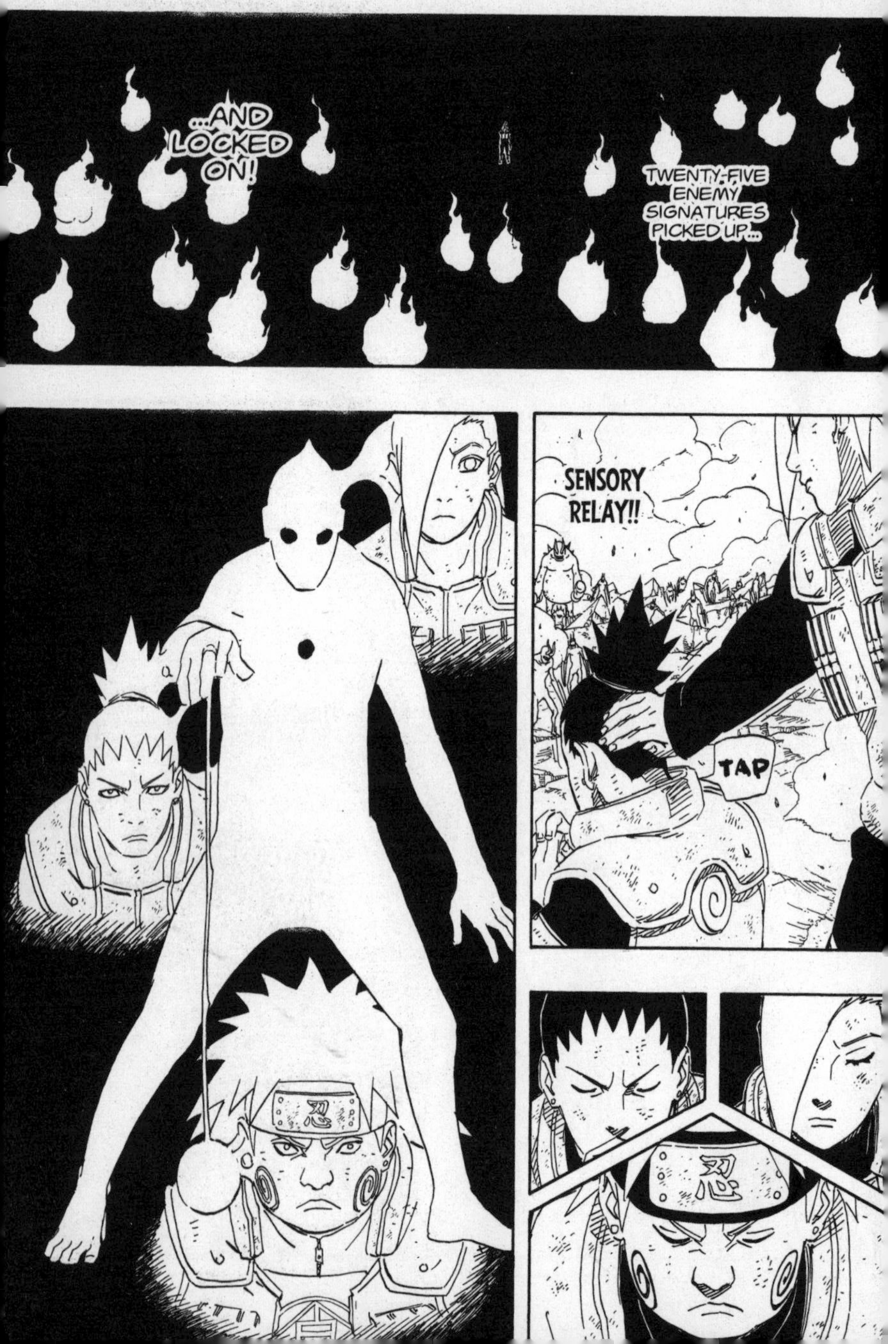
TWENTY-FIVE ENEMY SIGNATURES PICKED UP...
...AND LOCKED ON!
SENSORY RELAY!!
TAP

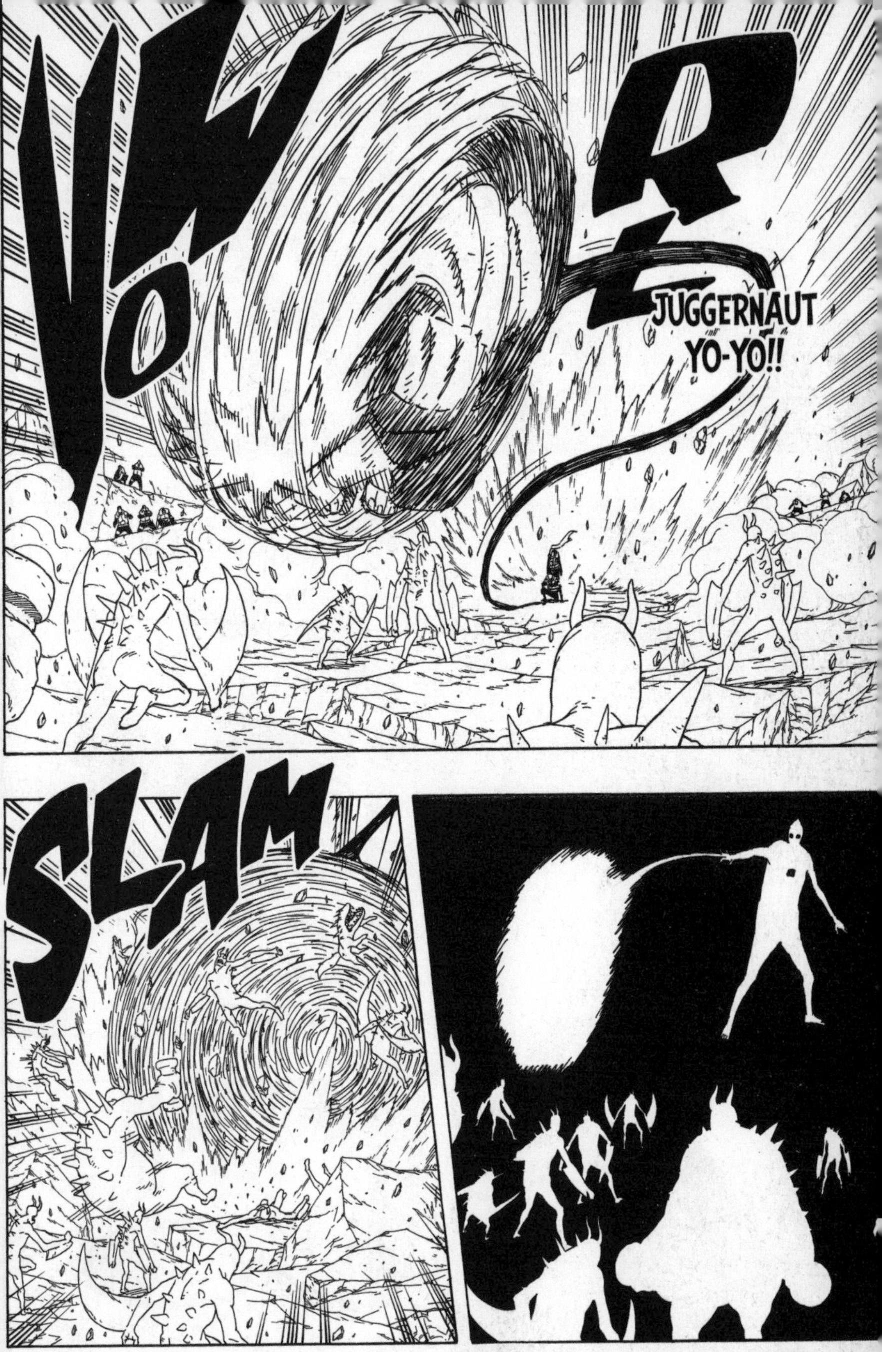
JUGGERNAUT YO-YO!!
SLAM

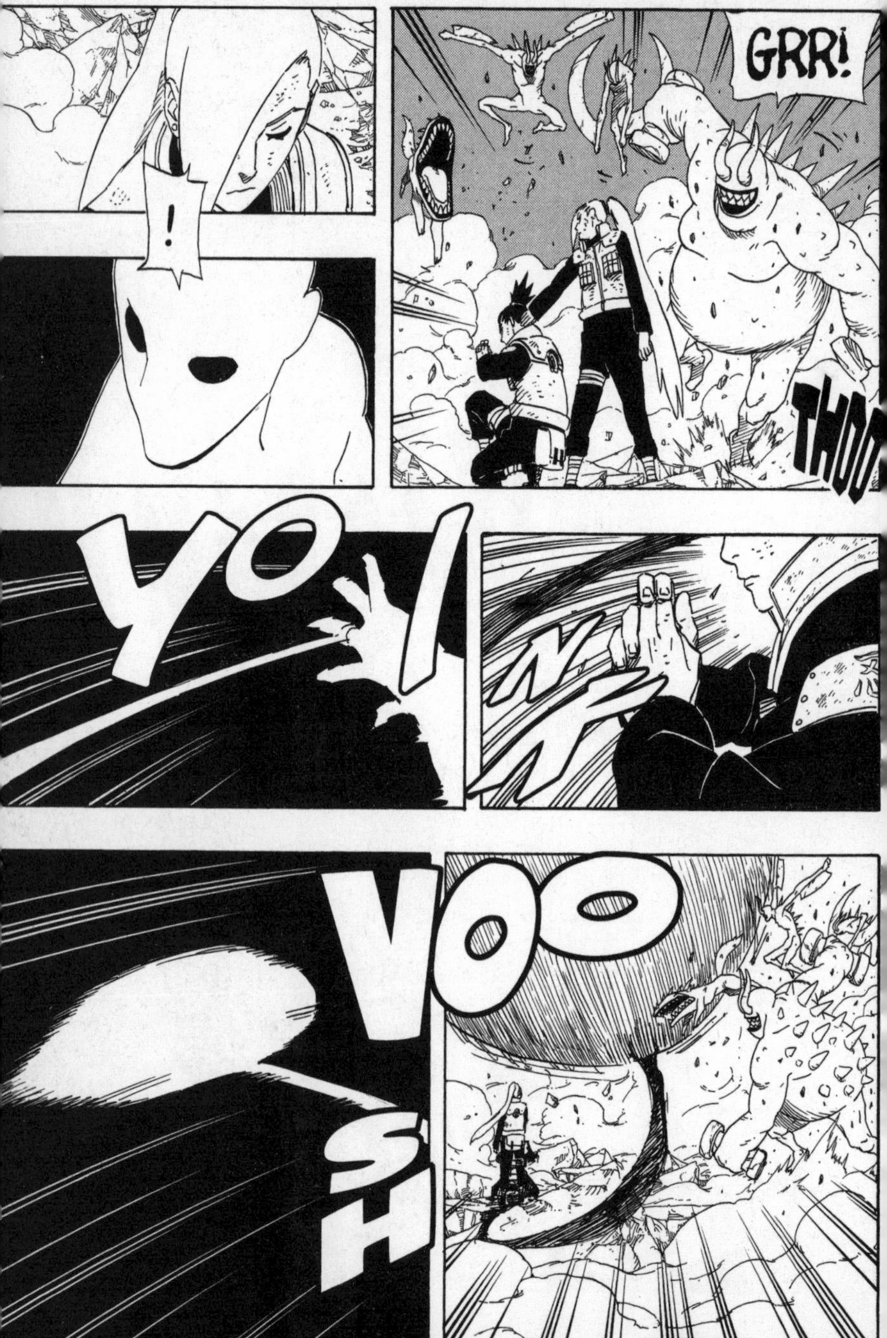
GRR!
THUD
!
YOIN
VOOSH

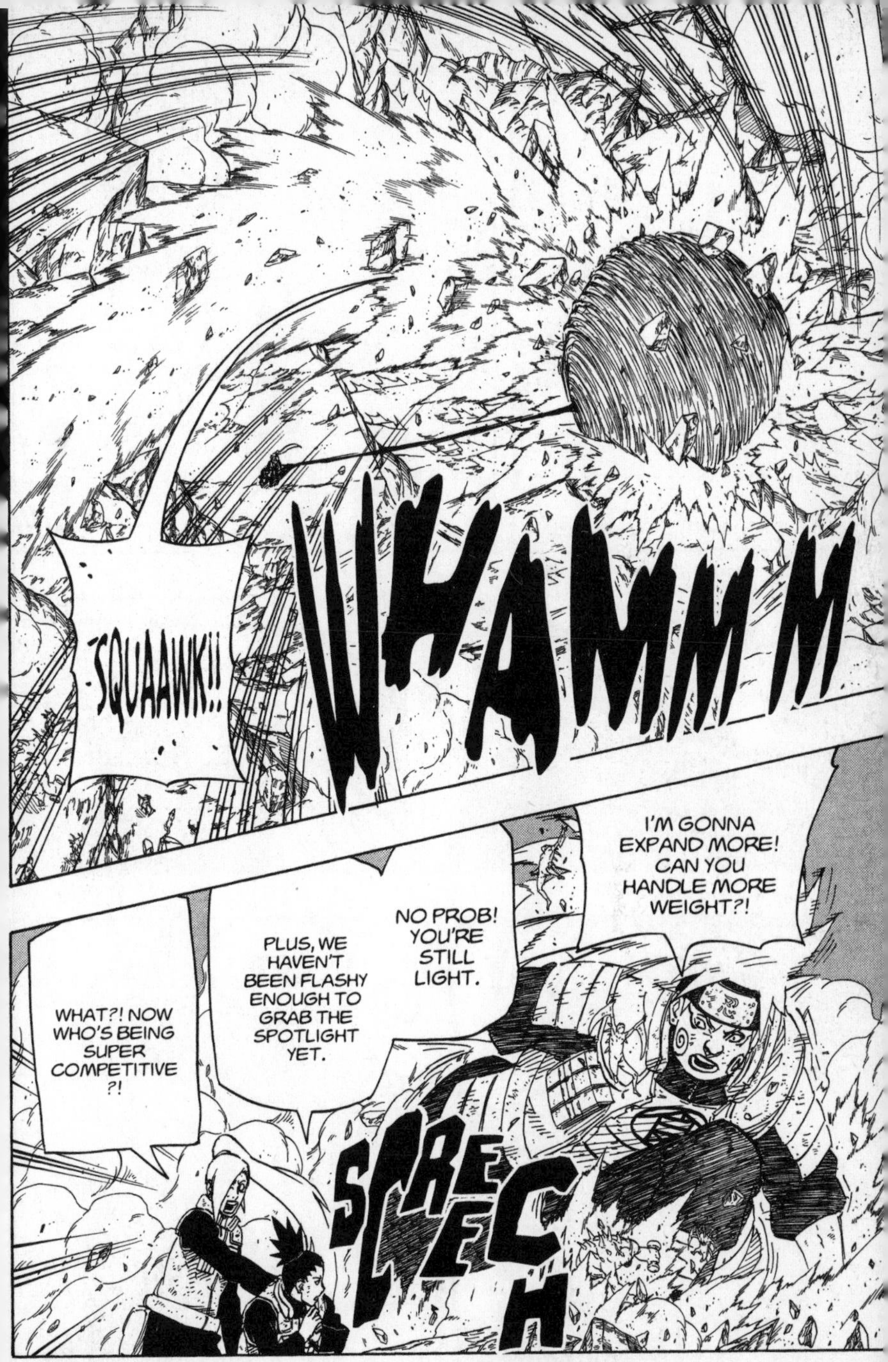
WHAMMMM
SQUAAWK!!
I'M GONNA EXPAND MORE! CAN YOU HANDLE MORE WEIGHT?!
NO PROB! YOU'RE STILL LIGHT.
PLUS, WE HAVEN'T BEEN FLASHY ENOUGH TO GRAB THE SPOTLIGHT YET.
WHAT?! NOW WHO'S BEING SUPER COMPETITIVE ?!
SCREECH

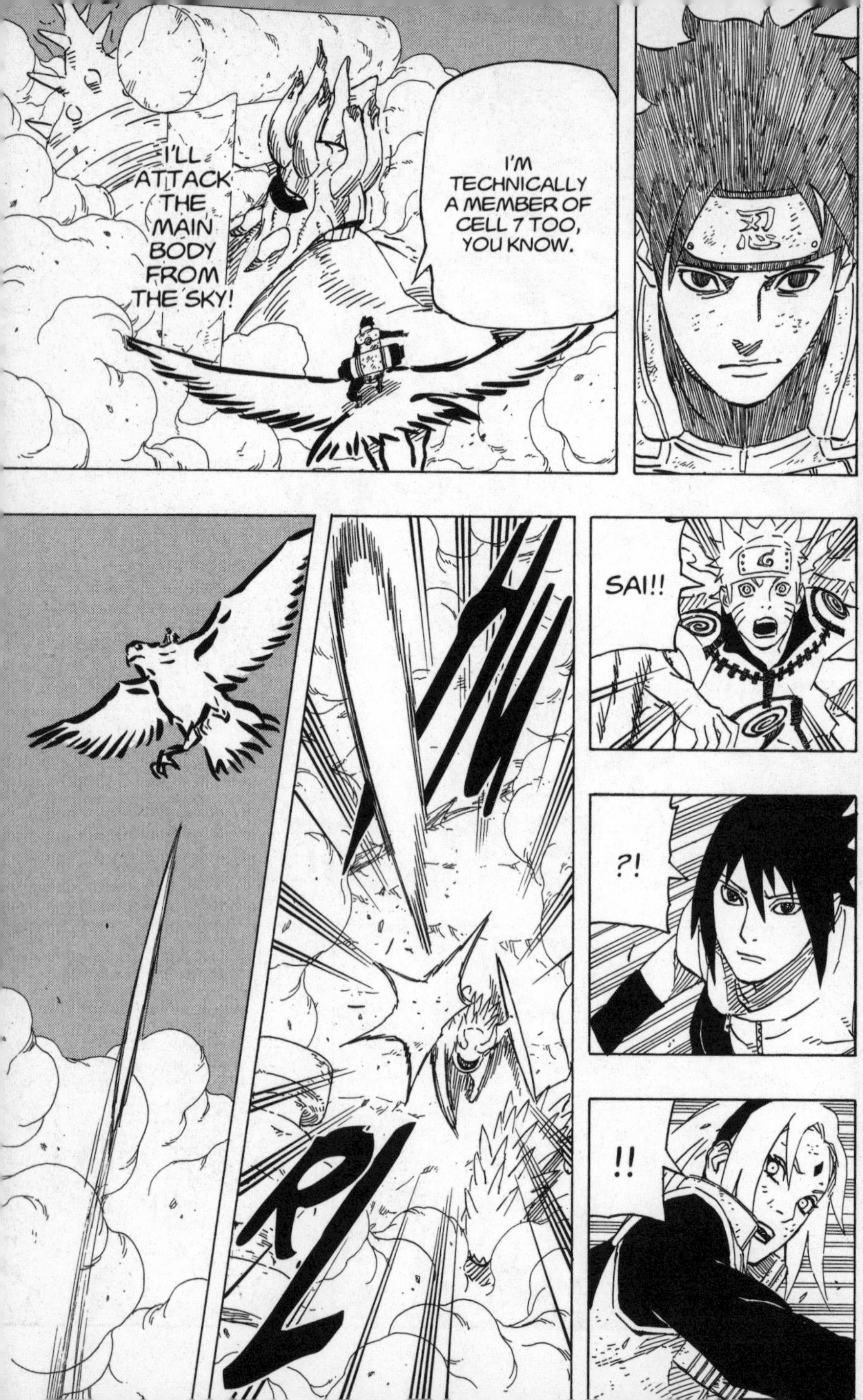
I'M TECHNICALLY A MEMBER OF CELL 7 TOO, YOU KNOW.
I'LL ATTACK THE MAIN BODY FROM THE SKY!
SAI!!
?!
!!

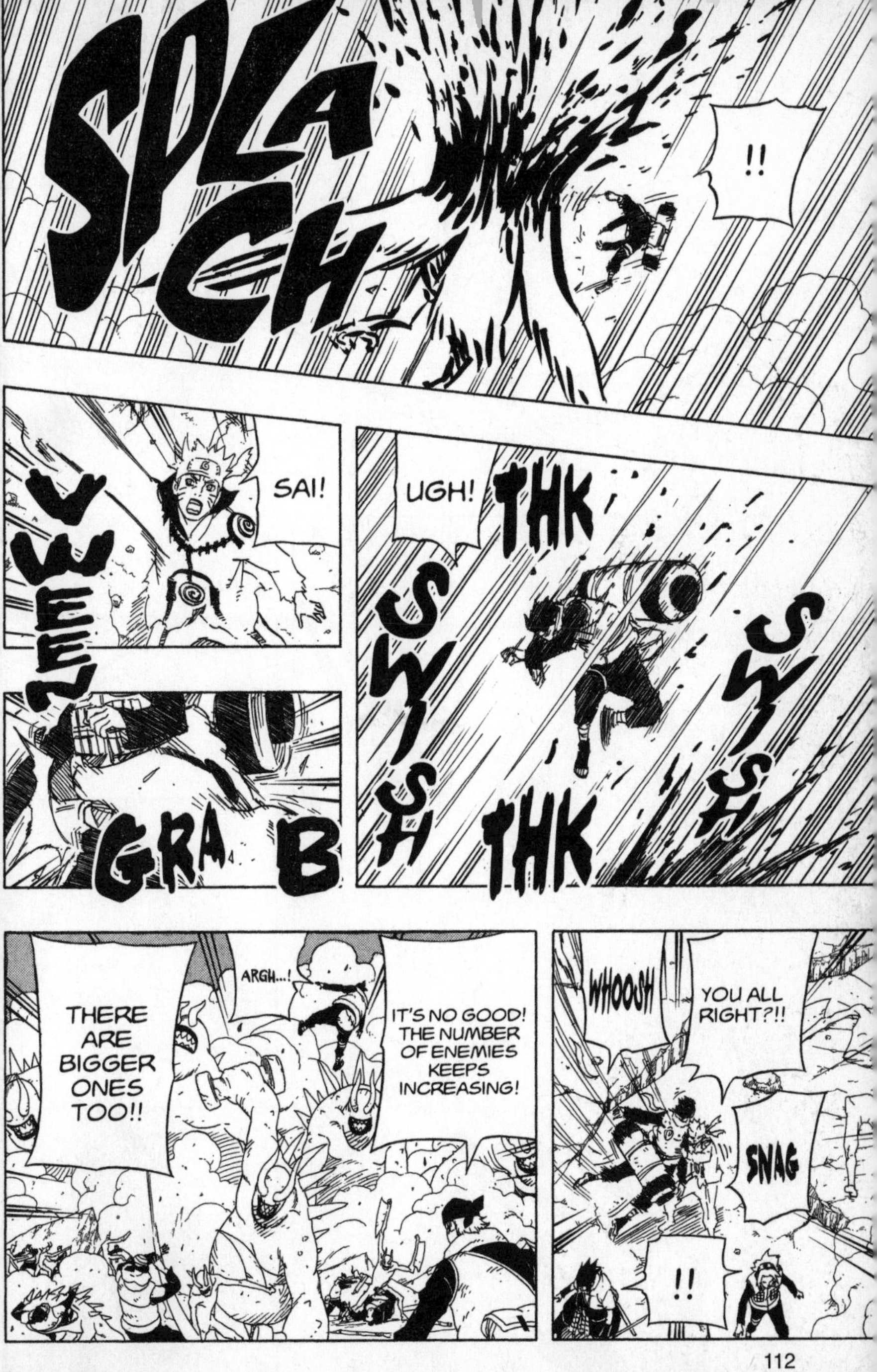
!!
SPLA SCH
UGH!
THK
SWSH
SWSH
THK
SAI!
GRAB
YOU ALL RIGHT?!!
WHOOSH
SNAG
!!
IT'S NO GOOD! THE NUMBER OF ENEMIES KEEPS INCREASING!
ARGH...!
THERE ARE BIGGER ONES TOO!!

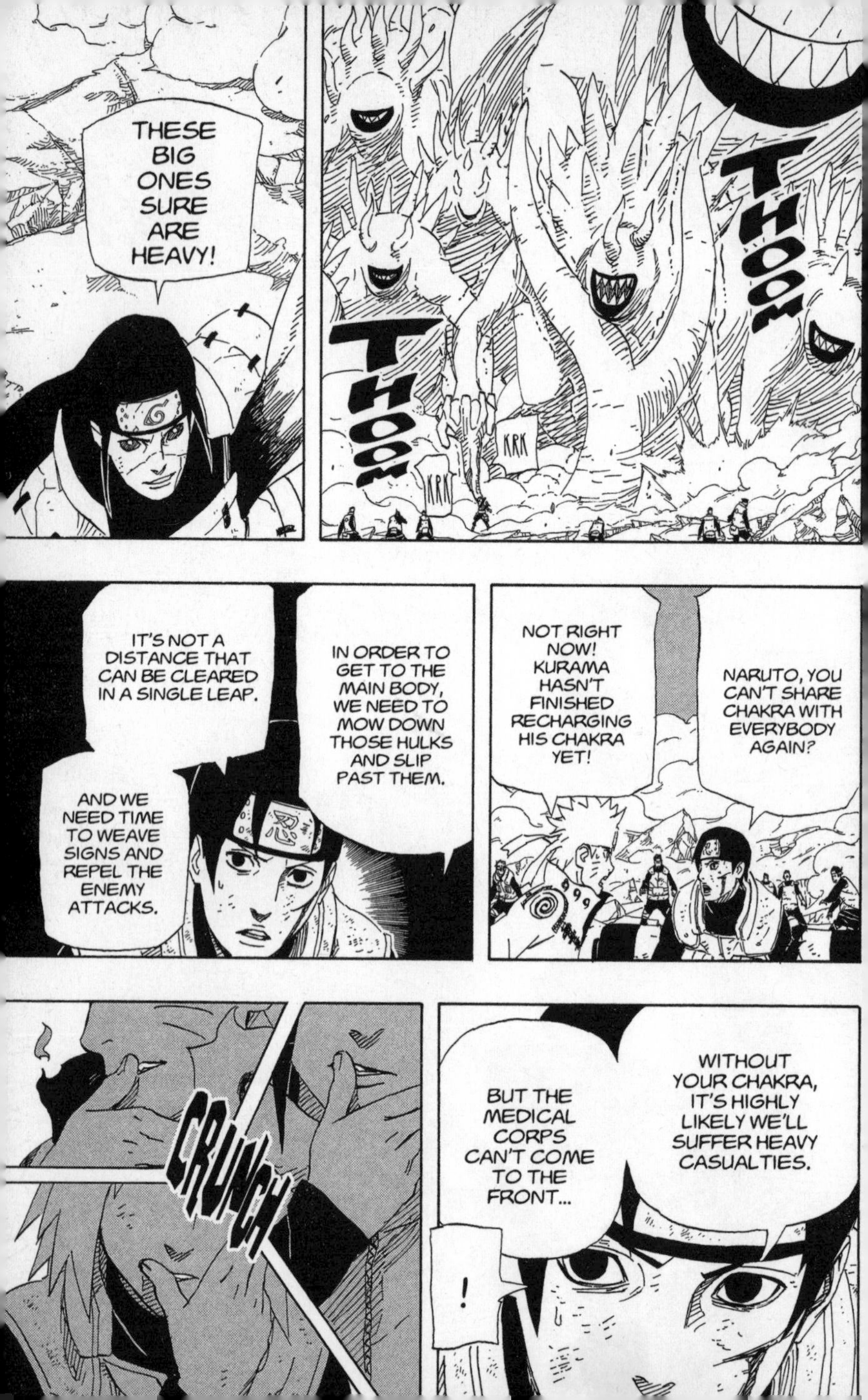
THOOM
THOOM
KRK
KRK
THESE BIG ONES SURE ARE HEAVY!
NARUTO, YOU CAN'T SHARE CHAKRA WITH EVERYBODY AGAIN?
NOT RIGHT NOW! KURAMA HASN'T FINISHED RECHARGING HIS CHAKRA YET!
IN ORDER TO GET TO THE MAIN BODY, WE NEED TO MOW DOWN THOSE HULKS AND SLIP PAST THEM.
IT'S NOT A DISTANCE THAT CAN BE CLEARED IN A SINGLE LEAP.
AND WE NEED TIME TO WEAVE SIGNS AND REPEL THE ENEMY ATTACKS.
WITHOUT YOUR CHAKRA, IT'S HIGHLY LIKELY WE'LL SUFFER HEAVY CASUALTIES.
BUT THE MEDICAL CORPS CAN'T COME TO THE FRONT...
!
CRUNCH

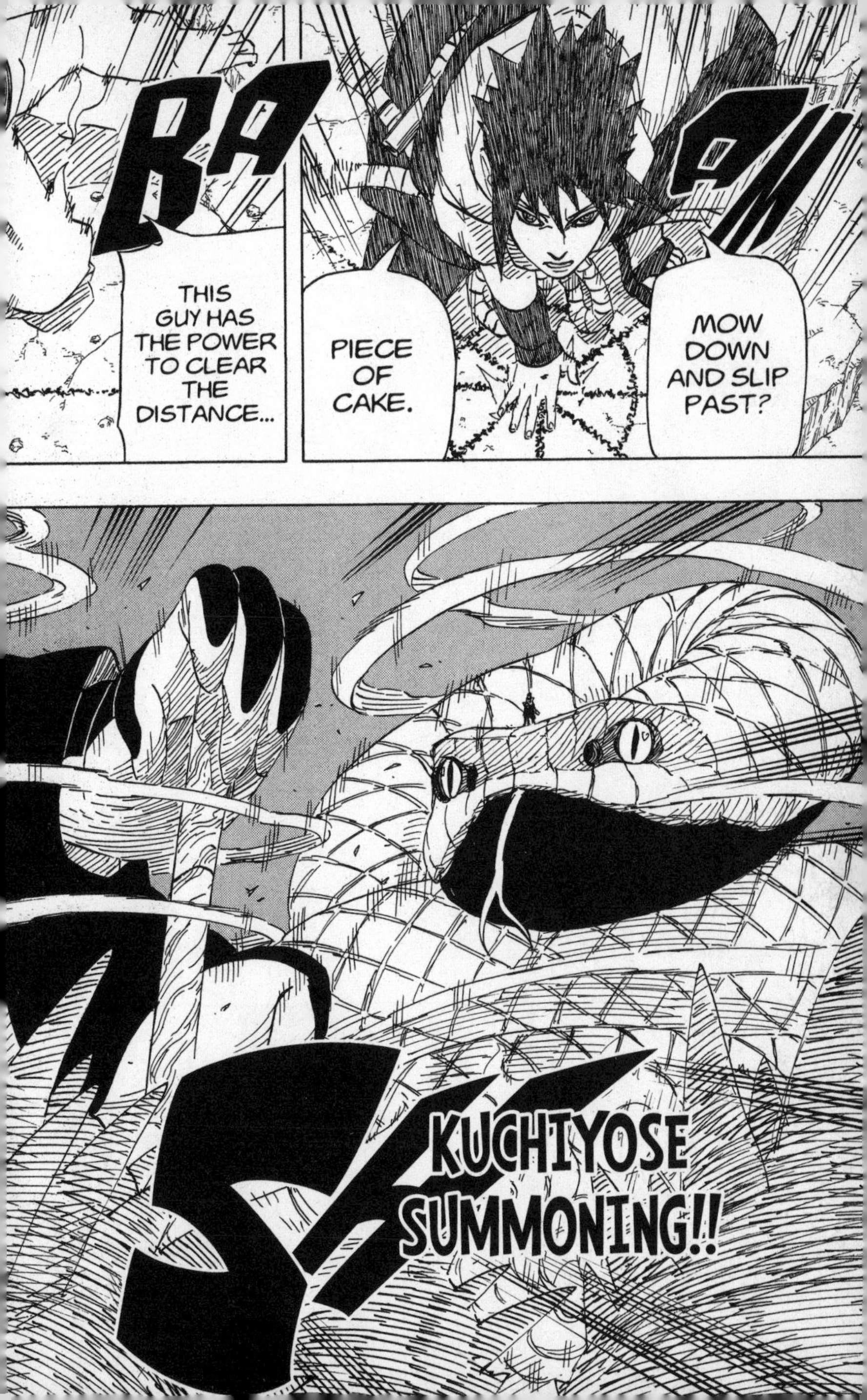
MOW DOWN AND SLIP PAST?
PIECE OF CAKE.
BA
AM
THIS GUY HAS THE POWER TO CLEAR THE DISTANCE...
KUCHIYOSE SUMMONING!!

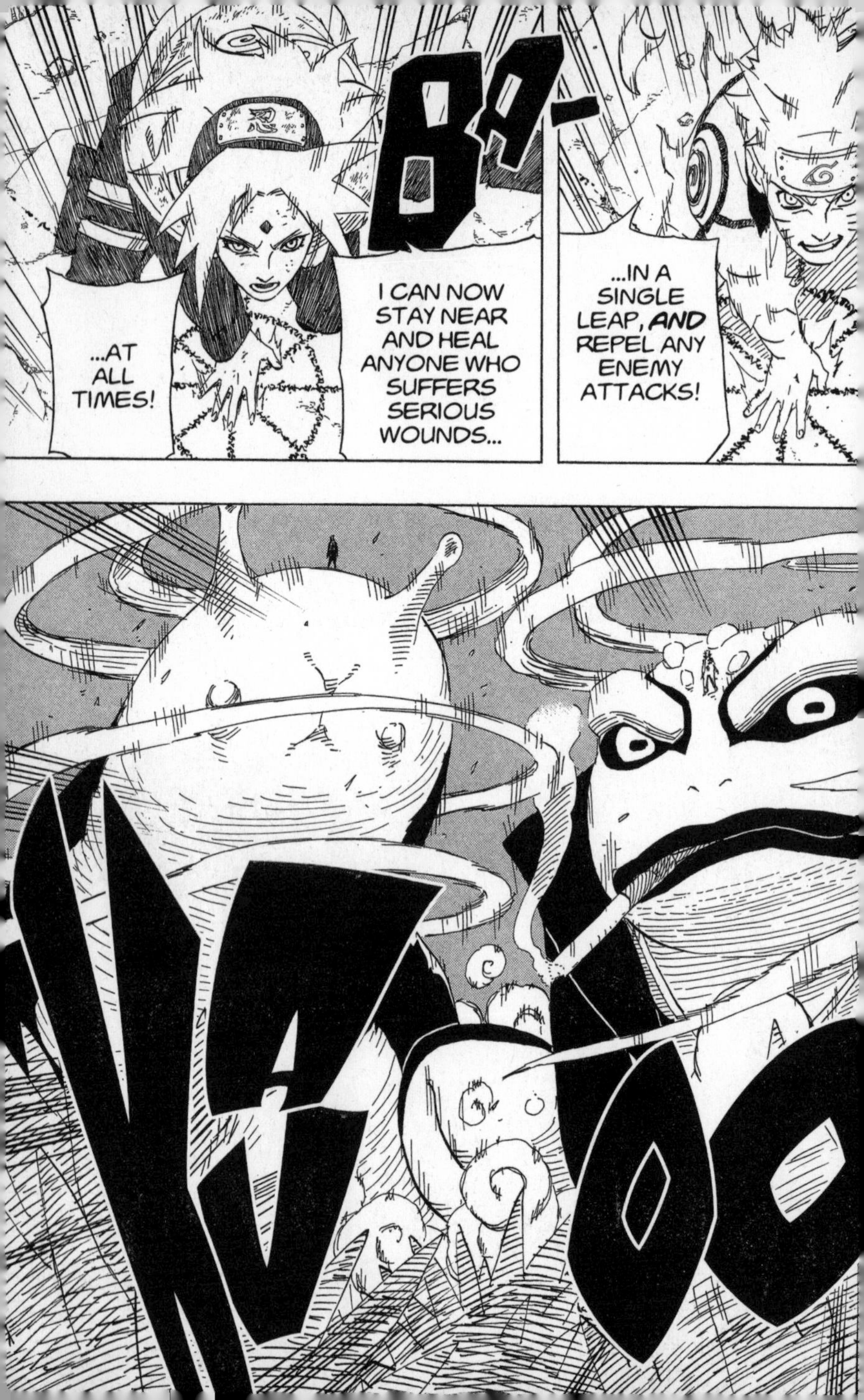
...IN A SINGLE LEAP, AND REPEL ANY ENEMY ATTACKS!
BA-
I CAN NOW STAY NEAR AND HEAL ANYONE WHO SUFFERS SERIOUS WOUNDS...
...AT ALL TIMES!

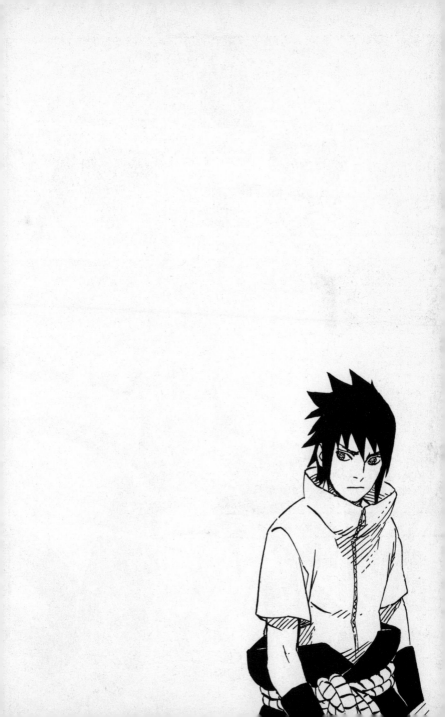

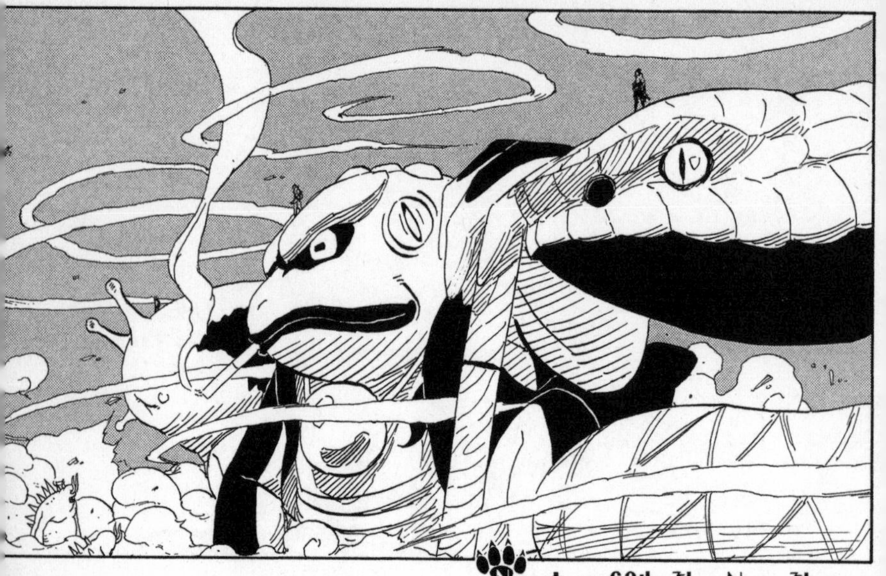

Number 634: The New Three

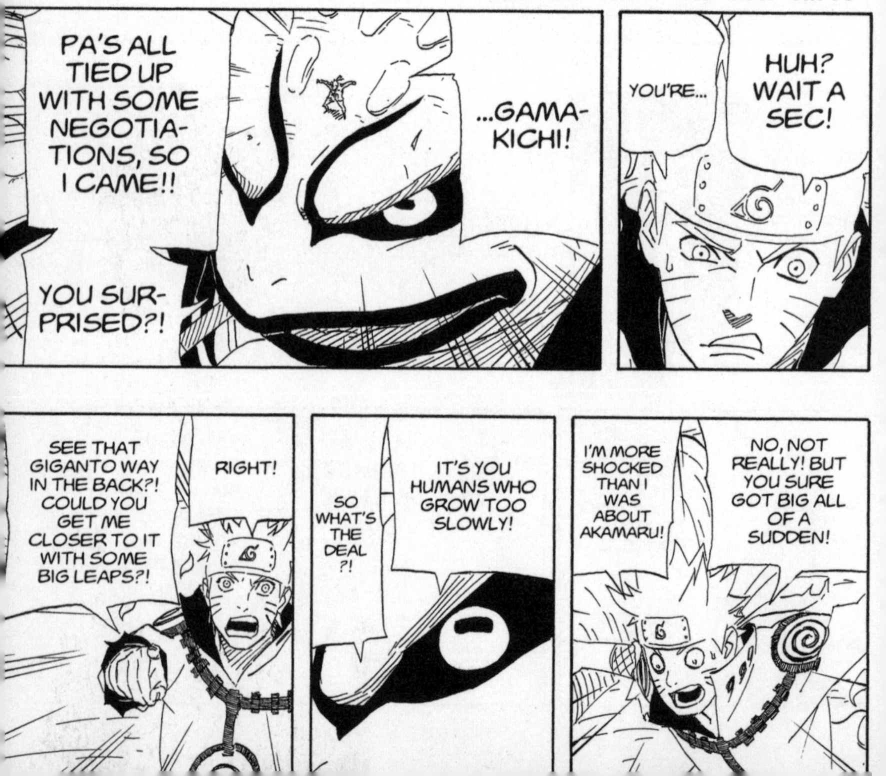
HUH? WAIT A SEC!
YOU'RE...
...GAMA-KICHI!
PA'S ALL TIED UP WITH SOME NEGOTIA-TIONS, SO I CAME!!
YOU SUR-PRISED?!
NO, NOT REALLY! BUT YOU SURE GOT BIG ALL OF A SUDDEN!
I'M MORE SHOCKED THAN I WAS ABOUT AKAMARU!
IT'S YOU HUMANS WHO GROW TOO SLOWLY!
SO WHAT'S THE DEAL ?!
RIGHT!
SEE THAT GIGANTO WAY IN THE BACK?! COULD YOU GET ME CLOSER TO IT WITH SOME BIG LEAPS?!

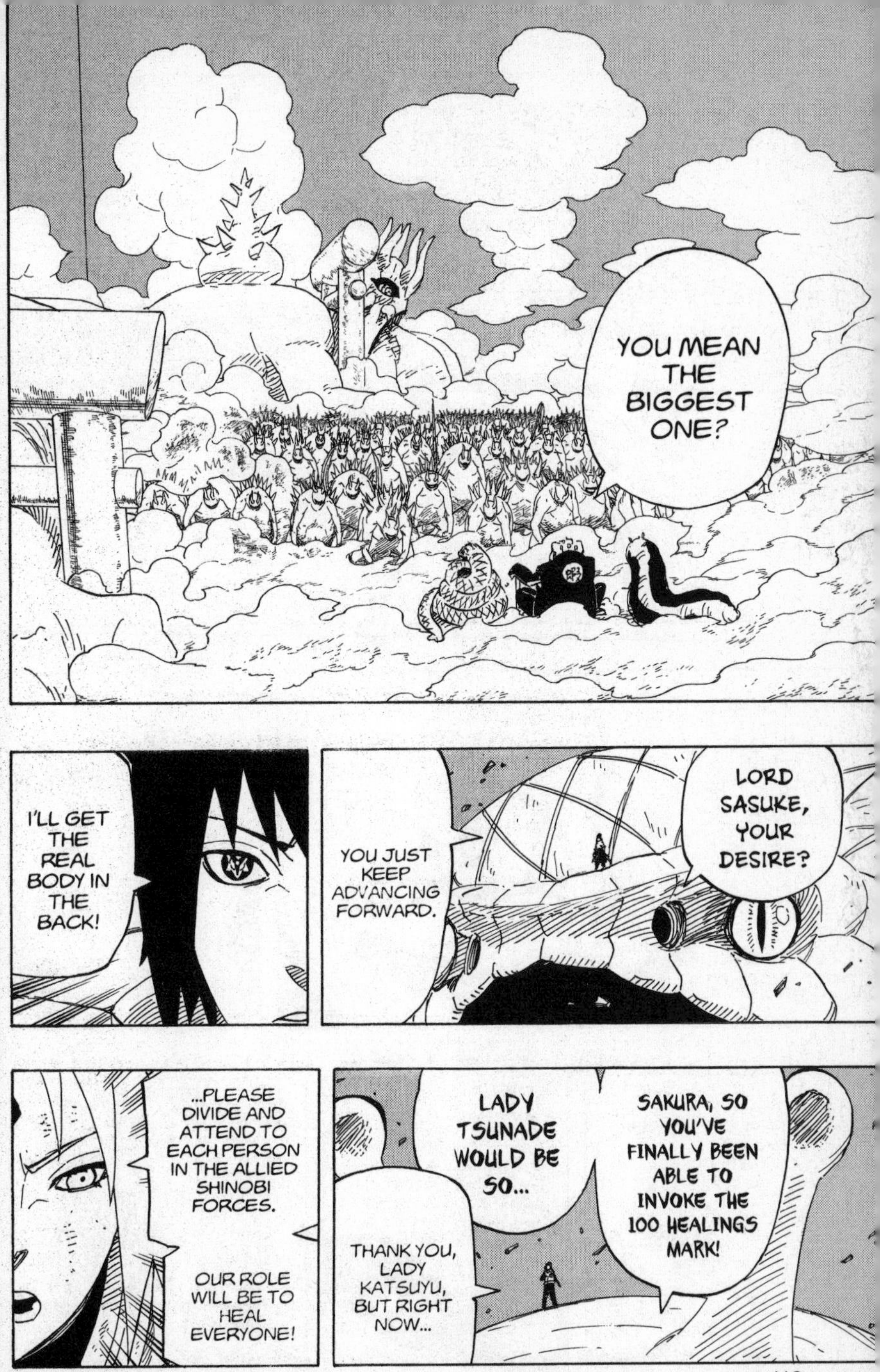
YOU MEAN THE BIGGEST ONE?
LORD SASUKE, YOUR DESIRE?
YOU JUST KEEP ADVANCING FORWARD.
I'LL GET THE REAL BODY IN THE BACK!
SAKURA, SO YOU'VE FINALLY BEEN ABLE TO INVOKE THE 100 HEALINGS MARK!
LADY TSUNADE WOULD BE SO...
THANK YOU, LADY KATSUYU, BUT RIGHT NOW...
...PLEASE DIVIDE AND ATTEND TO EACH PERSON IN THE ALLIED SHINOBI FORCES.
OUR ROLE WILL BE TO HEAL EVERYONE!

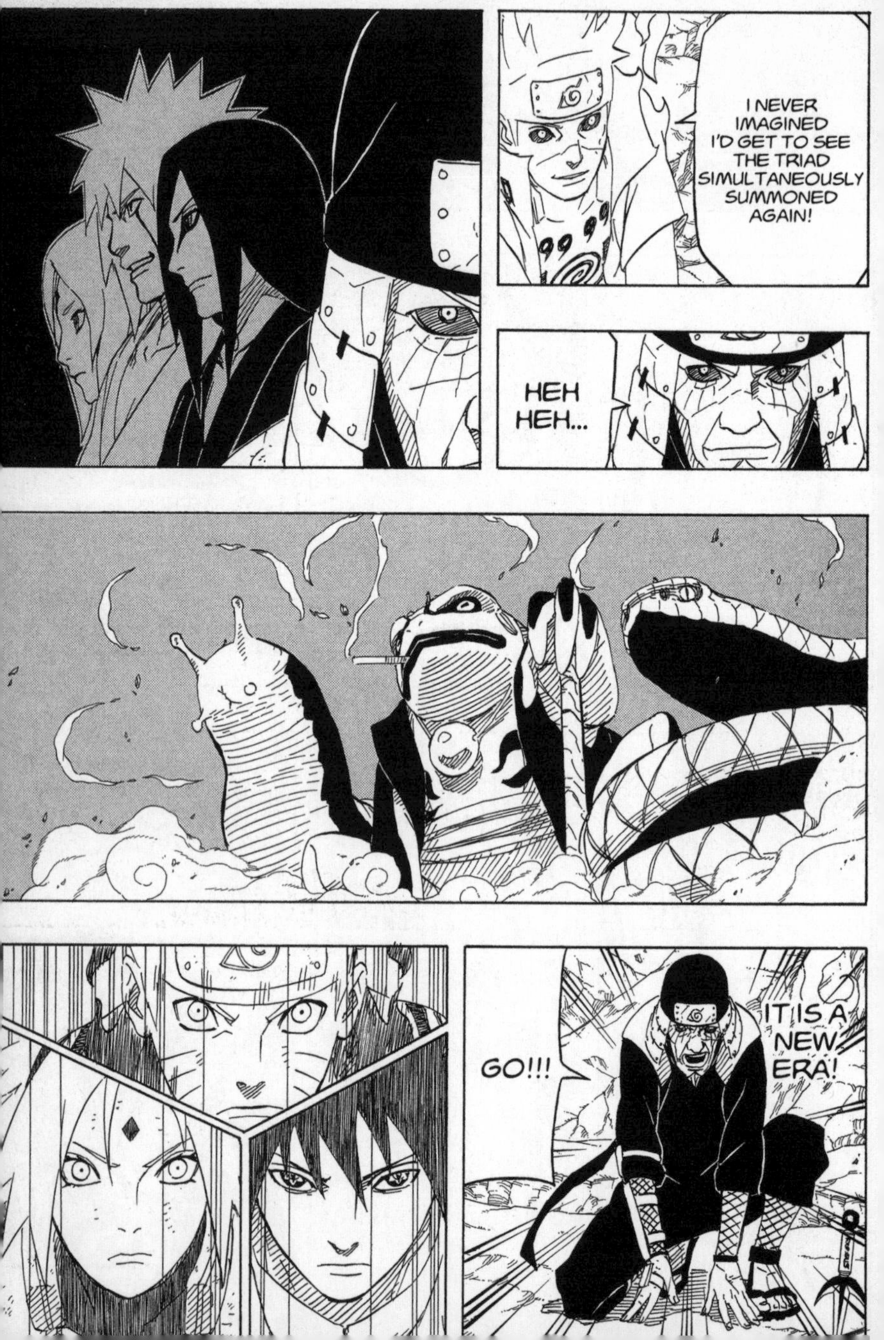
I NEVER IMAGINED I'D GET TO SEE THE TRIAD SIMULTANEOUSLY SUMMONED AGAIN!
HEH HEH...
IT IS A NEW ERA!
GO!!!

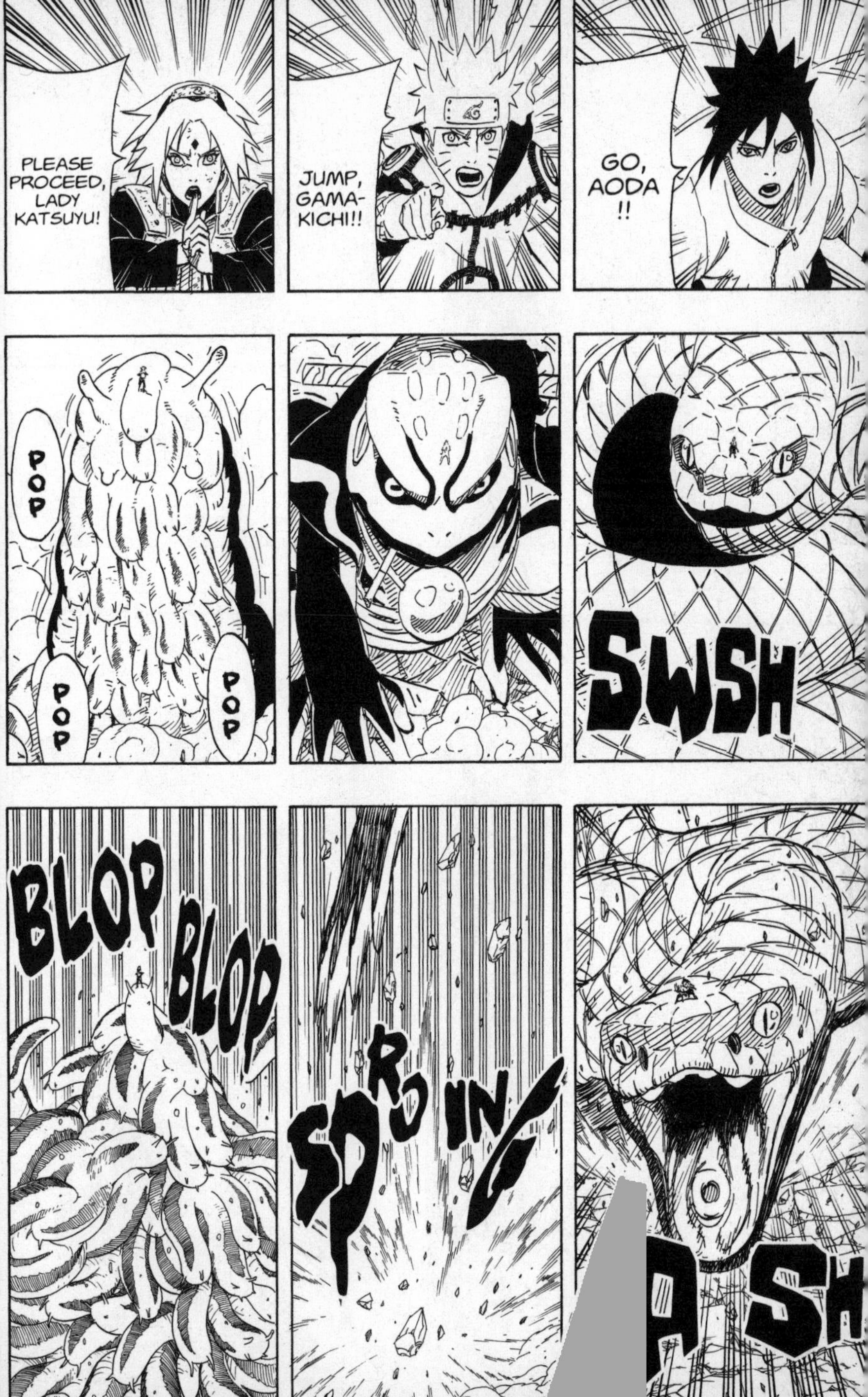
GO, AODA !!
JUMP, GAMA-KICHI!!
PLEASE PROCEED, LADY KATSUYU!
SWSH
POP
POP
POP
SPROING
BLOP BLOP

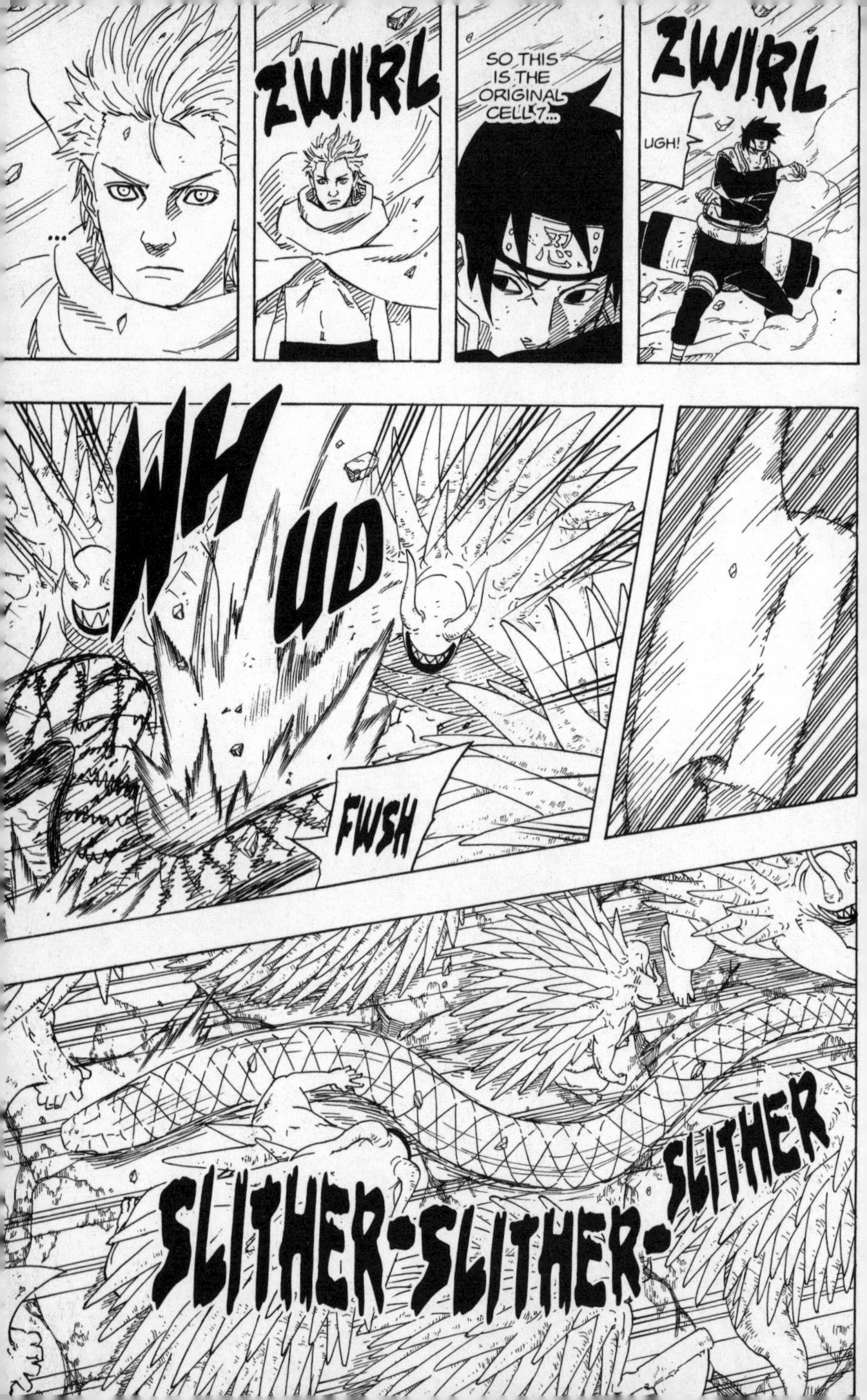

ZWIRL
UGH!
SO THIS IS THE ORIGINAL CELL 7...
ZWIRL
...
WHUD
FWSH
SLITHER-SLITHER-SLITHER

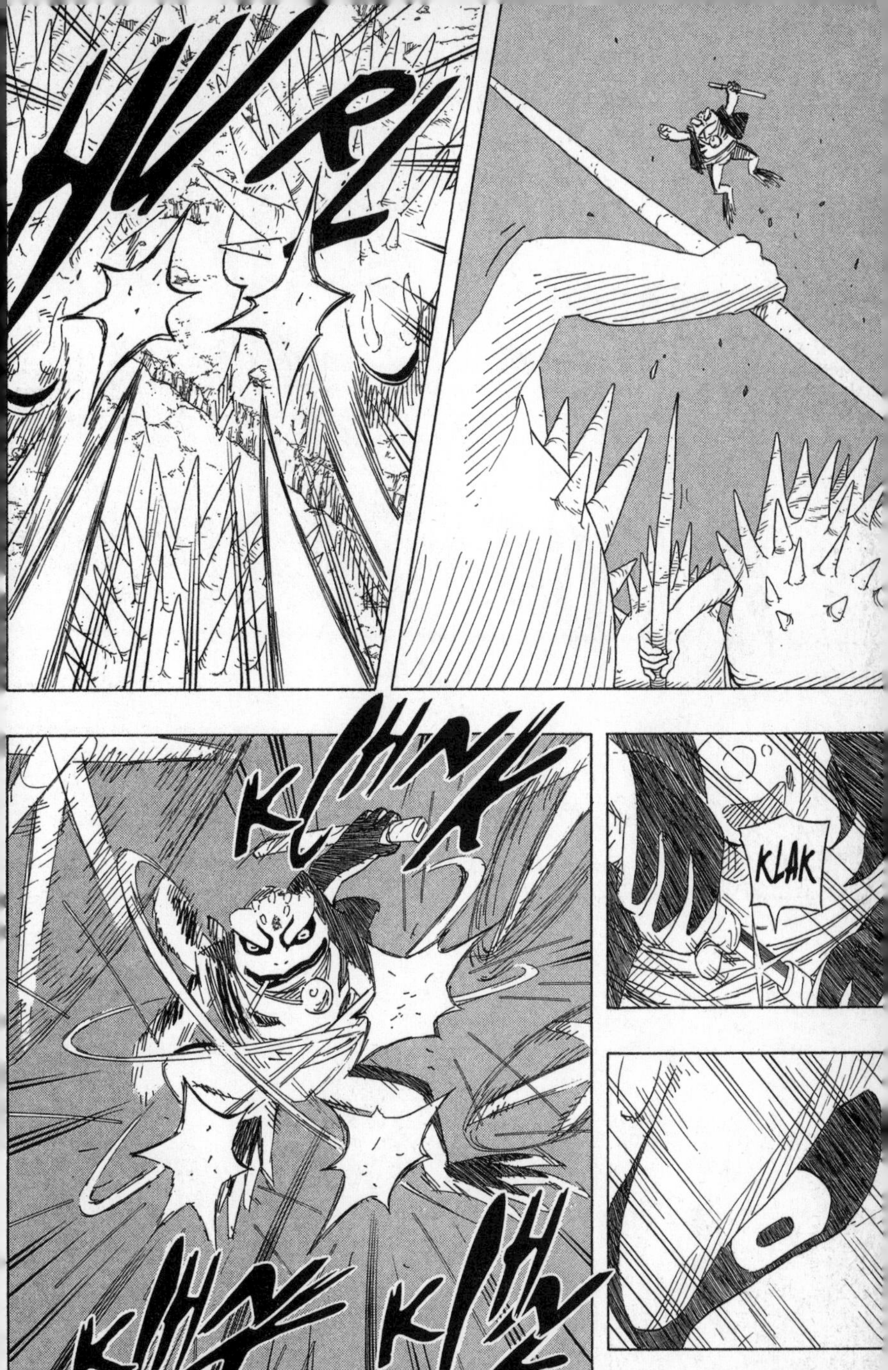
KLAK

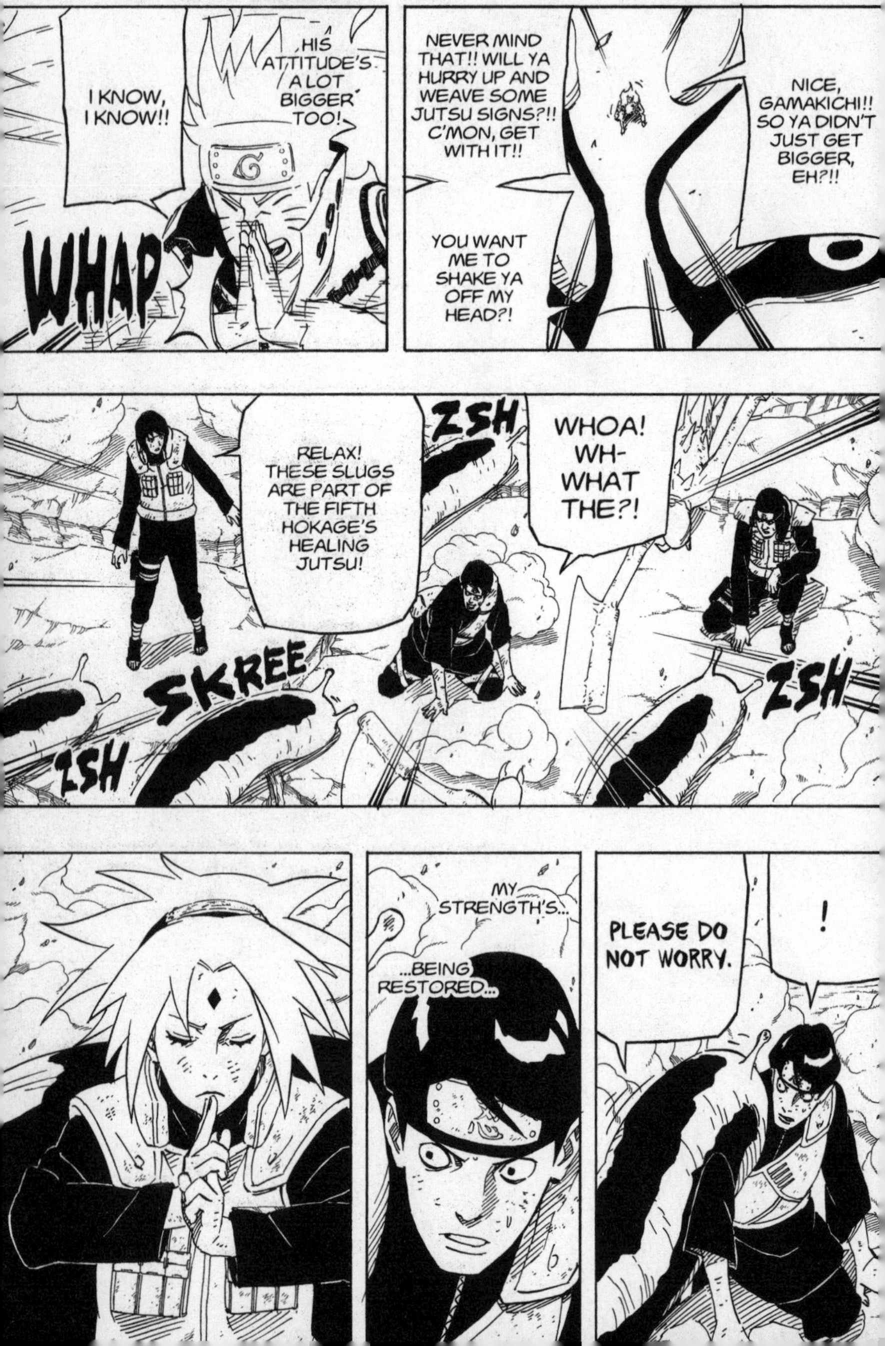
NICE, GAMAKICHI!! SO YA DIDN'T JUST GET BIGGER, EH?!!
NEVER MIND THAT!! WILL YA HURRY UP AND WEAVE SOME JUTSU SIGNS?!! C'MON, GET WITH IT!!
YOU WANT ME TO SHAKE YA OFF MY HEAD?!
HIS ATTITUDE'S A LOT BIGGER TOO!
I KNOW, I KNOW!!
WHAP
ZSH
WHOA! WH- WHAT THE?!
ZSH
RELAX! THESE SLUGS ARE PART OF THE FIFTH HOKAGE'S HEALING JUTSU!
SKREE
ZSH
!
PLEASE DO NOT WORRY.
MY STRENGTH'S...
...BEING RESTORED...

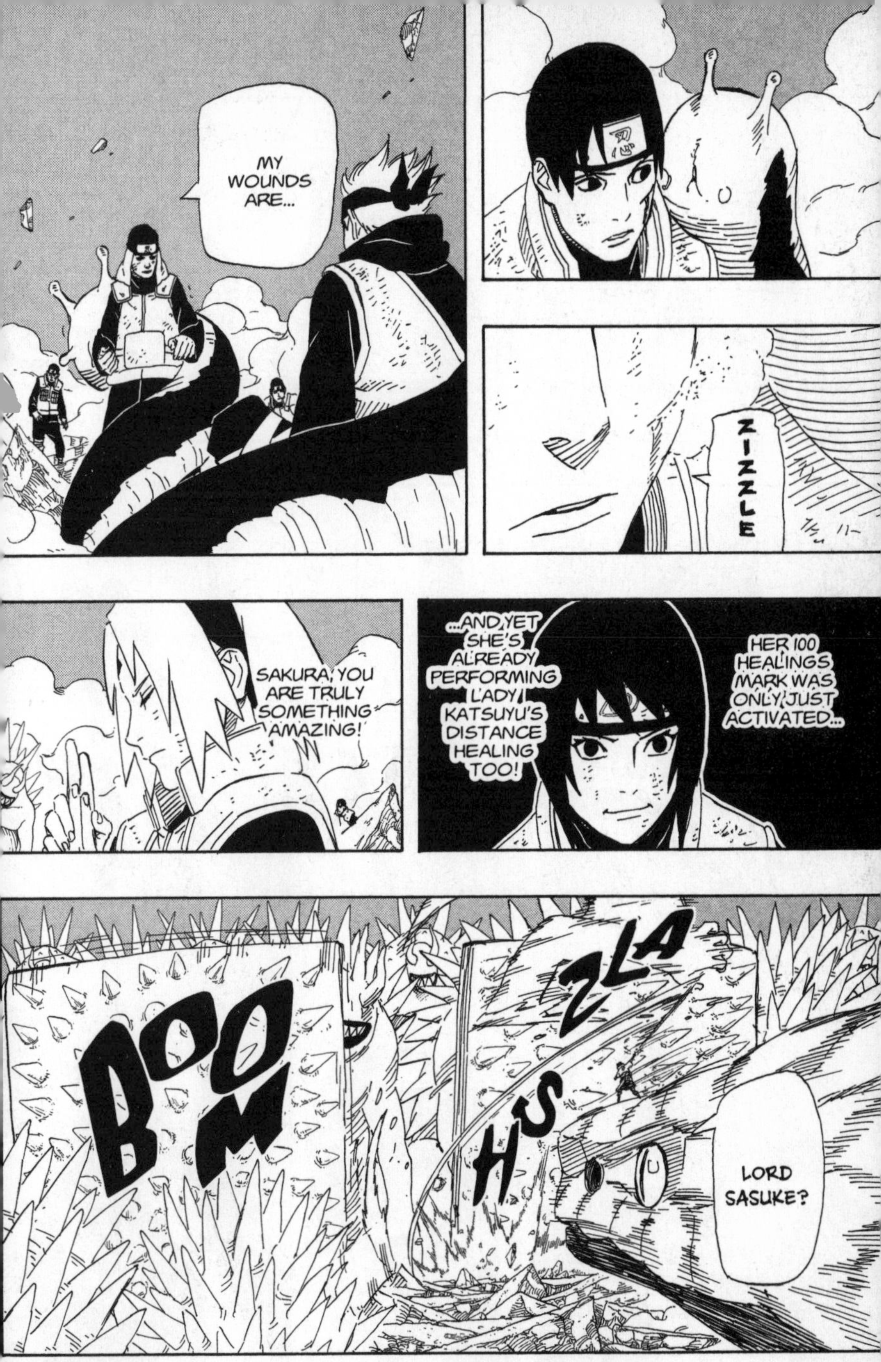
ZIZZLE
MY WOUNDS ARE...
HER 100 HEALINGS MARK WAS ONLY JUST ACTIVATED...
...AND YET SHE'S ALREADY PERFORMING LADY KATSUYU'S DISTANCE HEALING TOO!
SAKURA, YOU ARE TRULY SOMETHING AMAZING!
SHZZLA
LORD SASUKE?
BOOM

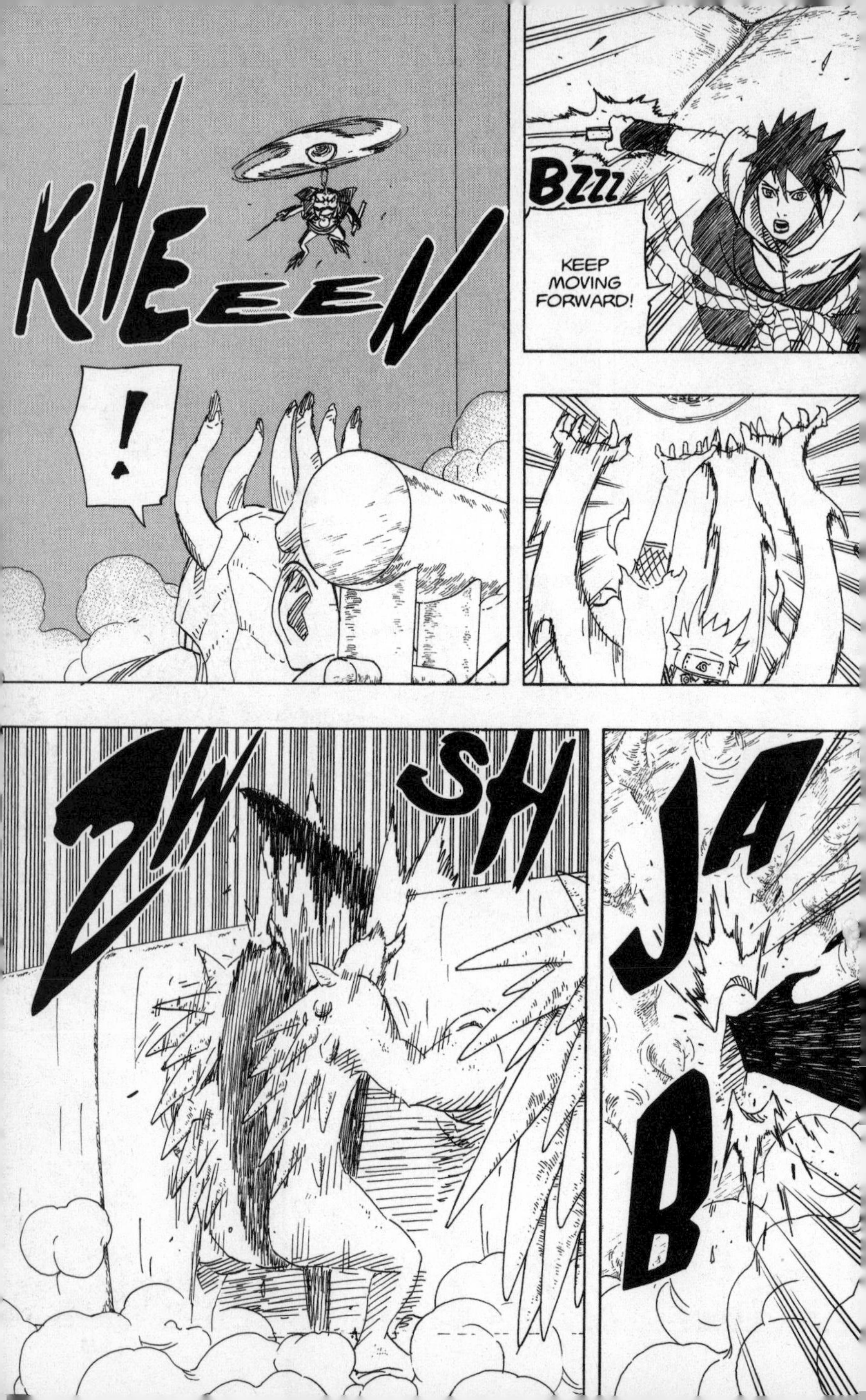
BZZZ
KEEP MOVING FORWARD!
KWEEEEN
!
JA
B
ZW
SH

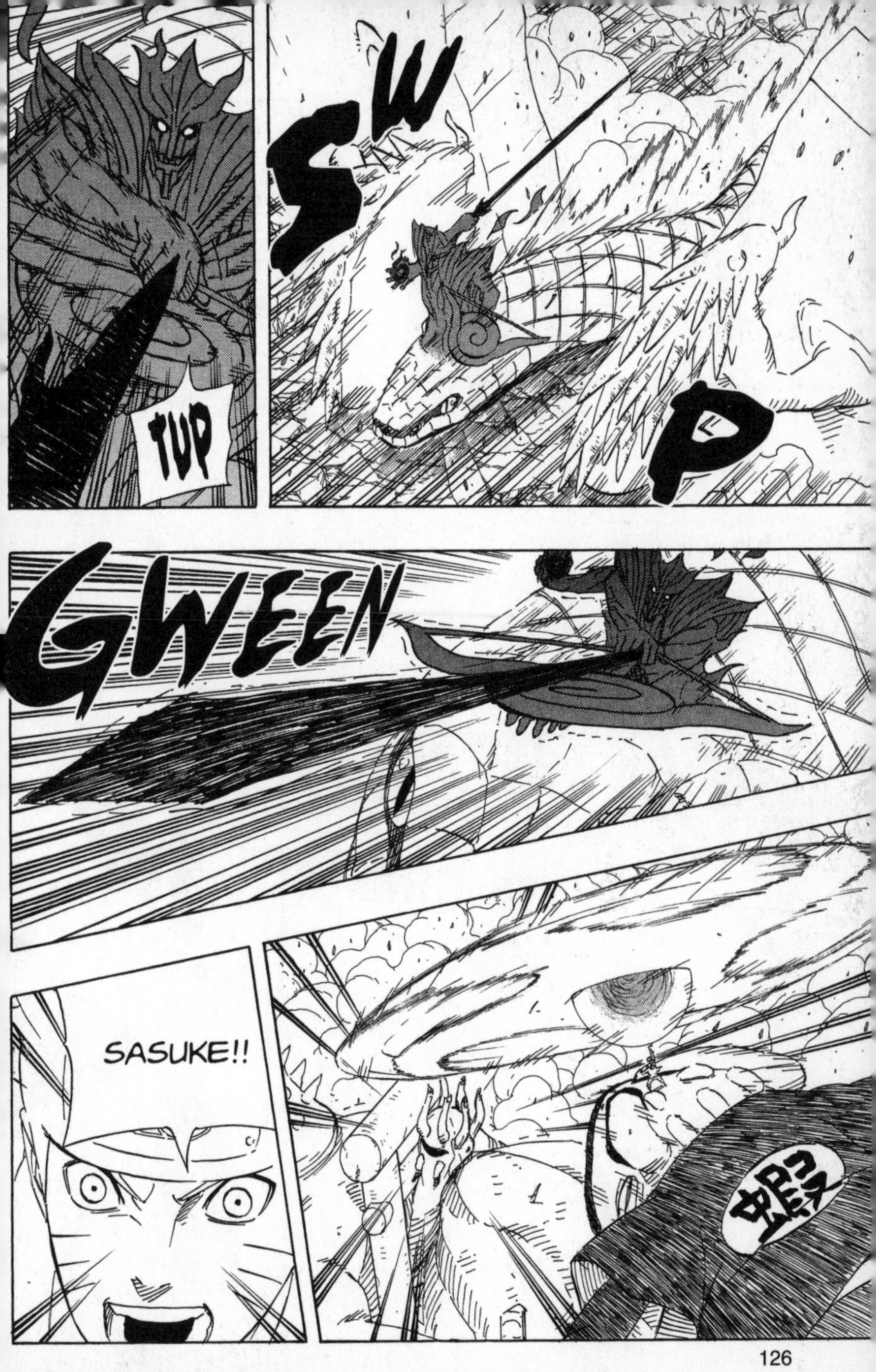
SWP
TUP
GWEEN
SASUKE!!

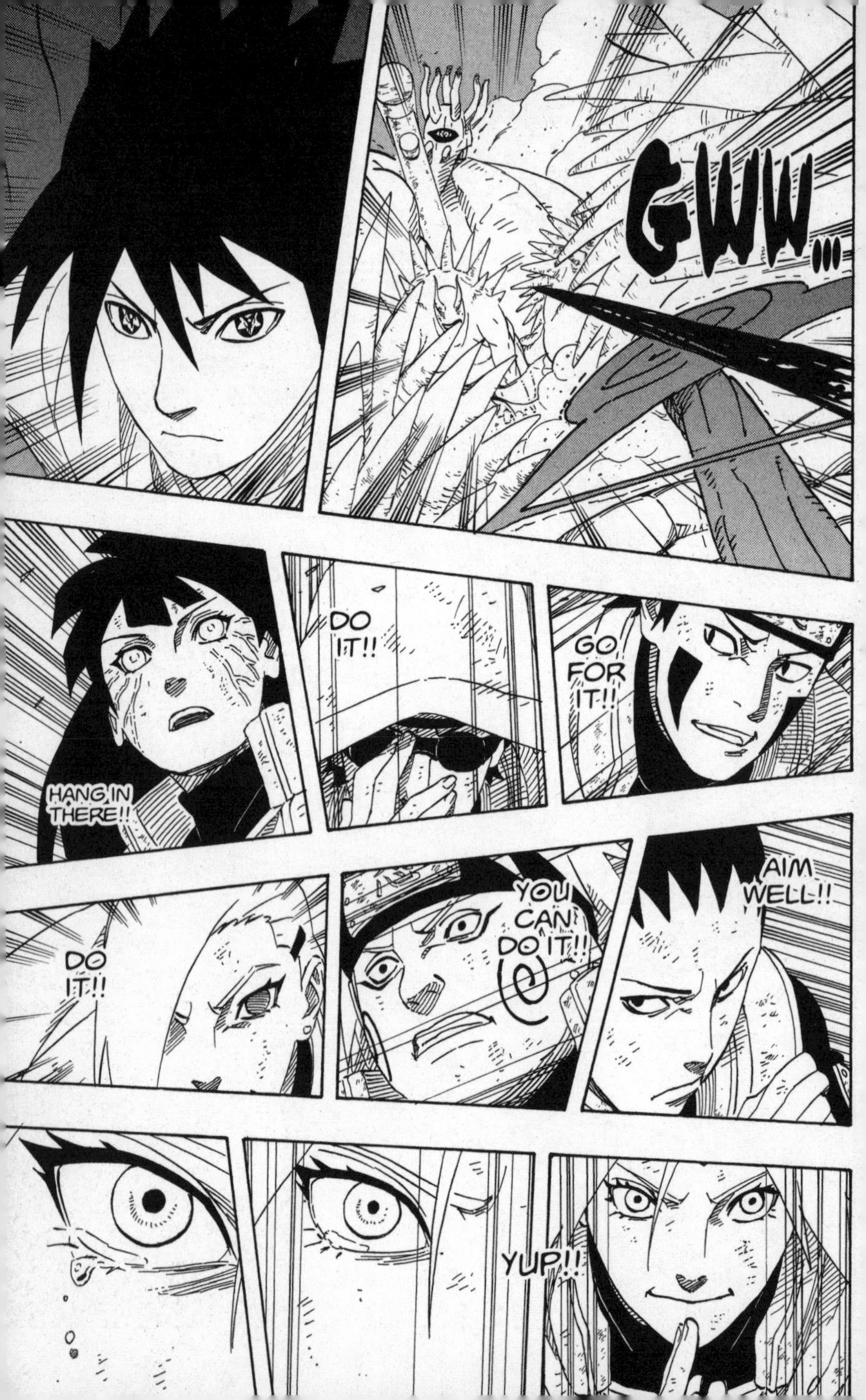
GWW!!!
GO FOR IT!!
DO IT!!
HANG IN THERE!!
AIM WELL!!
YOU CAN DO IT!!
DO IT!!
YUP!!

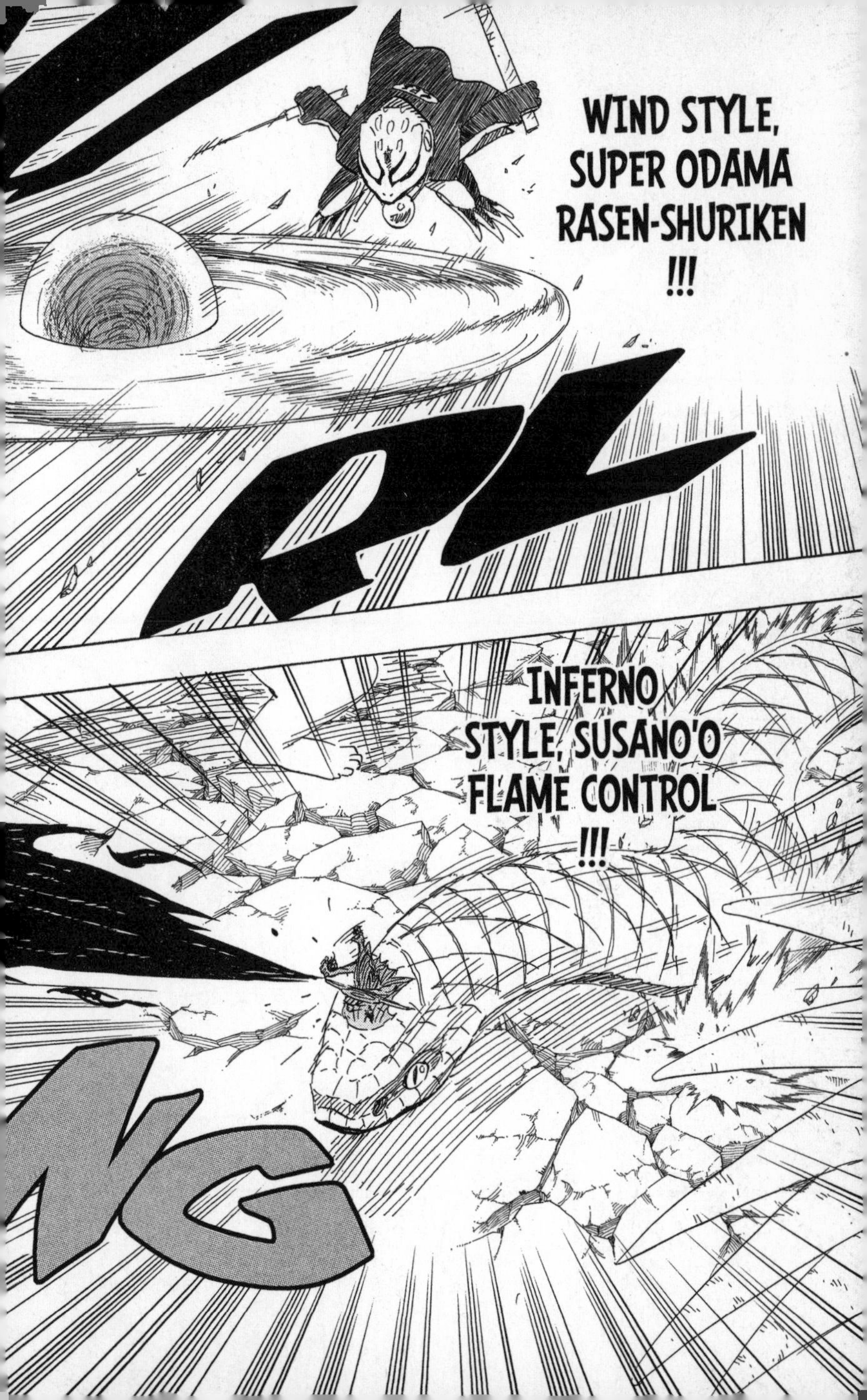
WIND STYLE, SUPER ODAMA RASEN-SHURIKEN !!!
INFERNO STYLE, SUSANO'O FLAME CONTROL !!!
NG

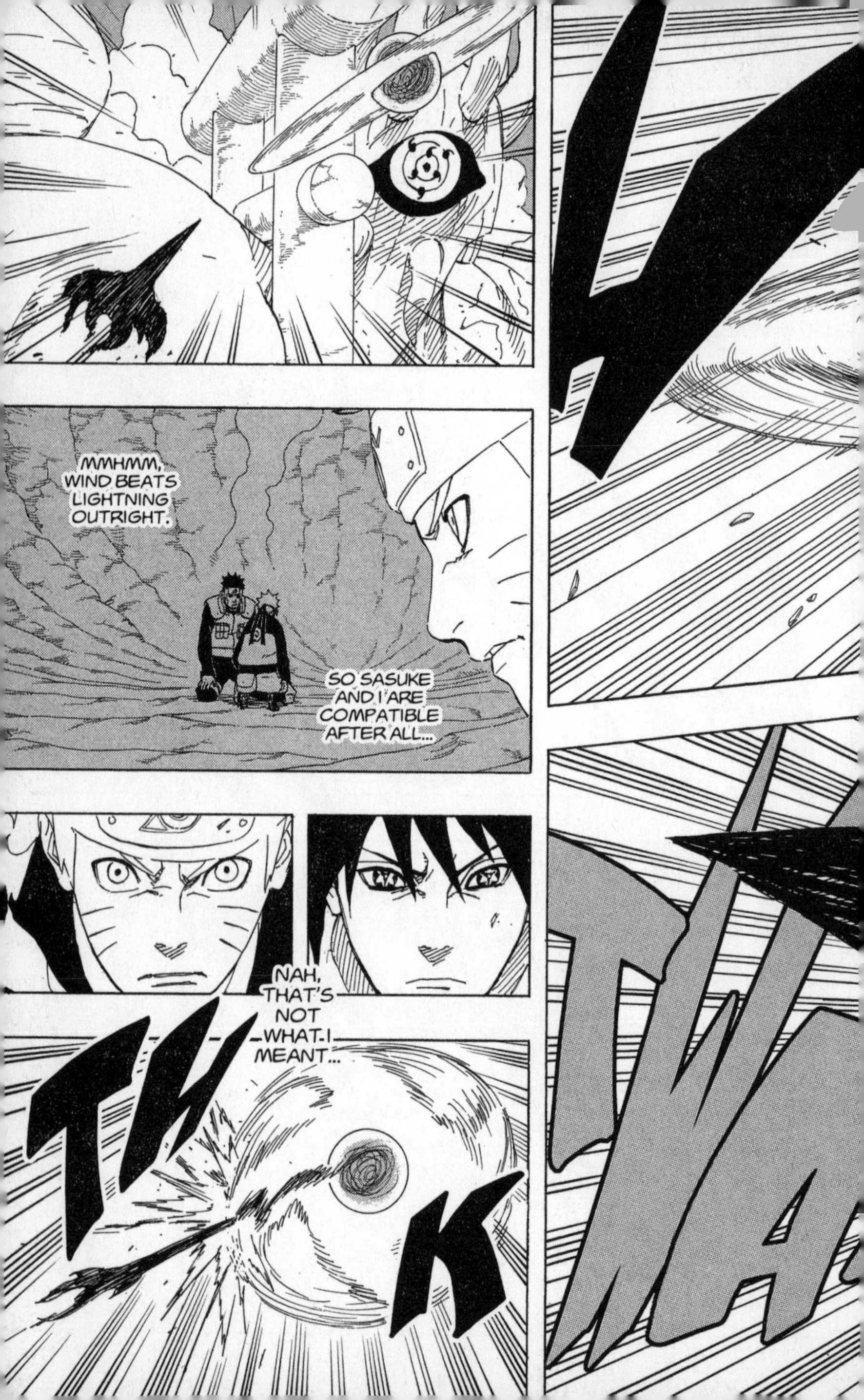
MMHMM, WIND BEATS LIGHTNING OUTRIGHT.
SO SASUKE AND I ARE COMPATIBLE AFTER ALL...
NAH, THAT'S NOT WHAT I MEANT...
THK

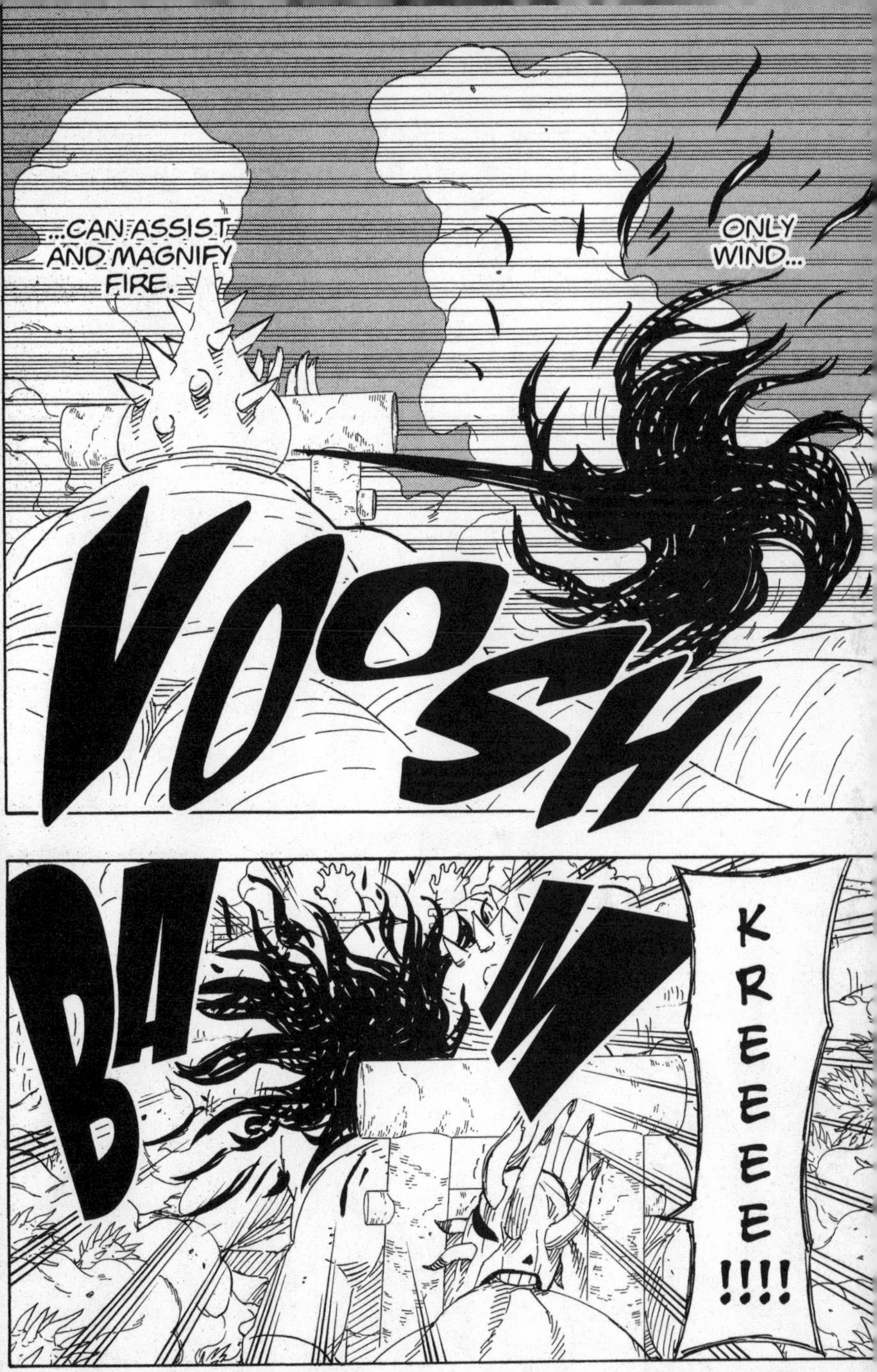
ONLY WIND...
...CAN ASSIST AND MAGNIFY FIRE.
VOOSH
KREEEE!!!!

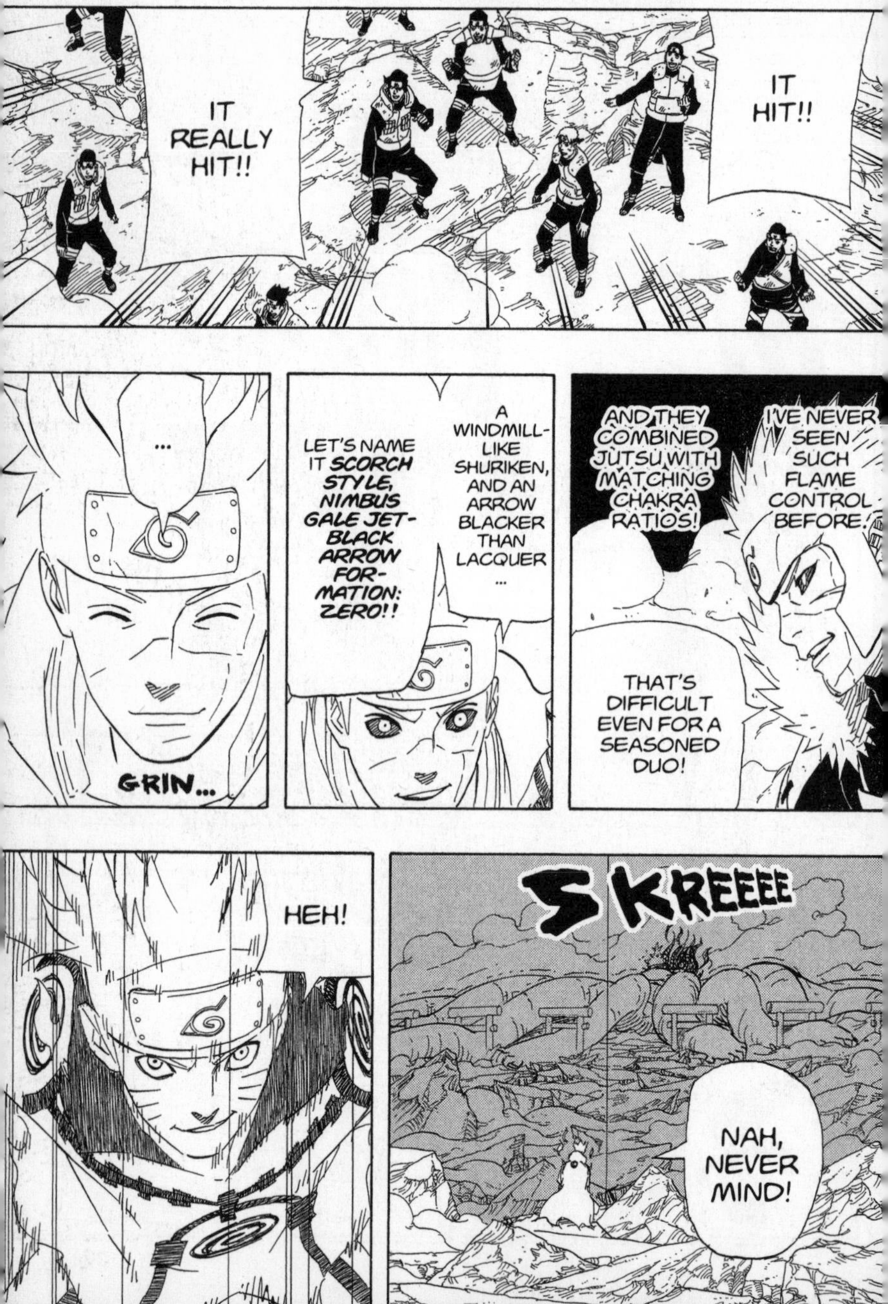

IT HIT!!
IT REALLY HIT!!
I'VE NEVER SEEN SUCH FLAME CONTROL BEFORE!
AND THEY COMBINED JUTSU WITH MATCHING CHAKRA RATIOS!
THAT'S DIFFICULT EVEN FOR A SEASONED DUO!
A WINDMILL-LIKE SHURIKEN, AND AN ARROW BLACKER THAN LACQUER...
LET'S NAME IT *SCORCH STYLE, NIMBUS GALE JET-BLACK ARROW FORMATION: ZERO!!*
...
GRIN...
SKREEEE
NAH, NEVER MIND!
HEH!

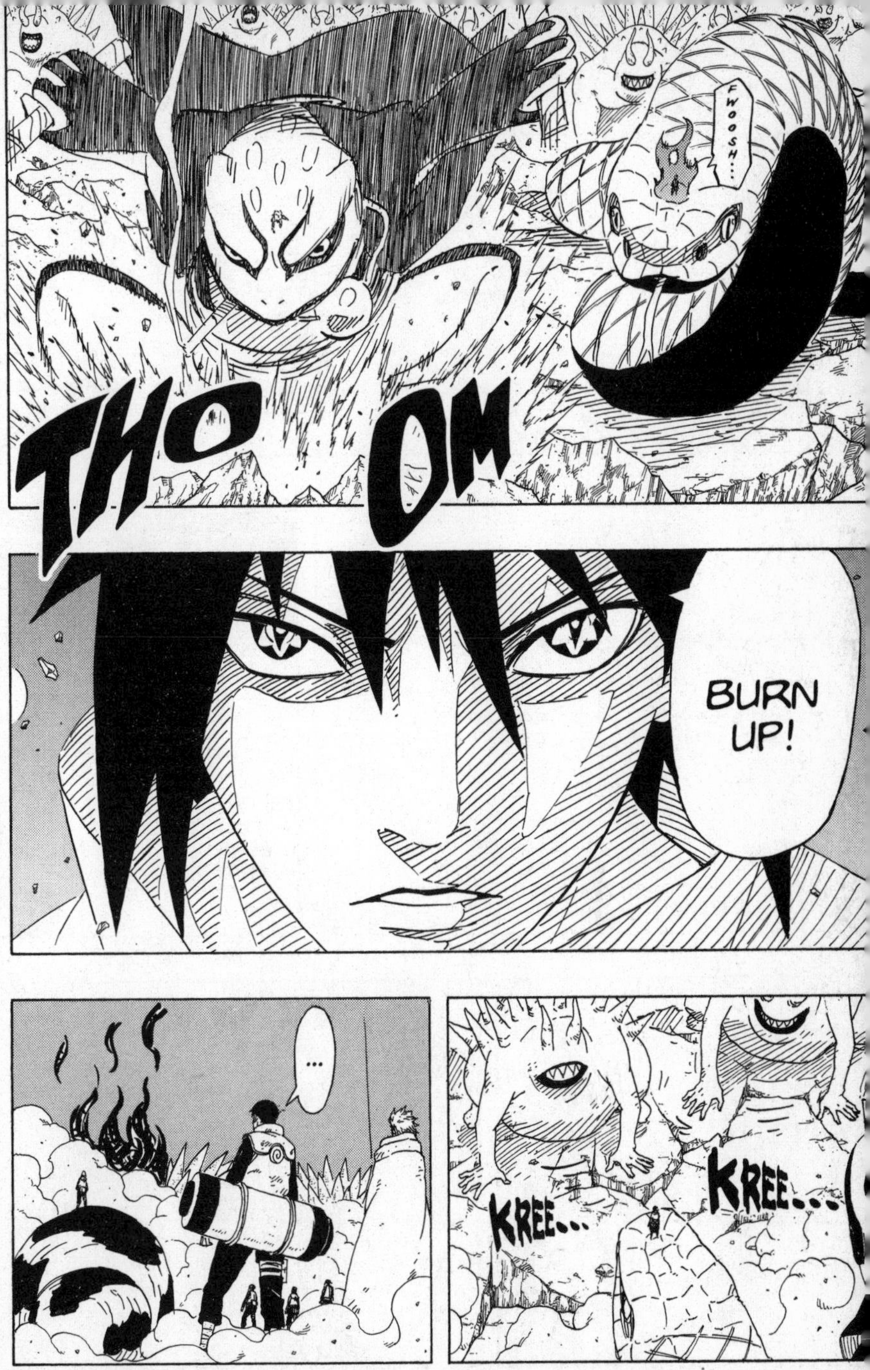
FWOOSH...
THOOM
BURN UP!
KREE...
KREE...
...

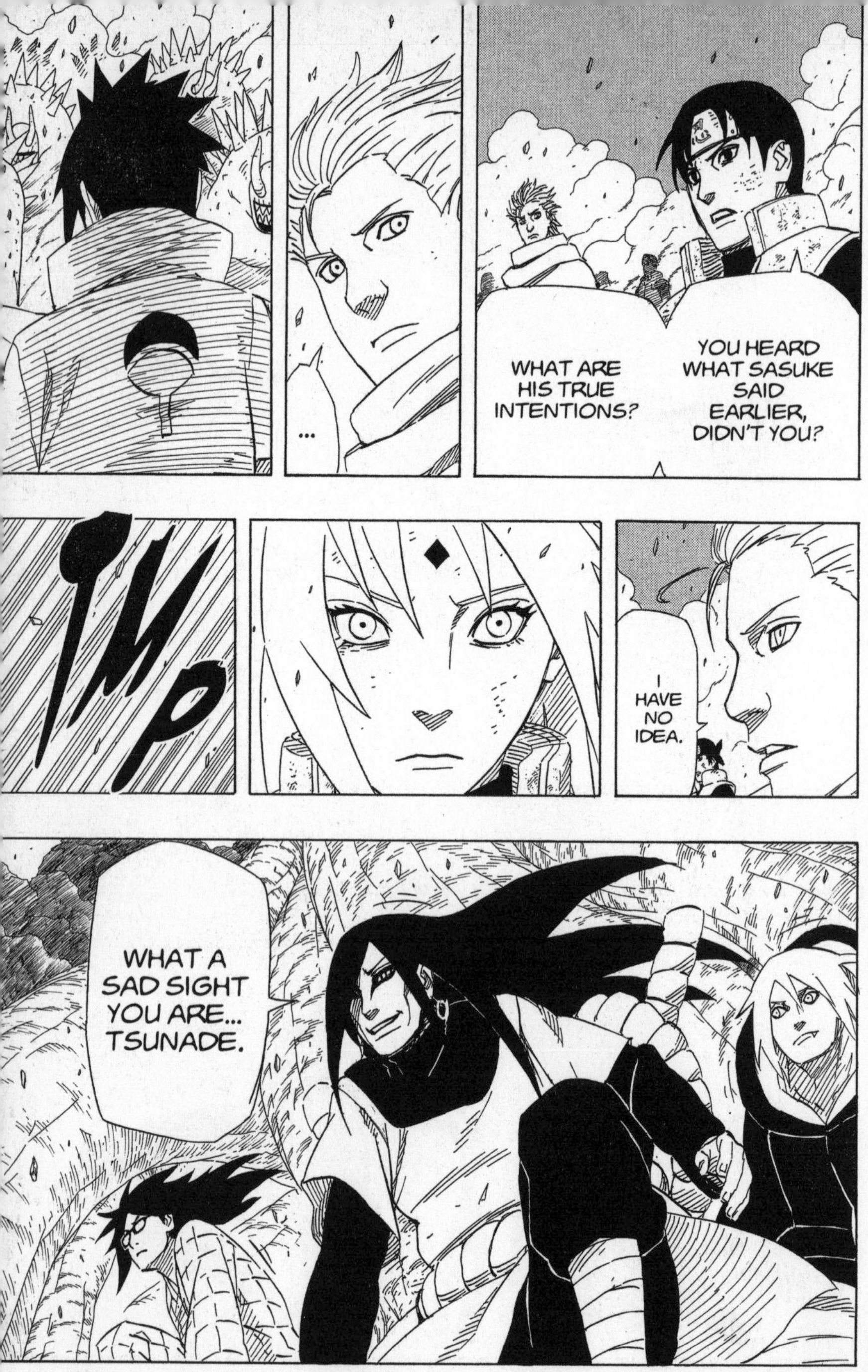
YOU HEARD WHAT SASUKE SAID EARLIER, DIDN'T YOU?
WHAT ARE HIS TRUE INTENTIONS?
...
I HAVE NO IDEA.
TMP
WHAT A SAD SIGHT YOU ARE... TSUNADE.

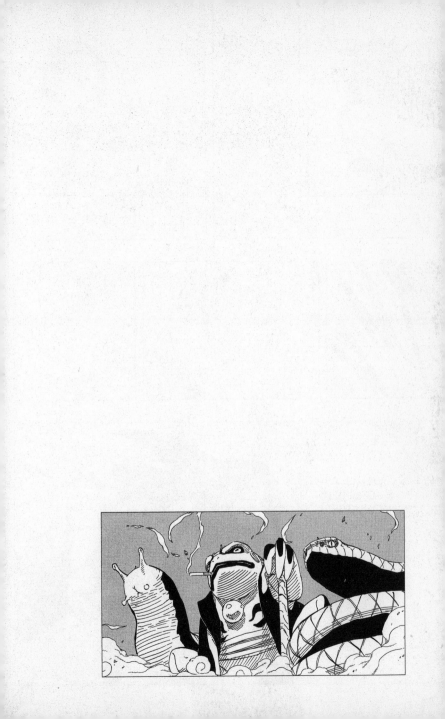

Number 635: A New Wind

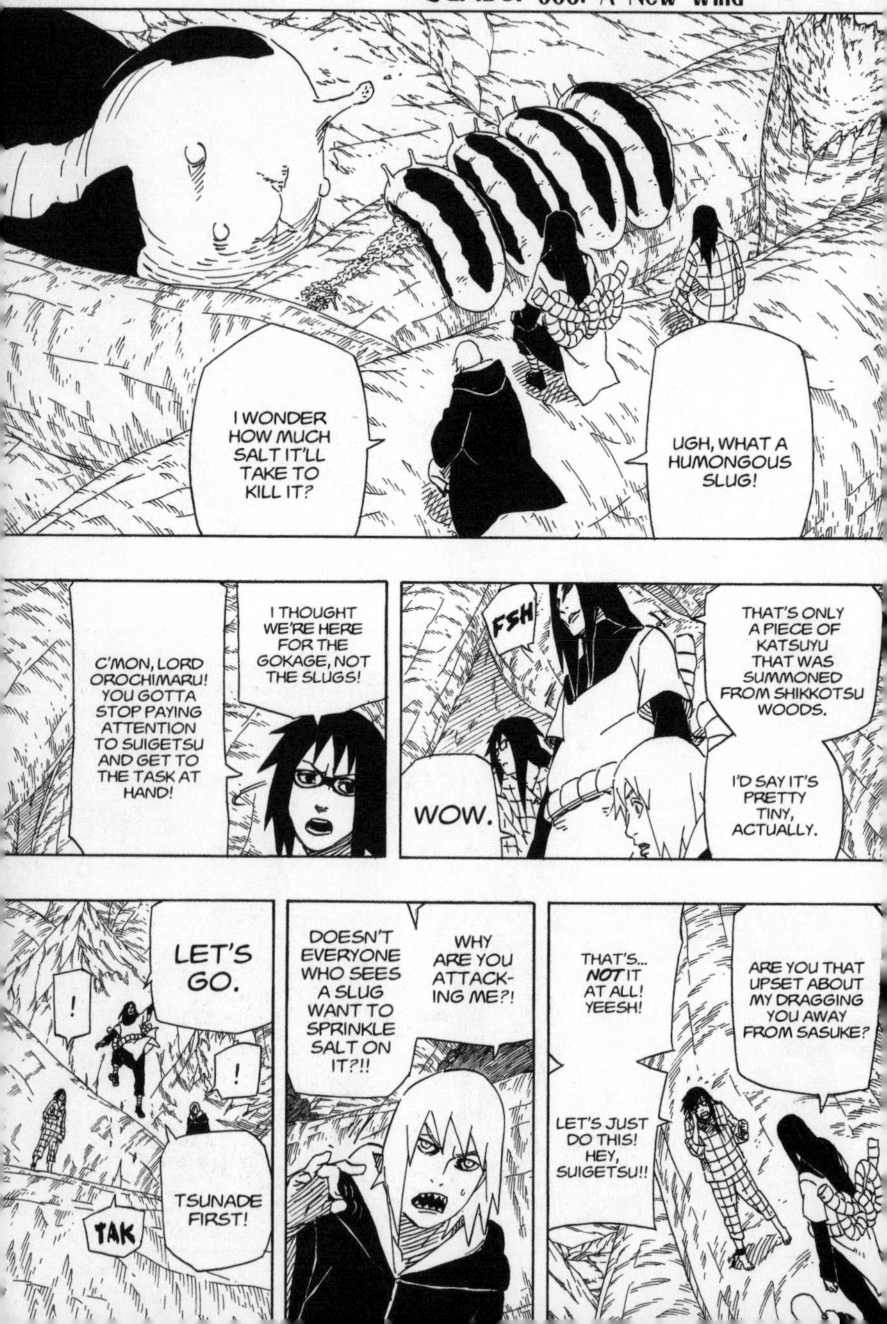
UGH, WHAT A HUMONGOUS SLUG!
I WONDER HOW MUCH SALT IT'LL TAKE TO KILL IT?
THAT'S ONLY A PIECE OF KATSUYU THAT WAS SUMMONED FROM SHIKKOTSU WOODS.
FSH
I'D SAY IT'S PRETTY TINY, ACTUALLY.
WOW.
I THOUGHT WE'RE HERE FOR THE GOKAGE, NOT THE SLUGS!
C'MON, LORD OROCHIMARU! YOU GOTTA STOP PAYING ATTENTION TO SUIGETSU AND GET TO THE TASK AT HAND!
ARE YOU THAT UPSET ABOUT MY DRAGGING YOU AWAY FROM SASUKE?
THAT'S... NOT IT AT ALL! YEESH!
LET'S JUST DO THIS! HEY, SUIGETSU!!
WHY ARE YOU ATTACKING ME?!
DOESN'T EVERYONE WHO SEES A SLUG WANT TO SPRINKLE SALT ON IT?!!
LET'S GO.
!
!
TSUNADE FIRST!
TAK

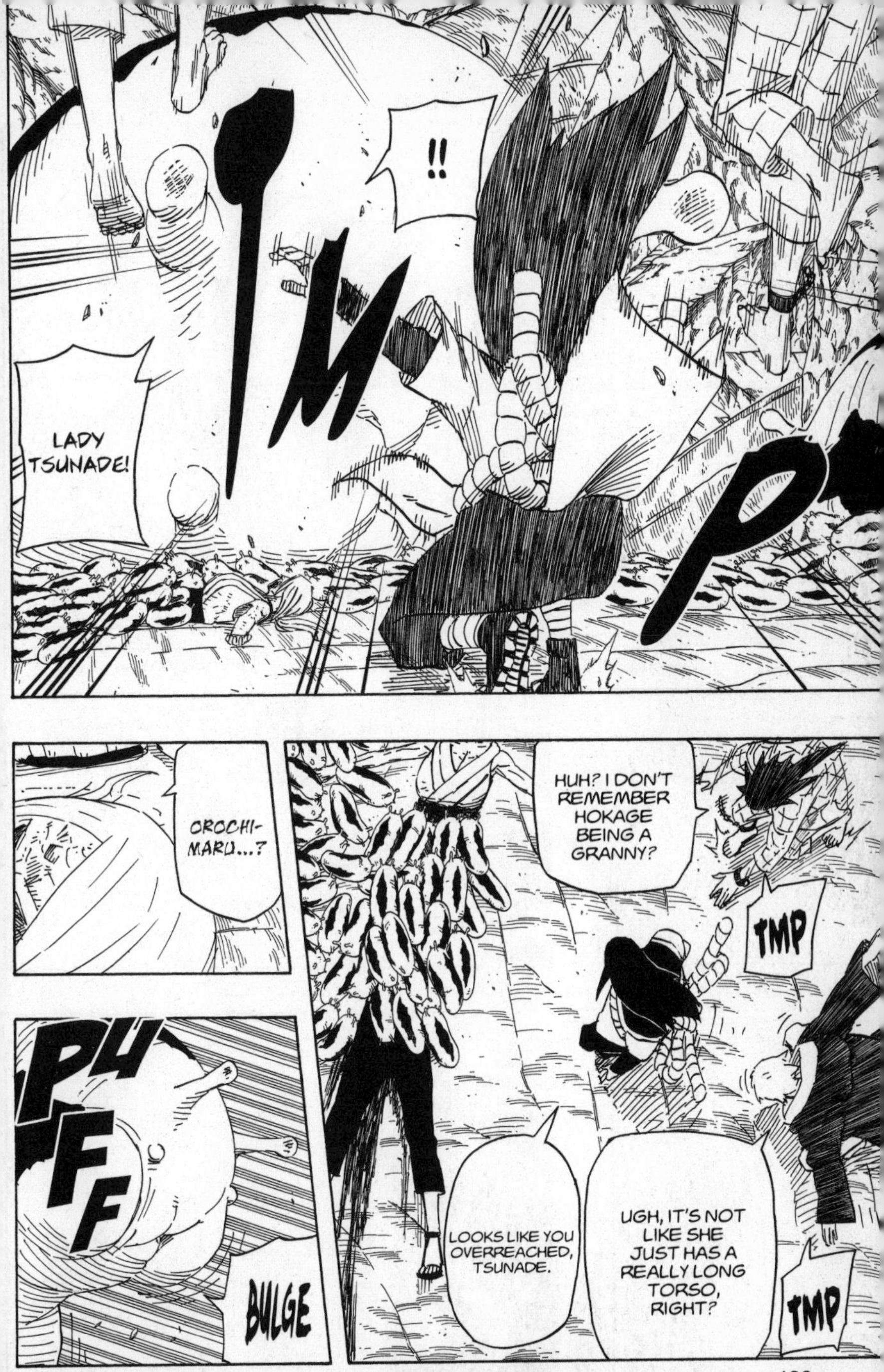
!!
LADY TSUNADE!
IMP
HUH? I DON'T REMEMBER HOKAGE BEING A GRANNY?
TMP
UGH, IT'S NOT LIKE SHE JUST HAS A REALLY LONG TORSO, RIGHT?
TMP
LOOKS LIKE YOU OVERREACHED, TSUNADE.
OROCHI-MARU...?
PUFF
BULGE

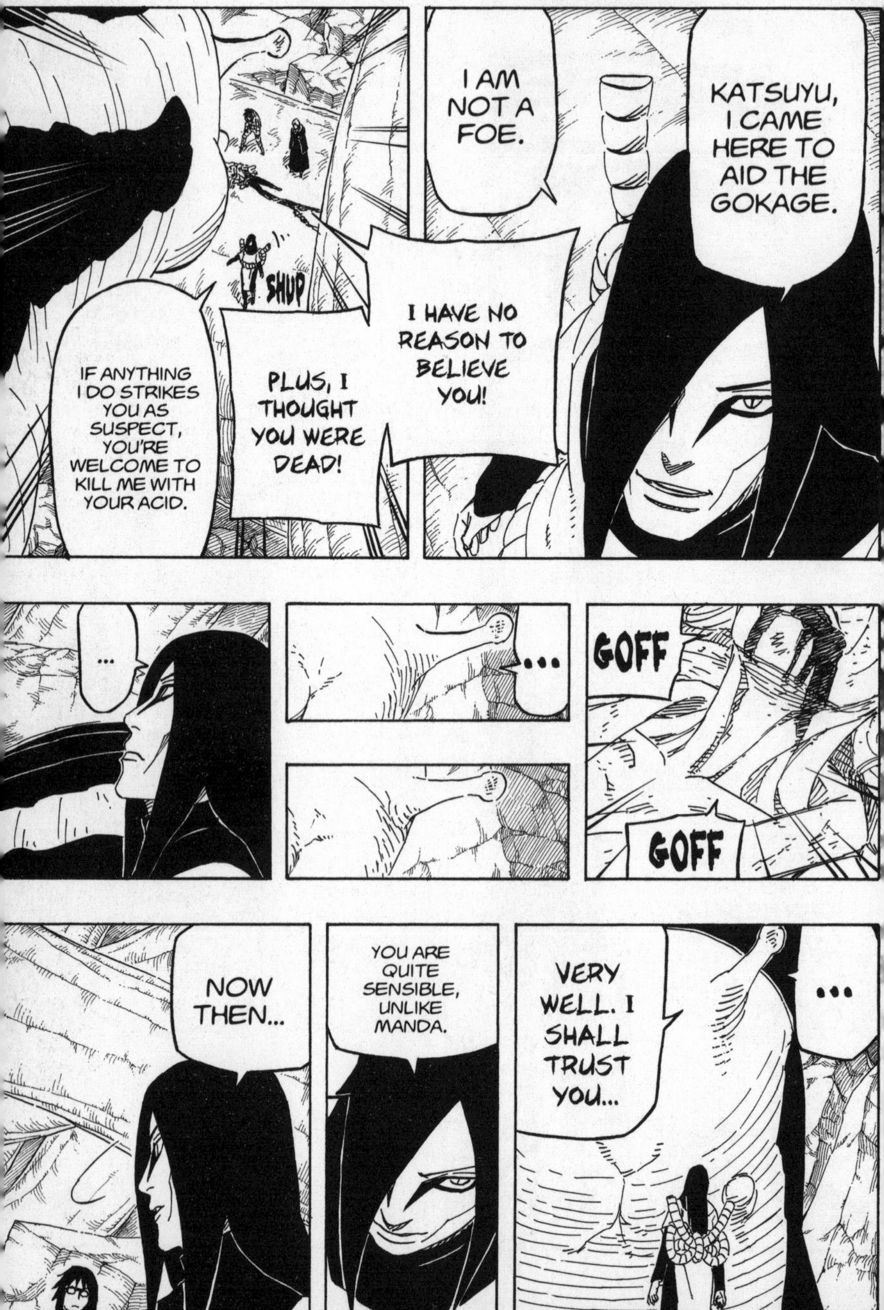
KATSUYU, I CAME HERE TO AID THE GOKAGE.
I AM NOT A FOE.
I HAVE NO REASON TO BELIEVE YOU!
PLUS, I THOUGHT YOU WERE DEAD!
SHUP
IF ANYTHING I DO STRIKES YOU AS SUSPECT, YOU'RE WELCOME TO KILL ME WITH YOUR ACID.
GOFF
GOFF
...
...
...
VERY WELL. I SHALL TRUST YOU...
YOU ARE QUITE SENSIBLE, UNLIKE MANDA.
NOW THEN...

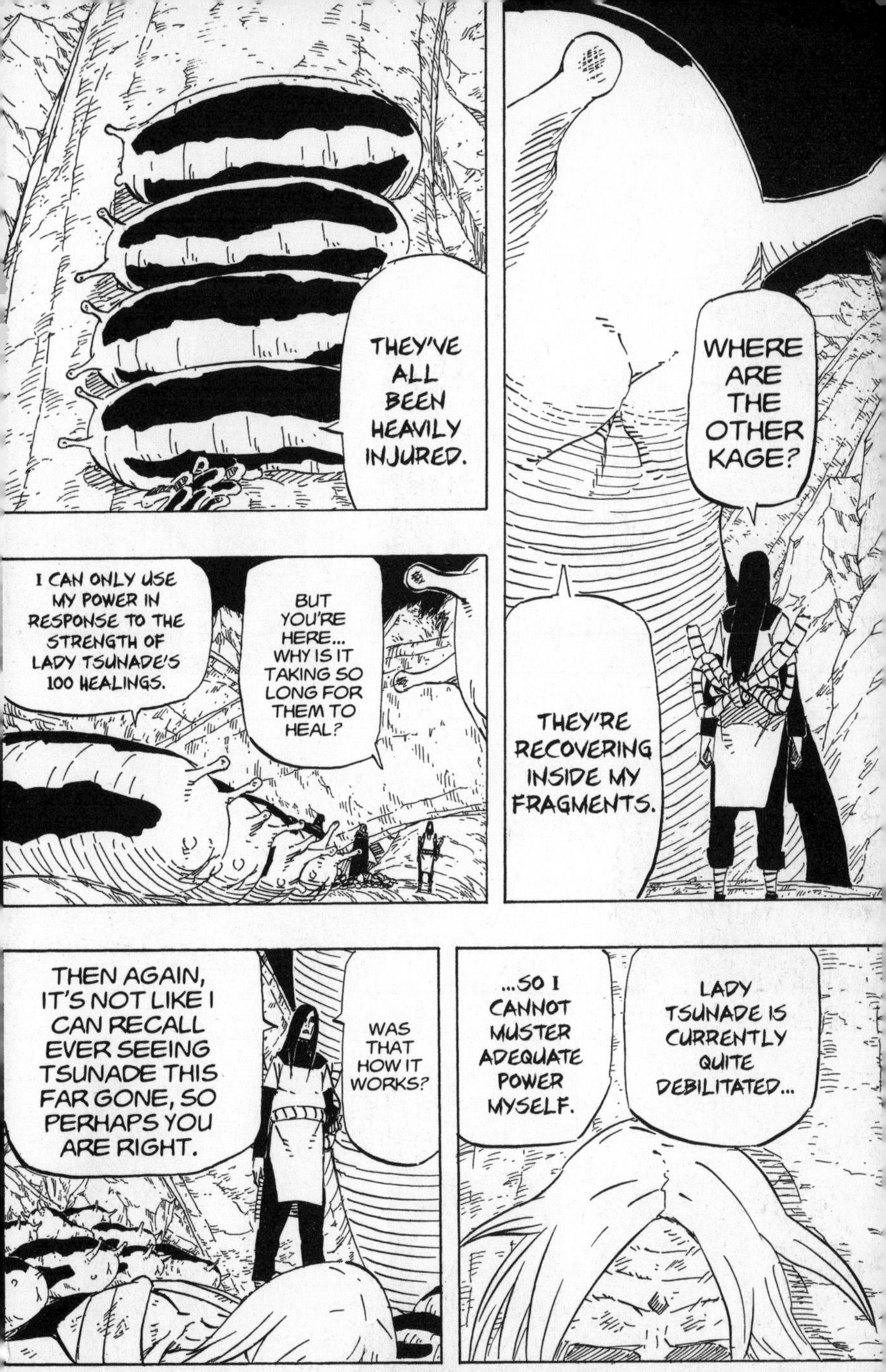
WHERE ARE THE OTHER KAGE?
THEY'RE RECOVERING INSIDE MY FRAGMENTS.
THEY'VE ALL BEEN HEAVILY INJURED.
BUT YOU'RE HERE... WHY IS IT TAKING SO LONG FOR THEM TO HEAL?
I CAN ONLY USE MY POWER IN RESPONSE TO THE STRENGTH OF LADY TSUNADE'S 100 HEALINGS.
LADY TSUNADE IS CURRENTLY QUITE DEBILITATED...
...SO I CANNOT MUSTER ADEQUATE POWER MYSELF.
WAS THAT HOW IT WORKS?
THEN AGAIN, IT'S NOT LIKE I CAN RECALL EVER SEEING TSUNADE THIS FAR GONE, SO PERHAPS YOU ARE RIGHT.

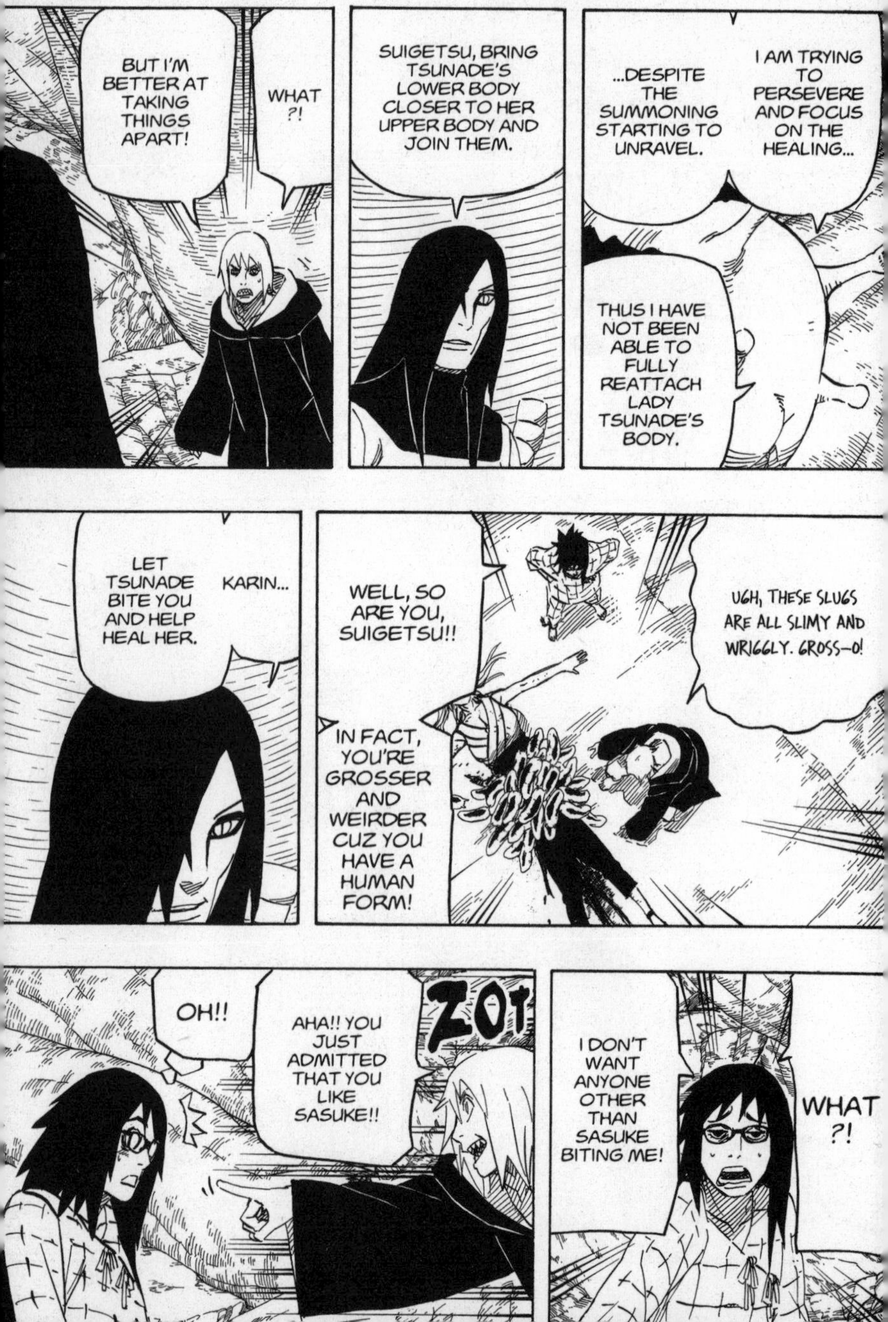
I AM TRYING TO PERSEVERE AND FOCUS ON THE HEALING...
...DESPITE THE SUMMONING STARTING TO UNRAVEL.
THUS I HAVE NOT BEEN ABLE TO FULLY REATTACH LADY TSUNADE'S BODY.
SUIGETSU, BRING TSUNADE'S LOWER BODY CLOSER TO HER UPPER BODY AND JOIN THEM.
WHAT ?!
BUT I'M BETTER AT TAKING THINGS APART!
UGH, THESE SLUGS ARE ALL SLIMY AND WRIGGLY. GROSS-O!
WELL, SO ARE YOU, SUIGETSU!!
IN FACT, YOU'RE GROSSER AND WEIRDER CUZ YOU HAVE A HUMAN FORM!
KARIN...
LET TSUNADE BITE YOU AND HELP HEAL HER.
WHAT ?!
I DON'T WANT ANYONE OTHER THAN SASUKE BITING ME!
ZOT
AHA!! YOU JUST ADMITTED THAT YOU LIKE SASUKE!!
OH!!

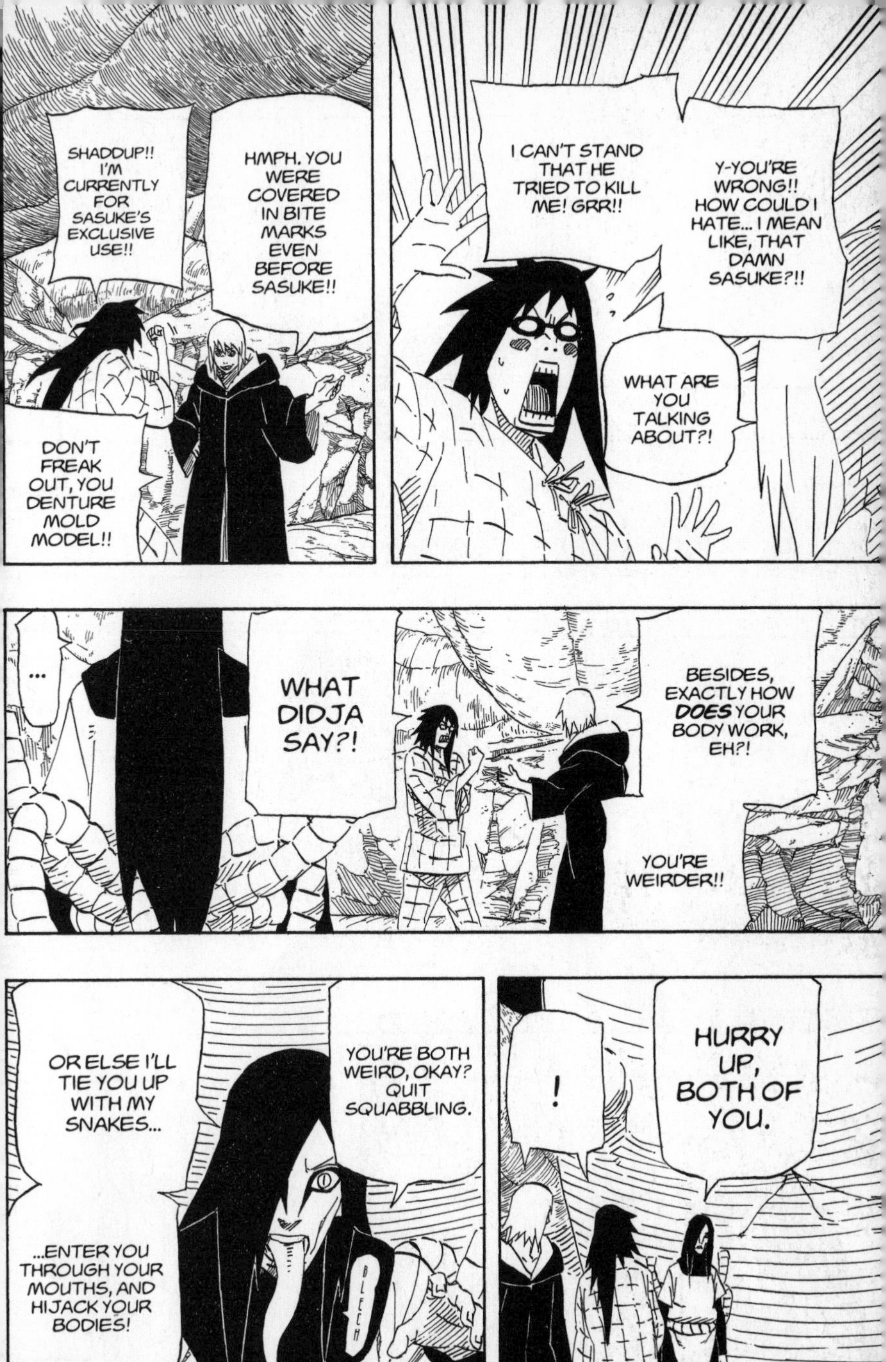
Y-YOU'RE WRONG!! HOW COULD I HATE... I MEAN LIKE, THAT DAMN SASUKE?!!
I CAN'T STAND THAT HE TRIED TO KILL ME! GRR!!
WHAT ARE YOU TALKING ABOUT?!
HMPH. YOU WERE COVERED IN BITE MARKS EVEN BEFORE SASUKE!!
SHADDUP!! I'M CURRENTLY FOR SASUKE'S EXCLUSIVE USE!!
DON'T FREAK OUT, YOU DENTURE MOLD MODEL!!
BESIDES, EXACTLY HOW **DOES** YOUR BODY WORK, EH?!
YOU'RE WEIRDER!!
WHAT DIDJA SAY?!
...
HURRY UP, BOTH OF YOU.
!
YOU'RE BOTH WEIRD, OKAY? QUIT SQUABBLING.
OR ELSE I'LL TIE YOU UP WITH MY SNAKES...
...ENTER YOU THROUGH YOUR MOUTHS, AND HIJACK YOUR BODIES!
BLECH

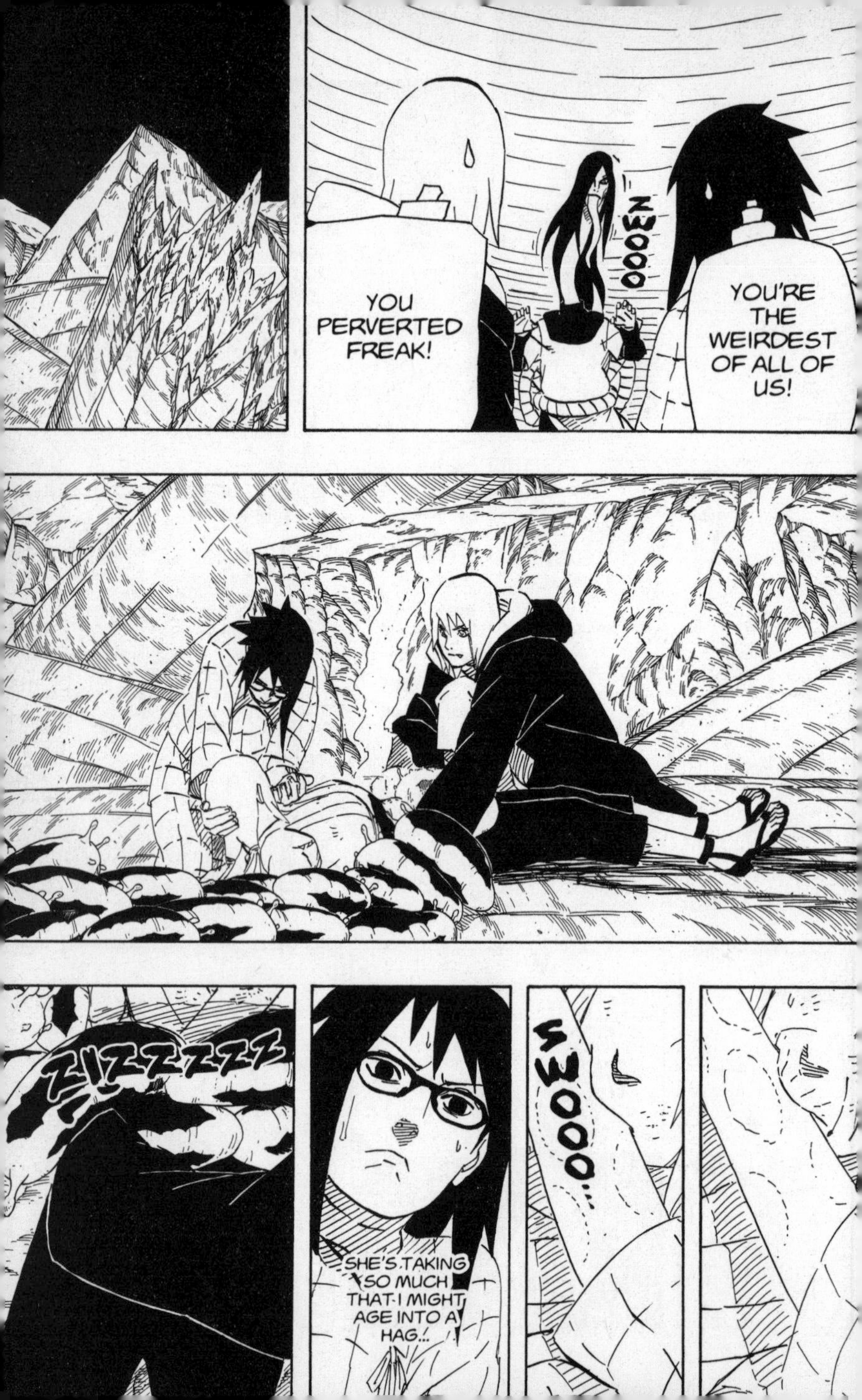
YOU'RE THE WEIRDEST OF ALL OF US!
ZWOOO
YOU PERVERTED FREAK!
SWOOOO...
SHE'S TAKING SO MUCH THAT I MIGHT AGE INTO A HAG..!
ZIZZZZZZ

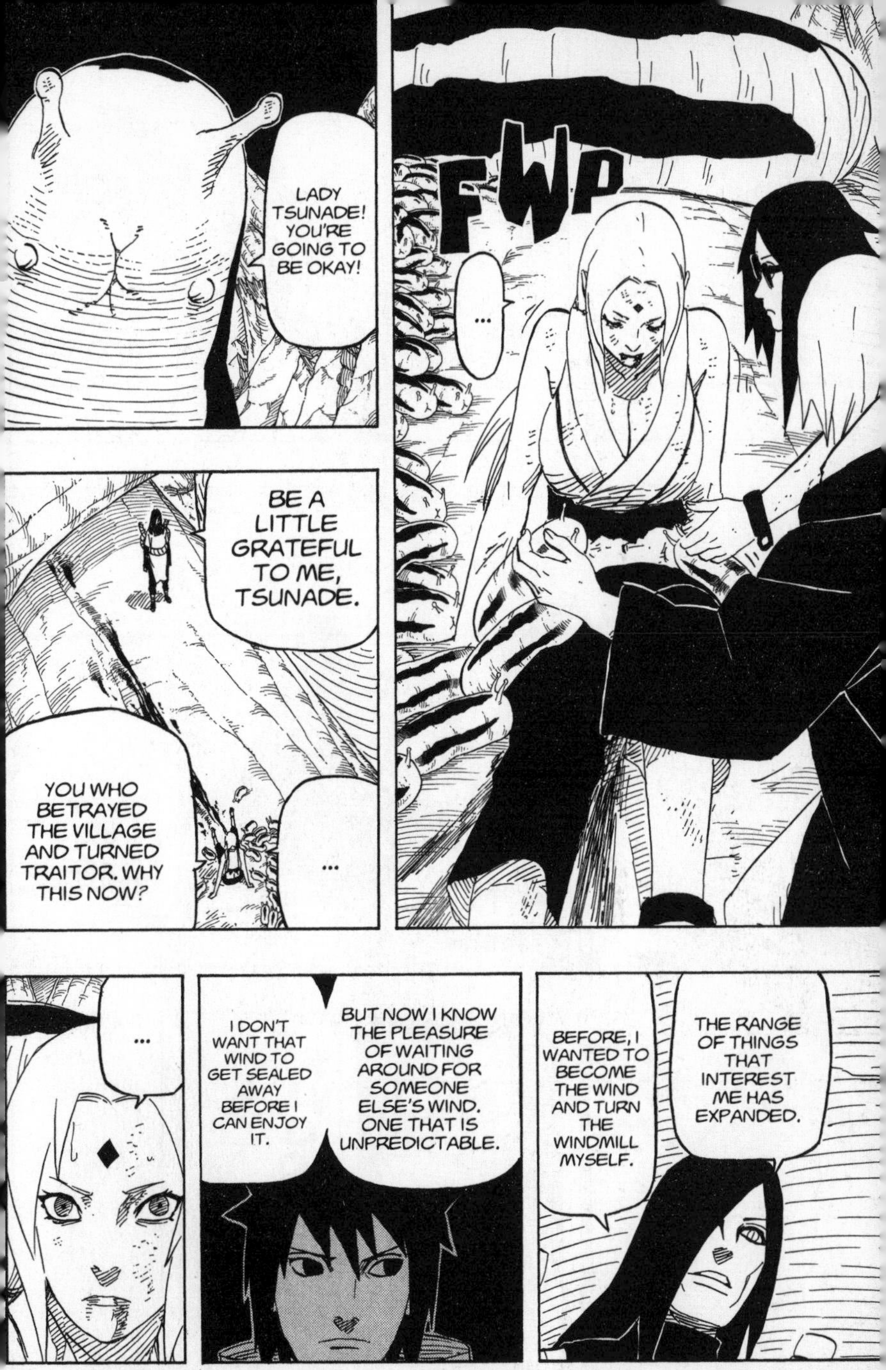
FWP
...
LADY TSUNADE! YOU'RE GOING TO BE OKAY!
BE A LITTLE GRATEFUL TO ME, TSUNADE.
...
YOU WHO BETRAYED THE VILLAGE AND TURNED TRAITOR. WHY THIS NOW?
THE RANGE OF THINGS THAT INTEREST ME HAS EXPANDED.
BEFORE, I WANTED TO BECOME THE WIND AND TURN THE WINDMILL MYSELF.
BUT NOW I KNOW THE PLEASURE OF WAITING AROUND FOR SOMEONE ELSE'S WIND. ONE THAT IS UNPREDICTABLE.
I DON'T WANT THAT WIND TO GET SEALED AWAY BEFORE I CAN ENJOY IT.
...

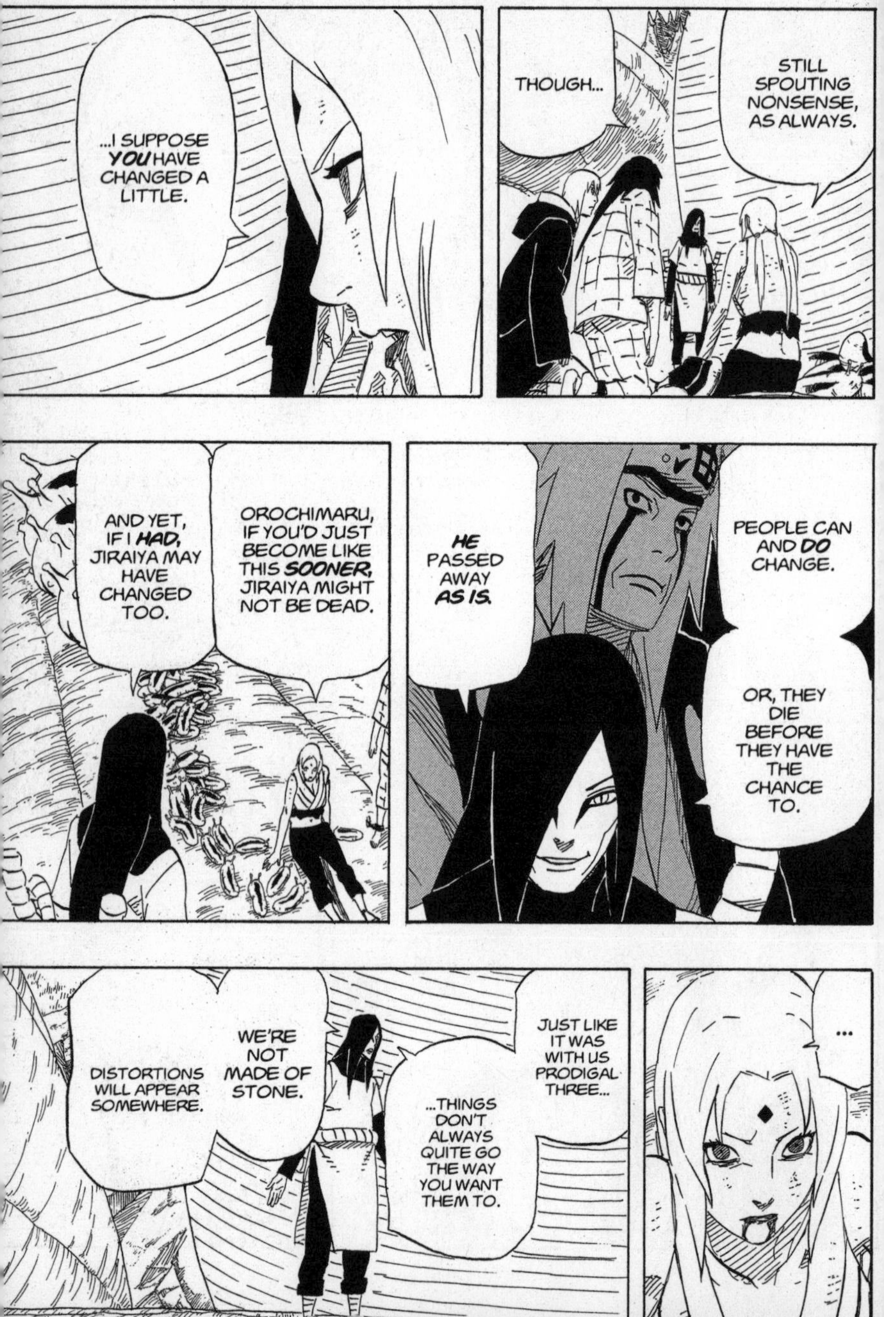
STILL SPOUTING NONSENSE, AS ALWAYS.
THOUGH...
...I SUPPOSE *YOU* HAVE CHANGED A LITTLE.
PEOPLE CAN AND *DO* CHANGE.
OR, THEY DIE BEFORE THEY HAVE THE CHANCE TO.
HE PASSED AWAY *AS IS.*
OROCHIMARU, IF YOU'D JUST BECOME LIKE THIS *SOONER,* JIRAIYA MIGHT NOT BE DEAD.
AND YET, IF I *HAD,* JIRAIYA MAY HAVE CHANGED TOO.
...
JUST LIKE IT WAS WITH US PRODIGAL THREE...
...THINGS DON'T ALWAYS QUITE GO THE WAY YOU WANT THEM TO.
WE'RE NOT MADE OF STONE.
DISTORTIONS WILL APPEAR SOMEWHERE.

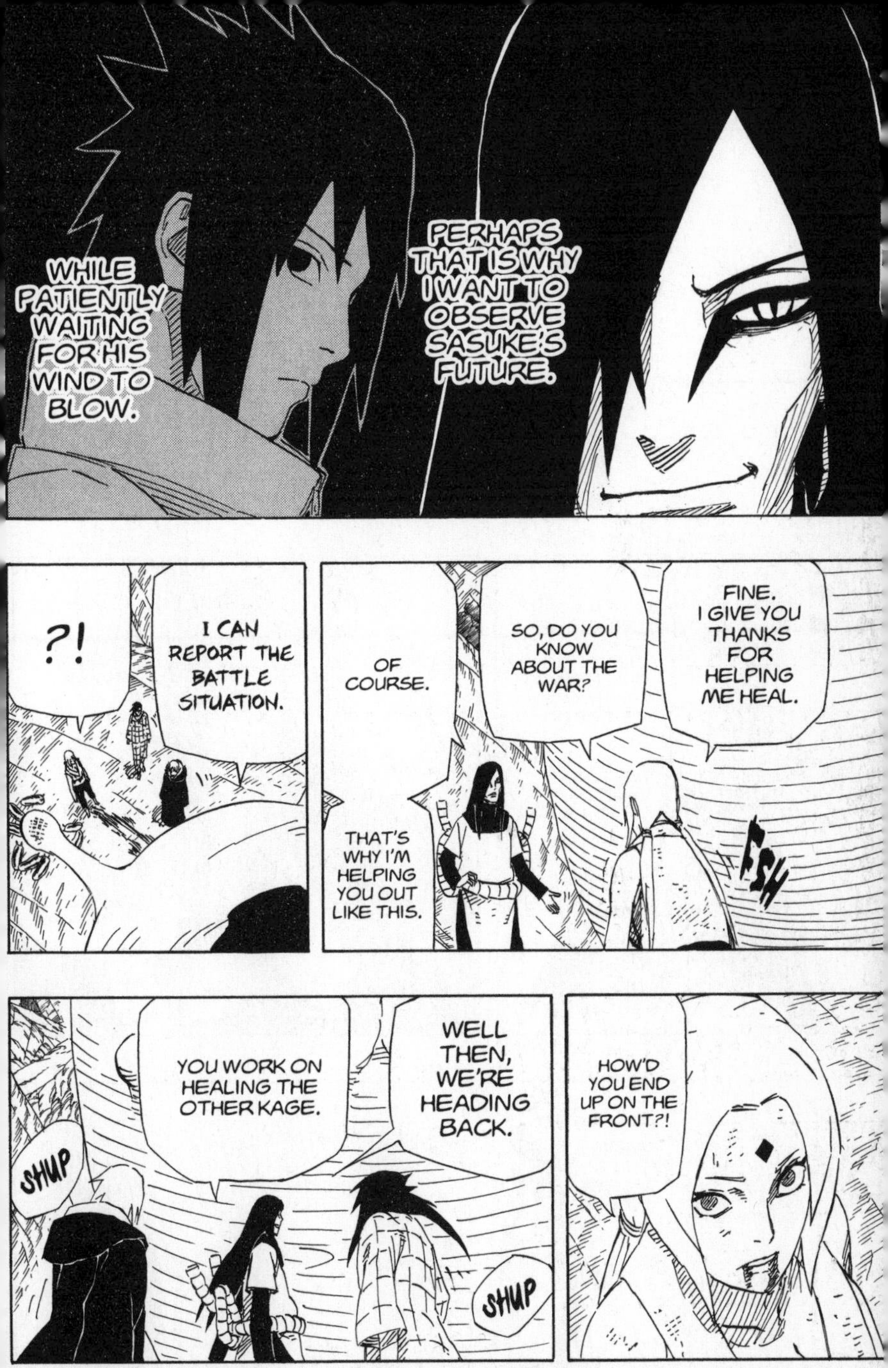
PERHAPS THAT IS WHY I WANT TO OBSERVE SASUKE'S FUTURE.
WHILE PATIENTLY WAITING FOR HIS WIND TO BLOW.
FINE. I GIVE YOU THANKS FOR HELPING ME HEAL.
FSH
SO, DO YOU KNOW ABOUT THE WAR?
OF COURSE.
THAT'S WHY I'M HELPING YOU OUT LIKE THIS.
I CAN REPORT THE BATTLE SITUATION.
?!
HOW'D YOU END UP ON THE FRONT?!
WELL THEN, WE'RE HEADING BACK.
YOU WORK ON HEALING THE OTHER KAGE.
SHUP
SHUP

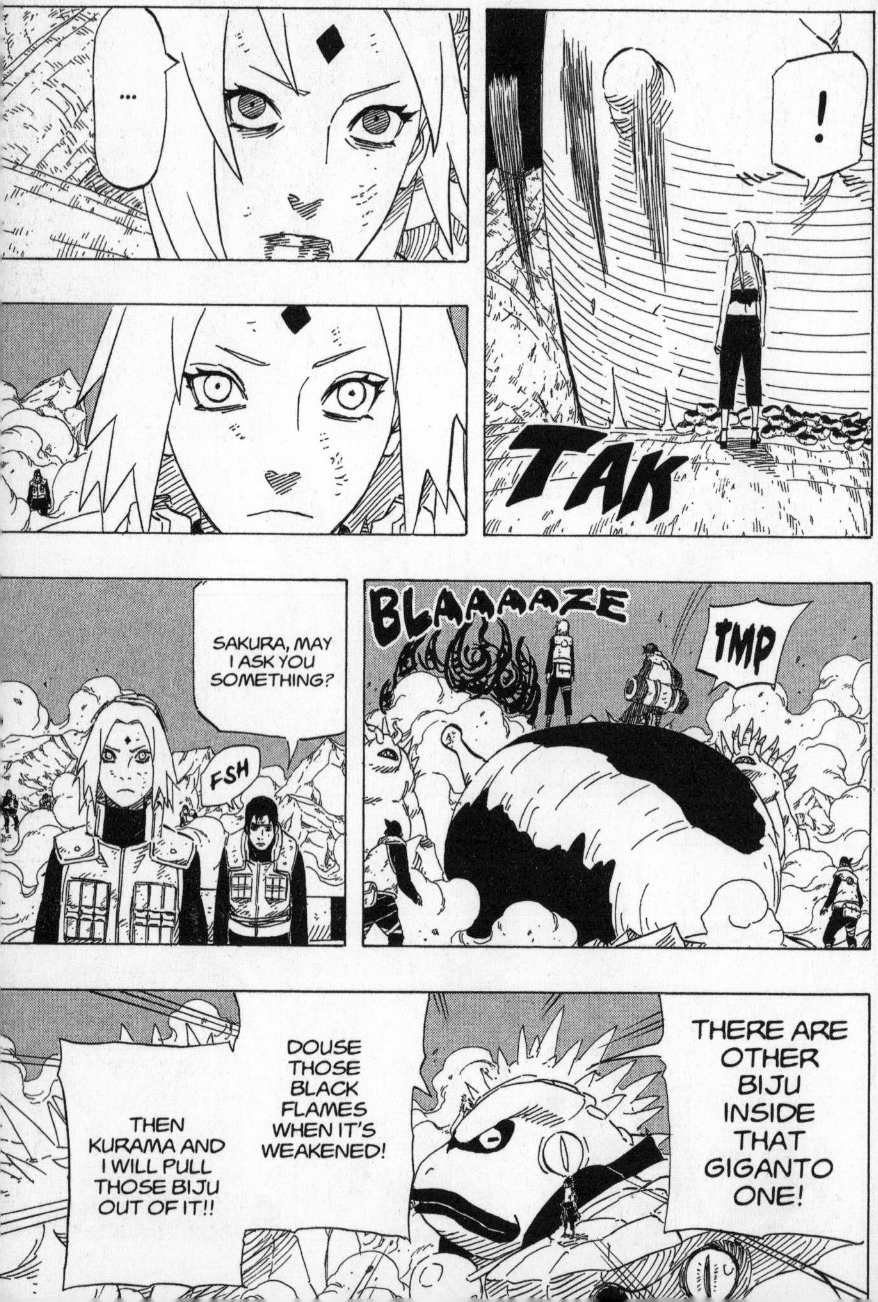
!
TAK
...
BLAAAAZE
TMP
SAKURA, MAY I ASK YOU SOMETHING?
FSH
THERE ARE OTHER BIJU INSIDE THAT GIGANTO ONE!
DOUSE THOSE BLACK FLAMES WHEN IT'S WEAKENED!
THEN KURAMA AND I WILL PULL THOSE BIJU OUT OF IT!!

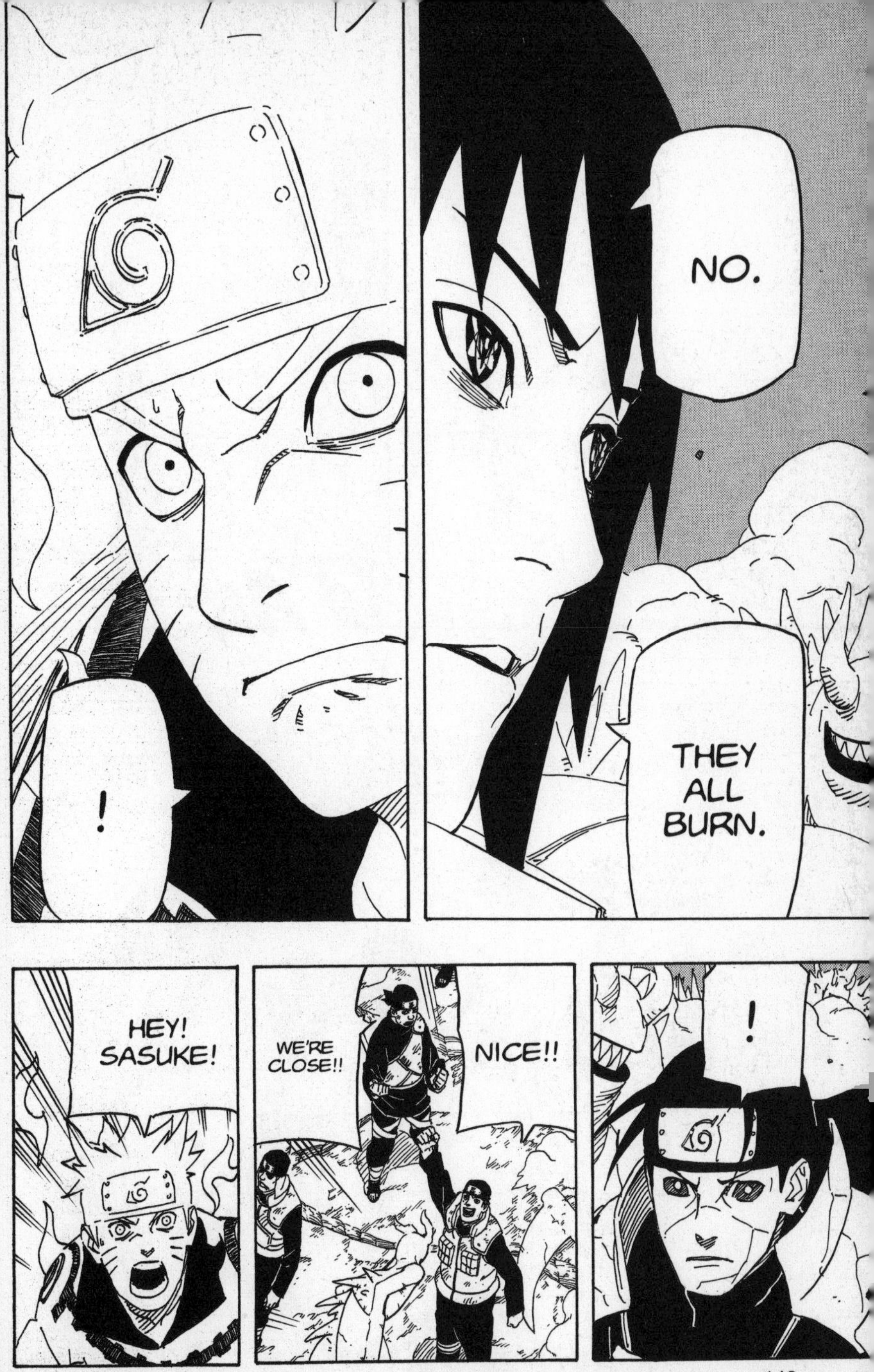
NO.
THEY ALL BURN.
!
!
NICE!!
WE'RE CLOSE!!
HEY! SASUKE!

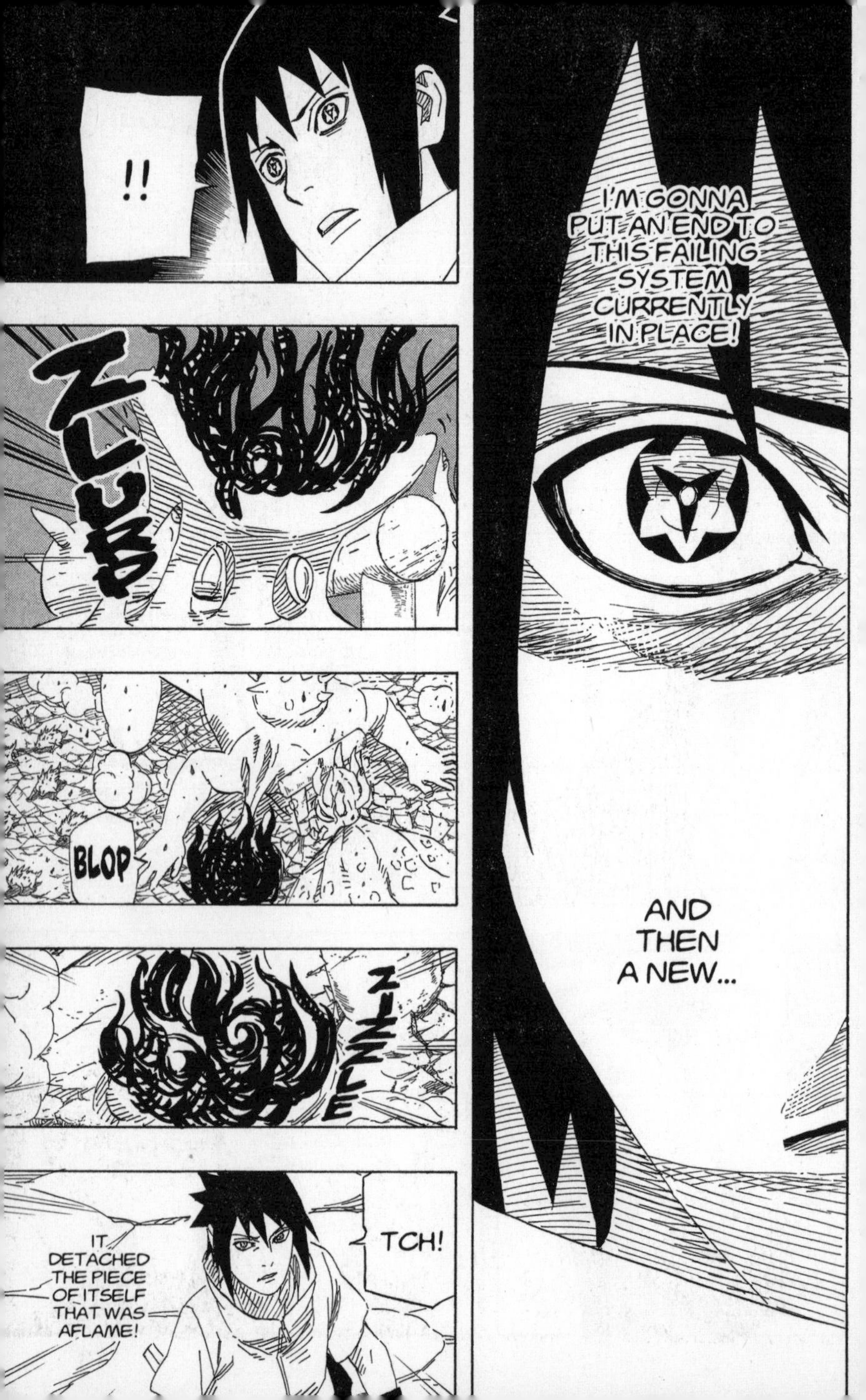
I'M GONNA PUT AN END TO THIS FAILING SYSTEM CURRENTLY IN PLACE!
AND THEN A NEW...
!!
BLOP
TCH!
IT DETACHED THE PIECE OF ITSELF THAT WAS AFLAME!

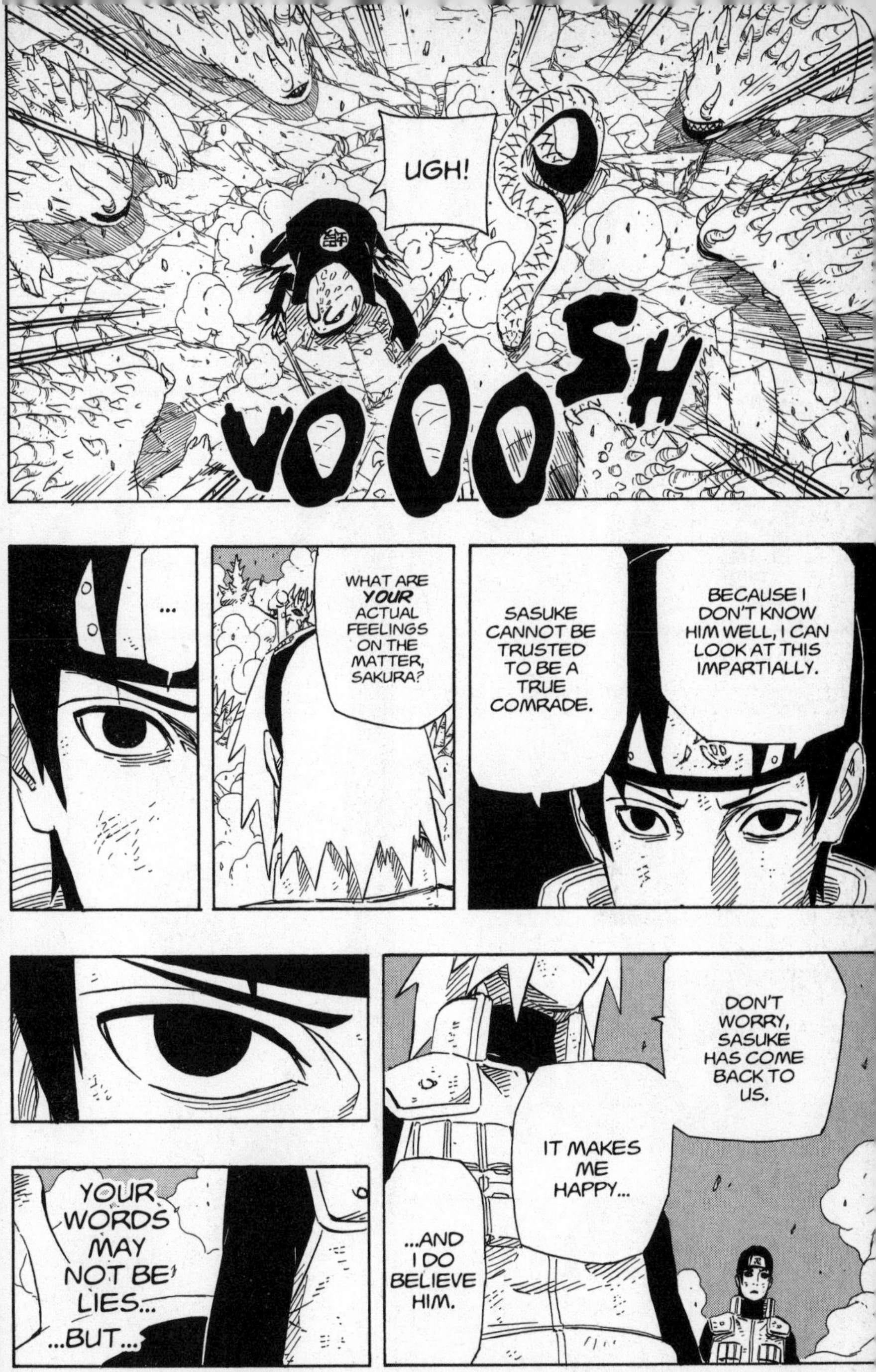
UGH!
VOOOSH
BECAUSE I DON'T KNOW HIM WELL, I CAN LOOK AT THIS IMPARTIALLY.
SASUKE CANNOT BE TRUSTED TO BE A TRUE COMRADE.
WHAT ARE *YOUR* ACTUAL FEELINGS ON THE MATTER, SAKURA?
...
DON'T WORRY, SASUKE HAS COME BACK TO US.
IT MAKES ME HAPPY...
...AND I DO BELIEVE HIM.
YOUR WORDS MAY NOT BE LIES...
...BUT...

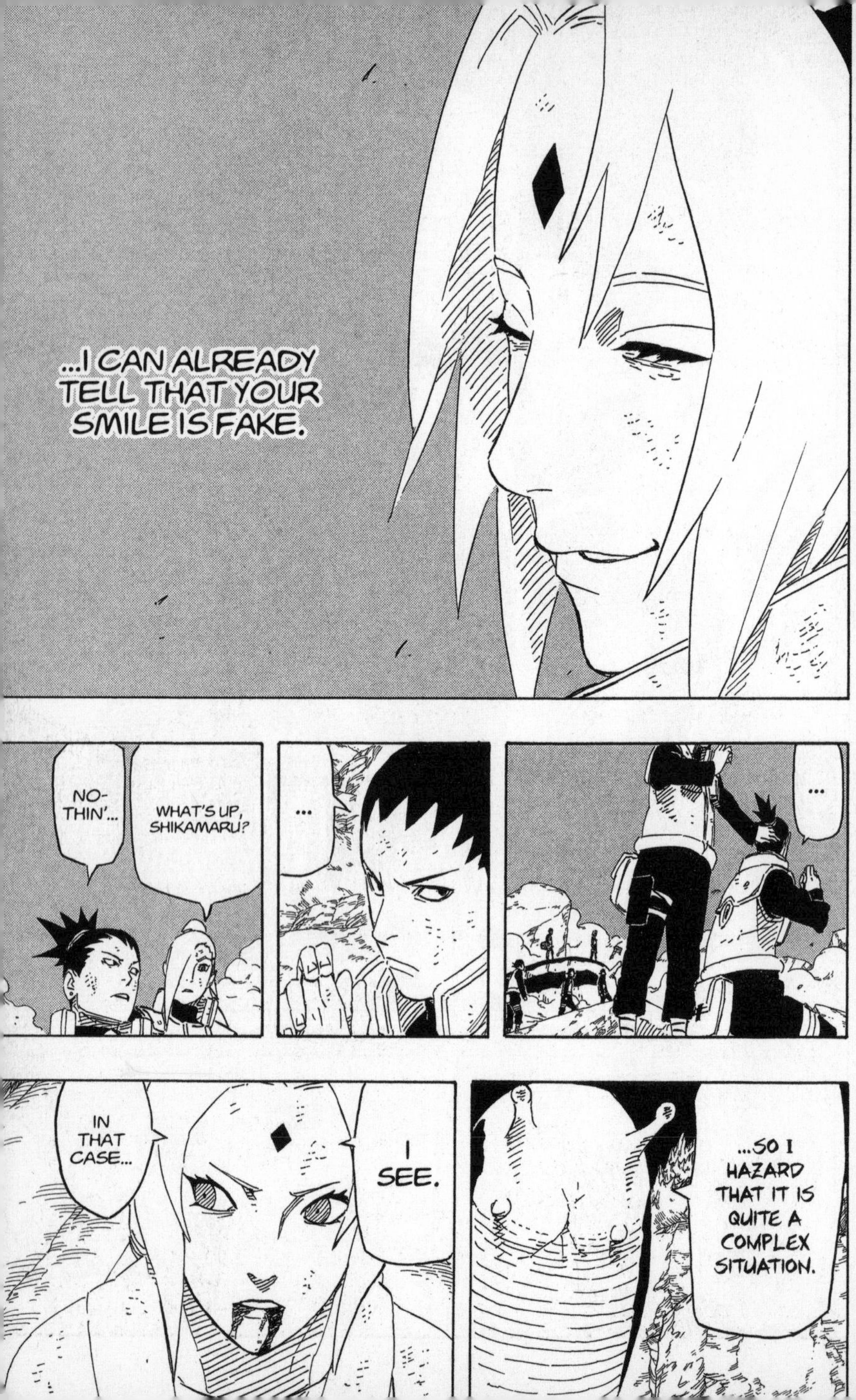
...I CAN ALREADY TELL THAT YOUR SMILE IS FAKE.
...
...
WHAT'S UP, SHIKAMARU?
NO-THIN'...
...SO I HAZARD THAT IT IS QUITE A COMPLEX SITUATION.
I SEE.
IN THAT CASE...

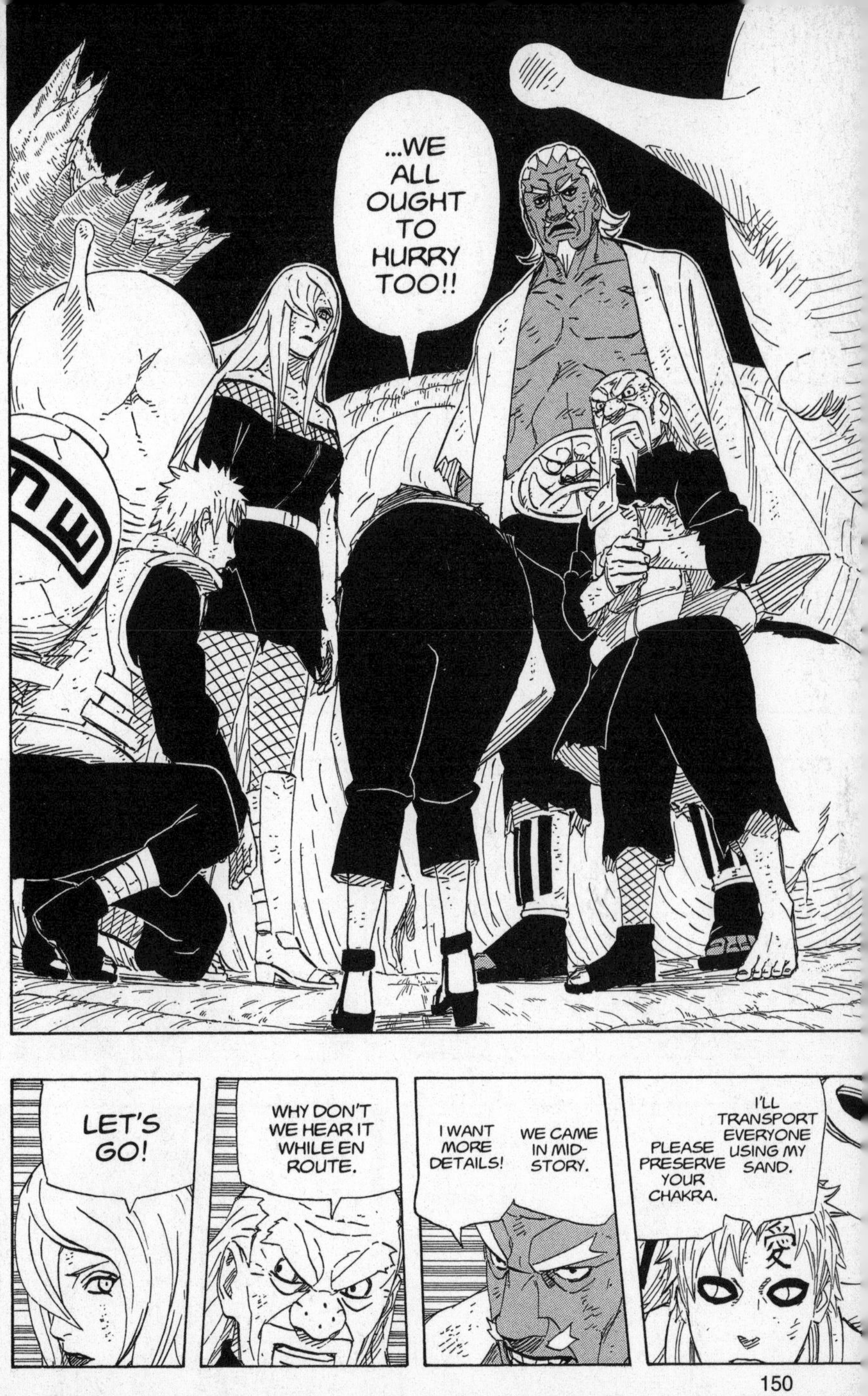
...WE ALL OUGHT TO HURRY TOO!!
I'LL TRANSPORT EVERYONE USING MY SAND.
PLEASE PRESERVE YOUR CHAKRA.
WE CAME IN MID-STORY.
I WANT MORE DETAILS!
WHY DON'T WE HEAR IT WHILE EN ROUTE.
LET'S GO!

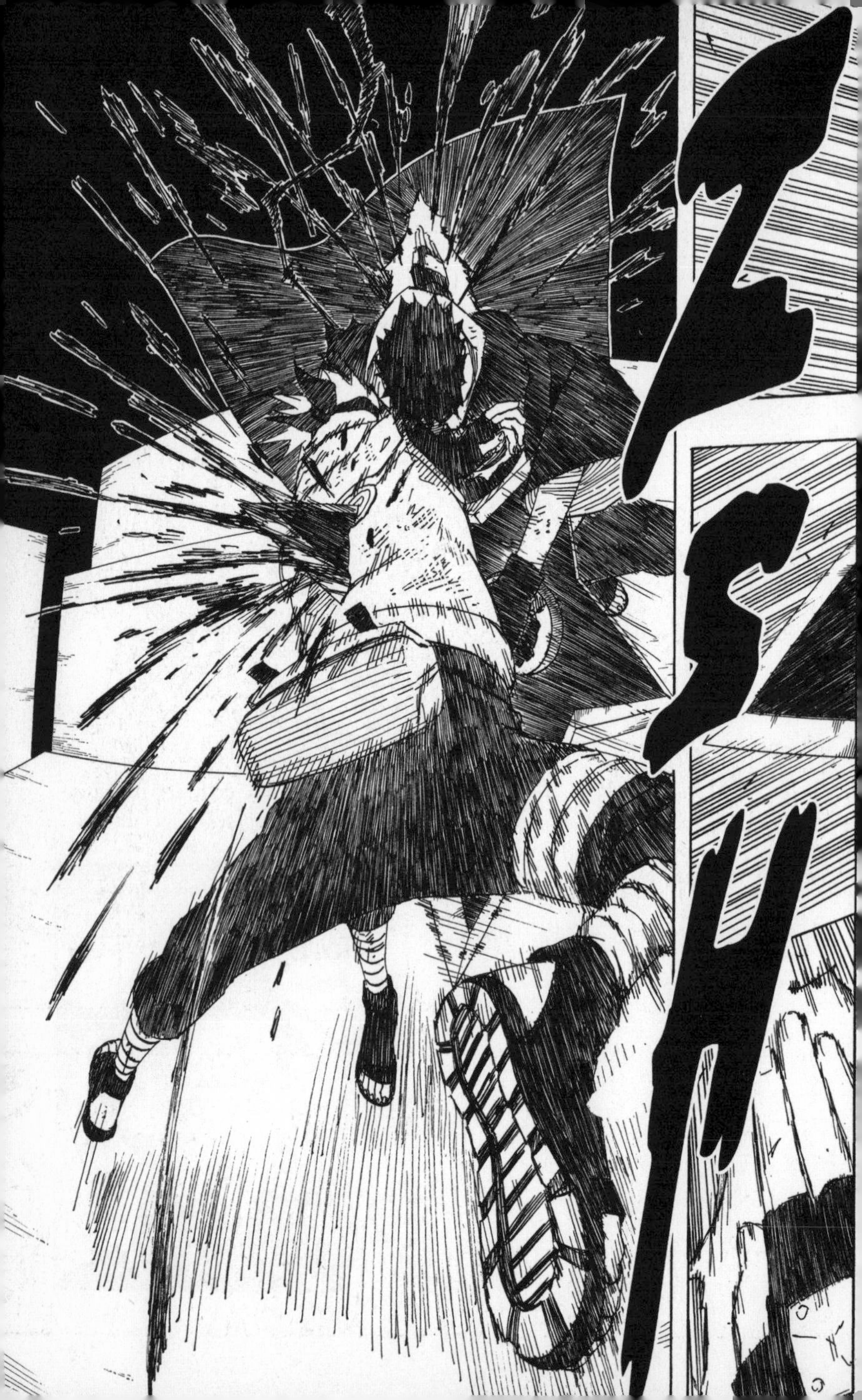

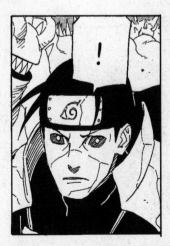

Number 636: The Current Obito

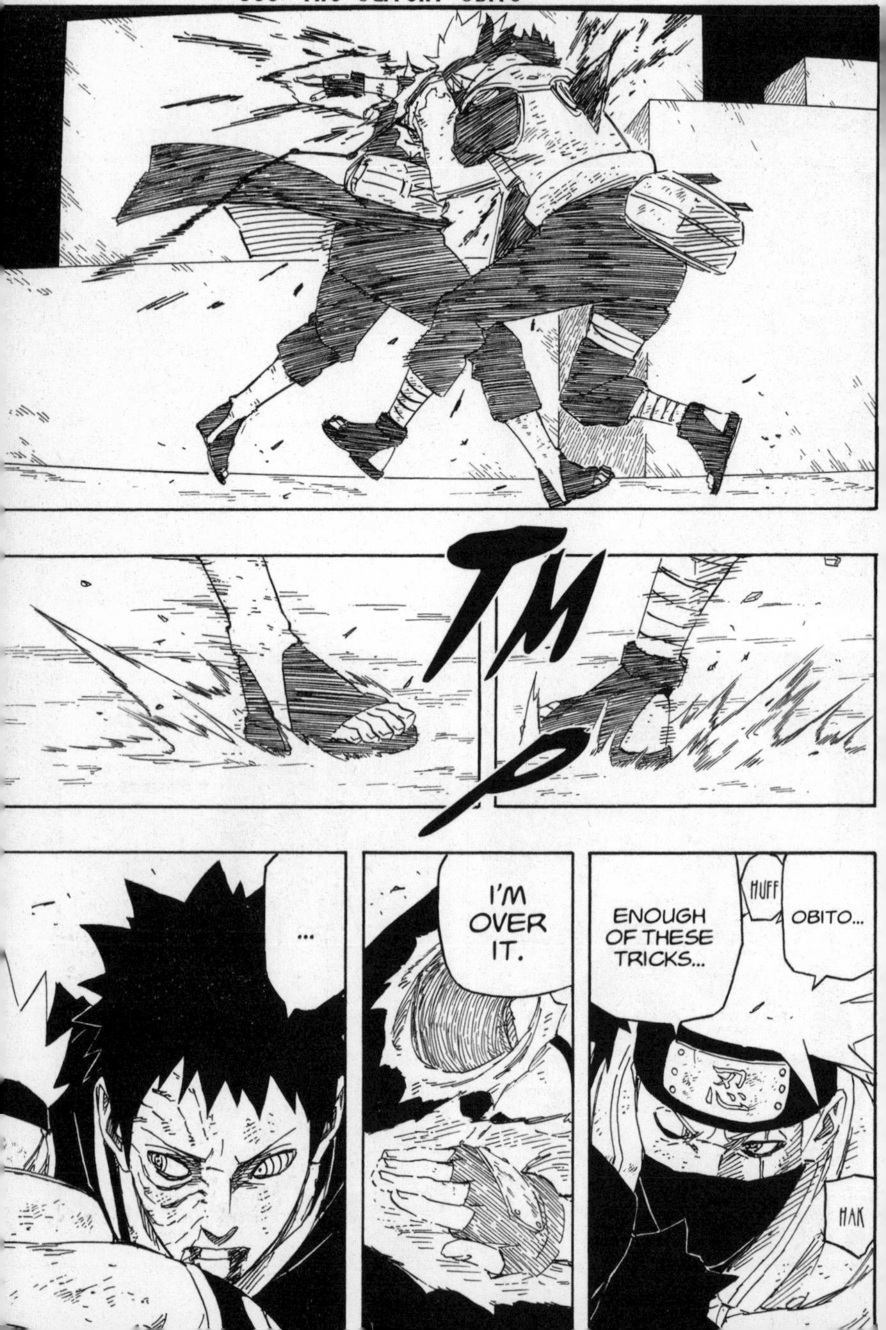
TMP
HUFF
OBITO...
ENOUGH OF THESE TRICKS...
HAK
I'M OVER IT.
...

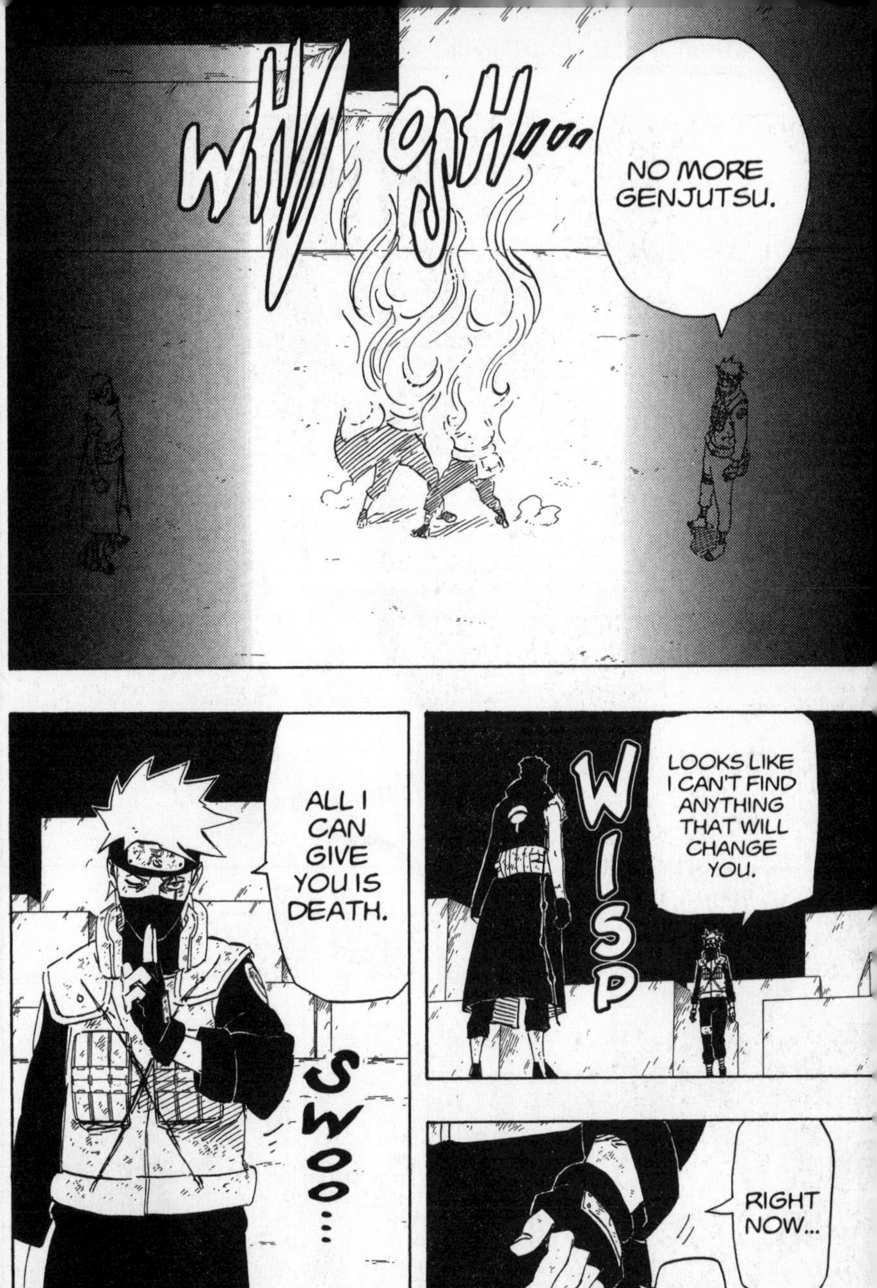
WHOOSH...
NO MORE GENJUTSU.
WISP
LOOKS LIKE I CAN'T FIND ANYTHING THAT WILL CHANGE YOU.
RIGHT NOW...
FSH
ALL I CAN GIVE YOU IS DEATH.
SWOO...

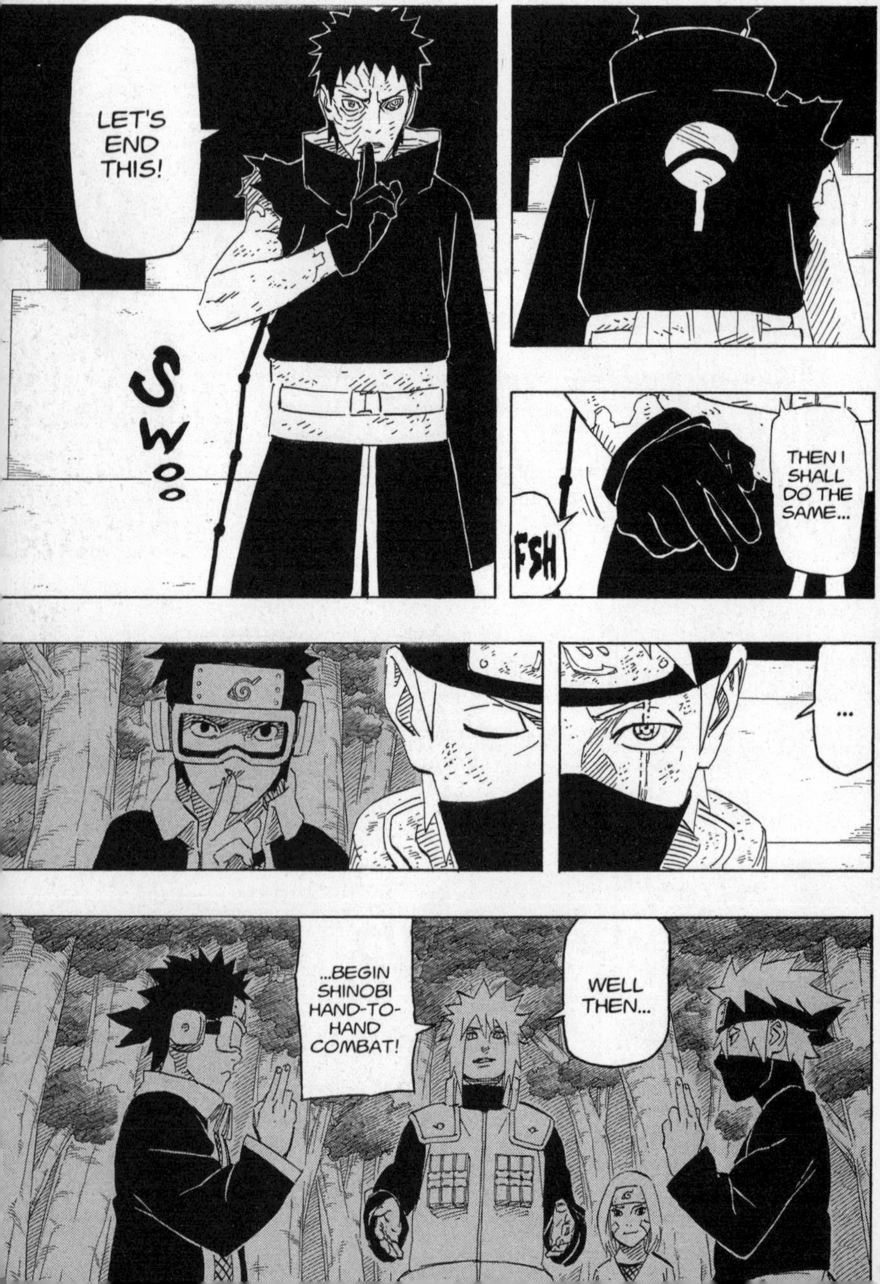
THEN I SHALL DO THE SAME...
FSH
LET'S END THIS!
SWOOO
...
WELL THEN...
...BEGIN SHINOBI HAND-TO-HAND COMBAT!

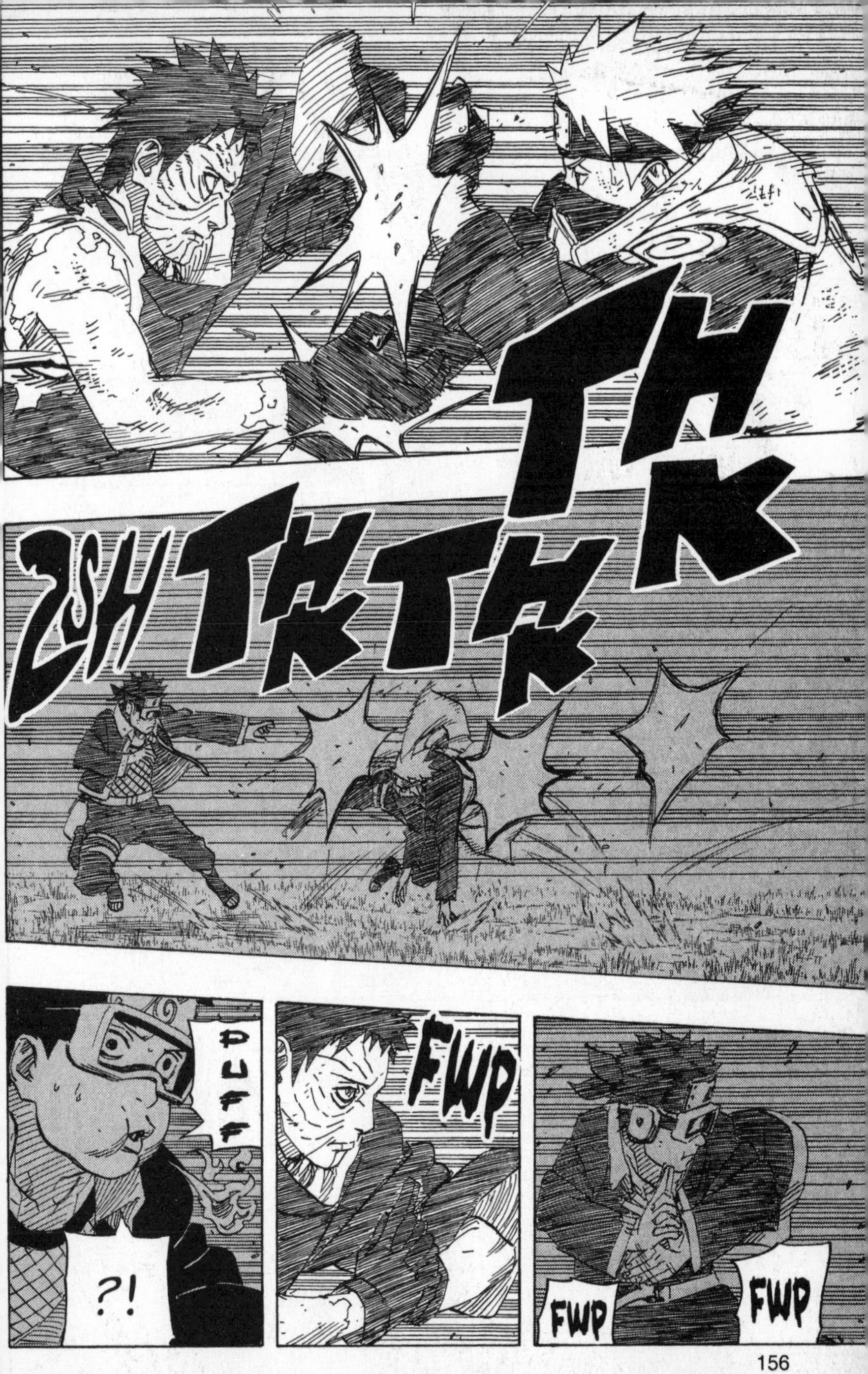
TK
TK
TK
TK
ZSH
FWP
PUFF
?!
FWP
FWP

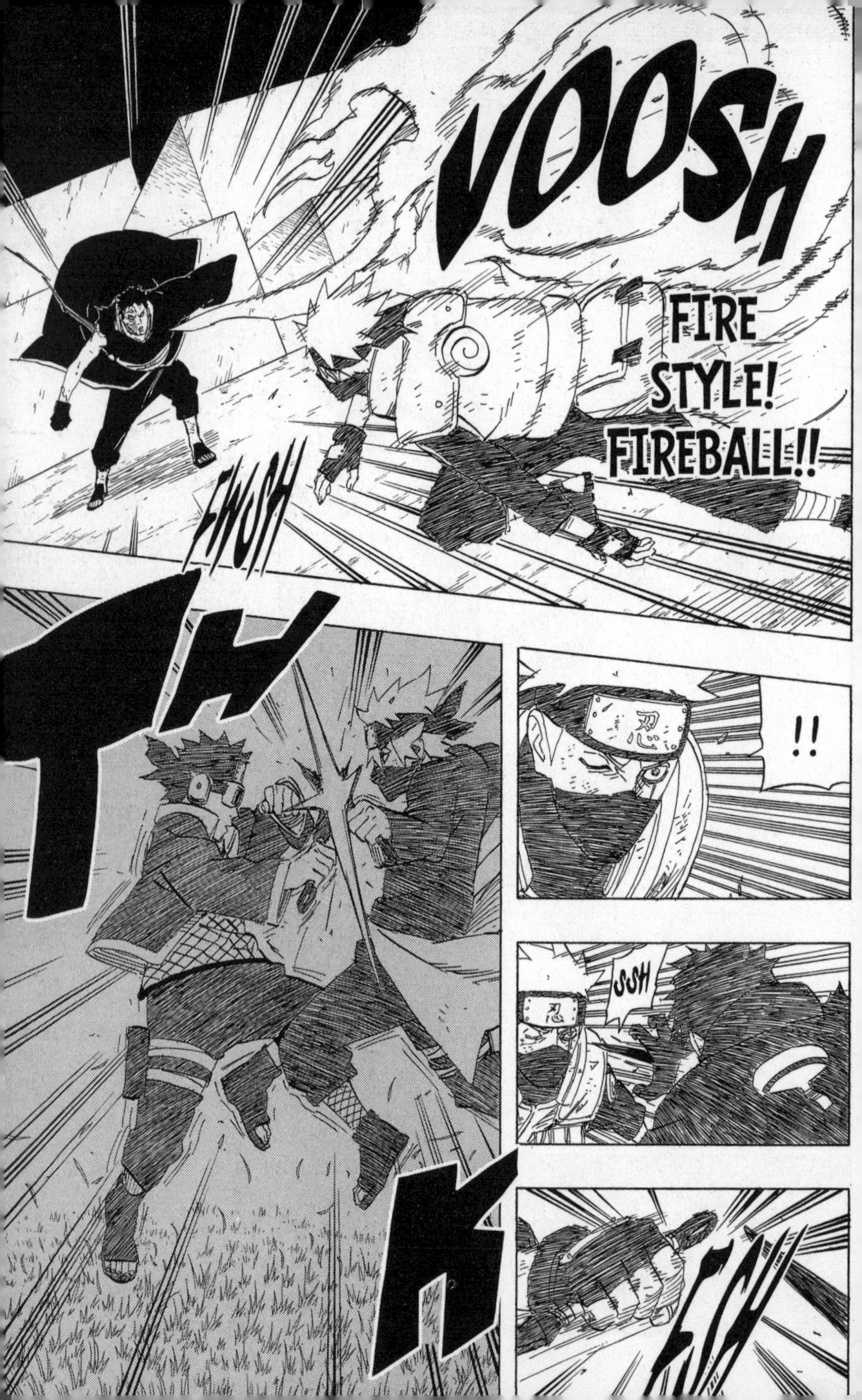
VOOSH
FIRE STYLE! FIREBALL!!
FWOSH
!!
SSH

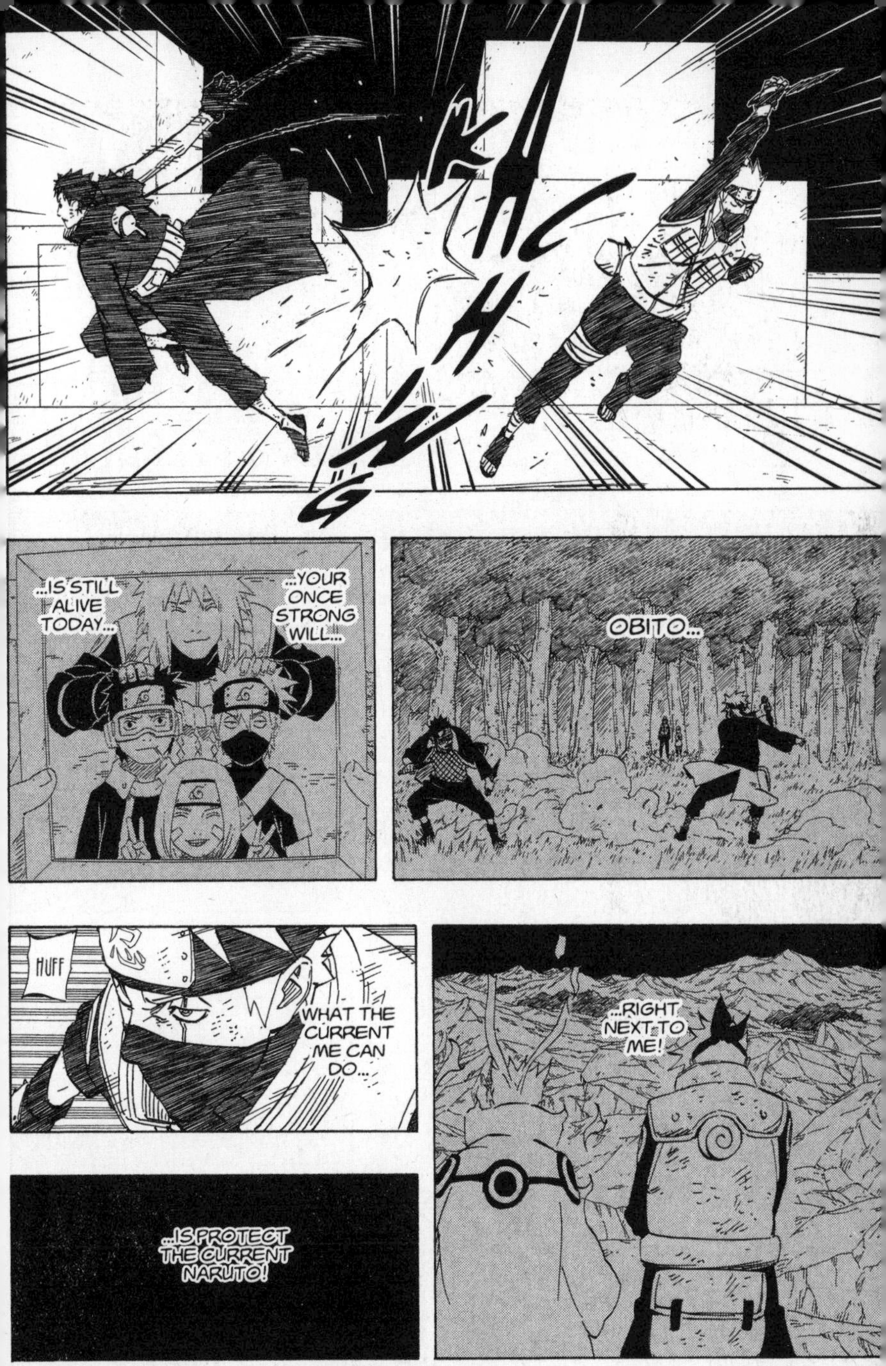
KACHINNG
OBITO...
...YOUR ONCE STRONG WILL...
...IS STILL ALIVE TODAY...
...RIGHT NEXT TO ME!
HUFF
WHAT THE CURRENT ME CAN DO...
...IS PROTECT THE CURRENT NARUTO!

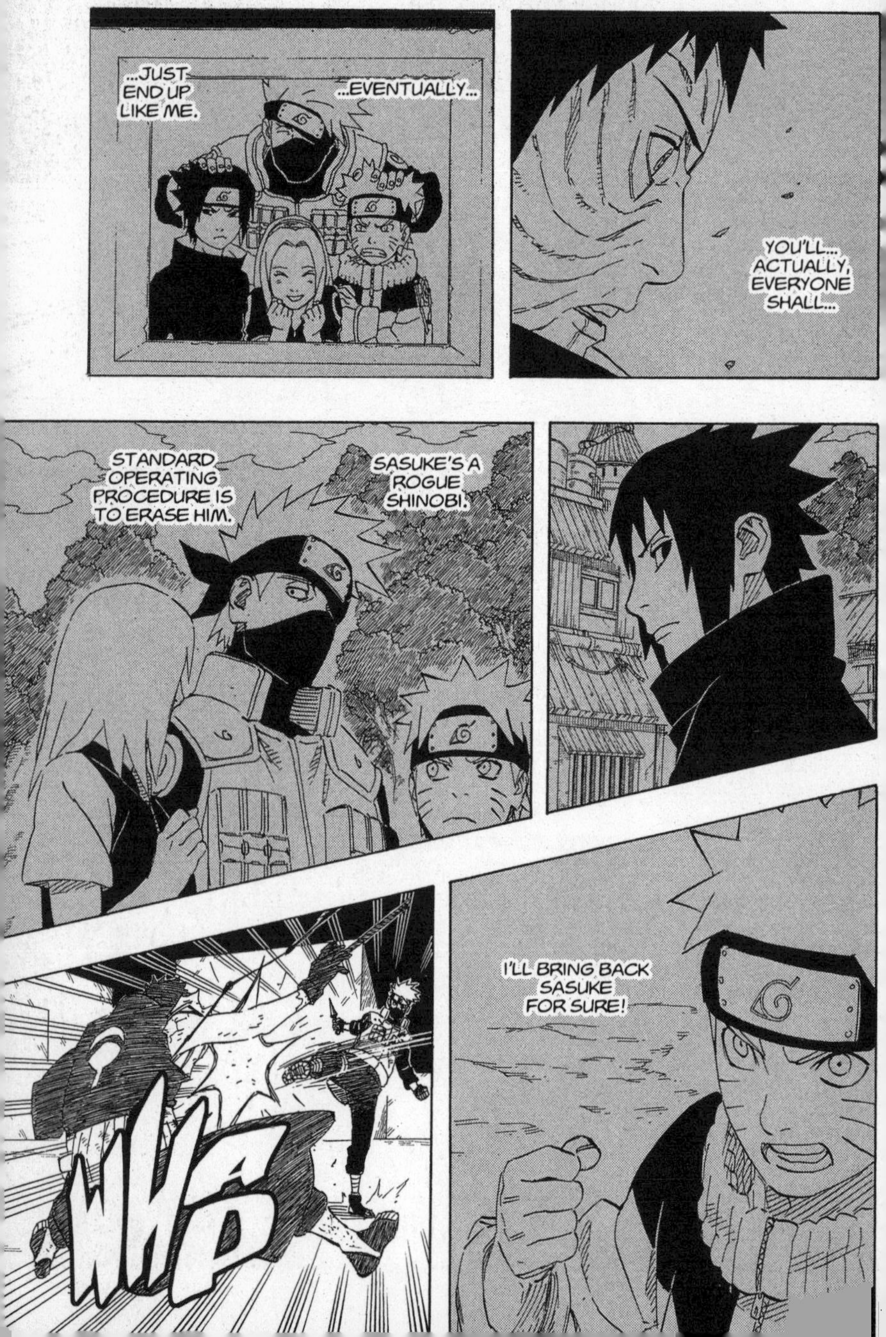
YOU'LL... ACTUALLY, EVERYONE SHALL...
...EVENTUALLY...
...JUST END UP LIKE ME.
SASUKE'S A ROGUE SHINOBI.
STANDARD OPERATING PROCEDURE IS TO ERASE HIM.
I'LL BRING BACK SASUKE FOR SURE!
WHAP

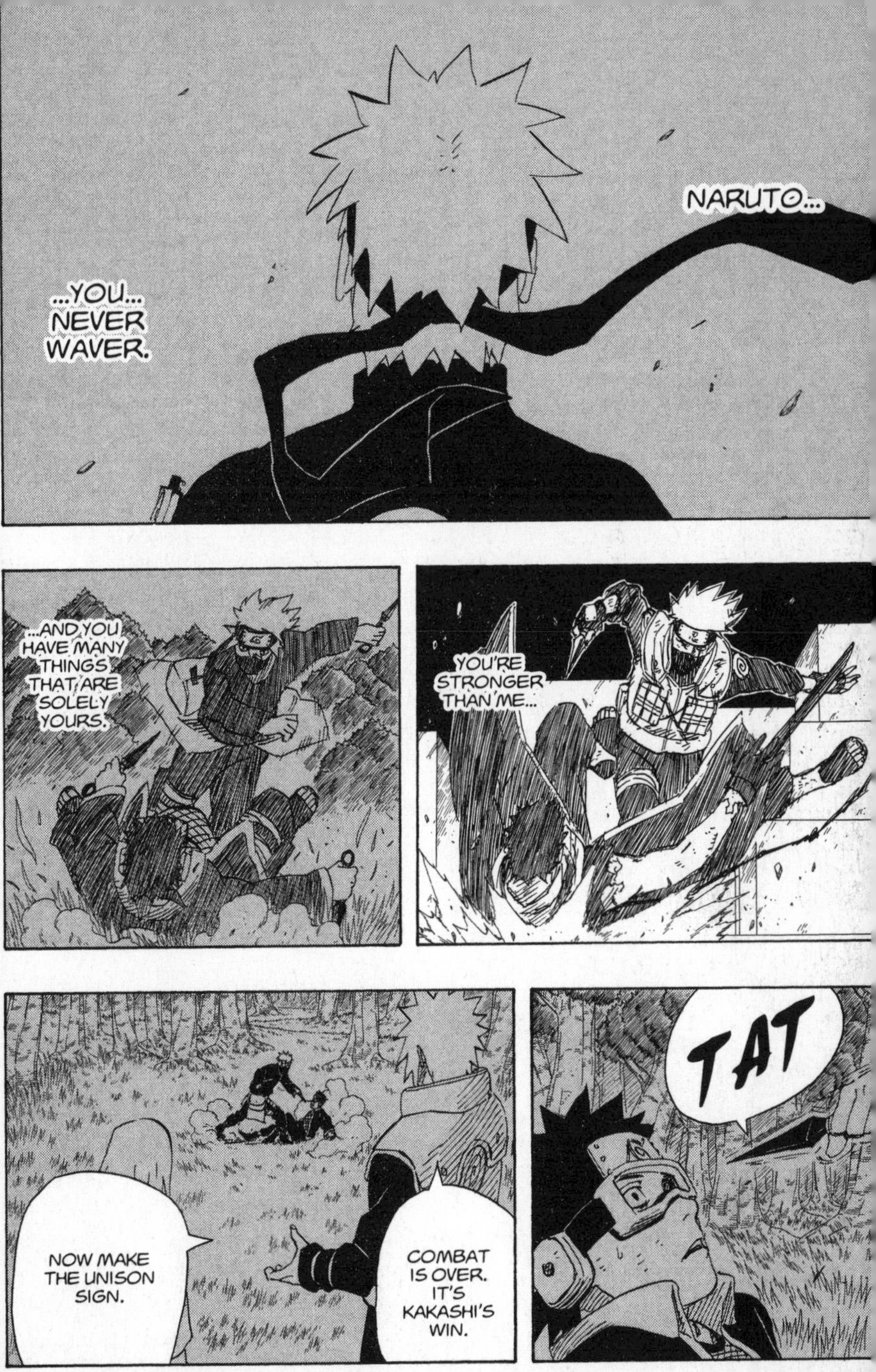
NARUTO...
...YOU... NEVER WAVER.
YOU'RE STRONGER THAN ME...
...AND YOU HAVE MANY THINGS THAT ARE SOLELY YOURS.
TAT
COMBAT IS OVER. IT'S KAKASHI'S WIN.
NOW MAKE THE UNISON SIGN.

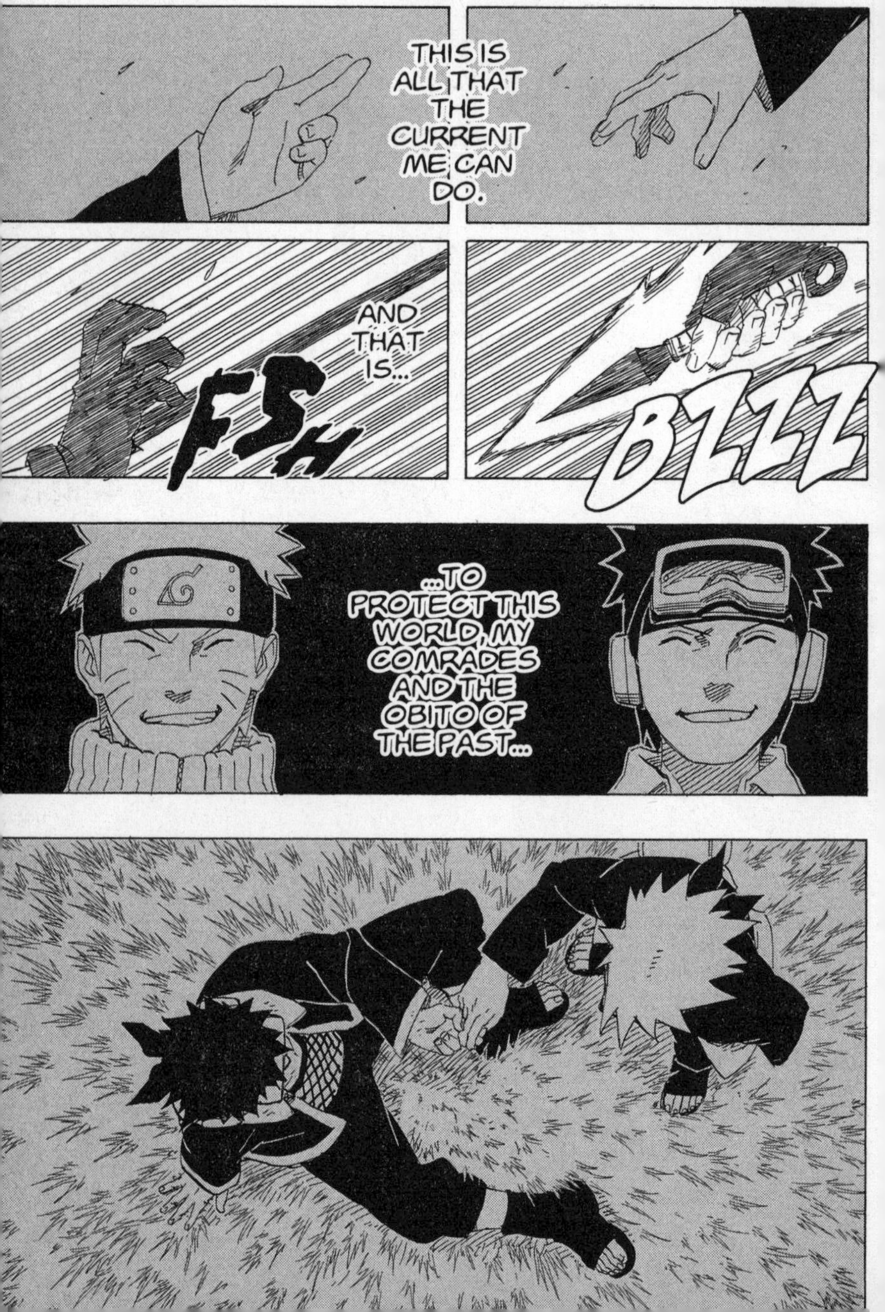
THIS IS ALL THAT THE CURRENT ME CAN DO.
BZZZ
AND THAT IS...
FSH
...TO PROTECT THIS WORLD, MY COMRADES AND THE OBITO OF THE PAST...

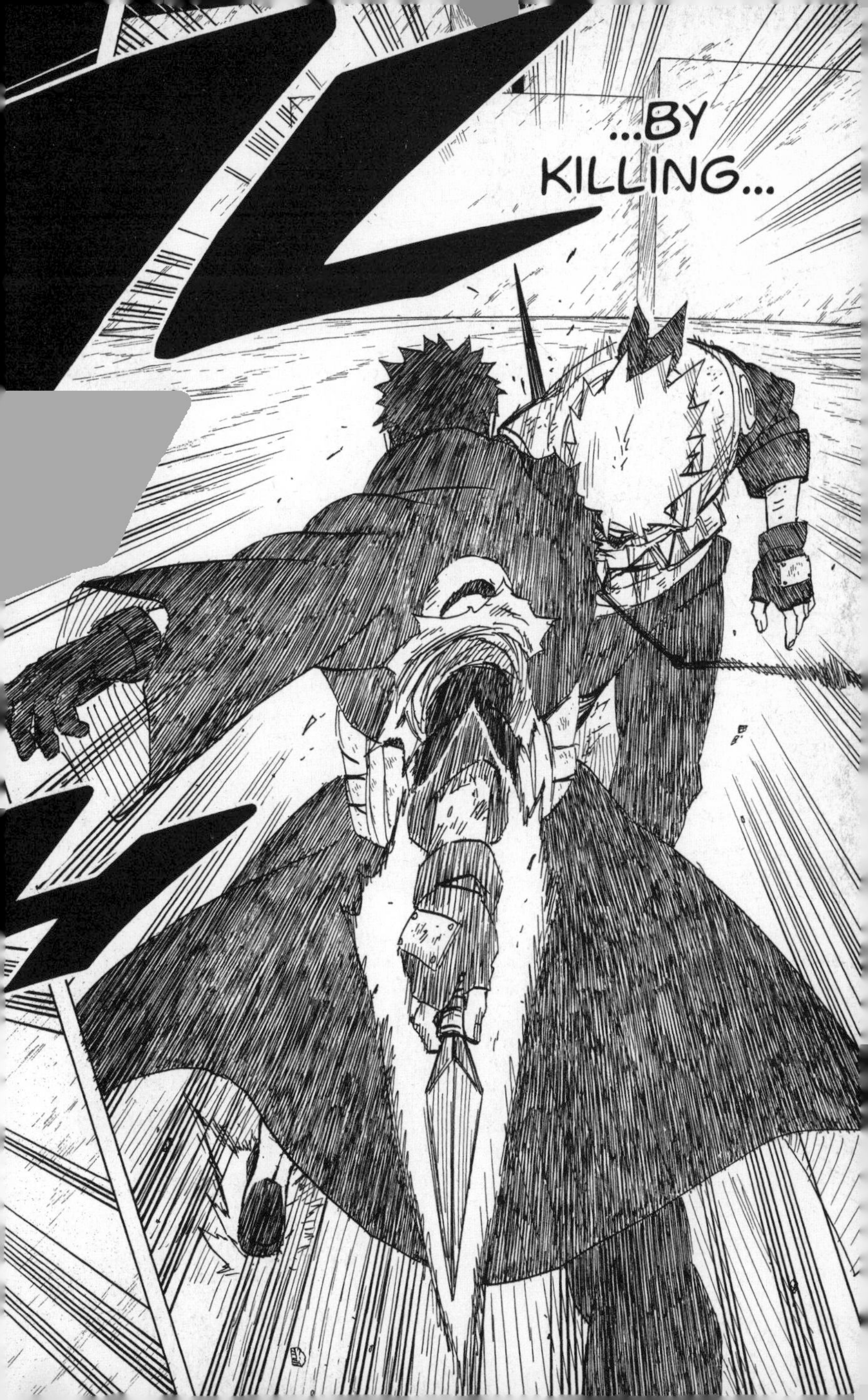
...BY KILLING...

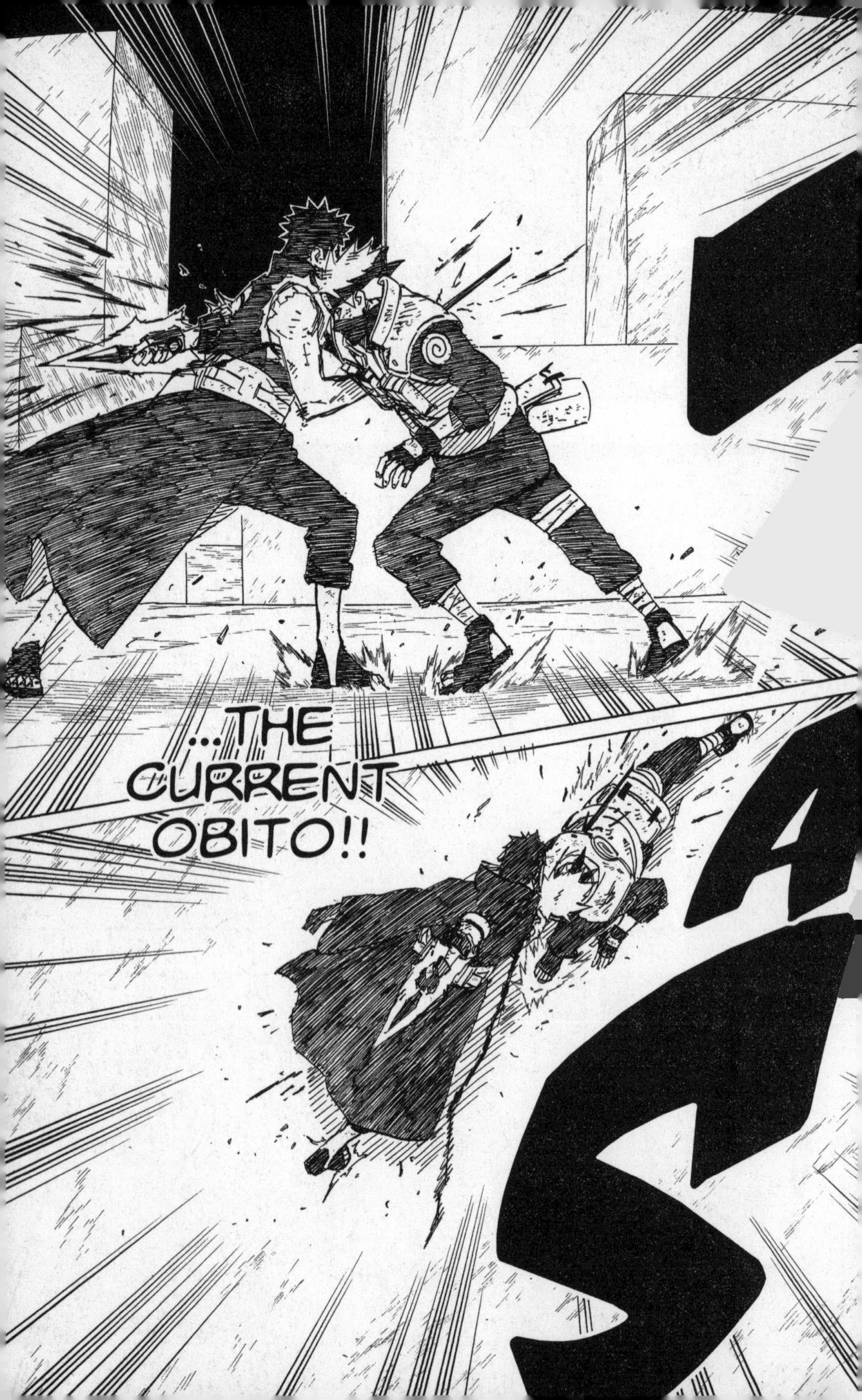
...THE CURRENT OBITO!!

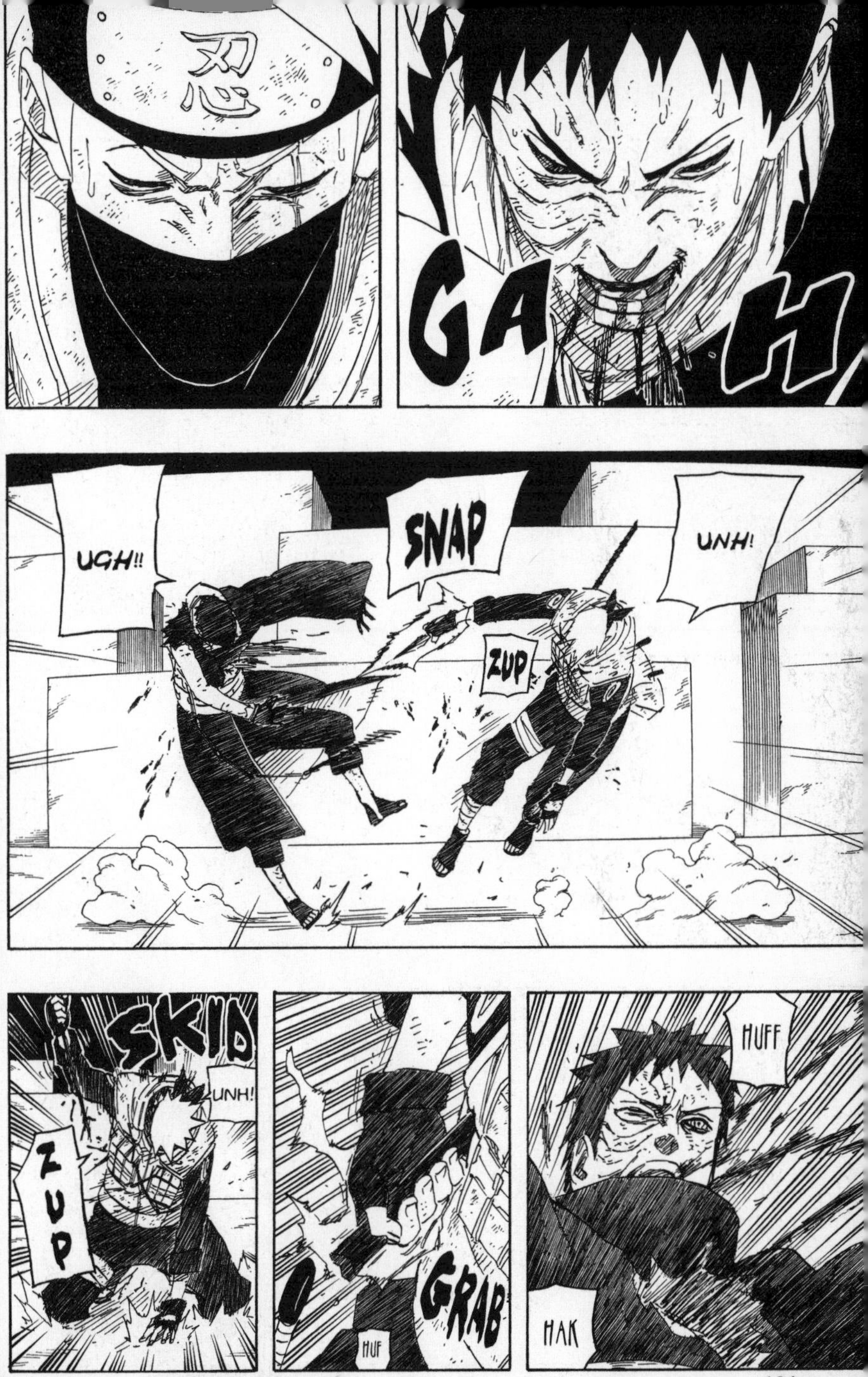
GA
H
UNH!
SNAP
ZUP
UGH!!
HUFF
HAK
GRAB
HUF
SKID
UNH!
ZUP

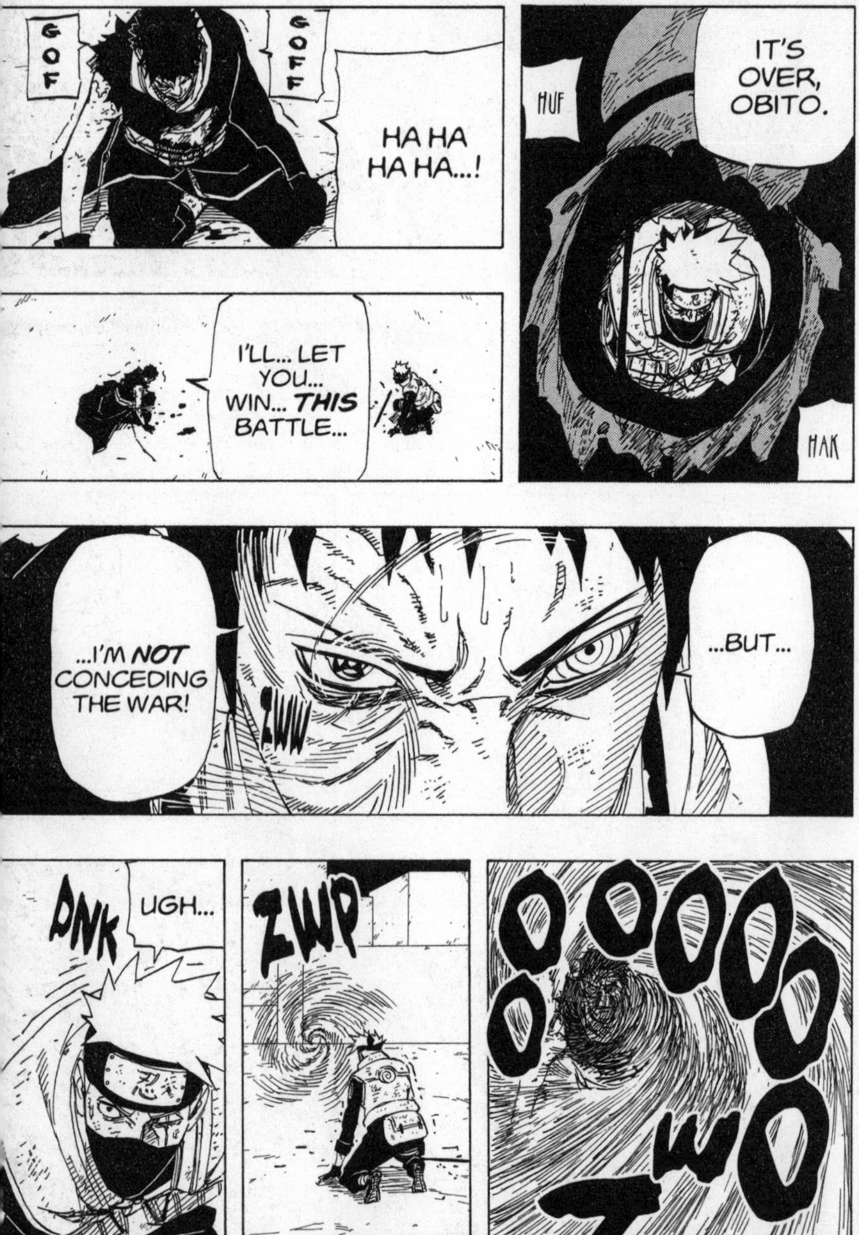

IT'S OVER, OBITO.
HUF
HAK
GOF
GOFF
HA HA HA HA...!
I'LL... LET YOU... WIN... *THIS* BATTLE...
...BUT...
...I'M *NOT* CONCEDING THE WAR!
ZWW
ZWOOOOOOOOOO
ZWP
DNK
UGH...

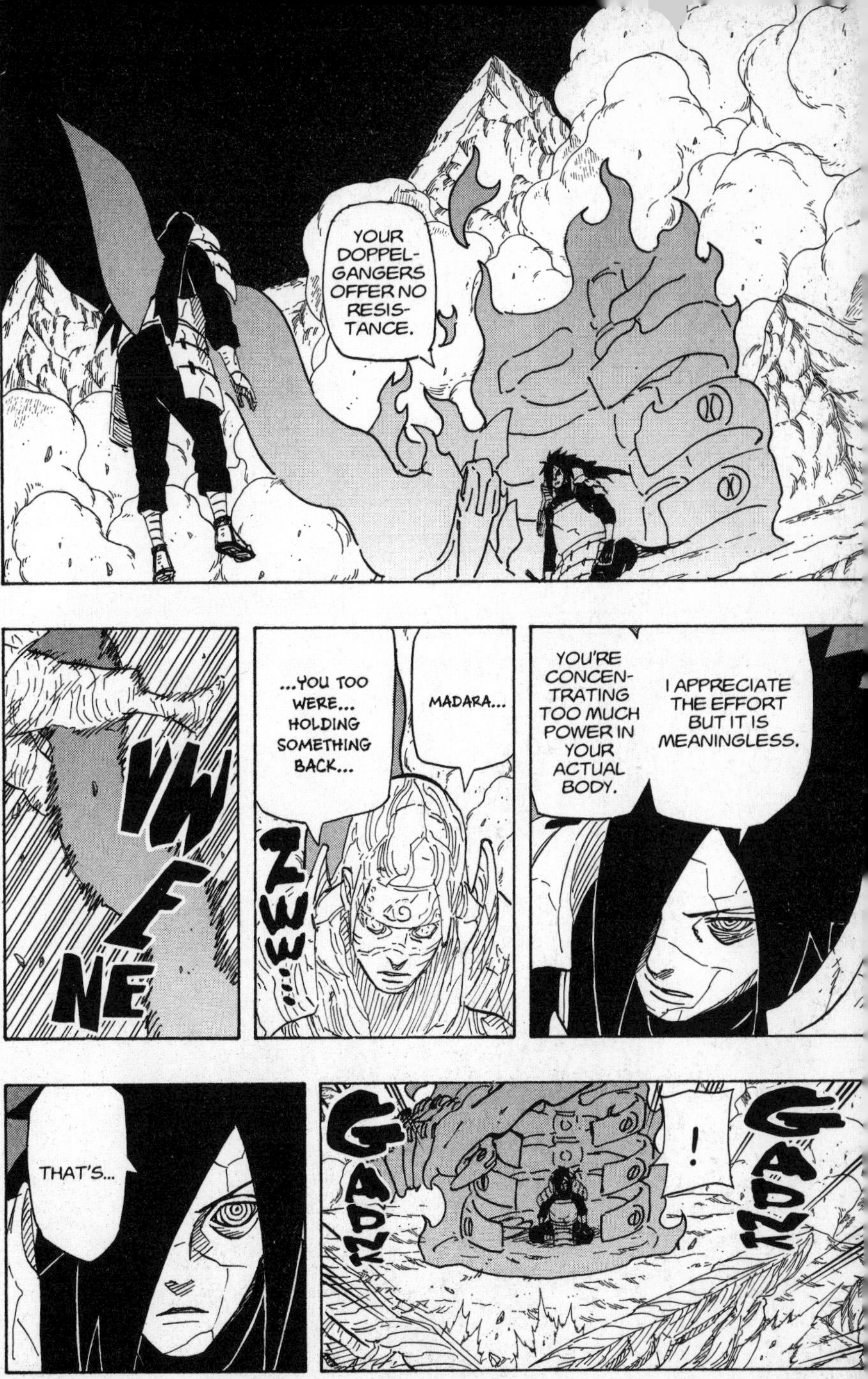
YOUR DOPPEL-GANGERS OFFER NO RESIS-TANCE.
I APPRECIATE THE EFFORT BUT IT IS MEANINGLESS.
YOU'RE CONCEN-TRATING TOO MUCH POWER IN YOUR ACTUAL BODY.
MADARA...
...YOU TOO WERE... HOLDING SOMETHING BACK...
ZWWW...
VWFNE
!
GADN
GADN
THAT'S...

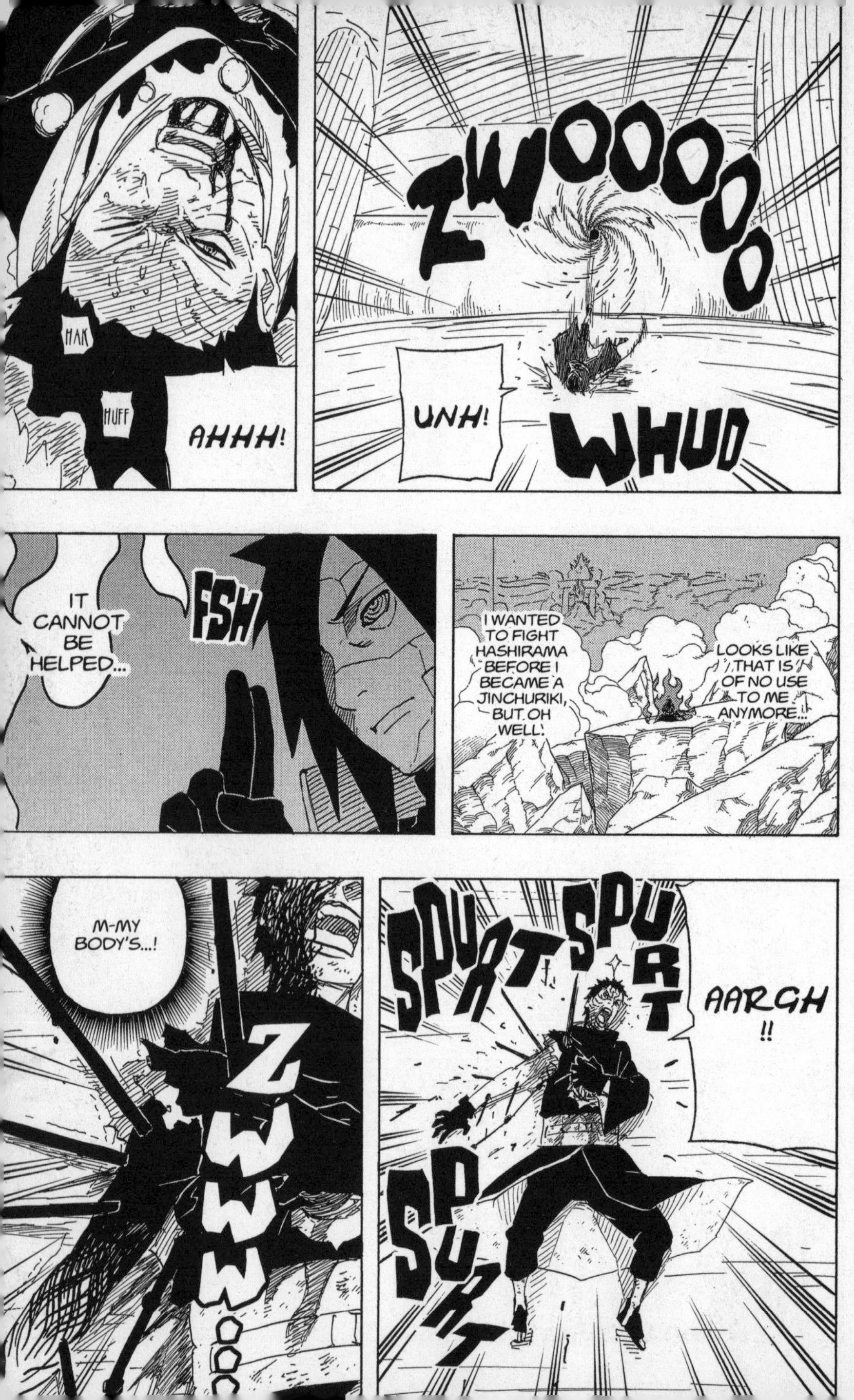
ZWOOOOO
UNH!
WHUD
HAK
HUFF
AHHH!
LOOKS LIKE THAT IS OF NO USE TO ME ANYMORE...
I WANTED TO FIGHT HASHIRAMA BEFORE I BECAME A JINCHURIKI, BUT OH WELL.
FSH
IT CANNOT BE HELPED...
SPURT
SPURT
AARGH!!
SPURT
M-MY BODY'S...!
ZWWWOOO

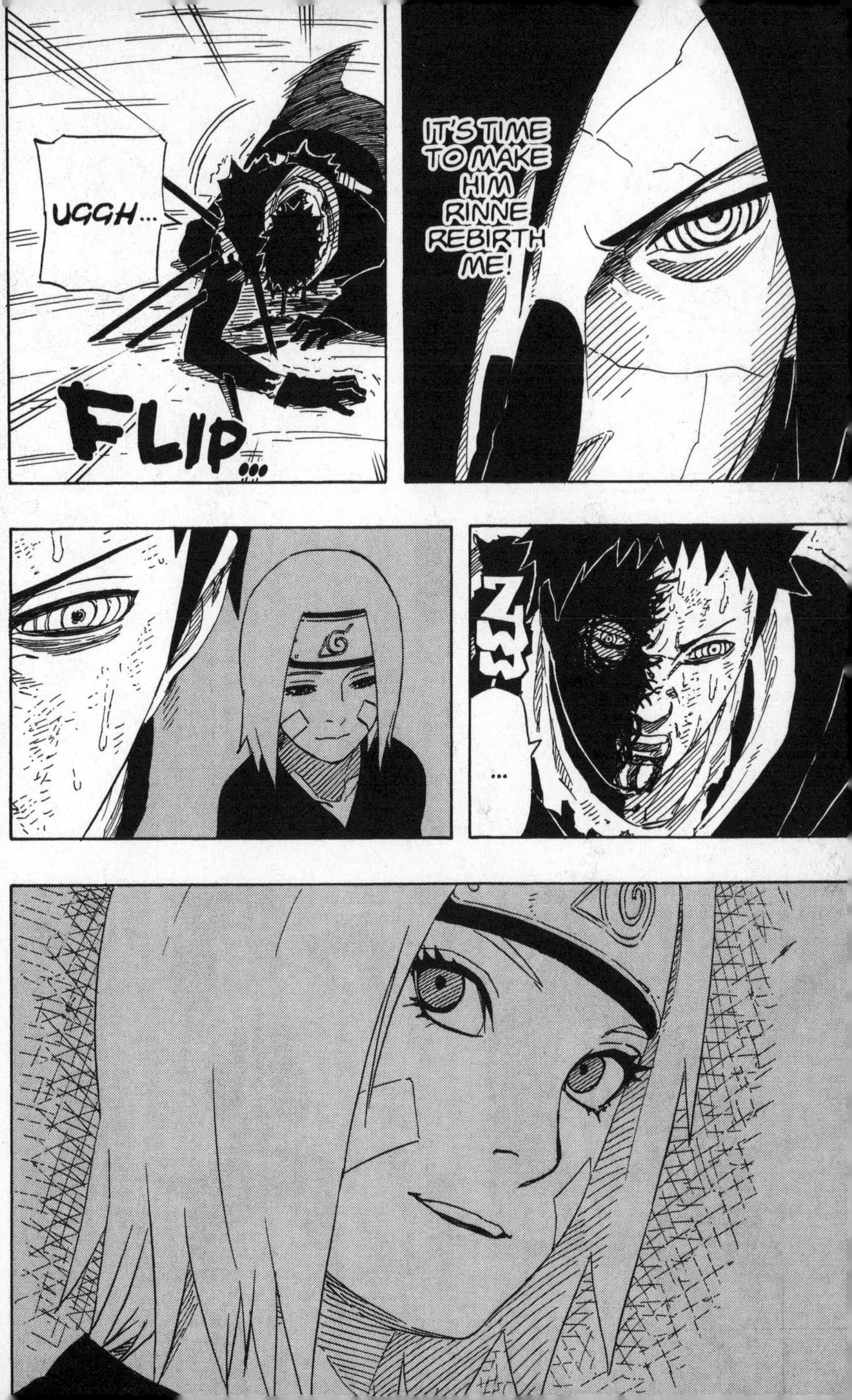
IT'S TIME TO MAKE HIM RINNE REBIRTH ME!
UGGH...
FLIP...
ZWW
...

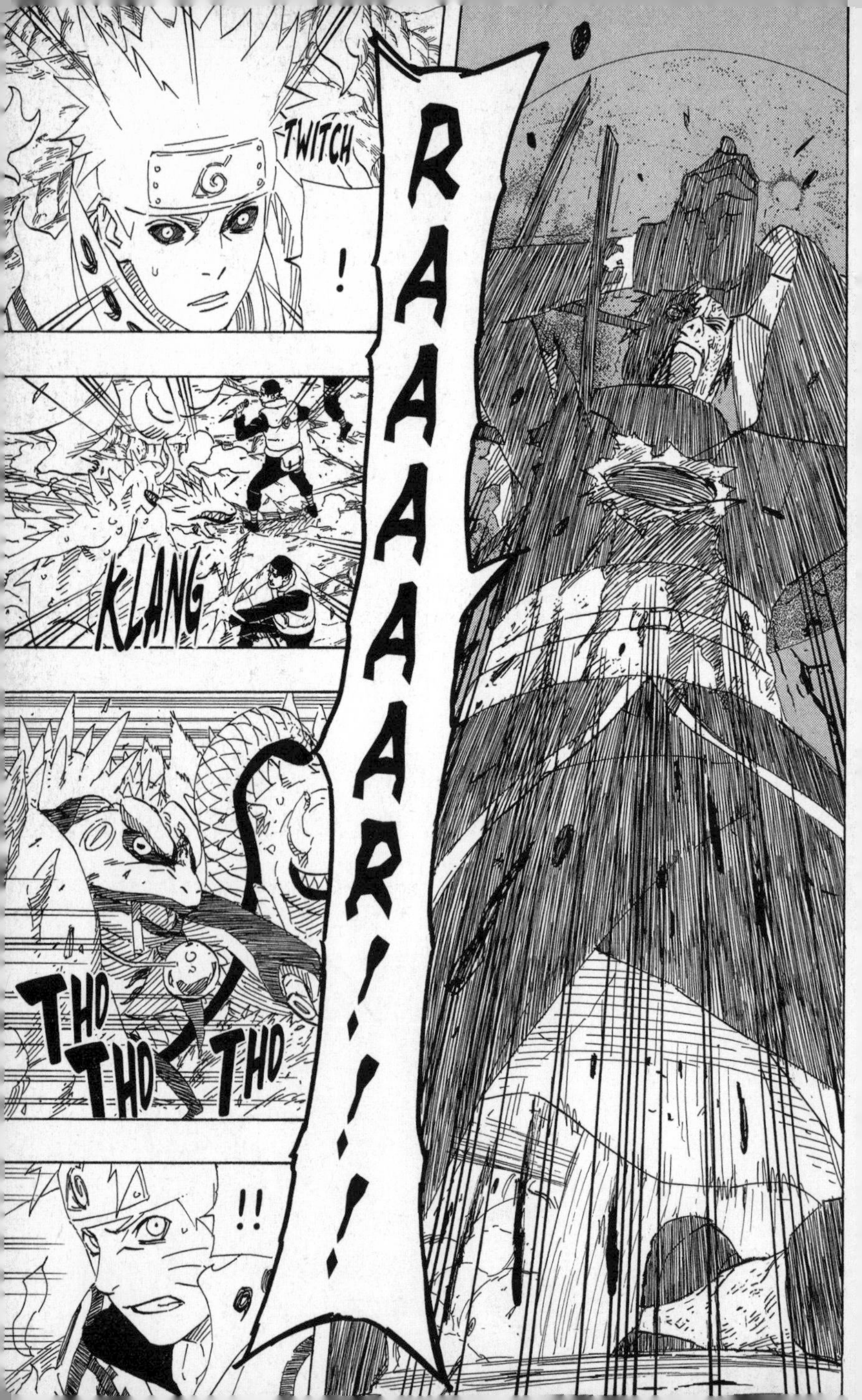
RAAAAAR!!!!
TWITCH
!
KLANG
THO THO THO
!!

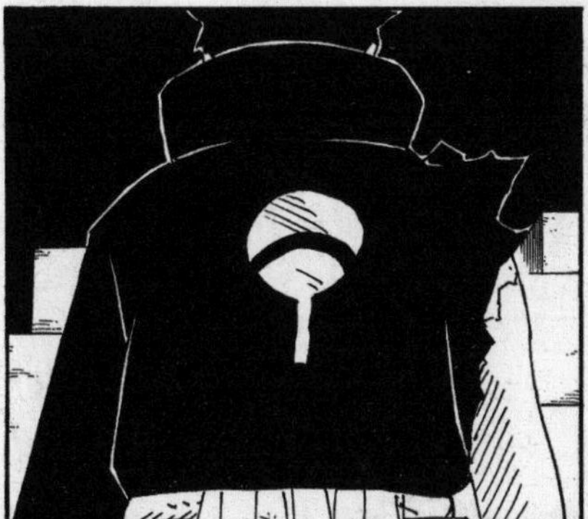

Number 637: The Ten Tails Jinchuriki

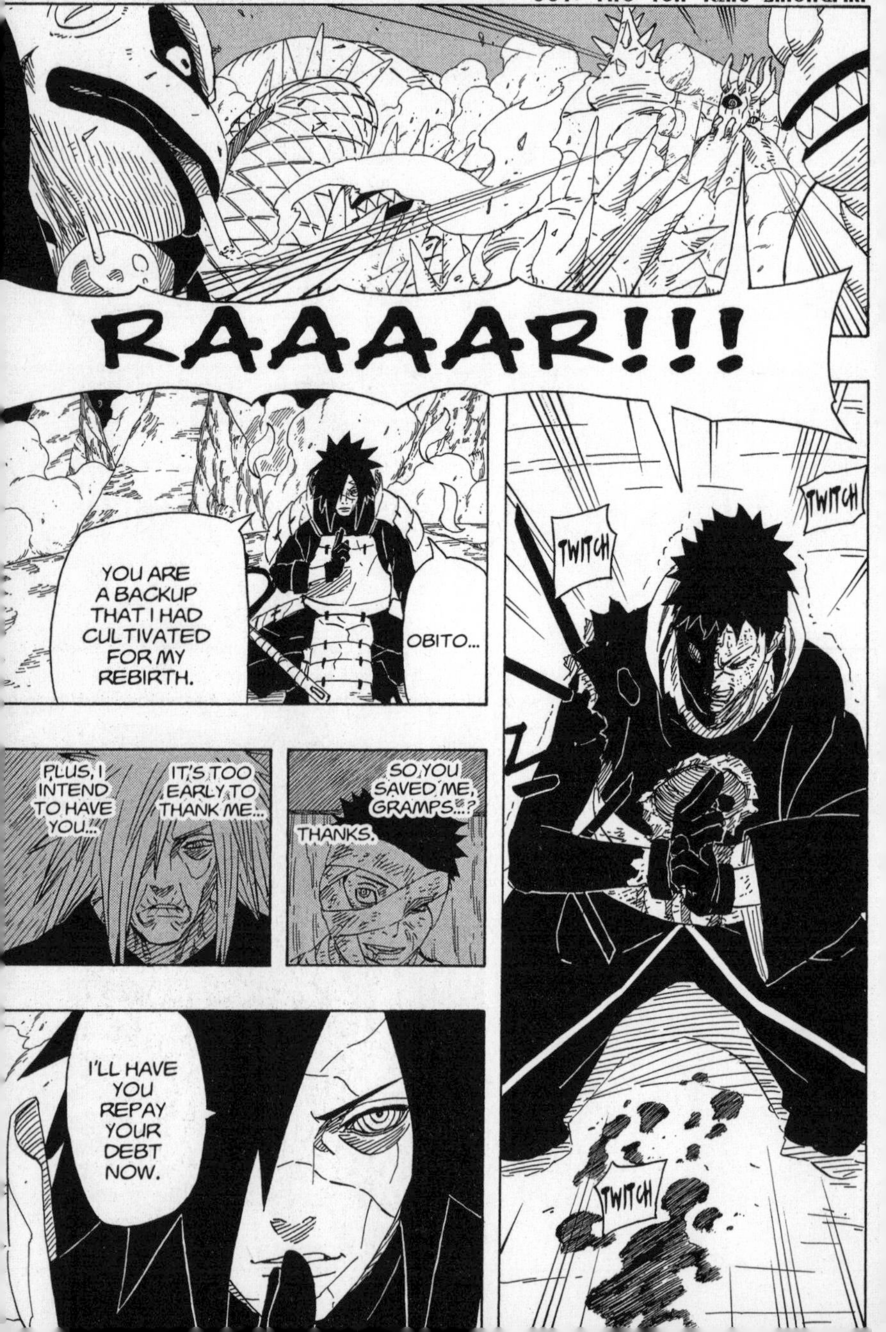
RAAAAR!!!
TWITCH
TWITCH
TWITCH
OBITO...
YOU ARE A BACKUP THAT I HAD CULTIVATED FOR MY REBIRTH.
SO YOU SAVED ME, GRAMPS...?
THANKS.
IT'S TOO EARLY TO THANK ME...
PLUS, I INTEND TO HAVE YOU...
I'LL HAVE YOU REPAY YOUR DEBT NOW.

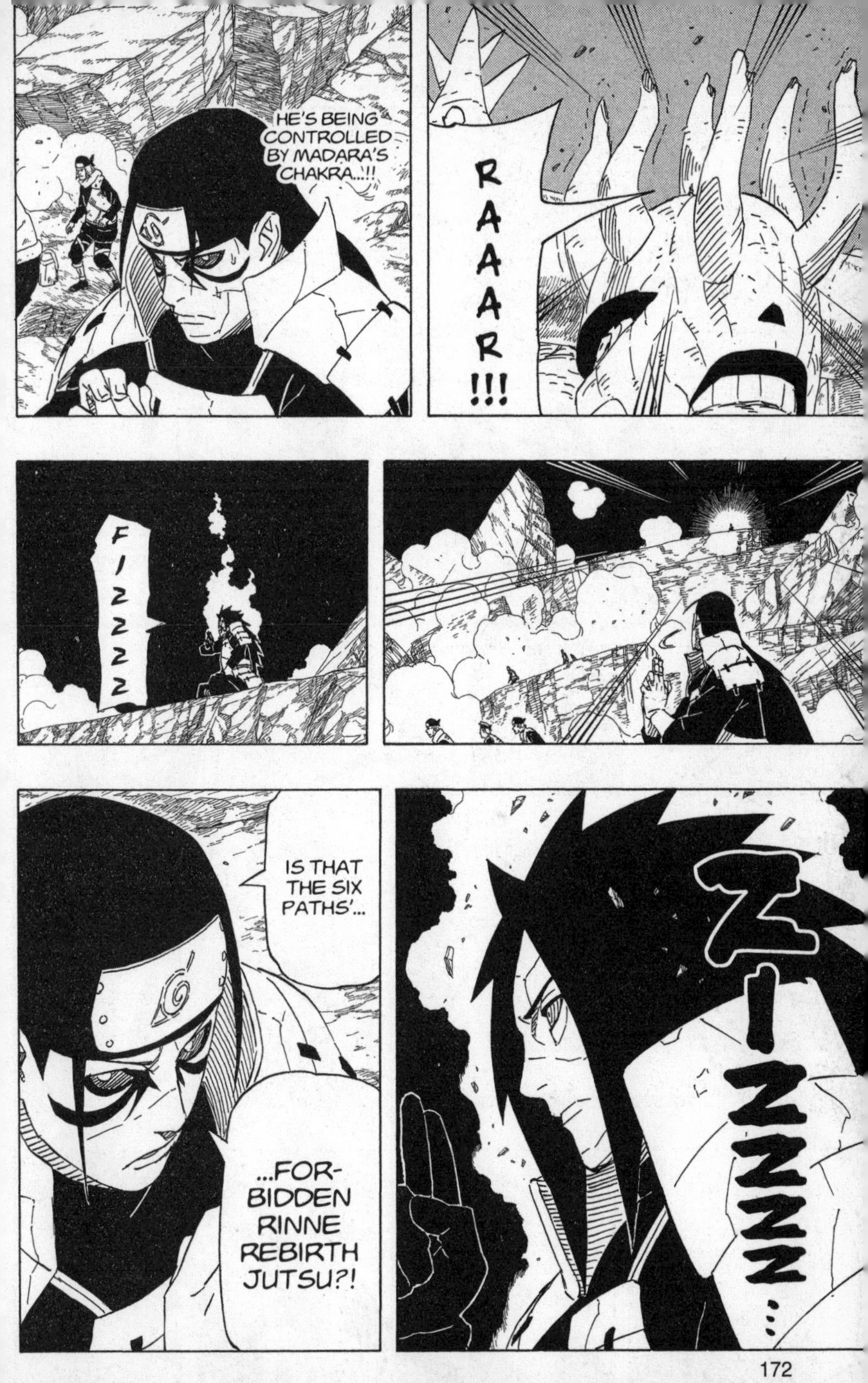
RAAAR!!!
HE'S BEING CONTROLLED BY MADARA'S CHAKRA...!!
FIZZZZ
Z-ZZZZ...
IS THAT THE SIX PATHS'...
...FOR-BIDDEN RINNE REBIRTH JUTSU?!

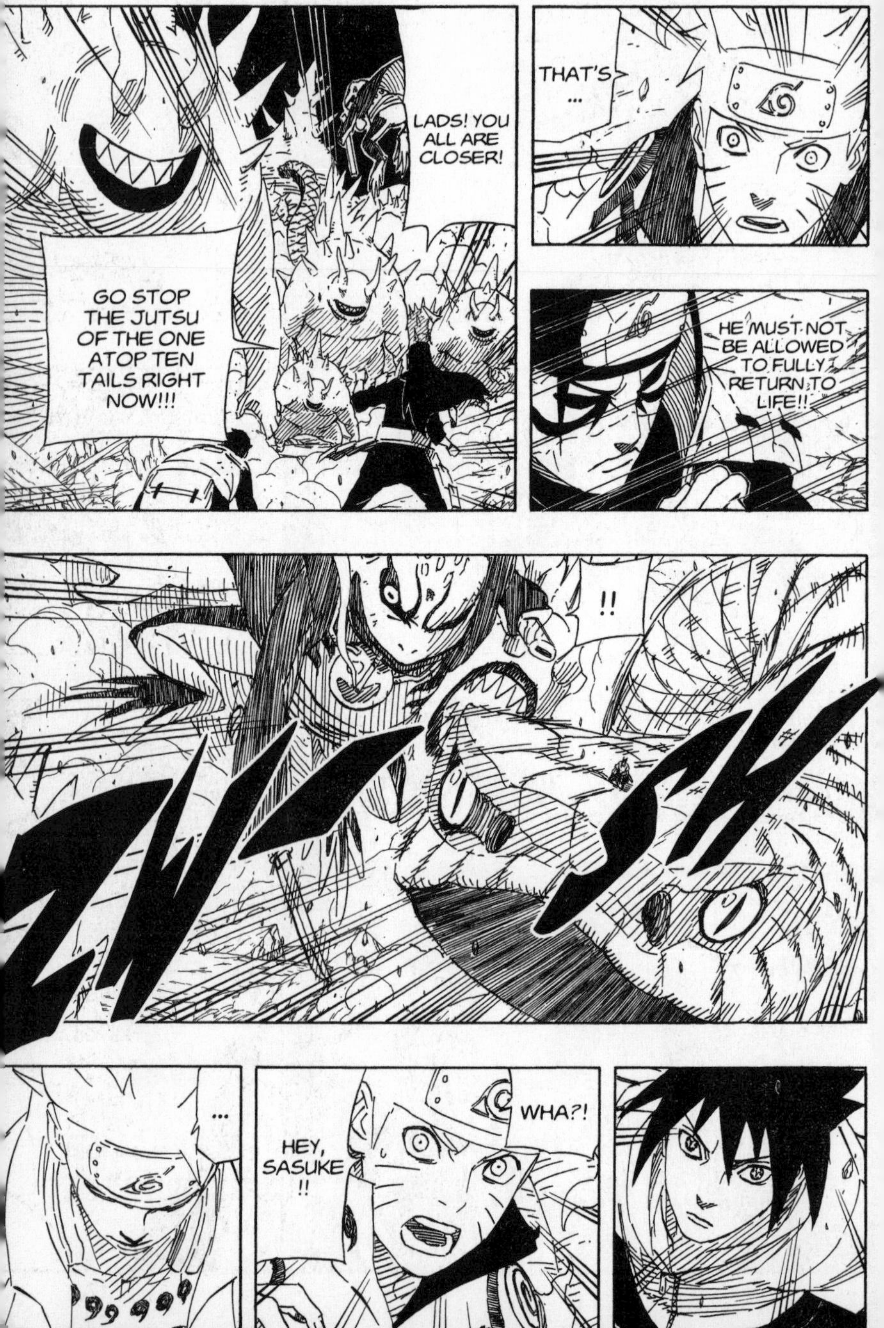
THAT'S ...
HE MUST NOT BE ALLOWED TO FULLY RETURN TO LIFE!!
LADS! YOU ALL ARE CLOSER!
GO STOP THE JUTSU OF THE ONE ATOP TEN TAILS RIGHT NOW!!!
!!
WHA?!
HEY, SASUKE !!
...

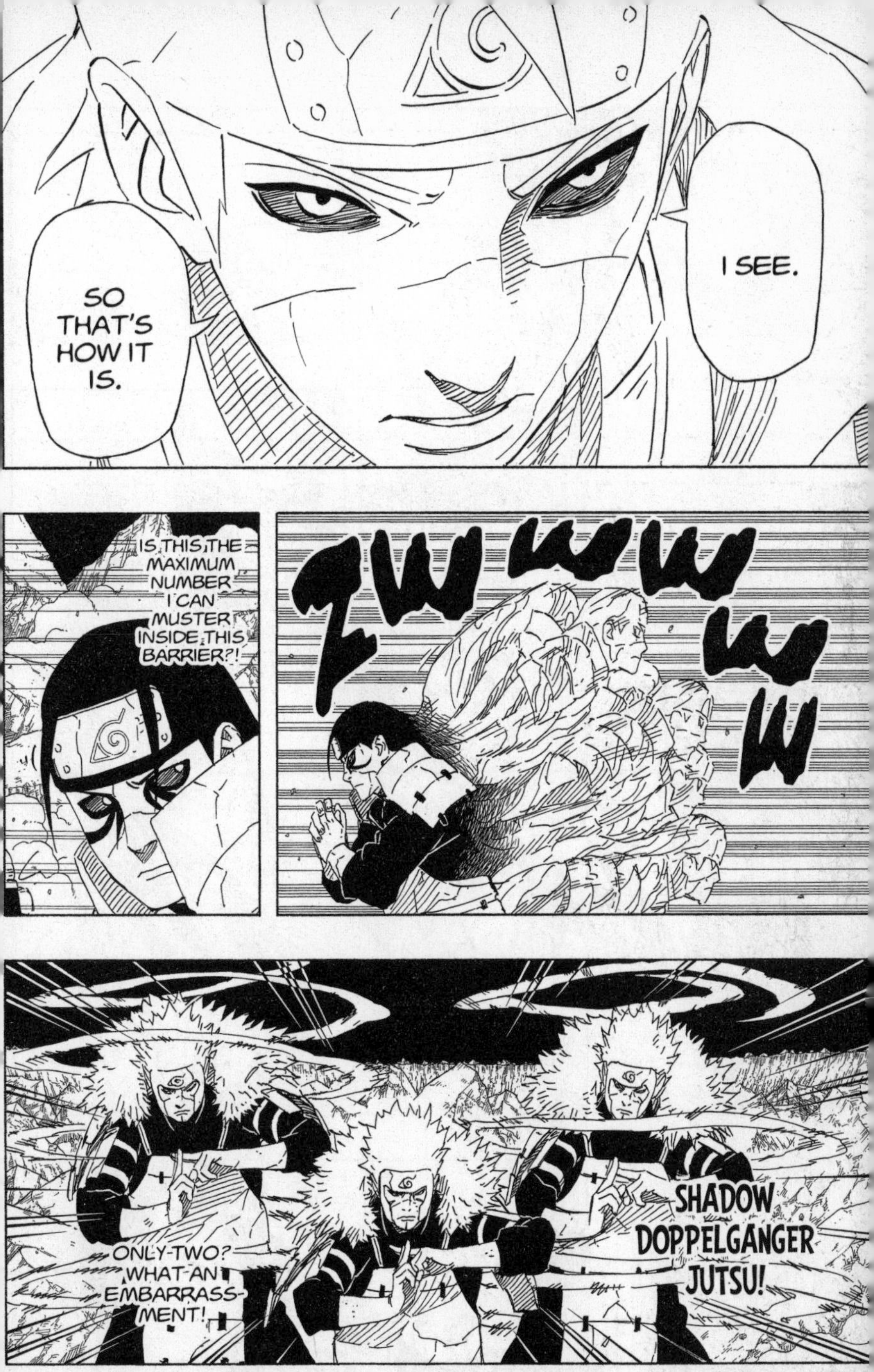
I SEE.
SO THAT'S HOW IT IS.
IS THIS THE MAXIMUM NUMBER I CAN MUSTER INSIDE THIS BARRIER?!
SHADOW DOPPELGANGER JUTSU!
ONLY TWO? WHAT AN EMBARRASSMENT!

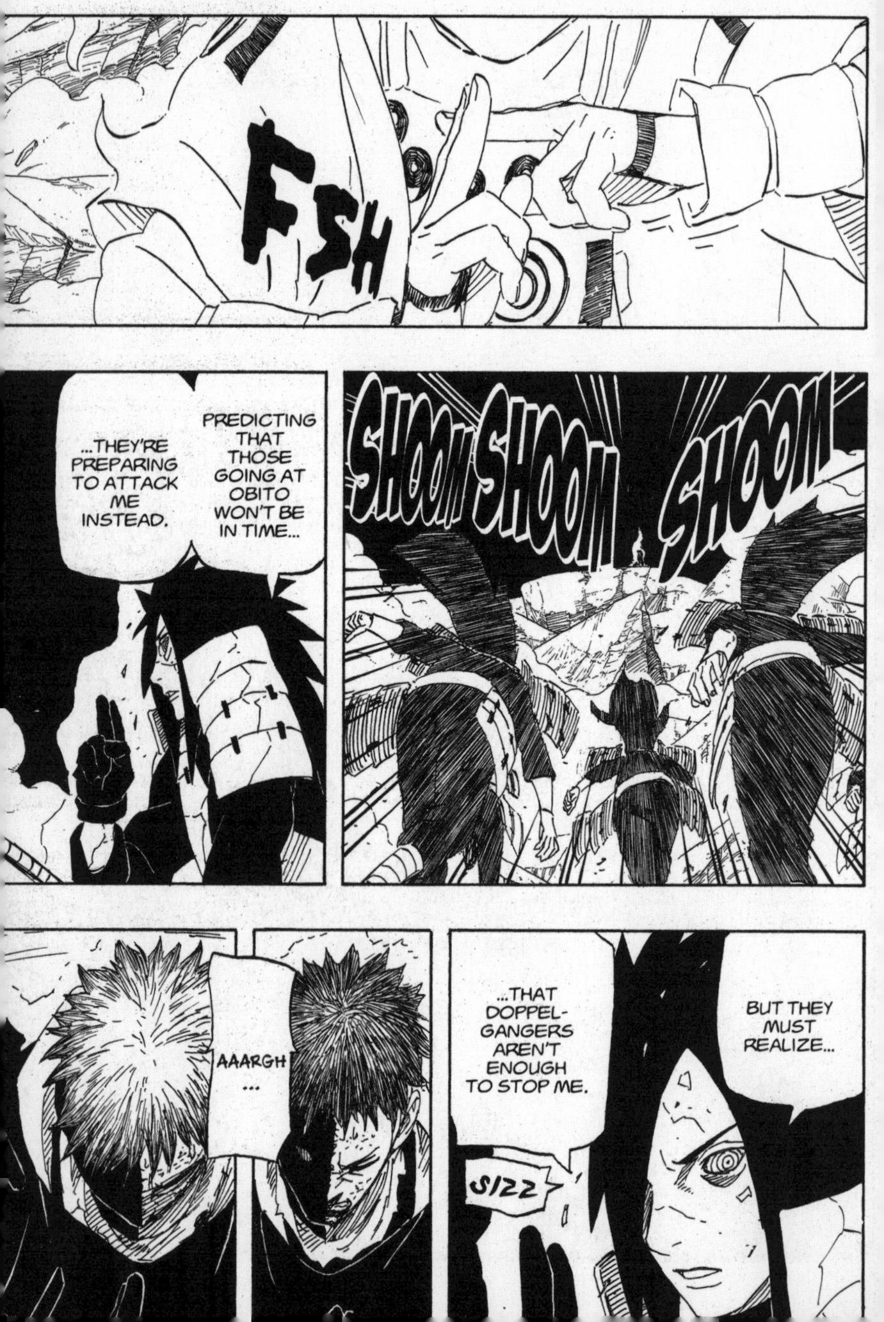
FSH
SHOOM SHOOM
SHOOM
PREDICTING THAT THOSE GOING AT OBITO WON'T BE IN TIME...
...THEY'RE PREPARING TO ATTACK ME INSTEAD.
BUT THEY MUST REALIZE...
...THAT DOPPEL-GANGERS AREN'T ENOUGH TO STOP ME.
SIZZ
AAARGH ...

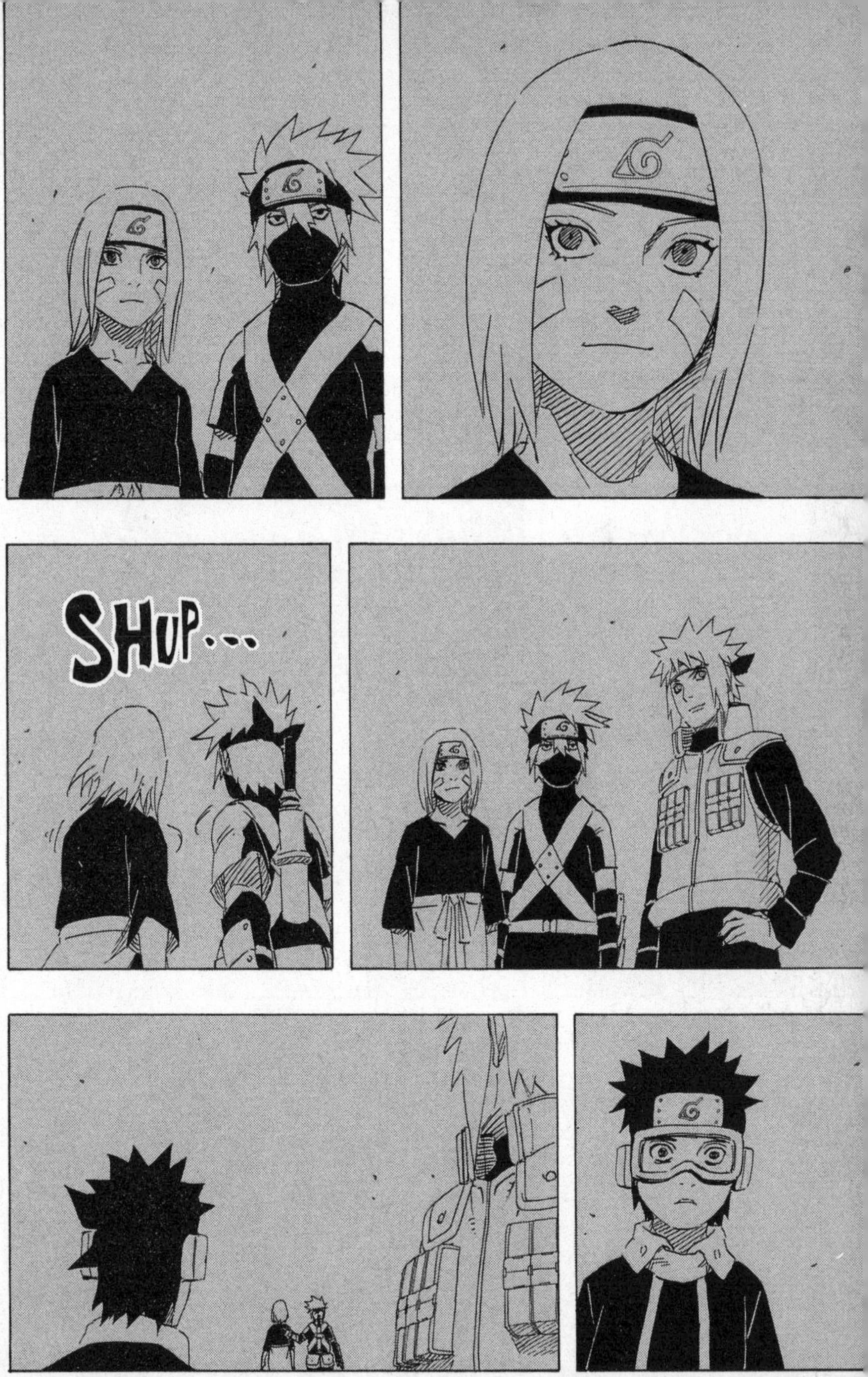
SHUP...

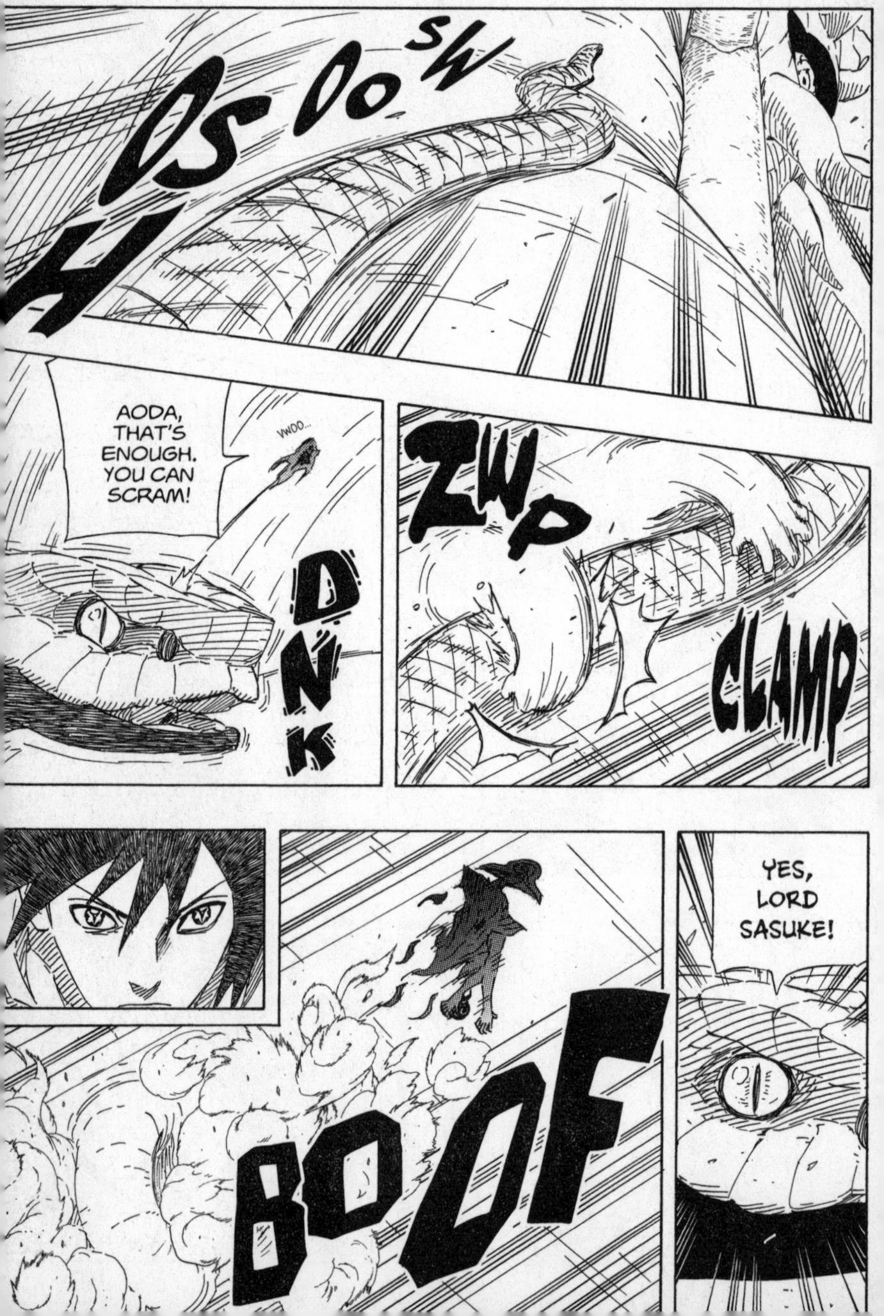
SWOOSH
ZWP
CLAMP
AODA, THAT'S ENOUGH. YOU CAN SCRAM!
VWOO...
DNK
YES, LORD SASUKE!
BOOF

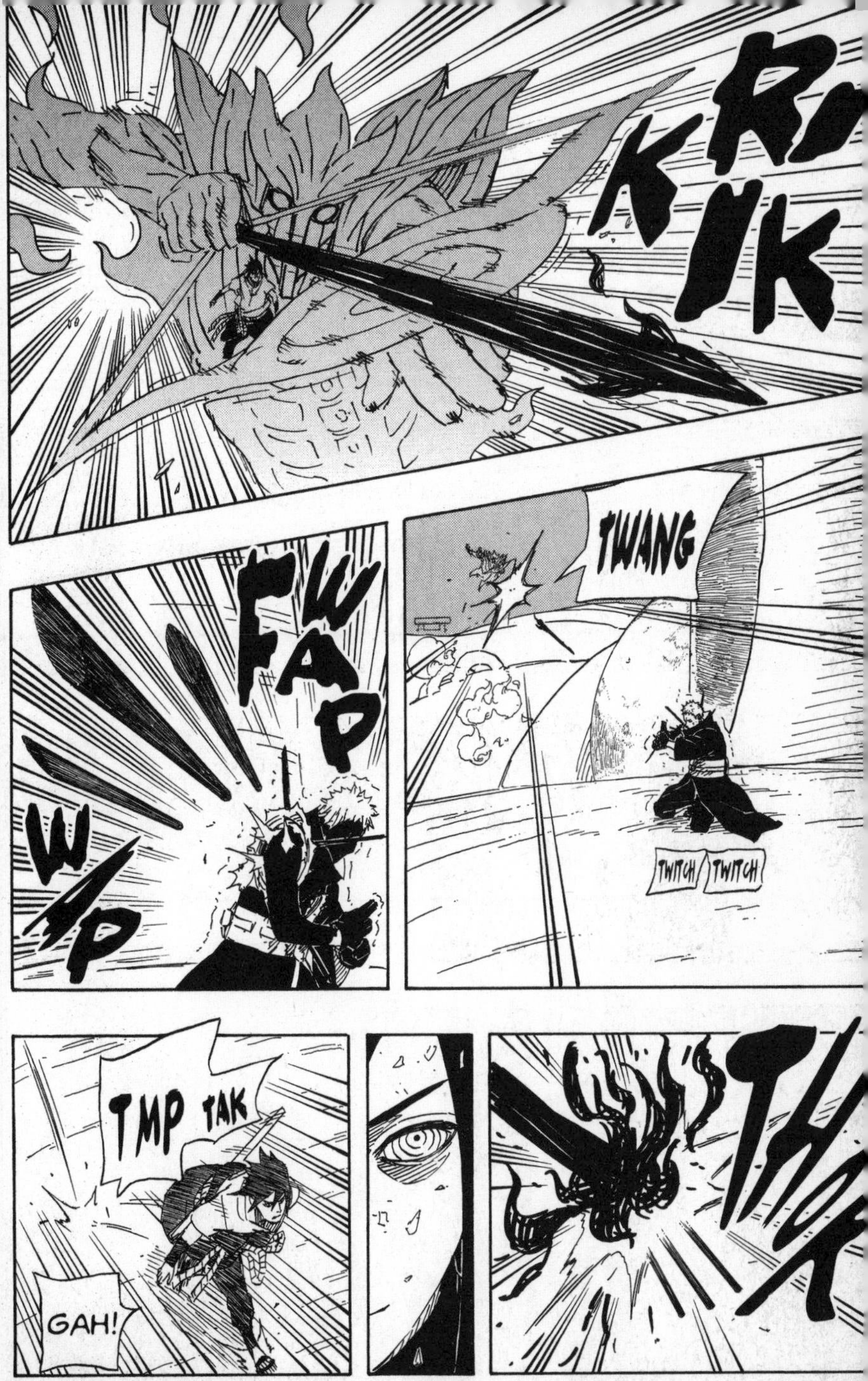

TWANG
TWITCH TWITCH
FWAP
TMP TAK
GAH!

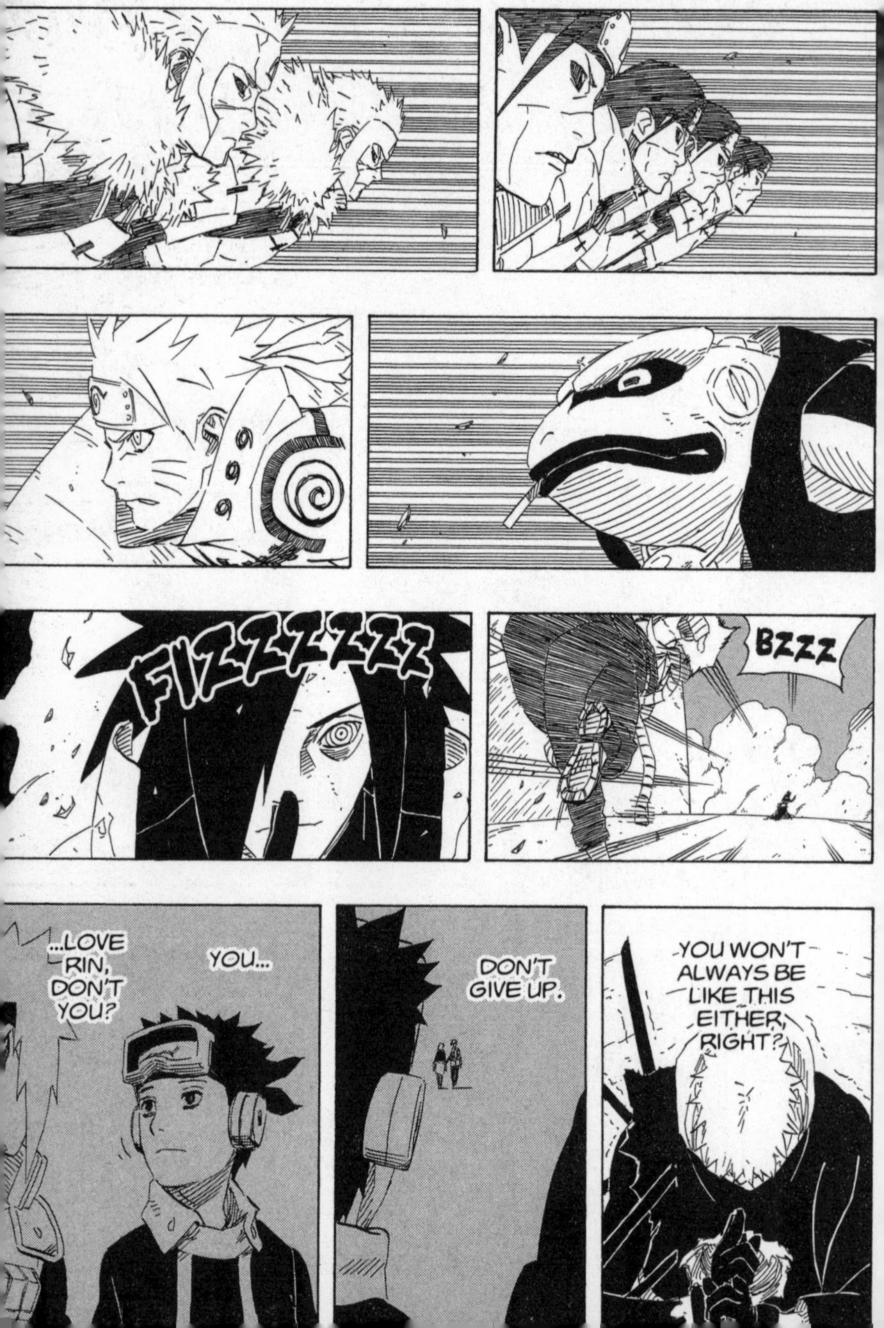
BZZZ
FIZZZZZZ
YOU WON'T ALWAYS BE LIKE THIS EITHER, RIGHT?
DON'T GIVE UP.
YOU...
...LOVE RIN, DON'T YOU?

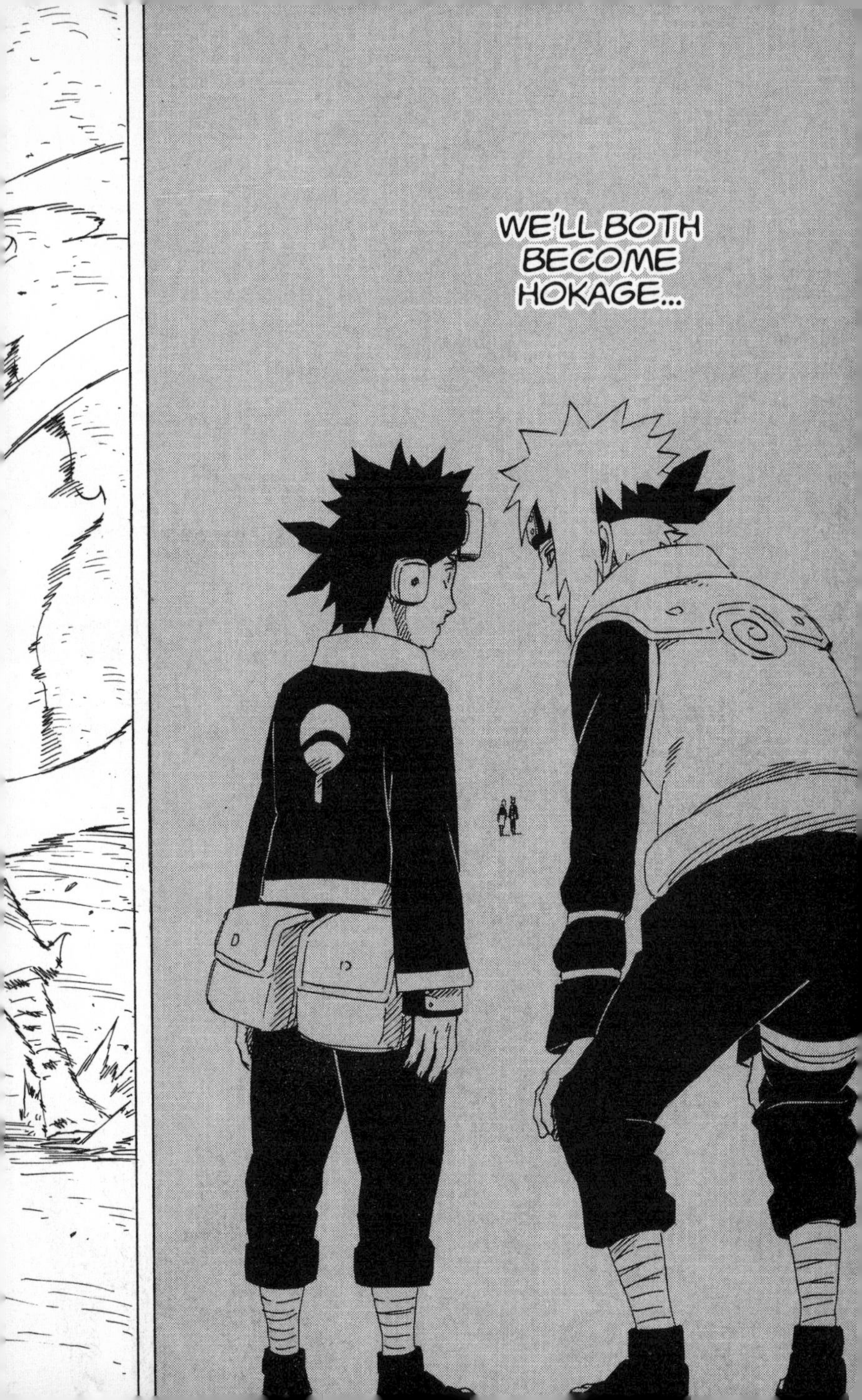
WE'LL BOTH BECOME HOKAGE...

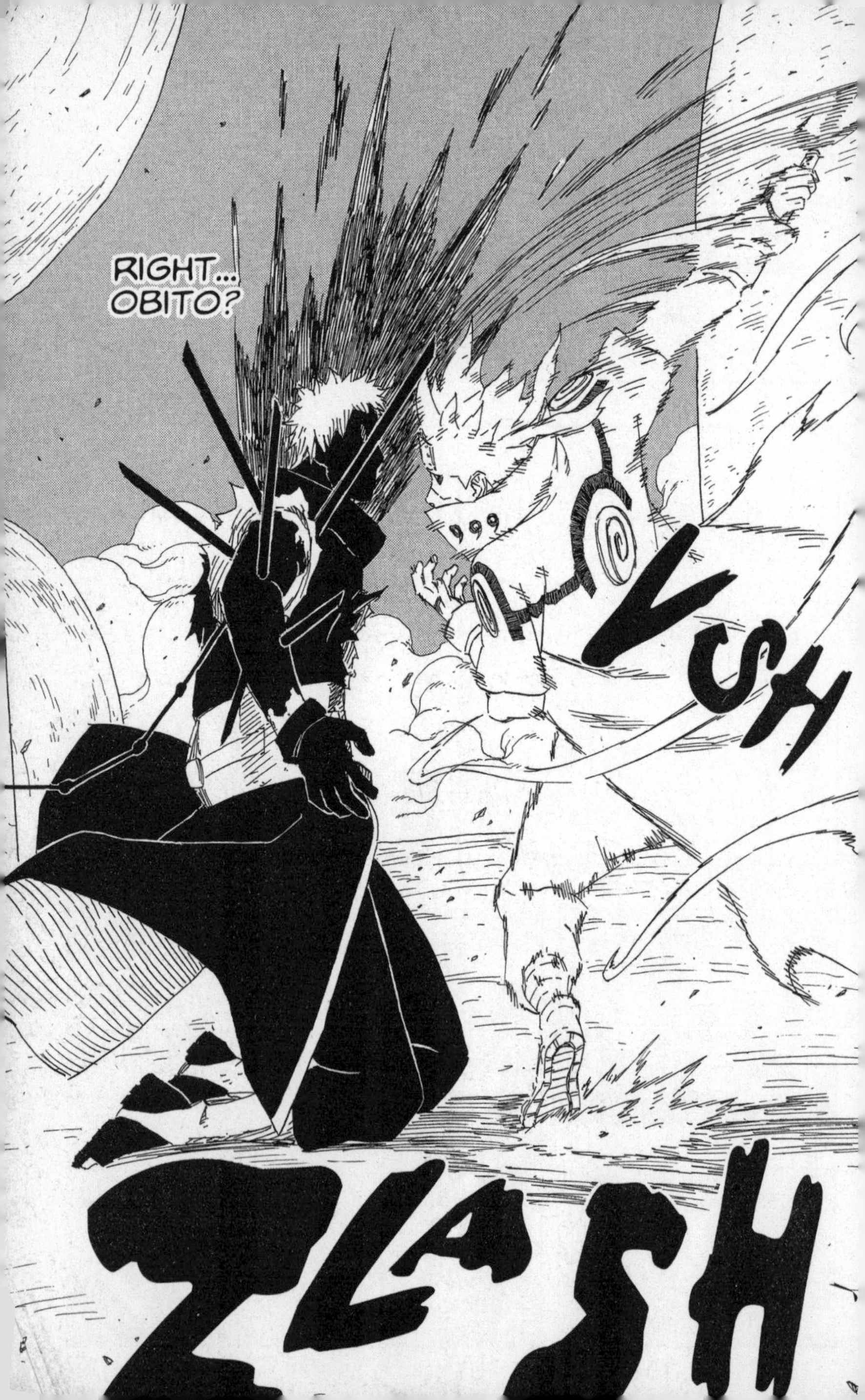
RIGHT... OBITO?
VSH
ZLASH

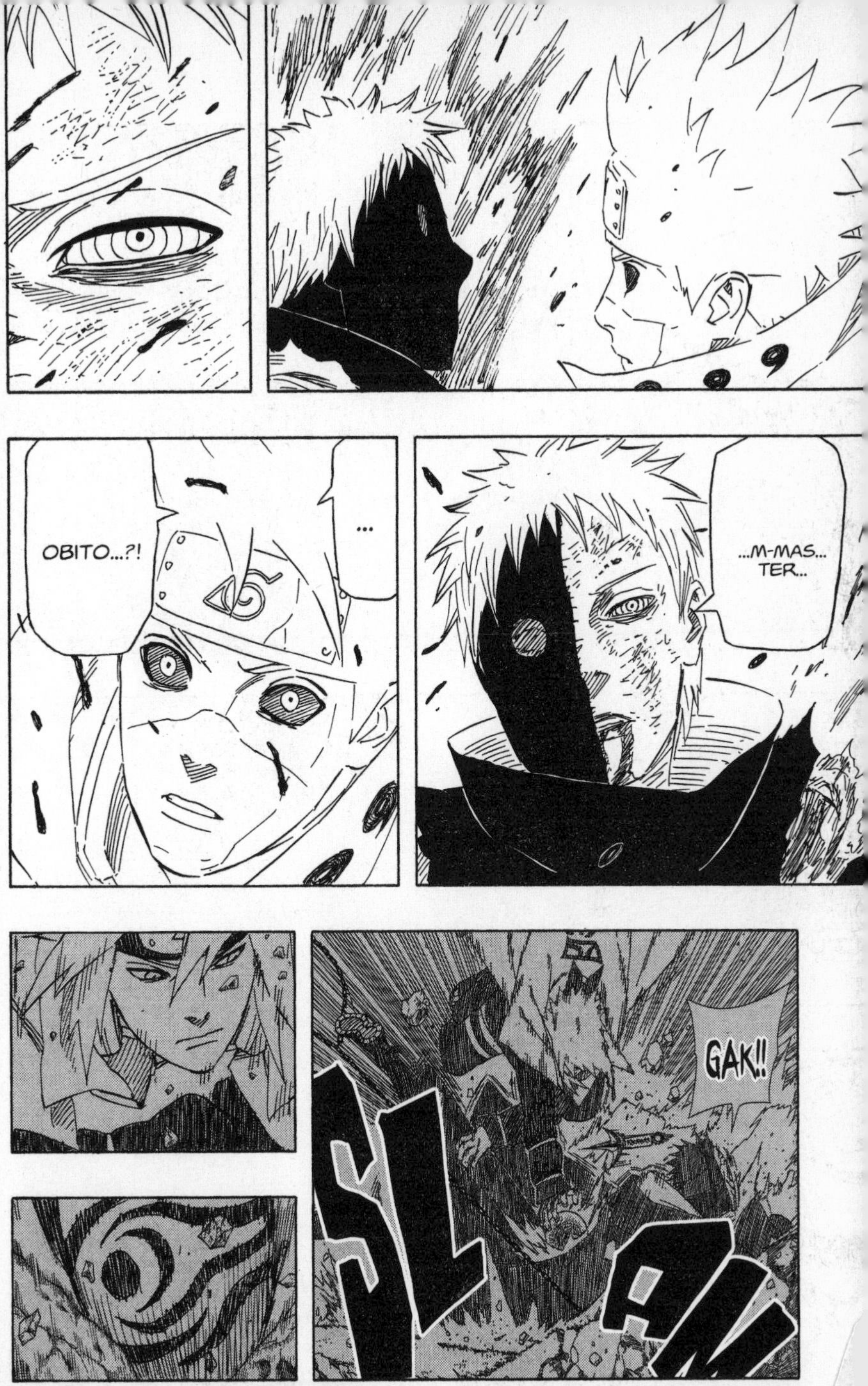
...M-MAS...
TER...
...
OBITO...?!
GAK!!
SLAM!

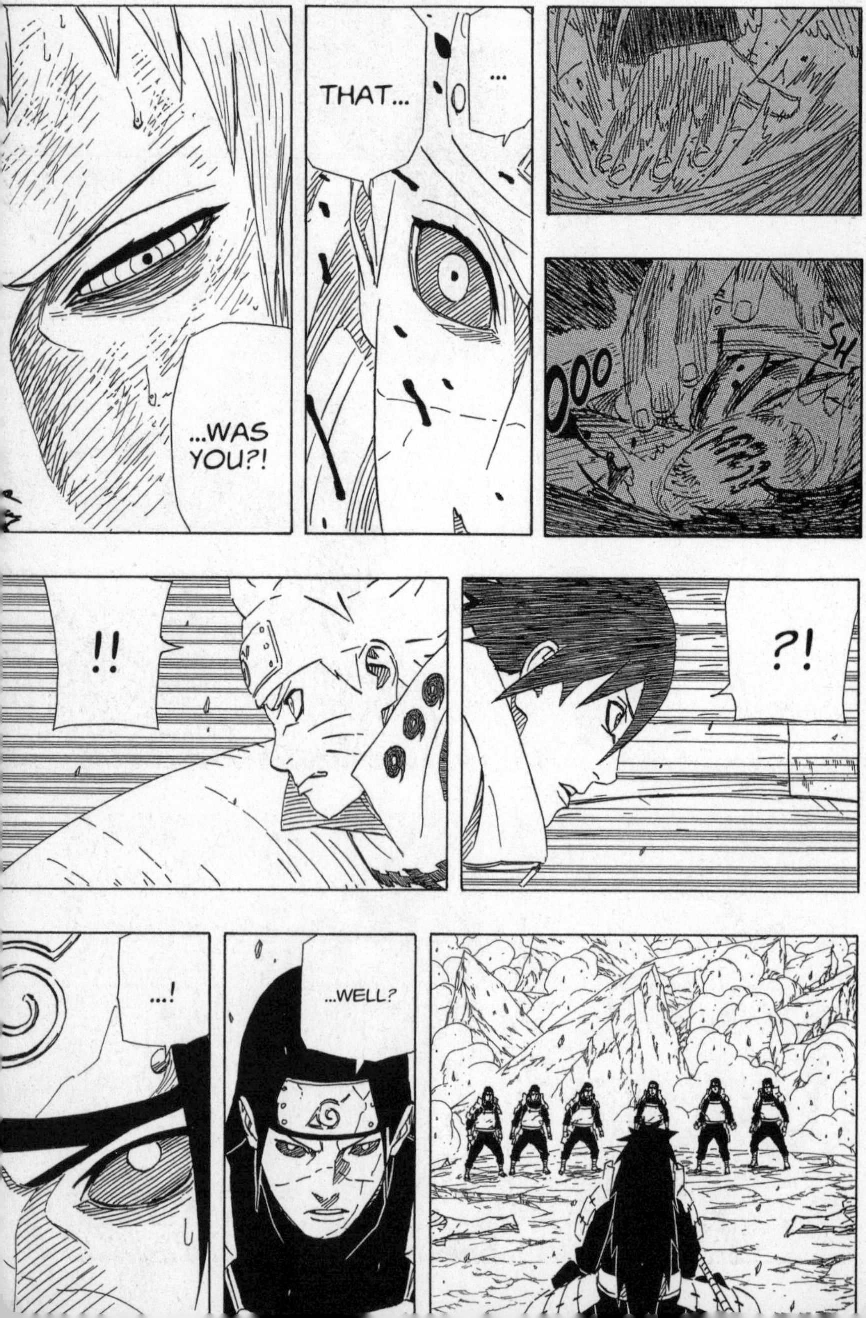
SH
OOO
...
THAT...
...WAS YOU?!
?!
!!
...WELL?
...!

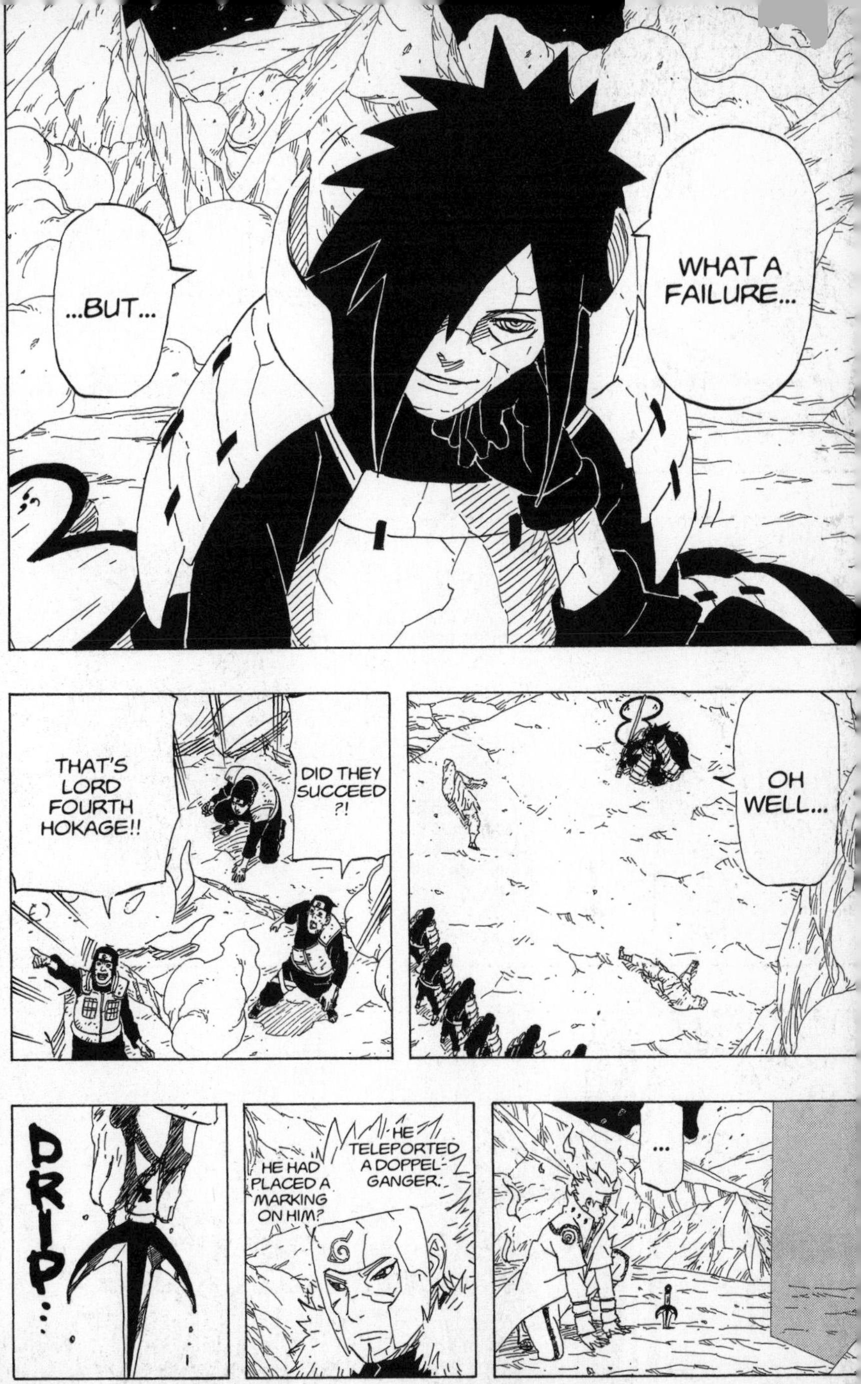
WHAT A FAILURE...
...BUT...
OH WELL...
DID THEY SUCCEED ?!
THAT'S LORD FOURTH HOKAGE!!
...
HE TELEPORTED A DOPPEL-GANGER.
HE HAD PLACED A MARKING ON HIM?
DRIP...

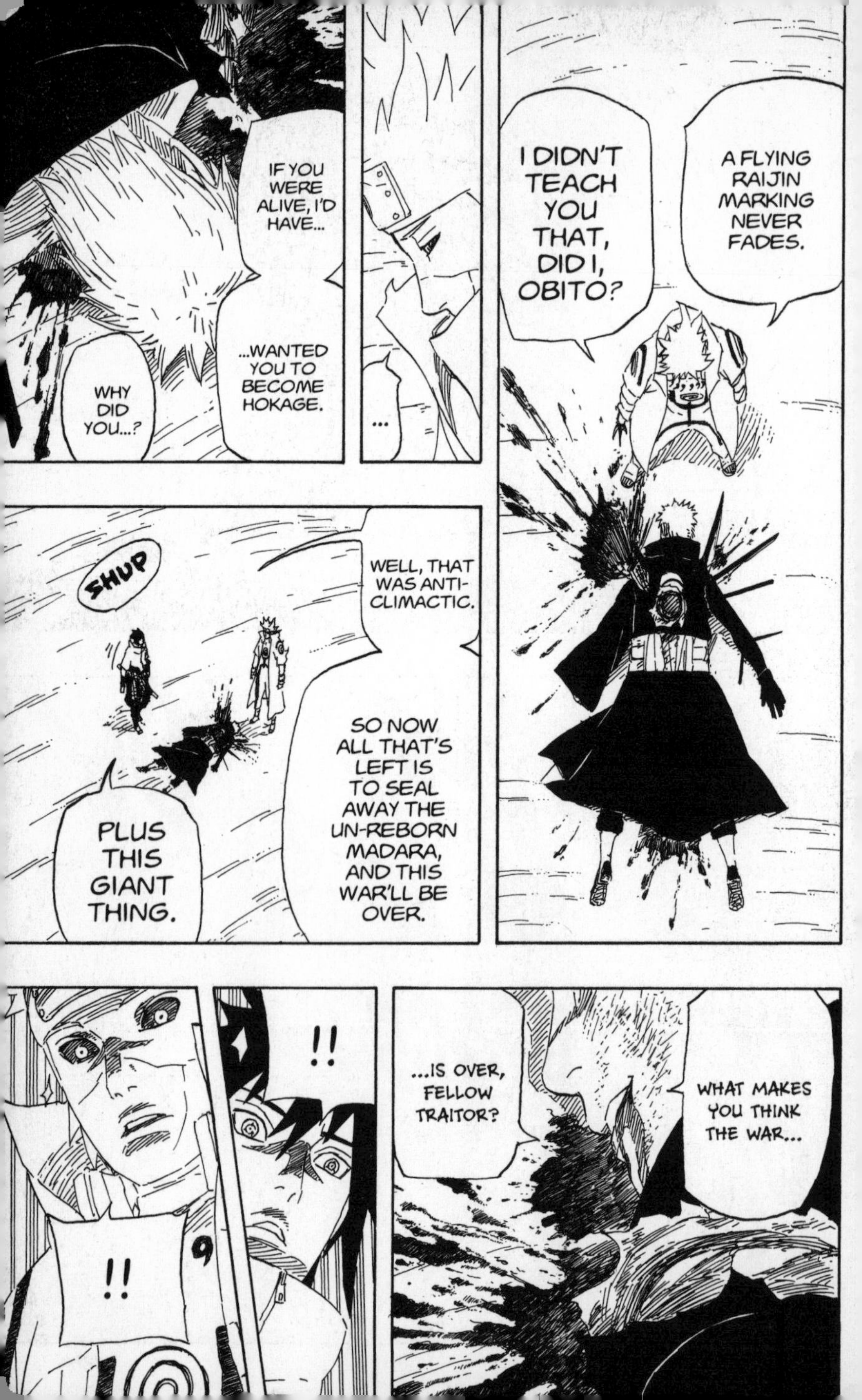
A FLYING RAIJIN MARKING NEVER FADES.
I DIDN'T TEACH YOU THAT, DID I, OBITO?
...
IF YOU WERE ALIVE, I'D HAVE...
...WANTED YOU TO BECOME HOKAGE.
WHY DID YOU...?
WELL, THAT WAS ANTI-CLIMACTIC.
SHUP
SO NOW ALL THAT'S LEFT IS TO SEAL AWAY THE UN-REBORN MADARA, AND THIS WAR'LL BE OVER.
PLUS THIS GIANT THING.
WHAT MAKES YOU THINK THE WAR...
...IS OVER, FELLOW TRAITOR?
!!
!!

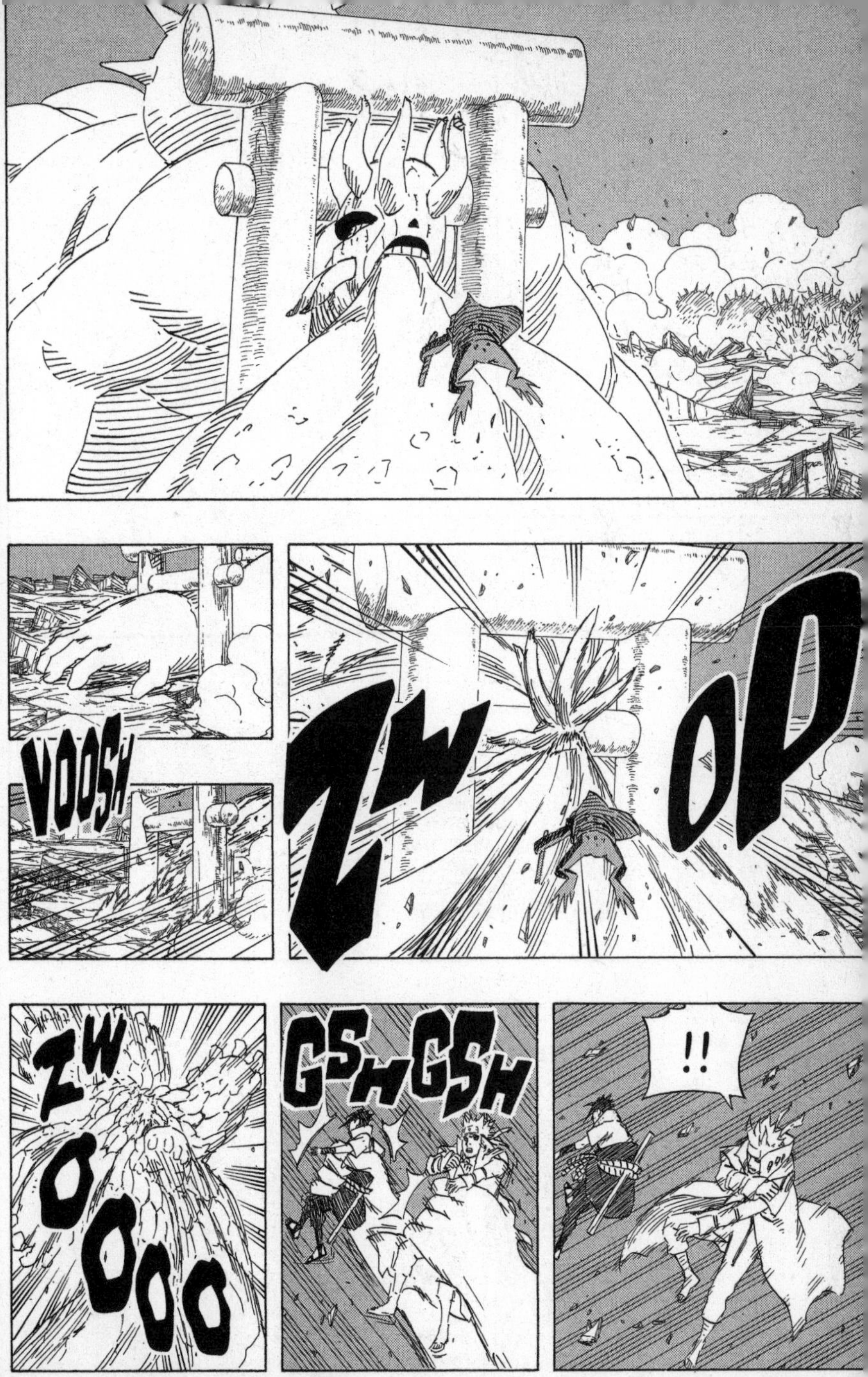
ZWOOP
VOOSH
!!
GSH GSH
ZWOOOO

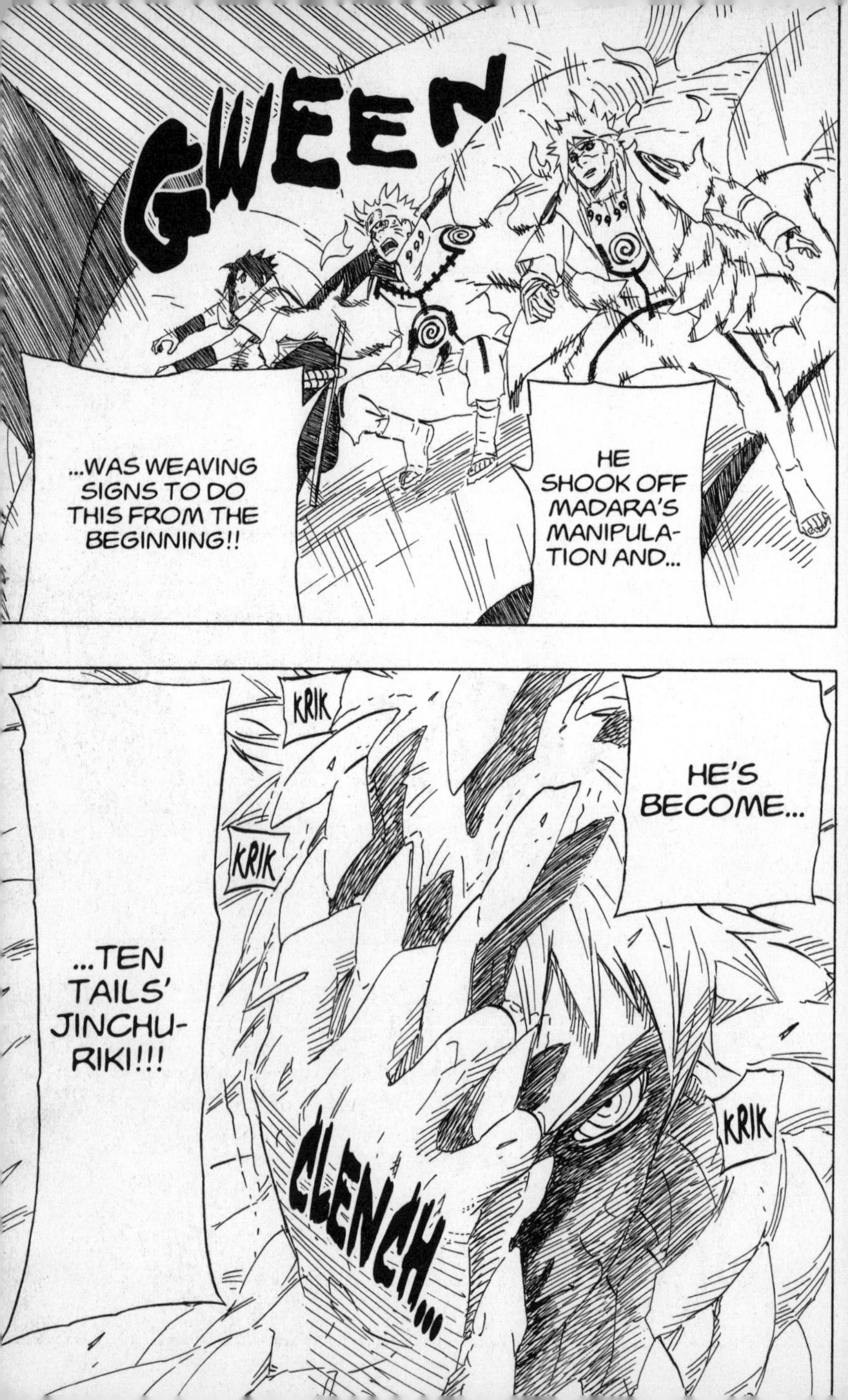
GWEEN
HE SHOOK OFF MADARA'S MANIPULATION AND...
...WAS WEAVING SIGNS TO DO THIS FROM THE BEGINNING!!
HE'S BECOME...
KRIK
KRIK
KRIK
...TEN TAILS' JINCHURIKI!!!
CLENCH...

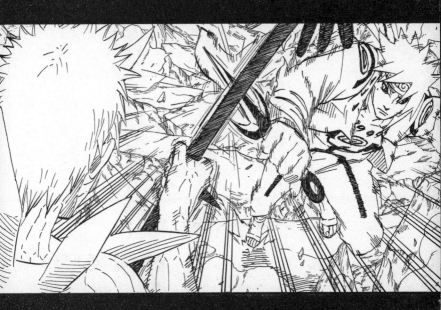

IN THE NEXT VOLUME...

AN OPENING

Just as victory seems at hand, Obito turns the tables on the Allied Shinobi Forces and becomes the Ten Tails jinchuriki. With the powers of the great Sage of Six Paths now under his control, Obito seems unstoppable. Naruto and his father will have to team up if they have any hope against this beast!

AVAILABLE OCTOBER 2014!

ᐯIZMᐯNGᐯ
Read manga anytime, anywhere!

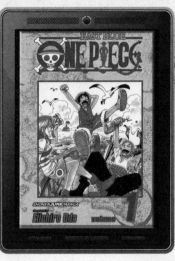

From our newest hit series to the classics you know and love, the best manga in the world is now available digitally. Buy a volume* of digital manga for your:

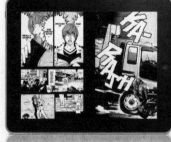

- iOS device (**iPad®, iPhone®, iPod® touch**) through the **VIZ Manga app**
- **Android-powered device (phone or tablet)** with a browser by visiting **VIZManga.com**
- **Mac or PC computer** by visiting VIZManga.com

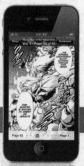

VIZ Digital has loads to offer:

- 500+ ready-to-read volumes
- New volumes each week
- FREE previews
- Access on multiple devices! Create a log-in through the app so you buy a book once, and read it on your device of choice!*

To learn more, visit www.viz.com/apps

* Some series may not be available for multiple devices.
 Check the app on your device to find out what's available.

RATED T FOR OLDER TEEN
ratings.viz.com

ᐯIZ media
viz.com/apps

DISCOVER ANIME
IN A WHOLE NEW WAY!

neon alley

www.neonalley.com

What it is...

- Streaming anime delivered 24/7 straight to your TV via your connected video game console
- All English dubbed content
- Anime, martial arts movies, and more

Go to **neonalley.com** for news, updates and to see if Neon Alley is available in your area.

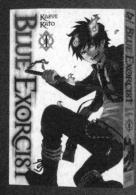
  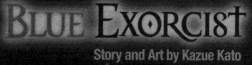

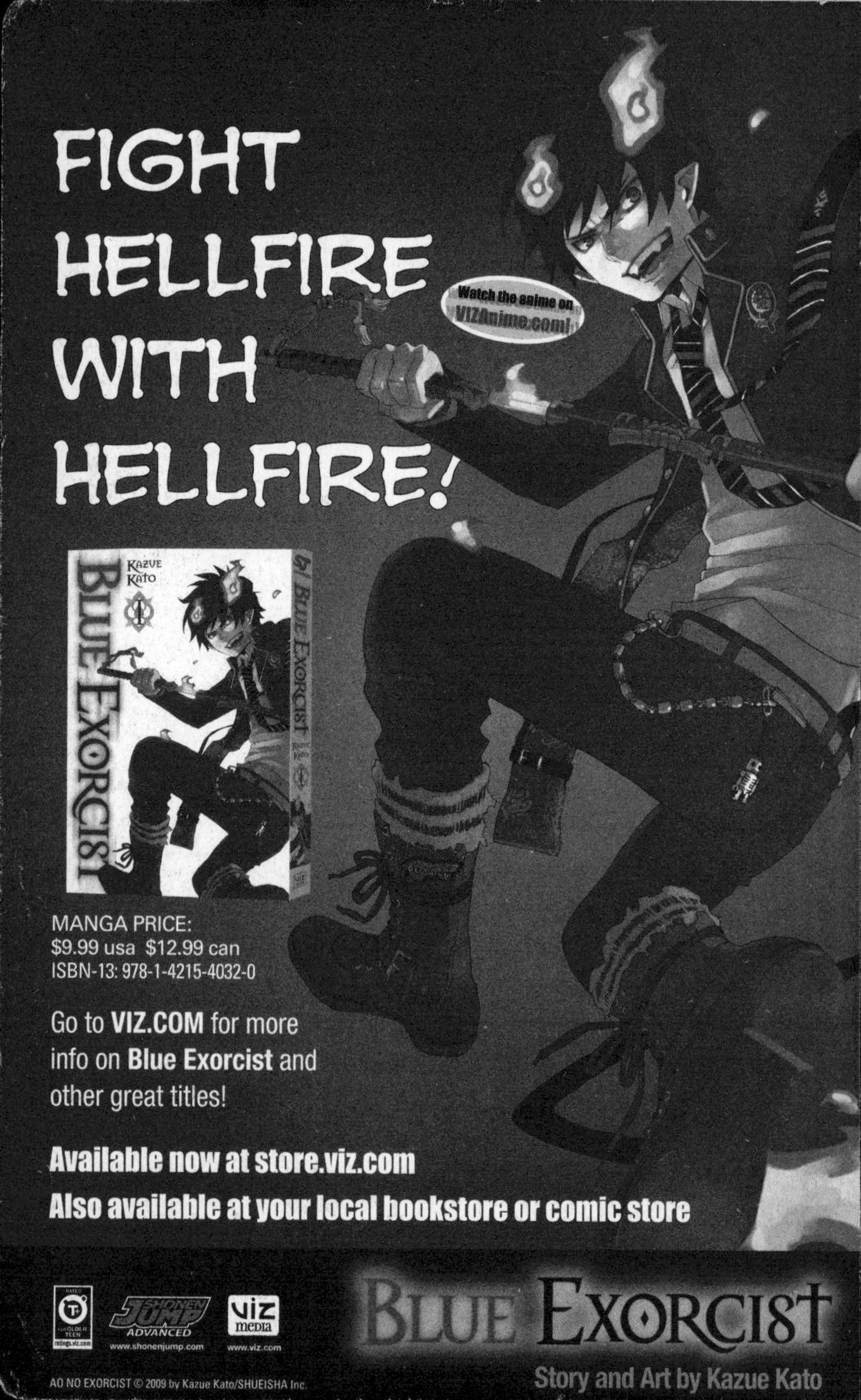

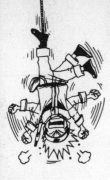

You're Reading in the Wrong Direction!!

Whoops! Guess what? You're starting at the wrong end of the comic!

...It's true! In keeping with the original Japanese format, **Naruto** is meant to be read from right to left, starting in the upper-right corner.

Unlike English, which is read from left to right, Japanese is read from right to left, meaning that action, sound effects and word-balloon order are completely reversed... something which can make readers unfamiliar with Japanese feel pretty backwards themselves. For this reason, manga or Japanese comics published in the U.S. in English have sometimes been published "flopped"—that is, printed in exact reverse order, as though seen from the other side of a mirror.

By flopping pages, U.S. publishers can avoid confusing readers, but the compromise is not without its downside. For one thing, a character in a flopped manga series who once wore in the original Japanese version a T-shirt emblazoned with "M A Y" (as in "the merry month of") now wears one which reads "Y A M"! Additionally, many manga creators in Japan are themselves unhappy with the process, as some feel the mirror-imaging of their art alters their original intentions.

We are proud to bring you Masashi Kishimoto's **Naruto** in the original unflopped format. For now, though, turn to the other side of the book and let the ninjutsu begin...!

—Editor

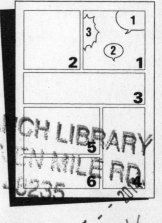